Iran's Final Solution for Israel

Also by Andrew G. Bostom

The Legacy of Jihad (2006/2008)

ISBN-10: 1591026024

ISBN-13: 978-1591026020

The Legacy of Islamic Antisemitism (2008)

ISBN-10: 1591025540

ISBN-13: 978-1591025542

Sharia Versus Freedom (2012)

ISBN-10: 1616146664

ISBN-13: 978-1616146665

The Mufti's Islamic Jew-Hatred (2013)

ISBN-13: 978-1493721924

ISBN-10: 1493721925

Iran's Final Solution for Israel

The Legacy of Jihad and Shi'ite Islamic Jew-Hatred in Iran

Andrew G. Bostom

Bravura Books

Washington, D.C.

Praise for

Iran's Final Solution for Israel

"SHINING THE LIGHT of meticulous, fearless scholarship that has made him one of the leading scholars of Islam of the post-9/11 era, Andrew G. Bostom accomplishes two key objectives in *Iran's Final Solution for Israel.* He uncovers the purely Islamic basis of Iran's annihilationist animus toward the Jewish state, and he debunks the gruesome apologetics the West relies on to avoid or hide Islam's animating role. In the end, a reader is left to ponder not only the peril of jihad from without, but what is surely the even greater peril of cowardice and submission from within. Essential reading for any person who wants to think past the denial and delusions of glib punditry and 'brokered agreements' -- before it's too late."

— **DIANA WEST, nationally syndicated columnist and author of *American Betrayal* and *The Death of the Grown-Up***

"ANDREW BOSTOM'S NEW book is a powerful antidote to the all-too-widespread view that Iran's rulers are capable of co-existing with non-Muslims on peaceful, equal terms. By quoting Islam's highest authorities extensively—including the major contemporary Shiite 'quietists'—he shows that the more committed someone is to being a faithful Muslim, the less tolerant he is of human beings who are not. Bostom shows that our problems with Iran's rulers and with other good Muslims is not one of policy but of civilization. For this we owe him our attention and our gratitude."

— **ANGELO M. CODEVILLA, Professor Emeritus of International Relations, Boston University**

"A BRILLIANT AND COMPREHENSIVE study of world issues. A must-read for whoever wants to understand the challenges and fights for civilization's survival in this century. Not everyone can face and contend with Evil so long and so consistently as Bostom has done to help us remain human, and free."

— **BAT YE'OR, author of *The Decline of Eastern Christianity Under Islam: From Jihad to Dhimmitude***

"THIS LATEST MASTERFUL work from Dr. Andrew Bostom, *Iran's Final Solution for Israel,* should leave no doubt about the genocidal intent of the Iranian regime towards the Jewish State of Israel, as Tehran drives to acquire and deploy nuclear weapons. Dr. Bostom's meticulous scholarship makes the inescapable case that Iran's aggressive ambitions are driven by Islamic doctrine and cannot be deterred by negotiations or sanctions. This is a superb book that should be required reading for U.S. leadership and all who are dedicated to the cause of human liberty and our freedom from Sharia."

— CLARE M. LOPEZ, **Senior Fellow, Center for Security Policy, and co-author of** *Sharia: The Threat to America*

"ANDREW BOSTON'S LATEST book, *Iran's Final Solution for Israel,* offers a brilliant and compelling case for the contribution of Islamic dogma to Iran's foreign policy. Iran's relentless determination to acquire nuclear weapons, Bostom argues, can be accounted for by its ancient twin theological passions of Jew-hatred and holy war dogma. It is Islamic theology, pure and simple, which accounts for Iran's often-repeated ambition to annihilate Israel. At the same time, Bostom laments the fact that Western states have been attempting to engage with Iran without understanding or appreciating its theological agenda. Of this little good can come."

— MARK DURIE, **author of** *The Third Choice: Islam, Dhimmitude, and Freedom*

"ONCE AGAIN, THE INDEFATIGABLE Dr. Andrew Bostom has exploded Western delusional fantasies about Islam with a compelling, source-based analysis of endemic Muslim antisemitism. The force of his rigorous arguments leads to only one conclusion: the Jew-hating Iranian regime must not be allowed to acquire nuclear weapons. A must-read for those who take seriously the moral of the Holocaust, 'never again.' "

— BRUCE THORNTON,, **author of** *The Wages of Appeasement: Ancient Athens, Munich, and Obama's America*

"A BRILLIANT, COMPENDIOUS, and exceptionally well-written piece of work, *Iran's Final Solution for Israel* is Andrew Bostom's most recent and probing analysis of Islamic Jew-hatred, as practiced by the so-called Islamic Republic of Iran. Bostom scrupulously examines the evidence for the pervasive duplicity underlying and facilitating Iran's nuclear program, along with American and Western delusional naivety in complying with Iranian diplomacy. He is very clear on 'the chronic plight of Iranian Jewry' and 'Iran's relentless effort to obtain nuclear weapons for the stated purpose of destroying Israel.' Bostom's exegesis and warning should be heeded if we wish to avert a future few of us would like to contemplate."

— DAVID SOLWAY, **author of** *Hear, O Israel!*

9

"WORKING FROM HISTORY, Islamic sacred and juridical writings, and the statements and actions of the current Iranian regime, Andrew Bostom lays out a compelling case that the current Iranian 'moderation' so widely touted in the mainstream media — and upon which Barack Obama is betting nothing less than the future of the free world — is a not-so-thinly-disguised exercise in divinely sanctioned Islamic deception designed to co-opt and victimize a complacent and willfully ignorant West. If our Senators and Representatives absorbed and acted upon the lessons of this monograph, we would not be in the fix we're in."

— ROBERT SPENCER, author of the New York Times bestsellers *The Politically Incorrect Guide to Islam (and the Crusades)* and *The Truth About Muhammad*

"A MUST-READ WARNING about the Iranian Shi'ite theocracy and its trustworthiness as a negotiating partner. The extensive research and analysis presented in this monograph should provide the West with an understanding of the Iranian threat and its ideological motivations: jihadism, annihilationist Islamic antisemitism, and general hatred of non-Muslims. There is no excuse for being entrapped into useless agreements with Iran."

— NONIE DARWISH, author of *The Devil We Don't Know: The Dark Side of Revolutions in the Middle East*

"DR. ANDREW BOSTOM IS undoubtedly the leading academic authority on all pertinent matters of Jihadist doctrine. He is a rare scholar, one who has been willing to undertake meticulous and exhaustive examination of what lies at the very core of consciousness of Israel's recalcitrant enemies, including, most prominently, the contemporary Shiite theocracy of Iran."

— LOUIS RENÉ BERES, Professor of International Law, Purdue University, author of *Force, Order and Justice: International Law in the Age of Atrocity*

"THERE ARE VERY FEW scholars with the depth of understanding about Islam possessed by Andrew Bostom. That knowledge is in full display in his new book, *Iran's Final Solution for Israel*. One ignores this extraordinary work at his own peril, for it contains precisely the kind of insight our policy analysts need."

— HERBERT LONDON, President, London Center for Policy Research

Published by Bravura Books

Washington, D.C., 2014

IRAN'S FINAL SOLUTION FOR ISRAEL

Bostom, Andrew G.

  Iran's Final Solution for Israel

ISBN-13: 978-1497362895
ISBN-10: 149736289X

First edition: March 2014

CONTENTS

ACKNOWLEDGMENTS

This book would not have been completed without the steadfast support of my beloved wife. It is dedicated to my dear children, who deserve a future free from the threat of Iran's annihilationist Islamic Jew-hatred.

Close friends Ruth King, Diana West, Jan Breslow, Allon Friedman, Tariq Ismail, Rabbi Jon Hausman, and Hillel Stavis provided invaluable advice, assistance, and encouragement.

Many thanks to JW and NM for their critical assistance with the book design, and production.

I am also indebted to the efforts of translators Sjimon den Hollander, Nidra Poller, and Yigal Carmon.

AUTHOR'S NOTE

By design, this book avoids discussion of the unique aspects of Shiite Islam, or its development, which do not pertain to the creed's interface with non-Muslims. For those other myriad aspects of Shi'ism, interested readers should consult the excellent general references by Donaldson,[n1] Madelung,[n2] and Nasr.[n3]

Diacritical marks were not used, except in some cases of block quotes that already contained them. The reader is asked to bear with instances of variant spelling of Islamic terms and Muslim names. This minor variation is readily decipherable.

AUTHOR'S UPDATED PREFACE

*T*hey [the Jews of Iran] live under profound oppression because they are
considered as outlaws or outcastes. [T]he capriciousness of the governor and
the pack of his subordinates weigh upon them [the Jews]; they use any pretext to
plunder the Jews with impunity, for there is no one to whom the Jews could turn
or dare to turn to complain of their oppression except the governor himself, who is
the judge of his own case...If a Jew crosses the road dressed decently or hazards
to mount a horse, the spectators complain that he dares to present himself as a
believer. If on the other hand he is wearing miserable rags, the young rascals of
the streets, excited by persons much older, pursue him throwing mud and stones
at him...In the cases of jurisprudence, the Jew cannot invoke in his favor the
benefits of the law; it is certain that the Muslim will testify against him, while one
cannot trust the latter's words nor that of his witnesses... One of the principal
causes of the misery of the Jews is stirred up by the priests and descendants
of the [Muslim] prophet, the Mullah and the Sayyids [Muslim clerics]. Living
in opposition to the government, they surround themselves with the riffraff of
society—brigands, highway robbers—to whom they throw as fodder all who fall
into their hands, above all the Jews, inoffensive human beings not protected by
the law... [E]ven the obtainment of a firman declaring the emancipation of the
Jews and the abolition of all exclusion and restriction in regard to them, would
not be sufficient to guarantee in the future its strict execution. Besides, the great
distances which separate from the capital the numerous agglomerations of Jews,
serve to give security if not a guarantee of impunity to the persecutors.

— JACOB EDUARD POLAK, 1865§

One year after the widely celebrated, yet dangerously de-stabilizing so-called P5 +1 Iranian nuclear weapons negotiations were announced, it was declared Monday November 24, 2014 that no final deal could be sealed. [up1] New interim (March 1, 2015) and final (July 1, 2015) deadlines for continued negotiations were proclaimed, instead. [up2]

Prior to the announcement, Israeli Prime Minister Benjamin Netanyahu had lauded this ultimate development as the preferred, if hardly ideal, outcome. [up3]

> *No deal is better than a bad deal. The right deal that is needed is to dismantle Iran's capacity to make atomic bombs and only then dismantle the sanctions. Since that's not in the offing, this result is better, a lot better.*

Expanding upon Mr. Netanyahu's observations, the lack of a signed agreement provides Israel with a fortuitous, if evanescent strategic opportunity.

Thursday, 11/20/2014, reviewing more than a decade of International Atomic Energy Agency (IAEA) analyses (and other investigative findings) a 104 page report concluded that the Iranian regime—despite repeated, disingenuous countervailing protests—had, "vigorously pursued its ambitions to obtain nuclear weapons." [up4] Tehran continued to engage in "systematic," "vigorous" combined military, and dual military-civilian efforts, "such as enrichment, weaponization, warhead, and delivery system at some stage," whose ultimate goal was procuring nuclear weapons capability. [up5]

> *In other words, Iran has worked on specific programs and projects to master all necessary aspects of obtaining a nuclear weapon*

Moreover, the November 20, 2014 report noted, there were, "no serious indications that Tehran has stopped or abandoned this project or intends to do so." [up6] Iran, on the contrary, "has resorted to further secrecy and concealment to keep its program intact and unhindered." Additional discoveries and data all underscore how "a military program and military related activities," remain "at the heart of the Iranian nuclear program." [up7]

Just 11 days earlier, on November 9, 2014, Iran's theocratic leader, Ayatollah Khamenei reiterated his ceaseless call for the jihad annihilation of Israel, via his twitter account, in a "question and answer" tweet: *Why should & how can #Israel be eliminated? Ayatollah Khamenei's answer to 9 key questions. #HandsOffAlAqsa "9 key questions about elimination of Israel".* Khamenei argued that the "only means" of halting alleged "Israeli crimes," was "the elimination of this regime." [up8] He recommended, specifically, for this purpose, [up9]

> *The West Bank should be armed like Gaza...those who are*

interested in Palestine's destiny should take action to arm the people of the West Bank.

Ayatollah Khamenei justified this call for an annihilationist jihad by concluding,[up10]

Yasser Arafat was poisoned and killed by Israel, while he had the most cooperation with the Zionists [which] proves that in the viewpoint of Israel, "peace" is simply a trick for more crimes and occupation.

It is imperative for all those who aren't ignoring the Iranian nuclear threat, or abiding complementary syndromes of dangerous delusion on the Left ("The Trusting Khomeini/Khamenei/Rouhani Syndrome" [up11]) and Right ("The Trusting Montazeri/Green Movement Syndrome" [up12]) to understand that Israel must strike, now, as a temporizing measure.

Caroline Glick's October 10, 2014 essay [up13] revealed a delusive mindset which continues to be championed by conservative Iran analysts (i.e., "The Trusting Montazeri/Green Movement Syndrome"), delaying the requisite, urgent Israeli military action. Glick endorsed the following dangerous nonsense espoused by self-avowed "Iran expert" Michael Ledeen: [up14]

Dr. Michael Ledeen, Freedom Scholar at the Washington-based Foundation for Defense of Democracies has been closely following the Iranian regime since he served in the Reagan administration in the 1980s. In 2009, he argued that even without US assistance, if Israel had been willing to help the Green Movement, with little effort, it could have empowered the opposition sufficiently to overthrow the regime. In a conversation this week, Ledeen said Israel still has the capacity to provide opposition forces the tools they require to overthrow the regime.

Pace reams of debunking evidence (including the captured scene, above), analysts such as Ledeen and Glick continue to grossly mischaracterize both the Iranian "Green Movement," up16 and its designated "spiritual father," Ayatollah Montazeri (d. December, 2009). up17 As embodied, legitimately, by Montazeri, the Green Movement's Iranian Shi'ite theocratic ideology deviated precious little from the bellicose and bigoted Sharia supremacist norms of the retrograde 1979 "revolution."

The following extracts from two Montazeri public addresses in 1987 (both verbatim translations, and contextual summaries, provided by the U.S. Central Intelligence Agency's open source translation office, the *Foreign Broadcast Information Service* [up18]), replete with sanctions from the Koran, hadith (traditions of Muhammad), and Islamic jurisprudence, make plain whom he viewed as the primary "infidel targets" for the Iranian Islamic Republic's jihadism (and Jew-hatred), i.e., Israel ("Jews"), and the U.S. Montazeri also enunciated an unabashed call for a global jihad.

> *"[O]ur war is against Israel, which has been created in the heart of Islamic countries by satans and superpowers in order to weaken Islam and Muslims...[T]he Jews of Medina at the time of the noble prophet [i.e., Muhammad] sided with the infidels against Islam and Muslims...Palestine will never be liberated through political games. The territories that have been seized from Muslims by force can be regained only through strength. If the Muslims unite and become harmonious with one another they can do anything...Allah willing, then all Muslims should come together against the usurping Israeli government. They should be convinced that Israel will be defeated."* [up19]

مرده آن است که نامش به نکویی نبرند

منتظری در حین تن زدن از دست دادن با یک
هموطن کلیمی بواسطه اعتقاد به نجس بودن
غیر مسلمانان و جلوگیری از باطل شدن وضو

**Ayatollah Montazeri, Green Movement 'Inspiration,'
Refusing to Shake the Hand of a Najis Jew**

Translation of Farsi caption, beneath image: *"This is Iran's deceased Ayatollah Montazeri (d. December, 2009) in the photograph where he rejected shaking the hand of a fellow Jewish Iranian. He declined the handshake because he did not want to become dirty (najis) and his cleanliness despoiled for his "Salaat" preparation (for prayer, as a Muslim), by contacting the (najis, infidel) Jew.* [up15]

*"The Muslims should clearly recognize the main danger to Islam and the Islamic lands, which is the United States and international Zionism"...Grand Ayatollah Montazeri emphasized: "One cannot fight against the United States and Zionism merely by holding meetings and chanting slogans. The ulema of Islam and all the Muslims should make some serious decisions."...The deputy leader then quoted a large number of traditions from the Prophet of Islam from both Shi'a and Sunni books...In the same connection, he referred to the need to establish Islamic governments and traditions and behaviors as did the noble prophet, and said that his holiness did not remain quiet in the face of oppression. He [Muhammad] did not sit in a corner and merely pray, although all his prayers would have been answered. **On the contrary, he [Muhammad] carried out an uprising and had about 80 military clashes**. He [Muhammad] called on the Muslims to arise, and he established a just government and powerfully implemented Allah's laws, injunctions, and justice among the people.*

*He [**Montazeri**] said: **"There are more than 300 verses in the Koran about jihad**, which are unfortunately forgotten, and about 60 books of Islamic jurisprudence are devoted to political issues, economics, judicial matters, punishments, and similar subjects. In view of this it is regrettable that the enemies of Islam and the colonialists succeeded in influencing the thoughts and attitudes of Muslims and of the ulema and Islamic writers and preachers. These enemies took away from them their Islamic character, and said that religion is separate from politics. By so doing, the colonialists succeeded in imposing corrupt leaders over Islamic countries, in placing a few million Zionists in charge of the destiny of the Muslims and Al-Aqsa Mosque...Because the United States and Zionism hve placed their agents in charge of the destiny of Islam and Muslims...the only way for the salvation of Islam and Muslims is for them to recognize their real enemy...and to strengthen genuine Islamic movements in Islamic countries...In the same way that today the stirrings of the Islamic Revolution can be seen in Lebanon, Palestine, and Afghanistan, and thanks to Allah, is growing strong in all of the Islamic countries, resistance cells and Islamic movements should receive scientific, spiritual, and material support. This is the duty of all of us and all the ulema of Islam to identify these cells of Islamic movement and revolution and to strengthen them as much as we can. Allah willing, they will gradually grow and expand so that the nations may be awakened and liberate Jerusalem from the claws of usurping Israel...*

If we assist the religion of Allah...and if we make use of all the forces fighting against the enemies of Islam and the Koran, most definitely the colonial thesis of 'divide and rule' will be defeated... Very soon through a billion strong march by all the Muslims of the world, we can liberate beloved Jerusalem, destroy usurping Israel, and place the destiny of Islam and the Muslims in their own hands." [up20]

As illustrated by interviews conducted in 2003 and 2006, Montazeri reiterated his ongoing support for Sharia supremacism, shared the current Iranian regime's opinion about (and negotiating tactics for procuring) the Islamic Republic's "right" to pursue "peaceful" nuclear technology, and re-affirmed his bigoted, strident opposition to Israel's existence.

[Montazeri]: You see, if people around the world want to say certain things about women for example being equal to men in matters of inheritance or legal testimony, because these issues pertain to the very letter of the Qur'an, we cannot accept them... **in Iran we cannot accept those laws that are against our religion....on certain occasions that these laws contradict the very clear text of the Qur'an, we cannot cooperate**

[Interviewer]: So in future generations, when the number of professors, physicians, high-ranking experts, etc, will be more women, will Islam be able to have an ijtihad and modify these unjust laws because they no longer correspond with reality?

[Montazeri]: **Those aspects of the Islamic law that are based on the very letter of the Qur'an, the answer is no...** [up21]

If the U.S. or Europe wants to force Iran to relinquish nuclear energy for peaceful purposes - that is meddling in Iran's affairs... *One of the ways of dealing [with the crisis] is to conduct a diplomatic dialogue..., if America tries to force its power on Iran so as to deprive it of the use of nuclear energy for peaceful purposes, it would be a deceit [sic] - because knowledge and technology are not a monopoly but the right of all people. How can Israel have nuclear energy, and even nuclear weapons, but we, who don't want [nuclear] weapons - why can't we have nuclear energy for peaceful purposes?...* **Israel is a usurper government, that conquered the Palestinians' lands and made them refugees. If not for Israel, we would have no problem with other countries.** [up22]

The Glick-Ledeen "Trusting Montazeri/Green Movement Syndrome" approach stands in stark contrast to what I advocate in brief at the conclusion of this book, updated and elaborated in an essay ("End the Bush-Obama Fecklessness: Destroy Iran's Nuclear Facilities Now"), published November 10, 2014. [up23] The November 24, 2014 pronouncements regarding extension of the P5 +1 negotiations make plain that only continued Iranian obfuscation and delay loom going forward. However, now that not even the façade of agreement currently exists, Israel has been granted another window of opportunity—i.e., there is no "deal" yet affirmed that the Israelis are "sabotaging," let alone bound to uphold.

The question arises as to why more than 12-years after the August 14, 2002 revelations about Iran's Natanz and Arak nuclear installations [up24]—6-years under the Bush II Administration, and another 6-years (and counting) during the Obama Administration—sound, practical U.S. geostrategic arguments, and actions, such as those advocated by Professor Matthew Kroenig, have been dismissed. [up25] My book examines at some length, the origins of this tragic, yet entirely avoidable failure of imagination, and will, rooted in intellectual sloth, and cowardice.

The case for limited, targeted military strikes on Iran's four known nuclear facilities has been made with pellucid cogency by Professor Kroenig, Georgetown University International Relations Professor, and expert on Iran's nuclear program. Kroenig's dispassionate May, 2014, study, *A Time to Attack*, elucidates the profoundly destabilizing threat posed by an Iran armed with nuclear weapons:[up26]

> *From Iran, a revisionist and risk-acceptant state, we can expect...reckless behavior. Iran will almost certainly be willing to risk nuclear war in future geopolitical conflicts, and this will mean that it will be able on occasion to engage in successful nuclear coercion. It also means that, in playing these games of brinkmanship, it will increase the risk of a nuclear exchange.*

Kroenig then outlines the tactical obstacles military strikes on Iran's four established nuclear facilities would confront, from the relative ease of attacking the surface Isfahan and Arak sites, to the difficulty of targeting the underground Natanz and Qom complexes.[up27]

> *...Isfahan and Arak are above ground and therefore are easy military targets. We [the U.S.] could easily destroy these facilities using air- or sea-launched cruise missiles, launched from U.S. B-52 bombers operating outside Iranian airspace or U.S. warships in the Persian Gulf.*
>
> *Natanz is buried under seventy feet of earth and several meters of reinforced concrete, and Qom is built into the aide of a mountain and is therefore protected by 295 feet of rock. To destroy these sites we would need to use the Massive Ordnance Penetrator, or*

MOP. The MOP weighs 30,000 pounds and according to open source reporting, is capable of penetrating up to 200 feet before exploding. Some simple arithmetic (200 feet is greater than 70+ feet) suggests that Natanz doesn't stand a chance. It is unlikely that the MOP could penetrate into the enrichment chamber of Qom in a single shot (295 feet is greater than 200 feet), but we could simply put subsequent bombs in the crater left from a previous bomb and thus eventually tunnel our way in. Putting multiple bombs in the same hole requires a fair bit of accuracy in our targeting, but we can do it. In addition to destroying their entrances, exits, ventilation heating and colling systems, and their power lines and sources. The MOP can only be carried on the U.S. B-2 stealth bomber. Since it can be refueled in midair, the B-2 can be sent on a roundtrip mission from U.S. bases in Missouri and Diego Garcia in the Indian Ocean to its targets in Iran and back home again without stopping. The B-2 could also be escorted by stealthy U.S. F-22 fighters, or F-16s, to protect it against fighter aircraft.

This relatively limited, and very brief campaign consisting of "a barrage of cruise missiles and bombing sorties," Kroenig observes, plausibly conducted in one night,[up28]

would almost certainly succeed in its intended mission and destroy Iran's key nuclear facilities.

Citing four historical precedents where pre-emptive bombing of nuclear facilities achieved the goal of non-proliferation, decisively—"Nazi Germany during World War II, Iran during the Iran-Iraq War, Iraq several times in the 1980s, 1990s, and 2000s, and Syria in 2007" [up29]—Kroenig concludes by enumerating the multiple benefits which would accrue from similarly destroying Iran's known nuclear installations: [up30]

There is absolutely no doubt that a strike on Iran's nuclear facility would significantly set back Iran's nuclear progress and create a real possibility that Iran would remain non-nuclear for the foreseeable future.

Moreover ... [a] strike ... would stem the spread of nuclear weapons in the Middle East and bolster the nonproliferation regime around the world.

Furthermore, a U.S. strike would also strengthen American credibility. We declared many times that we were prepared to use force if necessary to stop Iran from building nuclear weapons. A strike would demonstrate that we mean what we say and say what

*we mean and that other countries, friends and foes alike, would be
foolish to ignore America's foreign policy pronouncements*

Iranian Revolutionary Guard Corps Deputy Commander Brigadier-General
Hossein Salami made the following comments at a conference held in Tehran,
which aired on Al-Alam TV on March 11, 2014: [up31]

> *Despite the geographical distance, we are attached to the hearts
> of the Palestinians. How is it that our slogans and goals are
> identical to the slogans and causes of the Palestinians? Why do
> we strive to become martyrs and risk our lives for the Palestinian
> cause? The answer is that the religion of Islam has designated
> this for us – this goal, this motivation, this belief, this energy – so
> that we, here, can muster all our energies in order to annihilate
> the Zionist entity, more than 1,400 kilometers away. We are ready
> for that moment in the future.*

The "Trusting Khomeini-Khamenei-Rohani" brain trust shaping current Obama
Administration Iran policy maintains the good general Salami doesn't mean
any of this, and it is somehow mere "cultural bluster." Conservative "Trusting
Montazeri/Green Movement," self-styled "Iran shenasans" ("Iran experts")
would argue the good general is simply "distorting" Shiite Islam and we must
be patient, support the (Soylent) Green Movement [up32] of Iranian Jeffersonian
Democrats, and at some unstated future time point, "regime replacement" will
solve the Iranian nuclear weapons, and all other such problems engendered by the
"distortion of Shiite Islam." Accordingly, we must ignore the hard data that show
83% support for the Sharia in Iran, [up33] or the 63% of Iranians who insisted that
Iran should continue to develop its nuclear program, [up34] even at the height of the
period of strictest international economic sanctions against the Islamic Republic.

Till now, those are your Iran policy options from the ones who control
such discourse—and current or planned actions—across the political and
ideological spectrum. As a potential alternative to this dangerously misguided
policy morass, I queried Professor Kroenig (in early November, 2014) about
the possibility of urgent Israeli airstrikes. Kroenig's *A Time to Attack* argues
persuasively about the limitations of such an Israeli campaign, Israel lacking any
known capability, for example, to penetrate the deeply embedded fortifications
of Iran's Qom/Fordow uranium enrichment facility. [up35] However, given what
is truly needed two-years from now, hope against hope—a complete U.S.
political and policymaking class "regime change"—I offer Professor Kroenig's
temporizing solution until the U.S. regains its geostrategic and moral bearings:

> ***As a last resort, an Israeli strike, and the year or two of
> breathing space, at minimum, it would buy, would be preferable
> to acquiescing to a nuclear Iran.***

Finally, the American public, regardless of the attitudes of current political leadership and policymaking elites, appears fully cognizant of Iran's intentions, and the unacceptable security threat posed by an Islamic Republic armed with nuclear weapons. Polling data from a U.S. national sample of 1800 Americans completed Sunday, November 23, 2014, indicated the following: [up36]

- 85% of Americans do not believe the Iranians' assertions that their nuclear program is peaceful

- 81% of Americans do not believe the current government in Iran can be trusted to keep agreements

- 69% of Americans oppose any negotiated agreement leaving Iran with nuclear capabilities

Hope springs eternal such gimlet-eyed Americans will elect equally astute political leaders also endowed with the courage necessary to authorize targeted military strikes which complete a task Israel will have initiated by 2015: destroying, or severely damaging the Islamic Republic of Iran's current nuclear development facilities, forestalling, and perhaps even preventing long term, a nuclear weapons-armed Iran.

Andrew G. Bostom
November 26, 2014

REFERENCES FOR THE AUTHOR'S UPDATED PREFACE

§ Jacob Eduard Polak, "Persecution of Jews—Information About the Jews of Persia from an Eyewitness," Archives Israélites, Vol. 28, 1865, pp. 489-49. (English translation by Ibn Warraq). Polak (1820–1891), was a Jewish physician and writer. Born in Bohemia [central Europe, currently in the Czech Republic], Polak studied medicine and science in Prague and Vienna. During 1851 he was invited to Tehran by the Persian government to serve as professor of anatomy and surgery at the military college. By 1856 he was appointed court physician to Shah Nasr-el-Din. After Polak returned to Vienna in 1860 he was affiliated with the general hospital there, and simultaneously taught Persian at the University of Vienna. Polak composed important treatises in Persian on anatomy, surgery, ophthalmology, and military medicine, some of which became standard works. He also compiled a medical dictionary, Deutsch-persiches Konversationswoerterbuch (1914), in Persian, Arabic, and Latin which provided the Persian language with a system of medical terminology. A devout Jew, Polak drew the attention of European Jewry to the plight of their co-religionists in Persia, and his proposal that the Alliance Israélite Universelle send a Jewish representative to Tehran or establish a Jewish school in the city, ultimately came to fruition. {Biography per, Christoph Werner, "POLAK, Jakob Eduard," [www.iranicaonline.org], December 15, 2009 [http://www.iranicaonline.org/articles/polak-jakob-eduard]}

up1. Jim Sciutto, Nic Robertson, Holly Yan, "New Iran Nuclear talks deadlines: March 1, July 1, 2015," *CNN*, November 24, 2014 [http://www.cnn.com/2014/11/24/world/meast/iran-nuclear-talks/index.html?hpt=po_c1%20%E2%80%A6]; "P5 +1" = the U.S., Britain, France, Russia, China, i.e., the five permanent members of the U.N. Security Council, plus Germany.

up2. Ibid.

up3. Michael R. Gordon, David E. Sanger, "U.S. and Allies Extend Iran Nuclear Talks by 7 Months," *The New York Times*, November 24, 2014 [http://www.nytimes.com/2014/11/25/world/middleeast/iran-nuclear-talks.html?_r=2]

up4. "Examining 10 Warning Signs of Iran Nuclear Weapons Development," *International Committee In Search of Justice*, November 20, 2014 [https://drive.google.com/file/d/0Bxsknizg1bK8ekNnby1NSjJTRWJqM205WEZtREp6djc3Uktv/view?pli=1]

up5. Ibid.

up6. Ibid.

up7. Ibid.

up8. [https://twitter.com/khamenei_ir/status/531366667377717248/photo/1]

up9. Ibid.

up10. Ibid.

up11. Iran's Ayatollah Khomeini, Ayatollah Khamenei, and President Rouhani

up12. Iran's Ayatollah Montazeri, and the "Green Movement" he allegedly inspired.

up13. Caroline Glick, "Bringing happiness to Iran," October 10, 2014 [http://carolineglick.com/bringing-happiness-to-iran-2/]

up14. Ibid.

up15. Andrew Bostom, "Photo of Ayatollah Montazeri, (Soylent) Green Movement "Inspiration," Refusing to Shake the Hand of a Najis Jew," March 30, 2014 [http://www.andrewbostom.org/blog/2014/03/30/photo-of-ayatollah-montazeri-soylent-green-movement-inspiration-refusing-to-shake-the-hand-of-a-najis-jew/]

up16. Andrew Bostom, "Yippee 'Hizbullahi' and 'Chaadoris'?—Some Sad Realities About Irredentist Iran," *www.andrewbostom.org*, Iran, June 20, 2009 [http://bit. ly/1do3UtN]; "Mullah's Milk," www.andrewbostom.org, June 21, 2009 [http://bit. ly/JZ0mU2]; "Perpetuating Iran's Islamic Culture of Hate," *www.andrewbostom. org*, June 22, 2009 [http://bit.ly/1do5hsq]; and "The Squandered Emancipation of Iranian Women," *The American Thinker*, July 1, 2009 [http://bit.ly/1hnyGnj]; A. Savyon, "Elections in Iran – Part V: The Waning of the Protest Movement," *The Middle East Media Research Institute*, Inquiry & Analysis Series Report No. 529, June 29, 2009, [http://bit.ly/JZ3Zcr]

up17. Michael Ledeen, "Montazeri," *Pajamas Media*, December 21, 2009 [http:// bit.ly/1hcjEmW]; Michael Rubin, "Grand Ayatollah Hossein Ali Montazeri, R.I.P.," *National Review Online*, December 21, 2009 [http://bit.ly/JHy3bW]; Reuel Marc Gerecht, "The Bill O'Reilly Fallacy," *The New Republic*, October 16, 2010 [http://bit.ly/1n2gGT6]

up18. *Foreign Broadcast Information Service* (*FBIS*) daily reports 1974-1996 [electronic resource], Naples, FL: Readex

up19. "Ayatollah Montazeri Meets With Karrubi, Others," April 22, 1987; *FBIS*, April 23, 1987, LD 222336

up20. "Montazeri Address," November 27, 1987; *FBIS*, November 30, 1987, LD271348

up21. Goldbarg Bashi, "Eyewitness History: Ayatollah Montazeri," *Payvand Iran News*, March 8, 2006 (The interview was conducted in 2003) [http://www. payvand.com/news/06/mar/1067.html]

up22. "Iraqi News Agency Aswathura's Exclusive Interview With Grand Ayatollah Montazeri," *The Middle East Media Research Institute*, May 24, 2006, Special Dispatch No.1171 [http://www.memri.org/report/en/0/0/0/0/0/0/1699.htm]

up23 Andrew Bostom,"End the Bush II-Obama Administration Fecklessness: Destroy Iran's Nuclear Facilities, Now," *Pajamas Media*, November 10, 2014 [http://pjmedia.com/blog/end-the-bush-obama-fecklessness-destroy-irans-nuclear-facilities-now/]

up24 "Examining 10 Warning Signs of Iran Nuclear Weapons Development"

up25 Matthew Kroenig, *A Time to Attack: The Looming Iranian Nuclear Threat*, New York, N.Y., 2014.

up26 Ibid, p. 165.

up27 Ibid, pp. 172-173.

up28 Ibid, p. 173.

up29 Ibid, p. 182.

up30 Ibid, pp. 188-189.

up31 "IRGC Deputy Commander Hossein Salami: We Are Ready to Annihilate the Zionist Entity in the Future," *Middle East Media Research Institute*, March 11, 2014, Clip No. 4188 [http://www.memri.org/clip_transcript/en/4188.htm]

up32 See ref. 16, above.

up33 "Iranians' Views Mixed on Political Role for Religious Figures," *Pew Research Religion and Public Life Project*, June 11, 2013 [http://bit.ly/1j6pDKH]

up34 Mohamed Younis, "Iranians Feel Bite of Sanctions, Blame U.S., Not Own Leaders— Most support nuclear program despite sanctions," *Gallup World*, February 7, 2013 [http://bit.ly/1m59HW3]

up35 Kroenig, *A Time to Attack*, pp. 176-177.

up36 Bostom, "End the Bush II-Obama Administration Fecklessness: Destroy Iran's Nuclear Facilities, Now"

up37 David Horovitz, "69% of Americans oppose deal leaving Iran with nuclear capabilities," *The Times of Israel*, November 25, 2014 [http://www.timesofisrael.com/most-americans-oppose-deal-leaving-iran-with-nuclear-capabilities/]

AUTHOR'S ORIGINAL PREFACE

With great fanfare, and giddy expectations of continued diplomatic success, the so-called "P5 +1" interim agreement was announced on November 24, 2013. [p1] Ostensibly, these negotiations were going to eliminate Iran's ability to produce nuclear weapons, and constrain the regime's hegemonic aspirations, including its oft-repeated bellicose threats to destroy the Jewish State of Israel.

Less than three months later, punctuated by cries of "down with the U.S."—and "Death to Israel"—Iranians took to the streets en masse, February 11, 2014, commemorating the 35th anniversary of the 1979 Islamic putsch, which firmly re-established Iran's legacy of centuries of Shiite theocracy, transiently interrupted by the 54-year reign (r. 1925-1979) of the 20th century Pahlavi Shahs. [p2] Celebratory statements by "moderate" Iranian President Rouhani claimed Iran would pursue its nuclear program "forever," and decried Western economic sanctions, designed specifically to forestall Iran's nuclear weapons producing capability, as "brutal, illegal, and wrong." [p3] Major-General Yahya Rahim Safavi, a senior military aide to Iranian Supreme Leader Ayatollah Ali Khamenei, threatened that any Israeli effort to pre-empt Iran's relentless pursuit of nuclear weapons, meant for Israel's annihilation, would be countered by retaliatory "destruction of the Zionist regime by Hezbollah forces of Iran and the Lebanese Hezbollah." [p3] Simultaneous triumphal commemorative pronouncements (from 2/11/14) included: [p4]

- Iranian Defense Minister Hossein Dehquani's declaration that Iran's test firing of ballistic missiles including a long-range ballistic missile with radar-evading capabilities—was (somehow) an appropriate response to "unfounded allegations" by the U.S.

- Iranian Navy Commander Admiral Habibollah Sayari's confirmation that Iranian warships had been deployed toward the territorial waters of the U.S. Atlantic coast. The good Admiral announced: *"Iran's military fleet is approaching the United States' maritime borders, and this move has a message. Like the arrogant powers that are present near our maritime borders, we will also have a powerful presence close to the American [maritime] borders."*

Moreover, within eight-days after Iran's 35th anniversary celebrations of its retrograde "Islamic revolution," the following stories were reported:

- Iran's chief "P5 + 1" negotiator, Muhammad Javad Zarif derided (unusually candid) comments by U.S. lead negotiator with Iran, Wendy Sherman, that if Iran's nuclear program was only for peaceful purposes, the Islamic Republic "does not need" the fortified, underground uranium enrichment center at Fordow, or its plutonium heavy-water reactor at Arak. A defiant Zarif, referring explicitly to Sherman's observations, opined, *"Iran's nuclear technology is non-negotiable and comments about Iran's nuclear facilities are worthless and there is no need to negotiate or hold talks about them."* [p5]

- Iran's Deputy Foreign Minister, Abbas Aragchi stated Iran would not capitulate to pressure from the U.S. and the five other world powers to dismantle *any* of its nuclear facilities. [p6]

- Iran rejected the U.S. contention that its ballistic missile program must be included as a key component of negotiations on a permanent nuclear agreement. Abbas Aragchi stated on Iranian state television: *"The Islamic Republic of Iran's defensive issues are neither negotiable nor subject to compromise. They are definitely among our red lines in any talks. We won't discuss **any** issue other than the nuclear dossier in the negotiations."* [p7]

- Despite such brazen Iranian intransigence, White House National Security Spokesman Caitlin Hayden revealed the Obama Administration would not interfere with Iran's burgeoning oil sales, which are generating billions of additional revenues as economic sanctions collapse in the wake of the P5 + 1 interim deal. [p8]

- Ayatollah Khamenei, during an address on Iranian television, February 17, 2014, insisted it would be "impossible" to resolve the "nuclear issue," per "U.S. expectations." He claimed Iran had been insulted by a U.S. Senator who *"takes money from Zionists in order to go to the Senate and curse the Iranian nation."* Khamenei reminded his audience, *"the Americans are the enemies of the Islamic Revolution and of Iran. They are the enemies of the flag that you hold high, and these [negotiations] will not bring an end to this enmity."* [P9]

- President Rouhani, at an ancillary meeting with Palestinian Parliament Speaker Salim Zanoun on Wednesday 2/19/14, held during the Organization of Islamic Cooperation Inter-Parliamentary Union in Tehran, stated, *"One of the wishes of the Iranian nation is liberation of the Holy Quds [Jewish Jerusalem, Israel's capital]...the Palestinian nation and the entire Muslim world will find a serious solution to this occupation through unity and integrity."* [P10]

These, and many comparably alarming developments since the P5 +1 deal was announced (see Chapter 1), epitomize the abject failure of a delusive and dangerous policymaking mindset I have dubbed, "The 'Trusting Khomeini' Syndrome." This "Syndrome" is named after infamous Princeton International Law Professor Richard Falk's February 16, 1979 essay, "Trusting Khomeini," dutifully published in the *The New York Times* [P11] The parlous denial—born of willful doctrinal and historical negationism—evident in Falk's February, 1979 essay, now shapes formal U.S. policy toward Iran, merely updated as "Trusting Khamenei." I further maintain that the *sine qua non* of this crippling mindset—bowdlerization of Islam—currently dominates policymaking circles, running the gamut from Left to Right. The late Islamologist Maxime Rodinson warned 40-years ago of a broad academic campaign—which has clearly infected policymakers across the politico-ideological spectrum—"to sanctify Islam and the contemporary ideologies of the Muslim world." [P12] A pervasive phenomenon, Rodinson ruefully described the profundity of its deleterious consequences: [P13]

> ***Understanding [of Islam] has given way to apologetics pure and simple.***

A prototypical example of how this mindset has warped intellectually honest discourse about Iran by conservative analysts, was published February 17, 2014 in *The Weekly Standard.* [P14] The essayist decried what he saw as misguided appropriation of Cold War era paradigms—"wishful thinking built around **imagined Cold War analogies**"—even by members of the Israeli "security establishment," let alone their Obama Administration counterparts. [P15] Although correctly dismissive of the sham notion that Iranian President "Rouhani and his crowd are moderates," the essayist also insisted Iran's "ayatollahs" have somehow "perverted Shia Islam with the state takeover of religion." [P16] He then ads, "the

older quietist school [ostensibly of Shiite Islam] still has many adherents." [p17]
These glib, distressingly uninformed pronouncements on Shiite Islam are
immediately followed by the author's own Cold War era comparisons: [p18]

> *What produced a change in Soviet behavior was the willingness*
> *of the West, led by the United States, to fight the Cold War on the*
> *ground—and the willingness to fight it ideologically.... Reagan,*
> *after all, did not allow his desire for negotiations to prevent him*
> *from saying the Soviet Union was an "evil empire"...*

Thus we have a pathognomonic illustration of the author's "**imagined Cold War
analogies**"—views published in a flagship conservative/neoconservative journal,
[p19] and shared by a broad swath of like-minded conservative analysts.

What Ronald Reagan understood—and articulated—was characterized elegantly
by Robert Conquest, the nonpareil historian of Communist totalitarianism's
ideology, and resultant mass murderous depredations. [p20]

> *The Soviet Union, right up to the eve of its collapse, was committed*
> *to the concept of an unappeasable conflict with the Western world*
> *and to the doctrine that this could only be resolved by what Foreign*
> *Minister Andrey [Andrei] Gromyko described as officially as one*
> *could imagine, in his 1975 book **The Foreign Policy of the Soviet***
> ***Union**, as world revolution: "The Communist Party of the Soviet*
> *Union subordinates all its theoretical and practical activity in the*
> *sphere of foreign relations to the task of strengthening the positions*
> *of socialism, and the interests of further developing and deepening*
> *the world revolutionary process." One could hardly be franker.*

President Reagan's seminal March, 1983 speech to the National Association of
Evangelicals included this gimlet-eyed description of the "totalitarian darkness"
at Communism's ideological core:[p21]

> *...they [Communists] preach the supremacy of the state, declare*
> *its omnipotence over individual man, and predict its eventual*
> *domination of all peoples on the Earth.*

Reagan's address also invoked Communist apostate, Whittaker Chambers.
Chambers' own 1947 book review of Rebecca West's *The Meaning of Treason*
compared the violent fanaticism of the twentieth century's secular totalitarian
systems adherents, to the votaries of Islam. [p22] The modern totalitarians expressed
"new ideas" which were "violently avowed," and [p23]

> **the hallmark of their advocates was a fanaticism unknown since**
> **the first flush of Islam.**

Does Chambers's analogy between Islam and Communism—utterly ignored in the February 17, 2014 *Weekly Standard* policy analysis [24]—have doctrinal and historical validity? This critical question can only be answered when other related questions pertaining to Islam—in its Shiite Iranian context, and more generally (i.e., within the predominant Sunni sect)—are put forth, and addressed. Those relevant questions conclude the Preface. The remainder of this book—materials from Chapters 1-3, and the Conclusions section—will answer them.

Here are the questions:

What is the Sharia? What are the uniquely Islamic institutions of jihad, and its corollary institution, dhimmitude, and how do these institutions relate to the Sharia? What are the similarities and differences comparing Sunni (the [vast] majority sect of Islam) and Shiite (Shi'ism being Islam's largest minority sect) doctrine on jihad and dhimmitude? What is the Shiite doctrine of *najis*? What are the major antisemitic motifs in Islam's canonical texts—the Koran itself (i.e., as glossed in the major Koranic commentaries, classical and modern), as well as the "Traditions" of Islam's prophet, Muhammad, and the nascent Muslim community?

What are the similarities and differences comparing Sunni and Shiite eschatology—end of times theology—and how central are the Jews to this doctrine (i.e., what is their described role, and fate?), from the Sunni and Shiite perspectives? How were these doctrines applied in Iran, and what was their effect upon the Jews of Iran, between the 16th, and early 20th centuries? Are these living doctrines, espoused and *presently* applied in contemporary Iran? For example, has the Sharia been applied in Iran since 1979 (especially vis-à-vis non-Muslims), and what is its current popularity in the Islamic Republic (as measured objectively, not anecdotally)?

Most importantly, how is Iran's historical application of these doctrines, in aggregate, to its Jewish minority population, relevant—and manifest—in the contemporary Islamic Republic's posture toward Israel, and the U.S.?

What is takiya (taqiya; taqiyya), and what was the treaty of al-Hudaybiyya (al-Hudaybiyyah), and how might both be very relevant to the interim "P5 + 1" agreement?

Who was Shah Ismail, and what was his attitude towards Iran's Jews? Who were Mohammad Baqer Majlisi, Sayyid Muhammad Sadiq Husayni Shirazi, and Hussein [Hossein] Ali Montazeri, and what were their views on jihad, dhimmitude, and *najis*?

What is *Al-Mizan fi Tafsir al-Qur'an* ("The measure of balance in the interpretation of the Koran"), who was its author, and what views are espoused in this "monumental" 20th century work, on jihad, dhimmitude—and the Jews?

Finally, returning to *The Weekly Standard* essayist's allusion to the "quietist school" of Shiite Islam and its "many adherents," [p25] what is Shiite "quietism," who are exemplar Shiite "quietists," and what are their views on the Sharia, jihad, dhimmitude, *najis*, and the Jews?

Andrew G. Bostom
February 26, 2014

1

Introduction

THE 'TRUSTING KHOMEINI' SYNDROME, REDUX?

Part of the confusion in America about Iran's social revolution involves Ayatollah Ruhollah Khomeini. More than any third-world leader, he has been depicted in a manner calculated to frighten... **To suppose that Ayatollah Khomeini is dissembling seems almost beyond belief...** *He has little incentive suddenly to become devious for the sake of American public opinion. Thus the depiction of him as fanatical, reactionary and the bearer of crude prejudices seems certainly and happily false. What is also encouraging is that his entourage of close advisers is uniformly composed of moderate, progressive individuals.*

— RICHARD FALK, International Law Professor, Princeton University, February 16, 1979 [§]

*Islamic law [sharia] exists to serve the interests of the Muslim community and of Islam. [Therefore,] to save Muslim lives and **for the sake of Islam's survival it is obligatory to lie, it is obligatory to drink wine** [if necessary].*

— AYATOLLAH RUHOLLAH KHOMEINI, from his speech addressing Revolutionary Guard commanders, and others, July 31, 1981. [§§]

Overview

Less than three weeks after the November 24, 2013 announcement of an interim agreement between Iran, the U.S., and five other world powers, [1] during an interview which aired December 11, 2013, Iranian Middle East analyst Mohammad Sadeq al-Hosseini, provided a candid assessment of the negotiations. El-Hosseini, a former political advisor to both Iran's alleged reformist ex-President Khatami, and the Khatami regime's erstwhile Minister of Culture and Islamic Guidance, Ata'ollah Mohajerani (also deemed a "moderate"), underscored the ancient Islamic doctrinal bases for the contemporary Iranian theocracy's geo-politics. Invoking the armistice "Treaty of Hudaybiyya" agreement between Muhammad and the 7th century pagan Quraysh tribe of Mecca, which Islam's prophet-warrior unilaterally abrogated as soon Muhammad's jihadist forces achieved the military superiority needed to vanquish his Meccan foes, el-Hosseini declared: [2]

> ***This is the Treaty of Hudaybiyya in Geneva, and it will be followed by a "conquest of Mecca."***

Consistent with Muhammad's tactical formulation when waging jihad, "War is deceit" (from the canonical hadith "traditions" of the Muslim prophet),[3] the Islamic doctrine of takiya, or kitman ("concealment"; "disguise"),[4] and the modern parallel of Soviet Communist deceit and conspiracy (especially during arms control negotiations), [5] el-Hosseini also noted, [6]

> *Incidentally, for your information, when you conduct political negotiations with Iran, you lose even when you think you have won.* ***The [Iranians] have raised the level of uranium enrichment far beyond the level they really needed, so that when the level would be lowered, they would emerge victorious.***

El-Hosseini further insisted the Geneva deal augured America's eventual jihad conquest during Iran's ongoing "fierce war with Americans on all levels." [7] While this claim appears dubious, at present, El-Hosseini contended, appositely, that the agreement marked near-term U.S. capitulation to Iran's oft-repeated threat to destroy Israel by jihad [8]—including via nuclear weapons.

> *Obama had to make a great retreat. He was forced to accept a handshake from President Rohani [Rouhani], whom he considered a kind of Gorbachev or Sadat, so that the day would not come when he would be forced to kiss the hands of [Secretary General of Lebanese Hezbollah]Hassan Nasrallah and [Supreme Leader of Iran] Imam Khamenei, so that they would hold their fire* ***in the great war that was prepared to annihilate Israel.*** [9]

Eighteen months earlier (on June 6, 2012), Iran's Fars News agency published an interview with el-Hosseini during which he quoted sura (chapter) 59, verse 14 of the Koran, a reference to Muhammad's brutal, sanguinary jihad conquests of Arabian (especially Medinan) Jewry, which concluded with the capture of Jews' final refuge at the Khaybar oasis: [10]

> *This matter is exactly the meaning of the Koranic verse, "They will not fight against you all together except in fortified cities, or from behind walls."... The circumstances of Khaybar [are present today as well, because the Jews are fighting] from behind a wall. This means that they have reached the limit of their capabilities and options, and are no longer willing to leave their homes. Consider that Israel is a small and very narrow coastal country and does not have the strategic or geopolitical ability to defend itself, and it could disappear at any moment. These people could flee en masse. As [Yahya Rahim] Safavi said, under circumstances of all-out war, a million Israelis will flee the occupied territories [i.e., Israel] in the first week [of the war]. This is no exaggeration.*

Despite the prevailing media and policymaking elite narrative, [11] do el-Hosseini's countervailing understandings, claims, and arguments, expressed so unabashedly, withstand serious, objective scrutiny? This is a very basic, critical question given the reflexive tendency—born, I would argue, of sheer ignorance, denial, and delusion—to simply ignore, or dismiss such outspoken analyses.

In pursuing an intellectually honest answer to this query, these two ancillary questions must be addressed:

[I] Are there fundamental deficiencies in the "P5 +1" agreement with Iran, announced on November 24, 2013, which would allow the Shi'ite Islamic Republic to realize its full nuclear ambitions, including the procurement of nuclear weapons capability?

[II] What are the animating Islamic ideologies (i.e., formal, traditionalist doctrines) which underpin Iran's relentless pursuit of nuclear weapons (and missile delivery systems), and explain why Israel, repeatedly, and selectively, has been identified as their first specific target, should Iran procure them?

As I will demonstrate within the limited, introductory discussion, the answer to question [I] is "yes." But more significantly, and ominously, the dangerous agreement brokered at Geneva represents the apotheosis of a delusive policymaking mentality—shared by most conservative foreign policy analysts and pundits with equal stubbornness—which disregards question [II] altogether. This latter, profound failure of imagination will be made apparent by the monograph's central discussion of jihad, its corollary institution, "dhimmitude," and Islamic

Jew-hatred, particularly as manifested by the Iranian Shi'ite theocracy, across a half-millennium, through the present era.

'Don't You Let That Deal Go Down'
(apologies to the late Jerry Garcia)

An unlikely consensus was reached by Israel's Prime Minister Netanyahu, Iran's President Rouhani, Russian Foreign Minister Lavrov, and his Iranian counterpart Mohammad Javad Zarif, immediately upon the announcement of the interim agreement struck between Iran, the U.S. and five other world powers, early Sunday morning, 11/24/13: **Iran's nuclear enrichment program would continue apace.** [12]

United Against Nuclear Iran (UANI), a not-for-profit, non-partisan, advocacy group which seeks to thwart Iran's ambition to obtain nuclear weapons, issued a press release that same day highlighting the fundamental strategic failures of the interim 6-month pact: [13]

> *By not agreeing to dismantle a single centrifuge, Iran has not rolled back its nuclear infrastructure and with the many [i.e., an estimated 19,500]* [14] *centrifuges that it is currently operating, Iran retains the ability to breakout and produce enough weapons-grade uranium for a nuclear weapon in as little as 2 months. At the same time, the carefully constructed sanctions architecture developed over decades has been significantly rolled back.*

UANI argued further that the Geneva agreement provided Iran disproportionate sanctions relief, which would enable the Iranian economy (as gauged by the value of its currency, the rial) to recover to an extent that Iran's nuclear weapons development (i.e., nuclear enrichment, and plutonium generation) programs, would be abetted by this reduction in economic pressures. [15]

> *Six months from now we believe that the Iranian rial will have regained significant lost value and there will be far less economic pressure on the Iranian economy. And accordingly there will be far less pressure for Iran to actually dismantle a material number of centrifuges, much less end its nuclear enrichment and plutonium programs for which it has no practical purpose except to produce a nuclear weapon. If Iran's industrial-size nuclear program is not rolled back, Tehran will inherently maintain the breakout capacity to build such a weapon*

Over the next three months, a surreal tragicomedy of U.S. diplomatic failure would unfold. President Obama's administration (and its champions among the media and policymaking chattering classes) were confronted with the inescapable realities outlined in the schematic UANI press release. The most salient of these revelations and developments, which have validated UANI's concerns, are enumerated and elaborated, in the following discussion.

Theatrical masks of Tragedy and Comedy. Mosaic, Roman artwork, 2nd century CE
http://bit.ly/1hGRXA2

(i) Ayatollah Ali Khamenei's alleged "fatwa" proscribing nuclear weapons development

During 1988, while the Iran-Iraq war still raged, draining Iran's military and financial resources, Ayatollah Ruhollah Khomeini wrote a letter reproducing a written request by then commander-in-chief of the Islamic Revolutionary Guard Corps, Mohsen Rezaii (via Rezaii's letter, dated 6/23/1988) for the development of "a substantial number of laser and atomic weapons." [16] (Rezaii, as per Khomeini's rendition of his 6/23/1988 letter, also advised that the U.S. be evicted from the Persian Gulf.) [17] Khomeini's letter expressed no opposition to the idea of procuring or developing atomic weapons of mass destruction

(WMD), but rather understandable concerns about Iran's capability to purchase or produce such an arsenal. [17] Furthermore, Khomeini apparently never issued any subsequent written (or oral) fatwa prohibiting either the development or usage of nuclear (and other) WMD. [18]

Twenty-five years later, 11/27/13, within three days after the Geneva agreement was announced, the Washington Post's Glenn Kessler published an evaluation [19] of the purported fatwa banning nuclear weapons by Ayatollah Khamenei, Iran's current Supreme Leader, who succeeded Khomeini in 1989. [20] Kessler introduced his discussion by quoting the verbatim statement of President Obama, pertaining to his conversation with Iranian President Rouhani on 9/27/13, [21] and two statements issued the same day the "P5 +1" deal with Iran was made public (11/24/13), one by a senior Obama administration official, [22] and the other by Secretary of State Kerry. [23]

> *[President Obama] "Iran's supreme leader has issued a fatwa against the development of nuclear weapons."*

> *[Senior Obama administration official, quoted by Kessler] "The supreme leader of Iran has said that there is a fatwa to development of a nuclear weapon."*

> *[Secretary Kerry] "So I close by saying to all of you that the singular objective that brought us to Geneva remains our singular*

Iran's Supreme Leader Ayatollah Ali Khamenei delivering a speech on November 8, 2006, where he stated that his country would continue to acquire nuclear technology and challenge "Western fabrications." [23a]

objective as we leave Geneva, and that is to ensure that Iran does not acquire a nuclear weapon. In that singular object, we are resolute. Foreign Minister (Mohammad Javad) Zarif emphasized that they don't intend to do this, and the supreme leader has indicated there is a fatwa, which forbids them to do this."

According to Kessler's report, Caitlin Hayden, a White House spokeswoman for the National Security Council, after maintaining that the Iranian government was the optimal source for information on the fatwa, added: [24]

Many Iranian officials have spoken of the fatwa publicly, and their comments are publicly available. There are various descriptions of it in the public domain. And importantly, the Iranians have also referenced the fatwa in our negotiations.

Kessler's investigation confirmed [25] what independent analysts (including, notably, one he interviewed, Mehdi Khalaji) had established [26] earlier. Notwithstanding Obama administration claims—based simply upon regurgitating mendacious Iranian government propaganda, and in the absence of any textual evidence—no such fatwa has ever been produced. As Kessler observed, even "the slick new Iranian government website on its nuclear program," which asserts Khamenei's ostensible 2003 fatwa banning nuclear weapons was a juristic extension of the (non-existent [27]) fatwa of his predecessor, Khomeini, allegedly proscribing chemical weapons production,

*... **does not provide the text of the original fatwa** — and then mostly cites Western news reports as evidence that Khamenei has reiterated it on several occasions.* [28]

Providing original documentary substantiation (i.e., a confidential 2004 U.S. State Department cable released via Wikileaks [29]), Kessler also exposed Khamenei's mendacious statements denying Iran's history of chemical weapons production. [30]

After uncovering hard evidence of Iran's history of mendacity regarding WMD production, and the Obama administration's current willful blindness to the transparent Iranian deception regarding the alleged Khamenei nuclear fatwa, how does Kessler conclude his investigative report? He simply ignores the profoundly dangerous implications of this disingenuous U.S. policymaking effort for regional Middle East, and U.S. security interests. Kessler concludes that the Obama administration's statements and behaviors germane to the fatwa amount to a mere inconsequential "diplomatic MacGuffin," which fail to earn any "Pinocchios" for dishonesty. [31]

Just about every Alfred Hitchcock thriller had what he called a "MacGuffin" — a plot device that gets the action going but is

*unimportant to the overall story. The Iranian fatwa thus appears
to be a diplomatic MacGuffin — something that gives the
Americans a reason to begin to trust the Iranians and the Iranians
a reason to make a deal. No one knows how this story will end,
but just as in the movies, the fatwa likely will not be critical to
the outcome. Even if one believes the fatwa exists — and will not
later be reversed — it clearly appears to have evolved over time.
U.S. officials should be careful about saying the fatwa prohibits
the development of nuclear weapons, as that is not especially
clear anymore. The administration's statements at this point do
not quite rise to the level of earning Pinocchios, but we will keep
an eye on this issue.*

As Kessler's report did note, [32] Khalaji's 2011 analysis chronicles Khamenei's
"evolving" views on nuclear weapons. Initially, during the mid-1990s, Khamenei
denied accusations that Iran was attempting to produce WMD. [33] Subsequently,
between 2003 to 2006, Khamenei's pronouncements shifted from negating the
practical utility of such weapons, to an emphasis on claims that "Islam" forbade
both their production and usage. [34] However, by 2010, Khamenei's position
morphed again into simply proscribing the use of atomic weapons, without
mentioning prohibitions on their production, or stockpiling. [35] Khalaji also
observed, appropriately, [36]

> *Regarding WMD, even if one disputes the Islamic legality of **using**
> [emphasis in original] WMD, one cannot ignore the Quran's
> justification [as examples, see Koran 3:151, 8:12, 8:60, 33:26,
> 59:2, and 59:13] for the production of such weapons to terrify
> the enemy.*

He then refers to written statements by Ayatollah Mesbah Yazdi, a member of
Iran's Assembly of Experts, the religious body of 86 senior Shiite clerics which
monitors the Iranian Supreme Leader, and anoints his successor. [37] Yazdi also
directs a prominent Shiite Islamic think tank, the Imam Khomeini Education
and Research Institute, based in the holy city of Qom. [38] During Mahmud
Ahmadinejad's Presidency, Yazdi served as the former President's spiritual
mentor. [39] Yazdi's 2005 book, "The Islamic Revolution: A Wave of Political
Change in History," drew attention in 2010 for its brazen endorsement of WMD
development by Iran, likely motivated, and rationalized, Khalaji argued, by the
canonical Islamic (i.e., especially Koranic) invocations for striking terror into the
hearts of infidels. [40] Yazdi opined, [41]

> *The most advanced weapons must be produced inside our
> country even if our enemies don't like it. There is no reason that
> they have the right to produce a special type of weapons, while*

*other countries are deprived of it... Under Islamic teachings, all
common tools and materialistic instruments must be employed
against the enemy and prevent enemy's military superiority...
From Islam's point of view, Muslims must make efforts to benefit
from the most sophisticated military equipment and get specific
weapons out of the monopoly of powerful countries*

Khalaji concluded, [42]

*And should the needs of the Islamic Republic or the Muslim
umma [global community of Muslims] change, requiring the use
of nuclear weapons, the Supreme Leader could just as well alter
his position in response.*

Khalaji delves briefly into several other critically relevant matters, including two [43] not discussed at all by Kessler, [44] let alone enthusiastic promoters of the "P5 + 1" deal with Iran: the question of "non-combatants" in Islamic jurisprudence, and takiya/kitman.

Islam, Khalaji tacitly acknowledges, lacks any doctrine comparable to Western just war theory. [45] During jihad wars (to be discussed in depth later), the lives and property of non-Muslims—*without* excepting non-combatants (unless they are already under treaty protections of a Muslim state), so-called "harbis," within the dar al-harb ("infidel lands of war"), are licit. [45] Citing both the important 19th century Shiite jurist Sayyed Ali Tabatabai (d. 1816), who sanctioned *any means* that assured the ultimate victory of jihadists, [46] and opinions of prominent contemporary Iranian clerics (i.e., from the Assembly of Experts, the powerful Guardian Council, and even the lionized "moderate," Ayatollah Montazeri), Khalaji concedes, [47]

*[T]he forces of Islam would seem to have very wide latitude in
dealing with non-believers...[E]xamination reveals the concept
of "civilian noncombatants" as alien to the Islamic juridical
tradition...Given these parameters, it is difficult to define the
notion of God's enemy as* **excluding** *[emphasis in original]
noncombatant believers when Islam allows Muslims to use any
weapon against the "enemies of God."*

Khalaji's candid analysis further acknowledges the "influence," perhaps "important influence on Iranian nuclear decision making," of dissimulation, and the formalized practice of takiya/kitman, or deception for the purpose of self-protection. He argues that such practices have greater urgency when conducted for the perceived welfare of an Islamic state, or the global Muslim community. [48]

The classical Shiite theologian Amin al-Islam Tabarsi said that

*taqiyya [takiya] is permitted "in all cases if it is necessary." [49]
Some jurists argue further that in safeguarding the interest of the
Muslim community, taqiyya can be highly desirable. [50] ...Ayatollah
Khomeini himself stated publicly that rulers or subjects should
lie or even drink wine (read: violate sharia) when required for
the expediency of the Islamic government. [51] ...In Shia Islam, the
interests of the Muslim umma stand above the interests of each
Muslim individual. Hence, if Islamic law permits Muslims to
lie for the sake of their own personal interest or welfare, then
certainly Islamic governments can lie on behalf of the interests
of the Muslim umma. Ayatollah Khomeini repeatedly used such
logic in his statements. [52]*

(ii) Critical omissions from the from the Geneva "P5 + 1" deal

None of Iran's ~19,500 centrifuges (19,462, by one reported tally [53]) used for
uranium enrichment were to be physically dismantled as per the 11/24/13 Geneva
agreement. [54]Although centrifuges capable of uranium enrichment beyond 5%
were, by compromise, to be disconnected, that arrangement, simultaneously,
permitted 10,000 centrifuges to continue to enrich to 20% purity, a concentration
approaching weapons grade. [55] Regardless, the technology required to enrich
uranium (U-235) to 5% is identical to that required to enrich it to weapons-grade
80% or more—all that is needed is to recycle previously enriched uranium through
the centrifuge system, until the desired concentration is reached. [56] Moreover,
despite France's publicized alarm about the Iranian heavy water plutonium reactor
at Arak, just two weeks prior [57] to the announcement of the "P5 + 1" deal, Iran was
only required to suspend, not cease activity on such heavy water related products.
[58] Martin Sevior, a University of Melbourne physicist, immediately highlighted
the problems with such an arrangement: [59]

*Another sticking point in yesterday's agreement was that Iran
is constructing a heavy water reactor. Heavy water reactors
use heavy water (deuterium oxide) as coolant (opposed to light
water reactors, which use normal water) and employ natural
unenriched uranium as fuel and produce plutonium as a waste
product. Unlike light water reactors which typically take one to
three months to shut down and restart, heavy water reactors do
not need to be shut down in order to change fuel assemblies. Thus
heavy water reactors are much better suited for weapons-grade
plutonium production.*

The agreement brokered in Geneva omitted any mention of the military
production center at Parchin (southeast of Tehran), Iran's experimental high
explosives facility. [60] Iran has steadfastly refused to permit International Atomic

Energy Agency (IAEA) inspectors access to this key testing site, and the interim agreement apparently does not include such inspections going forward. [61]

No wonder the Foreign Minister Mohammad Javad Zarif, crowed, on November 24, 2013: [61]

> *None of the enrichment centers will be closed and Fordo and Natanz will continue their work... [T]he Arak heavy water program will continue in its present form*

Analyst Jonathan Spyer summarized the one-sided outcome of the negotiations—a diplomatic bonanza for Iran. [63]

> *So the core elements of the Iranian drive for a nuclear weapon remain entirely intact–the construction of centrifuges, the enrichment of uranium, the maintenance of the Arak reactor in its present state, and the unimpeded development of the technology and scientific capacity required to produce a nuclear explosive device... In return for a series of concessions which do not affect these core principles, the sanctions on Iran's gold and petro-chemicals exports are to be removed. Efforts to reduce Iranian sale of crude oil will be ended, and there will be no new sanctions. Sanctions will be reduced in a number of other related areas as well.*

(iii) Iran: Deal brokering in Geneva, while jointly developing long-range missiles in Pyongyang

As reported by defense analyst Bill Gertz (on 11/26/13), [64] groups of Iranian missile technicians from the Shahid [="Martyr"] Hemmat Industrial Group (SHIG)—a unit controlled by the jihadist Islamic Revolutionary Guard Corps, [65] and tasked with building Iran's liquid-fueled missiles—traveled to Pyongyang, North Korea within a month of the Geneva agreement. According to U.S. intelligence assessments, Iranian SHIG technicians were believed to be working on a new 80-ton rocket booster under development by the North Koreans. [66] Gertz noted, [67]

> *The booster is believed by U.S. intelligence agencies to be intended for a new long-range missile or space launch vehicle that could be used to carry nuclear warheads, and could be exported to Iran in the future.*

Gertz's Tuesday, November 27, 2013 report made plain what the ongoing, more than a decade long Iranian-North Korean cooperation on missile development [68] revealed, juxtaposed to the "P5 + 1" negotiations, and interim agreement with Iran: [69]

The Iranian cooperation reveals that the nuclear framework agreement concluded Sunday [11/24/13] in Geneva has not slowed Tehran's drive for missiles that can deliver a nuclear warhead to intercontinental range.

(iv) <u>Negotiations jihad: Falling for the diplomatic Three Card Monte played by Iran's Shiite theocracy</u>

Thursday, December 9, 2013, Ali Akbar Salehi, current head of the Atomic Energy Organization of Iran (AEOI), and touted as a "pragmatist," [70] proclaimed triumphantly, "Our centrifuges are working full capacity." [71] Within a week later, Marzieh Afkham, an Iranian Foreign Ministry spokeswoman, projecting Tehran's official narrative in reference to the Geneva accord, commented that there was in fact, "no treaty and no pact, only a statement of intent." [72] Echoing this line, the Iranian daily *Kayhan*, published by Supreme Leader Ali Khamenei's office, maintained in a Sunday, 12/15/13 editorial that the accord's six month time frame meant nothing, and it could "even take 20 years to negotiate" a final agreement. [73] Khamenei's mouthpiece *Kayhan* concluded bluntly, [74]

If our centrifuges do not continue to turn, no other wheel shall turn for our dignity, independence, power and security.

These statements were representative of a host of other similar pronouncements made by Iranian diplomats, politicians, clerics, and other officials, since the Geneva accord was announced (1/24/13), through the end of December, 2013, and well into January, 2014. Such rhetorical Iranian interpretation of the recent agreement was accompanied by actions demonstrating Iran was tenaciously pursuing the full gamut of its nuclear aspirations, undaunted. Other salient examples of this consistent Iranian trend—both rhetoric and actions—are presented below, chronologically:

- President Rouhani told the *Financial Times*, in an interview published 11/29/13, that dismantling Iran's nuclear facilities was a "red line" Iran would not cross, and that the nation would set its own concentration limits for uranium enrichment. [75]

- Mansour Haqiqatpour, Vice-Chairman of the Iranian Parliament's National Security and Foreign Policy Commission, told the *Fars News Agency* on 12/9/13, that "Iran's enrichment right," was "recognized," and "the Americans can't take this right away from us." [76] His declaration reiterated a prior statement made by Seyed Abbas Araqchi, a senior Iranian negotiator in the "P5 + 1" talks, who insisted Iran's right to enrich uranium was a (another) "red line" sanctioned by the Geneva deal itself. [77]

- On December 12, 2013, AEOI chief Salehi re-affirmed his 12/9/03 statement about the pace of uranium enrichment continuing at "full capacity," [78] dismissing as "baseless and wrong" contentions that aspects of Iran's nuclear activities had been slowed. [79] Iran "will never cross its red lines or give up its…inalienable right" to enrich uranium, Saleh added. Saleh also insisted "there will be no more inspection" of Arak's heavy-water plutonium reactor facilities. [80]

- December 16th and 17th, 2013, Iran's Foreign Minister Muhammad Zarif, protested [81] the move by the U.S. Congress to legislate a regimen of bolstered economic sanctions, while maintaining, defiantly, [82]

- *It shows a lack of understanding of how to proceed in order to resolve the nuclear issue. Some people are wedded to the idea that pressure will produce results. They are wrong. Pressure has produced 18,000 centrifuges in Iran. So if they want to continue that road – it is open to them, but it doesn't produce any results.*

- On December 27, 2013—capitalizing on an obvious loophole defect in the Geneva interim agreement—Salehi announced that Iran would be producing new, more sophisticated centrifuges, capable of enriching uranium faster. [83]

- By December 29, 2013, senior Iranian Parliamentarians announced they had obtained 200 co-sponsors from among their colleagues for a bill requiring Iran's government to enrich uranium to 60%, complete the nuclear infrastructures at the Fordo and Natanz installations, and launch the Arak heavy water plutonium reactor. [84] Saturday January 4, 2014, the Fars News Agency reported a claim by Seyed Mehdi Moussavinejad, a member of the parliament's Energy Commission, that this "double-urgency bill, signed by 218 legislators," was presented to the "Presiding Board," and submitted to the parliament's speaker, Ali Larijani. Iranian Deputy Foreign Minister and senior negotiator in the P5 +1 talks Araqchi further maintained that if the Iranian parliament approves the draft bill, it will be binding for the government. [84a]

- Friday January 3, 2014, parliamentarian and cleric Muhammad Nabavian stated brazenly (as per Iranian press reports, independently reviewed and translated by The *Washington Free Beacon*) that Iran would be able to build a nuclear bomb in "two weeks" if it obtains "access to 270 kilograms of 20 percent [enriched uranium], 10 tons of 5 percent, and 20 thousand centrifuges." Nabavian added, "We are not looking for a nuclear bomb, but having a nuclear bomb is necessary to put down Israel." [84b]

- By Tuesday, January 14, 2014, President Rouhani was brazen enough to gloat about the "P5 + 1" Geneva accord, via his twitter account (tweet reproduced below as text, and a screen shot). He crowed that the U.S. et al (at Geneva) had acquiesced to the "Iranian nation's" own perceived nuclear goals: [84c]

> *Our relationship w/ the world is based on Iranian nation's interests. In #Geneva agreement world powers surrendered to Iranian nation's will.*

- One day earlier (January 13, 2014), Iran's Foreign Minister Zarif was photographed in a Beirut, Lebanon suburb laying a wreath on the grave of Imad Mughniyeh, the Hezbollah jihadist leader who planned the 1983 "martyrdom" bombings of the U.S. embassy, and Marine barracks, which, in sum, killed over 350 persons. [84d] Mughniyeh also orchestrated the 1992 and 1994 Buenos Aires bombings which targeted the Israeli embassy, and Asociacion Mutual Israelita Argentina (AMIA), respectively, murdering 114 people between the two attacks. [84e] According to a 2006 indictment by the Investigations Unit of the Office of the Attorney General of Argentina, the ultimate decision to bomb the AMIA center was not only made by Khamenei, and then-president Ali Akbar Hashemi Rafsanjani, but the "determining factor" which motivated the attack, was [84f]

> *the Argentine government's unilateral decision to terminate the nuclear materials and technology supply*

> *agreements that had been concluded some years*
> *previously between Argentina and Iran...[A]t this period*
> *the Iranian government felt that it was crucial for Iran to*
> *develop its nuclear capacities.*

- Saturday, January 18, 2014, the Fars News Agency reported the comments of a senior Iranian Parliamentarian, Mohammad Hassan Asafari, who serves on the Parliament's National Security and Foreign Policy Commission. Describing Foreign Minister Zarif's recent trip to Lebanon, which included a meeting with Hezbollah Secretary General Hassan Nasrallah, Asafari claimed, [84g]

> *During this meeting, the (Iranian) foreign minister*
> *reiterated that support will continue for the resistance*
> *movement Hezbollah, which seeks to establish peace in*
> *Lebanon and fight hegemony.*

- A day earlier, Friday January 17, 2014, Israeli Middle East security analyst Avi Issacharoff reported that despite the ongoing internecine Shiite-Sunni carnage in Syria, (Shiite) Hezbollah was still committing "more than a third" of its forces on the Lebanese border with Israel. These forces were engaged in "massive excavations" in Shiite towns and villages along the southern border, including shelters, storage facilities for an estimated 100,000 rockets, and the possible construction of tunnels for attacks into Israel. Citing a recent Nasrallah speech during which he declared that Hezbollah "has an old, new, and renewed score to settle," Issacharoff suggested [84h] the jihadist organization was preparing for a new round of "limited," but damaging assaults, short of all out warfare.

- By January 20, 2014, even as Iran claimed to have begun halting its production of 20% enriched uranium "in the Fordow and Natanz sites," the New York Times reported another glaring deficiency acknowledged by the International Atomic Energy Agency, as per the 11/24/13 "P5 + 1" joint plan of action for monitoring Iranian compliance: [84i]

> *Iran did not agree to all of the intrusive inspection*
> *regime that the International Atomic Energy Agency had*
> *said was needed to ensure that the Iranian program is*
> *peaceful.*

- Interviewed on Wednesday, January 22, 2013, Iran's Foreign

Minister Zarif implored CNN Chief National Security correspondent Jim Sciutto to read the actual text of the (P5 + 1) agreement, to dispel false claims by the Obama Administration it compels Iran to "dismantle" (any of) its nuclear infrastructure: [84j]

> *The White House tries to portray it as basically a dismantling of Iran's nuclear program. That is the word they use time and again. If you find a single, a single word, that even closely resembles dismantling or could be defined as dismantling in the entire text, then I would take back my comment.*

- Just hours before President Obama delivered his State of the Union address (1/28/14), which included remarks lauding how the P5 +1 agreement "halted" Iran's nuclear weapons development program, a joint Congressional hearing [84k] demonstrated otherwise. Gregory S. Jones, a Senior Researcher at the Nonproliferation Policy Education Center testified [84L] that "the great flaw in the deal" was "it permits Iran to retain centrifuge enrichment." He added, pointedly,

> *This fact has been denied by Secretary of State Kerry [84m] but the Joint Plan of Action says in two separate places that the follow-on Comprehensive Solution would "involve a mutually defined enrichment programme...." Note that the text says "would," not "might" or "could." That the Comprehensive Solution will permit Iranian centrifuge enrichment was later confirmed by the Obama administration national security spokeswoman Bernadette Meehan who said, [84n] "We are prepared to negotiate a strictly limited enrichment program."*

Jones' written testimony concluded, [84o]

> *The only reasonable negotiating position is for the U.S. and the P5+1 to insist that Iran stops all uranium enrichment and dismantles its centrifuge enrichment facilities. President Obama and others have recognized that this would be the best outcome from the negotiations with Iran but have said that it is an unrealistic demand since Iran would never agree.*

The hearings also revealed that the White House was refusing to release the full written text of the agreement with Iran. House Foreign Affairs Committee (HFAC) member Rep. Ileana Ros-Lehtinen (R., Fla.) complained, [84p]

> *Why is it that members of Congress have to go to a super*
> *secret location, a cone of silence ... to look at the deal?...*
> *It's a very easy to read document; one doesn't have to*
> *be an expert. If this is such a great deal and so good*
> *for peace and diplomacy in our time why is it held in*
> *secret?...If the administration is proud of it, I think they*
> *should highlight it.*

Jones concurred, [84q] stating "It does bother me," that the deal has been kept secret, adding,

> *It appears to me the administration has negotiated*
> *an agreement it does not fully understand and I don't*
> *understand how that can happen...I don't see how there's*
> *going to be an agreement.*

• Pressed by the Senate Foreign Relations Committee, during hearings on February 4, 2014, U.S. chief negotiator with Iran Wendy Sherman conceded that the P5 + 1 agreement, failed to "shut down" Iran's continuing development of ballistic missiles. [84r] These weapons, which have long range capabilities, are the preferred devices for delivering a nuclear payload. Senator Bob Corker (R., Tenn.), the committee's ranking member, raised the appropriate questions, interspersed with relevant commentary: [84s]

> *Why did you all not in this agreement in any way address*
> *the delivery mechanisms, the militarizing of nuclear*
> *arms, why was that left off since they [Iran] breached*
> *a threshold everyone acknowledges.? They can build a*
> *bomb. We know that. They know that. They have advanced*
> *centrifuges. We have a major loophole in the research*
> *and development area that everyone acknowledges. We*
> *are going to allow them over this next year to continue*
> *to perfect the other piece of this, which is the [nuclear]*
> *delivery mechanism. Why did we do that?*

• Despite all these developments, President Obama's January 28, 2014, State of the Union speech not only claimed "American diplomacy" had somehow "halted the progress of Iran's nuclear program," he peevishly threatened, [84t]

> *[L]et me be clear: if this Congress sends me a new*
> *sanctions bill now that threatens to derail these talks, I*
> *will veto it.*

Ironically, polling results were also published on January 28, 2014 which indicated robust public rejection of the Obama Administration's misbegotten negotiations strategy toward Iran. The National Omnibus Poll, conducted by McLaughlin Associates, surveyed a sizable, representative nationwide   sample of 1000 Americans, with the following demographic mix: Protestants (46%), Catholics (30%), Jews (3.6%), African Americans (13%), Hispanics (12%), Asians (3%) and Whites (70%). Forty-two percent (42%) of the respondents indicated they were Democratic party supporters, and 41% Republican party supporters. When asked, "Iran continues to call for Israel's destruction and calls America the Great Satan. Do you believe that President Obama has done all he can to prevent Iran developing nuclear weapons?," 51% responded that the President has not done all he can to prevent Iran from developing nuclear weapons, as opposed to 28% who believe that he has. Queried, "Should the United States pass stronger sanctions against Iran or should they weaken sanctions in order to convince Iran to stop developing nuclear weapons?," 59% replied that the U.S. should impose stronger sanctions, while only 17% indicated the U.S. should weaken sanctions on Iran. [84u]

Christopher Hellman, a veteran energy industry reporter, wrote an analysis immediately after (i.e., 11/25/13) the P5 +1 agreement was announced, which suggested that the negotiations with Iran, and resulting elimination of sanctions, could lead to massive investment in Iranian oil drilling, and related infrastructure. This development, in turn, would unleash enormous supplies of easily recoverable Iranian oil, with very deleterious effects on the "economics of the tight oil plays that have sprung up across the United States in recent years." [85] Hellman's assessment highlighted these potential short, intermediate, and long term consequences for "America's great oil and gas renaissance," which has been bolstered by the sanctions: [85a]

> *In the short term, the Iran deal will ease the political risk premium baked into oil prices. In the medium term a comprehensive deal could add 1 million or more barrels per day to the market. In the long-term a gush of Iranian oil could soften oil prices enough to kill the economics of America's tight oil boom.*

By early to mid-December, 2013 reports and analyses underscored how the prospective lifting of economic sanctions on Iran was immediately redounding to Iran's financial benefit. [85b] Analyst Ilan Berman summarized the Iranian windfall, thusly: [86]

> *Already, the Iranian regime itself has received a much-needed economic reprieve. On the heels of the accord, the Obama administration released billions of dollars in blocked Iranian oil assets as a goodwill gesture. That, however, is just the beginning. According to Iranian officials, the Iranian government will gain*

access to as much as $15 billion of oil revenues over the next half-year under the terms of the Geneva deal. As a result, Iran is poised to receive at least $20 billion-worth of economic relief — equivalent to nearly half of the country's hard-currency reserves (currently estimated at some $50 billion) and far greater than originally envisioned by the White House.

These developments have not gone unnoticed. More and more corporations and sovereign states alike are now making plans based on the assumption that eroding sanctions will again make Iran a lucrative commercial market — and a global energy player. As a result, Iranian officials are waxing optimistic. According to Hadi Ghavami, head of the Iranian parliament's Plans, Budget, and Auditing Commission, the country's economy, currently shrinking by 5.8 percent annually, is expected to grow 2.2 percent in the coming year.

Amir Taheri concurred with Berman's assessment that the P5 +1 agreement was already having a salutary effect on Iran's economy: [87]

The perception that the crisis is cooling down has already halted the Islamic Republic's economic free fall. The national currency, the rial, lost 80 percent of its value over four years, but now appears to have stabilized.

Most significantly, Taheri's pellucid, if trenchant analysis exposed how U.S. (and European) diplomacy was easy prey for Iran's negotiations jihad, "Three Card Monte" tactics: [88]

Having claimed that he had halted Iran's nuclear project, Secretary of State John Kerry might want to reconsider. He and his European colleagues, like many of their predecessors, may have fallen for the diplomatic version of the Three Card Monte played by the mullahs since they seized power in 1979. ***Khomeinist diplomacy has never aimed at reaching agreement with anyone. Instead, the regime regards negotiations as just another weapon in the jihad for ensuring the triumph of "true Islam" across the globe.*** *The regime can't conceive of give-and-take and compromise even with Muslim nations, let alone a bunch of "Infidel" powers. If unable to impose its will on others, the regime will try to buy time through endless negotiations. In Three Card Monte, suckers stay in the game in the hope of getting it right next time. A similar hope ensures outsiders' participation in Khomeinist diplomacy's version of the trick.*

Taheri's acid commentary recalls the ignored, but profoundly relevant warnings of Igor Lukes about Cold War era negotiations with the former Soviet Union, written 25 years earlier. [89]

> *We ought to remember that the Soviets conduct "total" politics. Whenever Kremlin representatives sit down to negotiate, we can assume that they were instructed to insist on superiority for the Soviet side. In order to achieve that objective, a whole scale of techniques (from regular diplomacy talks to walk-outs and threats of the use of force) will be applied. In the negotiating process, the West must demonstrate as much patience as it can muster. Open societies tend to expect instant results. But the issues involved in East-West relations are far too complex to be solved during a few meetings. In any case, summits are not solutions in and of themselves. Poorly prepared summits can seriously destabilize international relations.*

Historian Robert Conquest identified a salient feature of the delusive mindset of apologists for Soviet era Communist totalitarianism shared by today's useful idiots for totalitarian Islam—willing intellectual and ethical blindness. [90]

> *[A] con job needs a con man **and** a sucker. In their case many suckers even managed not to take in what they saw with their own eyes, or rather somehow to process unpleasantness mentally into something acceptable...Mind-set seems too strong a word: these were minds like jelly, ready for the master's imprint...[T]his was an intellectual and moral disgrace on a massive scale.*

Richard Falk's Mindset Lives
(and Thrives, Across the Political Spectrum)

International Law Professor Richard Falk has become infamous for his calumnies against Israel, based upon deliberately (and transparently) deceitful "investigations." [91] An eternal written testament to Falk's sheer, triumphal idiocy—and a harbinger, perhaps, of his moral cretinism as well—was published in the *New York Times* February 16, 1979. The very title of Falk's opinion editorial, "Trusting Khomeini," [92] is pathognomonic of two devastating Western maladies—cultural self-loathing, and jihad denial. Indeed these trends have worsened over the intervening three decades, as the civilizational war [93] waged by Shiite and Sunni jihadists —consistent with Islam's classical jihad theory [94]—has intensified. [95]

Distressingly uninformed, ebullient appraisals [96] of the interim Geneva agreement may represent the acme of perverse tendencies Falk epitomized 35 years ago.

However intellectually (and ethically) deficient Falk and his New York Times editorial page abettors were—and remain—it is still worth reflecting upon their clear, and nefarious goal, as elucidated by Protestant theologian and social critic Jacques Ellul. [97]

> *The goal of modern propaganda is no longer to transform opinion but to arouse an active and mythical belief.*

Bernadette Meehan, President Obama's National Security Council spokeswoman, issued a statement on Friday January 10, 2014 that was a striking example of such propaganda efforts.[98] Hectoring Congressional advocates of continued economic sanctions against Iran (i.e., S. 1881: "Nuclear Weapon Free Iran Act of 2013," [99], which target (albeit with dubious "success" [100]) Iran's relentless development of nuclear weapons-related materials and technology, Meehan accused them of being "warmongers," deliberately sabotaging the Obama administration's demonstrably feckless—and dangerous—"diplomacy": [101]

> *If certain members of Congress want the United States to take military action, they should be up front with the American public and say so. Otherwise, it's not clear why any member of Congress would support a bill that possibly closes the door on diplomacy and makes it more likely that the United States will have to choose between military options or allowing Iran's nuclear program to proceed.*

Sunday January 12, 2014, Meehan's diatribe was cited approvingly in a Fars News Agency report, which also quoted senior Iranian Parliamentarian Esmayeel Jalili's defiant pronouncement made that same day: [101a]

> *If the US congress doesn't abide by the policies of the [Obama] administration and approves new sanctions, the parliament will be ready to declare Iran's exit from the nuclear negotiations with the Group 5+1 (the US, Russia, China, Britain and France plus Germany)*

The Fars News Agency report also included comments made in December 2013 about S. 1881 by the Iranian Parliament Speaker's top advisor for international affairs, Hossein Sheikholeslam. These "relevant remarks," in the Fars News Agency's characterization, were redolent with Iran's pervasive, conspiratorial Jew-hatred. [101b]

> *Capitalism, and not democracy, has the last say in the US and the US congressmen should also pursue the goals and words of the US capitalists which are mostly Zionists. The Zionist lobbies are highly powerful in the US Congress, hence we always witness*

> *the US Congress moves against Iran. And there are many cases in*
> *which the American nation's interests are sacrificed for the sake*
> *of the Zionist regime's goals.*

National Security Council spokeswoman Meehan's deliberate misrepresentation of S. 1881, her vicious attack on its Senate sponsors, and the endorsement of these views by "senior" Iranian Parliamentarians, epitomizes Obama Administration policy toward Iran. The destructive repercussions of this mindset, and the behaviors it engenders, were illuminated by the third of Robert Conquest's three laws of politics: [102]

> *The simplest way to explain the behaviour of any bureaucratic*
> *organisation is to assume that it is controlled by a cabal of its*
> *enemies.*

What follows are extracts from Richard Falk's February, 1979 *New York Times* essay. [103] Tragically, Falk's warped vision of Khomeini and his "revolution," from 35 years ago, is no more ludicrous—or dangerous—than the mindset guiding current U.S. policy toward the Iran of Khomeini's successors, and ideological devotees. Summary, corrective annotation is provided documenting some of Khomeini's longstanding, clearly articulated views (as well as the views of what Falk terms his "entourage" of "moderates and progressives"). What actually befell non-Muslim minorities, and "the Left" under the Shiite theocracy Khomeini re-installed, is also introduced. The best source on the human rights tragedy engendered by Iran's retrograde 1979 Khomeini "revolution" remains historian Reza Afshari's seminal 2001 publication, *Human Rights in Iran: The Abuse of Cultural Relativism.* [104] "Promises Before and Results After Khomeini's Islamists Took Over," [105] is a very compendious online source of refutations to the fatuous claims by Falk, cited in addition. Further, more specific sources will be discussed within the expansive analysis of the chronic plight of Iranian Jewry (before and) after Khomeini and his clerical entourage seized control of Iran's government.

> [**Falk**] *Part of the confusion in America about Iran's social*
> *revolution involves Ayatollah Ruhollah Khomeini. More than any*
> *third-world leader, he has been depicted in a manner calculated*
> *to frighten....In recent months, before his triumphant return*
> *to Tehran, the Ayatollah gave numerous reassurances to non-*
> *Moslem communities in Iran. He told Jewish community leaders*
> *that it would be a tragedy if many of the 80,000 Jews left the*
> *country. Of course this view is qualified by his hostility to Israel*
> *because of its support of the Shah and its failure to resolve the*
> *Palestinian question.* [105a]

Shortly after the executions of Jewish community leaders, on manufactured charges of "espionage," following Khomeini's ascension to power, in fact 75%

of the Jewish community did flee. [106] These events, the overall plight of Jews (shared, to a great extent, by other non-Muslims in Iran, notably, Zoroastrians, Bahai, and Christians [107]), and Khomeini's genocidal Islamic supremacist views about the Jews of Israel because they did not live as "dhimmis," subjugated under the Sharia, Islamic Law—sentiments that were independent of the so-called "Palestinians," or any relationship between the Shah and "Zionists"—will be elaborated upon subsequently.

> *[Falk] He [Khomeini] also indicated that the non-religious left will be free to express its views in an Islamic republic and to participate in political life, provided only that it does not "commit treason against the country" by establishing foreign connections—a lightly-veiled reference to anxiety about Soviet interference. [107a]*

Reza Afshari has summarized what actually transpired: [108]

> *Politically, the highly repressive character of the regime emerged during the process by which the clerics severely restricted the basic freedoms of political activists. They achieved their goal by forcibly removing all secular, leftist, and liberal political forces and individuals from the wide and unwieldy array of political activities that the revolution had opened up in 1979.*

International Law Professor Ann E. Mayer, and Afshari have elucidated the impact of Iran's theocratic constitution upon the rights and status of the "non-religious" (as well as non-Muslims), including Sharia-based punishments for "apostasy," and "blasphemy". [109] Amir Taheri wrote a complementary December, 2010 retrospective highlighting Khomeini's brutal campaign against the Left, involving murder, torture, and incarceration. This ruthless, bloody oppression followed close upon the heels of what Taheri aptly describes as "a revolution based almost entirely on deception." [110]

> *[Falk] To suppose that Ayatollah Khomeini is dissembling seems almost beyond belief. His political style is to express his real views defiantly and without apology, regardless of consequences. He has little incentive suddenly to become devious for the sake of American public opinion. Thus the depiction of him as fanatical, reactionary and the bearer of crude prejudices seems certainly and happily false. What is also encouraging is that his entourage of close advisers is uniformly composed of moderate progressive individuals...[T]hey are widely respected in Iran outside religious circles, share a notable record of concern for human rights and seem eager to achieve economic development that results in a modern society oriented on satisfying the whole population's basic needs. [110a]*

Apparently Falk saw nothing "fanatical, reactionary" or rife with "crude prejudices" in Khomeini's unabashed declaration of open-ended, offensive jihad genocide to achieve regional, then global Islamic hegemony; his views on Jews and other non-Muslims, including the dehumanizing Shiite concept of najis; his grotesque misogyny, which legitimized female child abuse; or his acceptance of animal sodomy. [111] (These traditionalist views were either broadly shared and sanctioned, or tacitly accepted, by his "entourage.") Falk's willful "intellectual and moral disgrace," in Conquest's apt formulation, [112] also disregarded the religiously sanctioned practice of takiya/ kitman to promote Islamic goals. [113]

The concluding sections of Falk's 1979 essay, below, reach such dizzying heights of voluntary delusion that no annotated comments are necessary.

> *[Falk] Ayatollah Khomeini said recently, in France, that in any well-governed society "the ruler does not live very differently from the ordinary person." For him, to be religious is to struggle for these political goals, yet the religious leader's role is to inspire politics, not to govern. Hence, it is widely expected that he will soon go to the holy city of Qum, at a remove from the daily exercise of power. There he will serve as a guide or, if necessary, as a critic of the republic. In looking to the future, Ayatollah Khomeini has spoken of his hopes to show the world what a genuine Islamic government can do on behalf of its people. He has made clear frequently that he scorns what he considers to be the so-called Islamic Governments in Saudi Arabia, Libya, and Pakistan. Despite the turbulence, many non-religious Iranians talk of this period as "Islam's finest hour." Having created a new model of popular revolution based, for the most part, on non-violent tactics. Iran may yet provide us with a desperately-needed model of humane governance for a third-world country. If this is true, then indeed the exotic Ayatollah may yet convince the world that "politics is the opiate of the people." [113a]*

I maintain that the cardinal feature of Richard Falk's damaging mindset vis-à-vis Khomeini and Iran—i.e., his bowdlerized "conception" of Islam in general, and Shiite Islam in particular—now compromises U.S. analyses of Iran across the politico-ideological spectrum.

As described near the beginning of this Introduction, United Against Nuclear Iran (UANI), the centrist, non-partisan (and eponymous) advocacy group, weighed in immediately about the gravely negative implications of the November 24, 2013 "P5 +1" deal with Iran. [114] A number of simultaneous assessments by avowed conservative analysts reiterated UANI's tocsin of looming geo-strategic calamity, regarding this interim agreement. [115] By December 17, 2013, the bipartisan Center for Strategic and International Studies (CSIS), issued a mammoth 228 pp. report entitled, "The US and Iran: Sanctions, Energy, Arms Control, and Regime Change." [116] Despite its equivocations (and inaccurate characterization [117] of the current Rouhani regime in Iran), the CSIS assessment shared many of the overriding concerns expressed by UANI and the politically conservative analysts. [118]

All these assessments from the center-right, expressed valid strategic concerns, at times punctuated by alarm, over the "P5 + 1" agreement. **However, uniformly omitted were any serious discussions of the Islamic ideology which animates Iran's relentless efforts to obtain nuclear weapons for the stated purpose of destroying Israel, and in pursuit of its larger regional, and global hegemonic aspirations.** [119] For example, one may or may not believe that a wave of actionable messianism ("Mahdism")—central to which, in either classical Sunni, or the more ill-defined (and much less historically significant) modern Shiite variant of Islamic eschatology, is the destruction of the Jews [120]—truly grips the Iranian regime, and its supporters. [121] But certainly the oft-repeated apocalyptic rhetoric of Jew-annihilation, [122] or, more importantly, the boilerplate, corporeal world Islamic Jew-hatred Iran churns out on a continual basis, [123] should have been acknowledged, and examined, in such analyses. Even this material was not discussed.

Sharia supremacism—in its Twelver Shiite guise—was the fervent motivation for the Shiite theocracy established by Iran's first Safavid Shah Ismail I, at the outset of the 16th century. [124] This belief system—which was always redolent with Islamic Jew-hatred in Safavid Iran, and across a 500-year continuum, ever since—remains the guiding ideology in the "Khomeini revival" (and post-Khomeini) era, at present.

Intentionally obfuscating apologetics, aside, Sharia, Islamic law, whether Sunni or Shiite, is not merely holistic, in the general sense of all-encompassing, but totalitarian, regulating everything from the ritual aspects of religion, to personal hygiene, to the governance of a Muslim minority community, Islamic state, bloc of states, or global Islamic order. Clearly, this latter political aspect is the most troubling, being an ancient antecedent of more familiar modern totalitarian systems. Specifically, Sharia's liberty-crushing and dehumanizing political aspects feature: open-ended jihadism to subjugate the world to a totalitarian Islamic order; rejection of bedrock Western liberties—including freedom of conscience and speech—enforced by imprisonment, beating, or death; discriminatory relegation of non-Muslims to outcast, vulnerable pariahs, and even Muslim women to subservient chattel; and barbaric punishments which violate human dignity, such as amputation for theft, stoning for adultery, and lashing for alcohol consumption. [125] Regarding post-Khomeini Revolution Iran, and its "Guardianship of the Jurist" application of the Sharia, Abbas Amanat acknowledged that, [125a]

> *The doctrine of the "Guardianship of the Jurist" was informed above all by a Shi'i legal mindset that was essentially alien to modern notions of plurality and democratic leadership.*

Moreover, during interactions with non-Muslims, Shiites add strict doctrinal adherence to the odious concept of "najis," the physical as well spiritual "impurity" of the infidel, which results in a series of dehumanizing practices directed toward these "infidels." [126] The British scholar, E.G. Browne provided this eyewitness account of how najis regulations impacted non-Muslims—mirroring centuries of their continuous application—through the end of the 19th century: [126a]

> *While I was in Yezd [a center of Zoroastrian culture, 170 miles southeast of Isfahan] a Zoroastrian was bastinadoed [beaten with a cudgel on the soles of the feet] for accidentally touching with his garment some fruit exposed for sale in the bazaar, and thereby, in the eyes of the Musulmans [Muslims], rendering it unclean and unfit for consumption by true believers [i.e., the Muslims]*

The contemporary Iranian Shiite theocracy has revitalized the ugly doctrine—and practice—of najis.

I will conclude the Introduction with a small, yet representative series of examples which demonstrate the failure of center-right policymakers and analysts to consider Iran's Sharia supremacism and intrinsically-related jihadism and Islamic Jew-hatred. These consistent analytical lacunae—born of equal parts ignorance, doctrinaire cultural relativism, and magical thinking—help perpetuate ineffectual, and ultimately dangerous policies.

The CSIS's expansive December 17, 2013 analysis includes no mention of "jihad," "Jews," or "antisemitism"—not a single reference to the individual words throughout its entire 228 pp.[127] Absent any discussion of Iran's virulent jihadism and canonical antisemitism directed at Israel, which is intermingled with unequivocal calls for the Jewish State's destruction, the CSIS authors nevertheless advocate that the U.S. prevent any Israeli attempt at preemptively delaying (or destroying) Iran's nuclear weapons program, because, they allege, "that would probably end any chance of negotiations succeeding." [128] On p. 140, the CSIS analysis makes its sole, anodyne reference to "Sharia," citing President Rouhani's theological training, as follows: "his background in theology and Sharia comforts religious Iranians." [129] Rouhani (continuing the discussion on p. 140) is described as embodying a "measured pragmatism," as purportedly evidenced by appointments to his cabinet, which, "further reflected this commitment to a technocratic over ideological government." The CSIS authors, noting former President Rafsanjani's so-called moderation, add: "Many key appointees served under former **moderate** [emphasis added] President, Ali Akbar Hashemi Rafsanjani." [130] Rouhani's *Weltanschauung* and key utterances are elaborated in the discussion which follows.

But contra the CSIS characterization of Rafsanjani's ostensible "moderation," the former Iranian President made this bigoted and bellicose proclamation, televised on April 17, 2005: [130a]

> *The biggest problem of the Islamic world today is global Zionism and the Great Satan, America. They are our enemies ... they have no religion and they do not accept Allah. ... Some are called Christians and some Jews ... every passing day the people's hatred festers, especially among the youth in Islamic countries. This hatred of the Great Satan and global Zionism constantly intensifies ...*

Pace the CSIS analysts' assessment, the "measured pragmatist" Rouhani (as reported in *Kayhan*, the Iranian regime's house media organ, Saturday June 22, 2013) attributed his June, 2013 electoral victory to the influence of the 12th Shiite Imam, whose "occultation" [130b] dates from the end of the 9th century (~874 C.E.):

> *This victory and the epic saga is without a doubt due to the special kindness of the Imam Zaman (Mahdi) and the measures taken by the supreme leader, especially his guidance and words. ... Without his management then it was not clear if the people of Iran would witness such a day filled with joy* [130c]

Possible messianic allusions, and their significance, aside, *The New York Times* published a story on August 2, 2013 (that was briefly revised later), which included this ominous (and ugly) real world observation by Rouhani: [131]

> *Ahead of his inauguration, Iran's new president on Friday called Israel an "old wound" that should be removed, while tens of thousands of Iranians marched in support of Muslim claims to the holy city of Jerusalem. Hassan Rouhani's remarks about Israel — his country's archenemy — echoed longstanding views of other Iranian leaders. "**The Zionist regime has been a wound on the body of the Islamic world for years and the wound should be removed,**" Rouhani was quoted as saying by the __semi-official [Iranian State News Agency] ISNA news agency__.*

ISNA claimed later that they (and not Western editors) had mistranslated Rouhani's quote and then issued corrections claiming **he had merely called Israel a "sore"** and had not said it should be removed–though one wonders what he thinks should be done with sores if they are not to be made to disappear. The original Times story was then replaced with a piece containing revised language, albeit based on the most dubious of claims. But the argument that the alleged mistranslation should not be used to debunk Rouhani's reputation as a moderate was undermined by the fact that, as even the revised Times story said, he had denounced Israel "in several books." [132] **None of the material from this prominent New York Times story about Rouhani, reported just 4-months earlier, appeared in the December, 2013 CSIS analysis.**

Hassan Rouhani has a lengthy history in Iranian politics, having served as the Secretary of Iran's Supreme National Security Council for more than 16 years. He was also a former deputy speaker of the parliament. During Mohammad Khatami's Presidency, in 2003, Rouhani became Iran's chief nuclear negotiator. Rouhani maintained the post for two years before being replaced by Ali Larijani when Mahmoud Ahmadinejad assumed the presidency in 2005. He is also a member of Iran's Expediency Discernment Council, an advisory body to the Supreme Leader, Ayatollah Ali Khamenei, as well as the Assembly of Experts, a body vested with the power to elect and remove the Supreme Leader. Rouhani is reputed to be close to both Ayatollah Ali Khamenei and former President Akbar Hashemi Rafsanjani, the Chairman of Expediency Discernment Council. [133]

Until his election to the presidency, Hassan Rouhani headed the Tehran-based think tank, the Center for Strategic Research. [134] Rouhani, in a 2009 monograph published by the Center for Strategic Research, "Islamic Political Thought, Volume I: Theory," extolled Iranian theocrat Ayatollah Khomeini's alleged enlightened "vision" for Islamic governance, as follows: [135]

> *It appears distancing from any fundamental ideals of the Islamic Revolution, would only mean to be held in the prison of western politics, "politics without ethics" or a medieval European dungeon, "backward religious thoughts"...And we all have witnessed and taken notes of the warning of great architect of the Islamic government, Ayatollah Khomeini, that we avoid falling over that cliff...[T]he Islamic Revolution and its theorists, and above all, Imam Khomeini, were exemplary leaders who were the first projected, defined and implemented a superb divine Islamic model for all humans and all times. (translation kindly provided by Amil Imani)*

The CSIS analysis did not include these 2009 observations by Rouhani which capture, unequivocally, his ongoing reverence for Khomeini's ideology.

Not surprisingly, and entirely consistent with policies of the Iranian regime since Khomeini's retrograde "revolution," Rouhani is a strong proponent of Iran's nuclear weapons program, regardless of Western, or international objections, as evidenced by these multiple statements from 2004—**none of which was included in the CSIS analysis:** [136]

> *We will go ahead with confidence-building and will endeavor to build up our [nuclear] technical capability to restore our national*

rights in the context of the international conventions. This is our diplomacy: to proceed [in] both directions simultaneously.

We only agreed to suspend activities in those areas where we did not have technical problems. This is what they are saying now in their negotiations. We completed the Isfahan project, which is the UCF [uranium concentration facility] where yellowcake [uranium ore concentrate, or UOC] is converted into UF4 [uranium tetrafluoride] and UF6 [uranium hexafluoride] during suspension. While we were talking with the Europeans in Tehran, we were installing equipment in parts of the facility in Isfahan, but we still had a long way to go to complete the project. In fact, by creating a calm environment, we were able to complete the work in Isfahan. Today, we can convert yellowcake into UF4 and UF6, and this is a very important matter. In fact, UF6 is what the centrifuges feed on; it is the feed material for centrifuges. Therefore, it was important for us to conclude that process.

I think we should not be in a great rush to deal with this issue. We should be patient and find the most suitable time to do away with the suspension. If we decide to start enrichment in the face of opposition by the West, we must find the best time and the most favorable conditions, and if we decide to work with the West, we must utilize all our capabilities and everything that is in our power to achieve our objectives. We should not rush into this. We must move very carefully, in a very calculated manner.

If one day we are able to complete the fuel cycle and the world sees that it has no choice, that we do possess the technology, then the situation will be different. The world did not want Pakistan to have an atomic bomb or Brazil to have the fuel cycle, but Pakistan built its bomb and Brazil has its fuel cycle, and the world started to work with them. Our problem is that we have not achieved either one, but we are standing at the threshold.

One of the members indicated here that all this should have been done in secret. This was the intention; this never was supposed to be in the open. But in any case, the spies exposed it. We did not want to declare all this.

Rouhani's sentiments are apparently shared by the majority of Iranians. According to Gallup polling data from February, 2013, almost 2/3 were willing to pay the high price of sanctions. Sixty-three (63%) percent claimed that Iran should continue to develop its nuclear program, even given the scale of sanctions imposed on their country because of such efforts. [137] No wonder Iranian public reaction was effusively positive [138] now that the feckless Obama administration has proven willing to abandon even this tame disincentive to the popular sentiment for Iran's nuclear weapons program. **It is also noteworthy how center-right analysts routinely ignore the broad-based Iranian public support for Iran's nuclear program**. (Polling data reveal a seemingly perverse "show of support" for Iran's nuclear weapons program which transcends the Sunni-Shiite divide, amongst Palestinian Muslims. Sixty percent, whether living in the disputed territories, or within Israel's "Green Line," favor Iran's procurement of nuclear technology— despite the existential threat nuclear weapons deployed against Israel might pose to them! [138a])

During the summer of 2009, much ink was spilled over the "secular" revolution allegedly occurring in Iran. Indeed, President Obama has been excoriated ever since by conservatives for his failure to unabashedly support the so-called "Green revolution," which I argued at the time [139] — and still maintain — was not a mass movement of true Western freedom aspirants against Sharia totalitarians (i.e., in their Shiite incarnation), but merely a power struggle between rival Sharia supremacist factions. [140]

Despite the overwrought hyperbole of some conservative analysts, a very staid assessment (published June 29, 2009) by A. Savyon, Director the Middle East Media Research Institute's Iranian Media Project, noted that the "Green" protest movement's leaders, Mir Hossein Mousavi, Mehdi Karroubi and Mohammad Khatami, were "not interested in a change of regime in Iran, and have never called to topple Supreme Leader Ali Khamenei." [141] Furthermore, Savyon reported that Khatami and Rafsanjani, who operated behind the scenes of the protests, proved unable "to recruit the support of any senior ayatollah against Khamenei." [142] Savyon added, that former President Hashemi Rafsanjani, at that time, the second most powerful figure in the regime, who then headed two of its most important bodies (the Experts Assembly and Expediency Council), never, [143]

> ... *purported to lead a movement presenting an alternative to the regime. Despite his blatant disagreements with the Supreme Leader, he hasn't openly challenged the latter's decision to accept the [2009] election results, though, according to reports, he has sought to recruit senior ayatollahs to join his camp within the regime.*

Savyon's June 29th, 2009, report concluded, [144] "... the protest movement leaders never advocated a regime change in Iran; their campaign is part of a struggle between two streams within the regime."

Politically expedient hypocrisy compounds the deliberate intellectual blindness of conservative/ neoconservative analysts who persist in their misrepresentations of the 2009 Iranian "Green Movement," while continuing to chastise President

Obama for his refusal to assist this alleged "freedom movement." These same conservative "experts" conveniently ignore the George W. Bush Administration's abject failure to eliminate Iran's nuclear threat while the U.S. had more than one hundred thousand troops (and all forms of supportive military air, sea, and land firepower) strategically positioned in neighboring Iraq, for the five years between 2003 and 2008. Specifically, conservative Obama Administration critics of this ilk are silent about the following:

- The George W. Bush Administration negotiated a November, 2008 "SOFA" (status of forces agreement) with our "Iraqi allies" which, as per Article 27, paragraph 4 *("Iraqi land, sea and air shall not be used as a launching or transit point for attacks against other countries.")* **prohibited** the US from attacking, for example, Iranian nuclear production facilities, from Iraqi bases and airspace. [144a]

- Revelations from former Bush and Obama Administration Defense Secretary Robert Gates' recently published memoir (as reported by the Washington Post's Walter Pincus), **about President Bush being convinced by Gates to forestall a pre-emptive Israeli attack on Iran's nuclear facilities, and the (absurd) "geo-strategic rationale" for this executive decision**—*"Gates writes that his most effective argument was that an Israeli attack on Iran that overflew Iraq* **would endanger what the surge had achieved with Baghdad. Bush then 'emphatically said he would not put our gains in Iraq at risk,'** *according to Gates."* [144b]

Iran's backward "revolution" in 1978-1979 simply returned Iranian society to its longstanding status as a Shiite theocracy (i.e., from 1501/1502, to 1925; interrupted between from 1722-1795, after an Afghan invasion in 1719, subsequent Ottoman and Russian forays, and internecine struggle, combined with Nadir Shah's [(r. 1734-1747] religious "experimentation"), [145] following a relatively brief flirtation with Westernization and secularization under Pahlavi rule from 1925 to 1979. [146] In addition, as my colleague, journalist Alyssa Lappen and I discovered in early July of 2009, upon interviewing the leader of a genuine Western-oriented, secular (and non-Communist) Iranian political party, [147] Roozbeh Farahanipour, [148] this courageous man and his followers unfortunately represent only a small minority of Iran's overwhelmingly traditionalist Shiite Muslim masses

Yet after more than three decades of strict re-application of the Sharia in Iran (which has included stoning to death for adultery, execution for homosexuality, abrogation of freedom of conscience and religious minority rights, etc.), [149] and notwithstanding wishful arguments that these phenomena had spawned mass public rejection of Islamic Law, Pew polling data released June 11, 2013 (from face-to-face interviews with 1,522 adults, ages 18 years of age and older), revealed a sobering reality. [150] When asked, "Do you favor or oppose the implementation of Sharia law, or Islamic law in our country?", **83% favored its application**. A largely concordant finding demonstrated that only 28% of Iranians were at all concerned (i.e., 9% "very," and 19% "somewhat" concerned) about "extremist religious groups" in the nation. [151]

These data provided the context in which the June, 2013 Presidential election of Hasan Rouhani—an unabashed Ayatollah Khomeini-supporting Shiite cleric, and long term political apparatchik of the theocratic regime—must be viewed. Simply put, Rouhani is not "moderate" by any objective, Sharia non-compliant standard. The conundrum is that while center to left U.S. (and other Western) policymaking elites insist upon Rouhani's "moderation," their conservative counterparts rigidly uphold the equally destructive fantasy that this modern avatar of traditionalist Shiite Sharia supremacism is somehow unrepresentative of the Iranian populace's abiding beliefs, and mores.

Another disturbing manifestation of the abject denial of Iranian Sharia supremacism by American conservatives came to light in October, 2013. A confluence of news stories the week of October 20, 2013, including, prominently, the release of a report by the U.N. Special Rapporteur on human rights in Iran, highlighted the plight of Iranian Christians. [152] The salient findings from Special Rapporteur Ahmed Shaheed's report (issued online Tuesday 10/22/13), were as follows: [153]

> *Sources communicate that at least 20 Christians were in custody in July 2013. In addition, violations of the rights of Christians, particularly those belonging to evangelical Protestant groups, many of whom are converts, who proselytize to and serve Iranian Christians of Muslim background, continue to be reported. Authorities continue to compel licensed Protestant churches to restrict Persian-speaking and Muslim-born Iranians from participating in services, and raids and forced closures of house churches are ongoing. According to sources, more than 300 Christians have been arrested since 2010, and dozens of church leaders and active community members have reportedly been convicted of national security crimes in connection with church activities, such as organizing prayer groups, proselytizing and attending Christian seminars abroad.*

His report further noted allegations of additional abuses, including "various forms of legal discrimination…in employment and education," as well as frequent cases of "arbitrary detention, torture and ill-treatment." [154]

Monday, 10/21/13, a day before the Special Rapporteur's report was issued, Eddie Romero, a retired California pastor, who managed to enter Iran surreptitiously, staged a protest before Iran's infamous Evin prison. [155] Repeatedly proclaiming, "Let my people go," in Farsi, Romero attempted to draw attention to the predicament of at least four Iranians, incarcerated for converting from Islam to Christianity—Farshid Fathi, Saeed Abedini, Mostafa Bordbar, and Alireza Seyyedian. [156] (Detained for 24-hours in Iran, Romero was released and returned safely to the U.S. by mid-week.) [157]

Shahrokh Afshar, a pastor for the Iranian Church On The Way in Los Angeles, maintained Christian converts in Iran were imprisoned simply because they practiced their new faith. "Their greatest sin was leaving Islam to follow Christ," he stated. [158] One of the four imprisoned Christians, whose plight Pastor Romero was protesting, is Saeed Abedini, a U.S. citizen who has been incarcerated for over a year in Iran. His wife, Naghmeh, wrote a poignant depiction (published 9/25/13) of her husband's ordeal on the bitter one year anniversary of his imprisonment. [159]

> *Without warning, members of the Revolutionary Guard pulled him off of a bus and put him under house arrest in his parents' home in Tehran. On September 26, 2012, members of the Guard came to the home and took him away — in chains — to Evin Prison, where he has remained ever since.*

The following day, Wednesday 10/23/13, Christian Solidarity International published a report about a "verdict" an Iranian court issued on October 6th, which the named defendants received October 20th. Four members of the Church of Iran—Behzad Taalipasand, Mehdi Reza Omidi (Youhan), Mehdi Dadkhah (Danial) and Amir Hatemi (Youhanna)—were charged with drinking alcohol **during a communion service**, and possession of a receiver and satellite antenna. The court sentenced them to receive 80 lashes each, for these alleged "offenses." Two of the "suspects," Behzad Taalipasand and Mehdi Reza Omidi (Youhan), had been detained December 31, 2012, during an Iranian government crackdown on house churches. [160] Chief Executive of Christian Solidarity Worldwide, Mervyn Thomas, declared forthrightly, [161]

> *The sentences handed down to these members of the Church of Iran effectively criminalize the Christian sacrament of sharing in the Lord's Supper and constitute an unacceptable infringement on the right to practice faith freely and peaceably. We urge the Iranian authorities to ensure that the nation's legal practices and procedures do not contradict its international obligation under the International Convent on Civil and Political Rights (ICCPR) to guarantee the full enjoyment of freedom of religion or belief by all of its religious communities.*

With depressing predictability, the Sharia-based dynamic [162] which underpins such blatant—and grotesque—religious persecution, was ignored by the mainstream media, including conservative outlets. Even the following specific (if merely allusive) statement contained within the Special Rapporteur's analysis itself, did not get repeated. [163]

> ...the [Iranian] Government...states that its Constitution recognizes only Zoroastrianism, Christianity and Judaism as minority religions and that adherents to those religions are entitled to manifest their beliefs, **"within the limits of the law"**, **which is governed by Islamic sharia**. [emphasis added]

For example, neither Benjamin Weinthal's blog at National Review Online ("Iran's Continued War on Christians," 10/25/13), [164] nor his lengthier Fox News piece ("Iran gives Christians 80 lashes for communion wine as UN blasts human rights record," 10/24/13) [165]—despite the fact that both accounts referenced Special Rapporteur Shaheed's report—mentioned, let alone honestly elaborated upon, Shaheed's allusion to Sharia.

Although Weinthal should not be singled out, per se, his omission—pathognomonic of this consistent lacuna in contemporary "reportage" on Iran's abuse of its vulnerable non-Muslim minority populations—was egregious, and unacceptable. Willful blindness to this reality by our media and policymaking elites—including conservatives—is a moral perversion that assures such Sharia-sanctioned oppression will continue indefinitely. Worse still, this tendency also augurs continued American policymaking failure vis-à-vis Iran, regardless of whether or not a "conservative" U.S. administration is elected. Reactions to the passing of Grand Ayatollah Hussein Ali Montazeri by U.S. conservative "Iran specialists," illustrate the latter point, starkly.

Decidedly hagiographic post-mortems written by American conservatives appeared immediately after the announcement of Montazeri's death at age 87, on December 20, 2009. Neoconservative Michael Ledeen opined, [166]

> Some of us who have long fought against the terrible regime in Tehran were fortunate to have received wise observations from Montazeri over the years, and I am confident that, with the passage of time and the changes that will take place in Iran, scholars will marvel at the international dimensions of the Grand Ayatollah's understanding and the range of his activities.

But perhaps the most curious of these early assessments includes a contention by Michael Rubin that "...the real Achilles Heel to the Iranian regime is Shi'ism." [167] Reuel Marc Gerecht, writing in October, 2010, ten months after Montazeri's death, dubbed the Ayatollah, simultaneously, "the spiritual father of Iran's Green Movement," and the erstwhile "nemesis of Ali Khamenei, Iran's ruler," whom Gerecht derided (in contrast to Montazeri), as "a very mediocre student of the Sharia." [167a]

These odd viewpoints were (and remain) merely the extension of a profoundly flawed, ahistorical mindset which denies the living legacy of Shiite Islamic doctrine and its authentic, oppressive application in Iran, particularly, since the advent of the Safavid theocratic state at the very beginning of the 16th century. A gimlet-eyed evaluation of Montazeri's recorded views—entirely consistent with traditionalist Shi'ism—does not comport with the conservative eulogies of the late Ayatollah by Ledeen, Rubin, Gerecht, and their ilk.

Consistent with the institutionalized codifications of Islam's classical Sunni and Shiite legists (to be elaborated in the next section), Montazeri's written views (from his *Islamic Law Codes* [*Resaleh-ye Tozih al-masael*]) on jihad war reiterate the doctrine of open-ended aggression to establish global Islamic suzerainty, and the universal application of Sharia: [168]

> [T]he offensive jihad is a war that an Imam wages in order to invite infidels and non-monotheists to Islam or to prevent the violation of treaty of Ahl-e Zemmah [Ahl-al-Dhimma, the humiliating pact of submission binding non-Muslim "dhimmis" vanquished by jihad]. In fact, the goal of offensive jihad is not the conquest of other countries, but the defense of the inherent rights of nations that are deprived of power by the infidels, non-monotheists, and rebels from the worship of Allah, monotheism, and justice. "And fight them until there is no more Fitnah (disbelief and polytheism: i.e. worshipping others besides Allah) and the religion (worship) will all be for Allah Alone [in the whole of the world].," (Koran 8:39) [168a] ... This verse includes defensive as well as offensive jihad. Jihad, like prayer, is for all times and is not limited to an early period of Islam, such as Muhammad, Ali, or the other Imams. Jihad is intended to defend truth and justice, help oppressed people, and correct Islam. **In the Mahdi's occultation period, jihad is not to be abandoned; even if occultation lasts for a hundred thousand years, Muslims have to defend and fight for the expansion of Islam.** Certainly, if in early Islam the goodness was in the sword, in our time the goodness is in artillery, tanks, automatic guns and missiles. . . in principle, jihad in Islam is for defense; whether defense of truth or justice, or the struggle with infidels in order to make them return to monotheism and the divine nature. This is the defense of truth, because the denial of Allah is the denial of truth.

How would non-Muslims fare under the Shiite Islamic order— forcibly imposed by jihad—as envisioned by Montazeri?

Sorour Soroudi and Eliz Sanasarian have analyzed Montazeri's views on najis ("impurity," a concept to be discussed at length subsequently), Sanasarian noting: [168b]

> *Montazeri saw nejasat [najis] in twelve items including blood, dogs, pigs, wine, and kafirs [i.e., primarily, non-Muslims]...A kafir's body, including hair, nails, and body fluids was to be avoided. The purchase, sale, or receiving of meat and fat from either non-Muslim countries or a kafir were forbidden.*

Montazeri further argued that a non-Muslim's (*kafir*'s) impurity was, **"a political order from Islam and must be adhered to by the followers of Islam, and the goal [was] to promote general hatred toward those who are outside Muslim circles."** This **"hatred"** was to assure that Muslims would not succumb to corrupt, i.e., non-Islamic thoughts. [169] Montazeri's Shiite Islamic political *Weltanschauung* was articulated in his 4 volume treatise on the "*Vilayat al-Faqih*" [Guardianship of the Islamic Jurists], a key rationale for the post-1979 Iranian Shiite theocracy. These views—openly antithetical to Western conceptions of individual liberty, religious freedom, and democracy—were aptly summarized by Montazeri's student, Iranian Sociology Professor Mahmood Davari, in 2005: [170]

> *According to Montazeri, Islamic rule differs from Western democracy in two matters. While the people in a democratic system are supposedly free to elect any person as their ruler, in a Shi'i society Muslims may not choose any other ruler except a just faqih. In a democratic society, people are free to legislate any law according to their collective wishes, whereas in an Islamic regime the legislation must be in accord with Islamic laws and ordinances. Therefore, according to Montazeri, Islamic rule is essentially different from democracy in the West.*

Montazeri also adhered—quite rigorously—to the traditionalist Shiite dogma regarding punishment for the offense of "sabb," or blasphemy. Kamran Hashemi's 2008 study summarized the relevant Shiite jurisprudence: [171]

> *... according to the majority of Shiite jurists, in cases of sabb, instant punishment [i.e., killing] of the offender, either Muslim or non-Muslim, is not only permissible, but also a religious obligation for any Muslim who realizes the offense, or any who comes to know about it. In this sense, as soon as the offense takes place, the offender must be killed immediately by any one who does not fear for his own life to be endangered.*

Hashemi goes on to illustrate the "consensus among contemporary Shiite jurists on the instant punishment of an offender in cases of sabb," [172] by referring to Montazeri's opinion, specifically: [173]

> *For example, in response to a question Ayatollah Montazeri [d. 2009] makes a reference to this issue: "In cases of sabb al-Nabi*

[blasphemy against a prophet, in particular Islam's prophet, Muhammad]…if the witness does not have fear of his or her life and also there is no fear of mischief [mafsadeh] it is obligatory for him or her to kill the insulter."

The practical consequences of Montazeri's bigoted Shiite Islamic authoritarianism—which Ledeen, Rubin, and Gerecht all ignored—were highlighted by Iranian Studies Professor Jamsheed Choksy. In an essay (written with Nina Shea), published July 22, 2009, Choksy observed, [174]

*Iran's constitution requires that laws and regulations be based on Islamic criteria, which mandate inferior status for three non-Muslim faiths, while withholding all rights and protections from all other faiths. Zoroastrian, Jewish, and Christian (specifically, Assyrian and Armenian) live in a modern version of **dhimmi** status — the…subjugated condition of "people of the Book" dating back to medieval times. While these three groups are allotted seats in the legislative assembly (a total of five out of 290 seats), they are barred from seeking high public office in any of the three branches of government….*

Non-Muslim communities collectively have diminished to no more than 2 percent of Iran's 71 million people. Forty years ago, under the Shah, a visitor would have seen a relatively tolerant society. Iran now appears to be in the final stages of religious cleansing. Pervasive discrimination, intimidation, and harassment have prompted non-Muslims to flee in disproportionately high numbers.

Choksy concluded with a reminder especially apposite for those who share the opinions of Ledeen, Rubin, and Gerecht: [175]

Iran's political dissidents are defended by the West. Its diverse non Muslim minorities ask why they've been forgotten.

And following Montazeri's death, Choksy made this sobering observation: [176]

[T]he religious minorities in Iran see little theological difference and only a marginal pragmatism among the various Shiite views. Montazeri's opinion was characterized by one Iranian Christian clergyman as "…rubbing salt into our wounds." Ultimately, Montazeri's tolerance of differences, especially religious ones, was far from acceptance.

Finally, during an online symposium published October 9, 2012, Ze'ev Maghen, Professor of Persian Language and Islamic History, made this trenchant reference to Montazeri's alleged "moderation," in the context of Iran's dogged quest for nuclear weapons capability: [177]

> *Now the Jewish state is facing a regime **the most moderate elements of which** regularly threaten to wipe Israel off the map and repeat citations of the following sort: **"His Excellency [the sixth Shi'ite Imam Ja'far] al-Sadiq affirmed thrice that those who will ultimately exterminate the Jews will be the clerics of [the Iranian Shiite shrine city of] Qom"** (cited approvingly in a public forum by supporter of the "Green Movement" Ayatollah Ali Hosayn Montazeri, **Memoirs**). Now those clerics are enriching uranium at a dizzying pace just outside of Qom at Fordu [Fordow].[Emphases added]*

Maghen's earlier remarks, from a 2009 essay, highlight the dire near-term predicament for Israel, which the disastrous "P5 + 1" agreement has exacerbated. [178]

> *The Iranians and their allies throughout the Muslim world are bent on making the abandonment of Israel the price of "peace in our time."... [A]n ideological, totalitarian state **is building upon an endemic antisemitism inculcated by centuries of religious indoctrination** [emphasis added] to create an atmosphere in which the massacre of large numbers of Jews and the destruction of their independent polity will be considered a tolerable if not indeed a legitimate eventuality.*

These 2009 observations by Maghen are an ideal segue to the remaining focus of this monograph: how Iran's native Islamic Jew-hatred has long impacted its indigenous Jews, and what this legacy, conjoined to resurgent Iranian jihadism, bodes for the Jewish State of Israel.

2

Jihad, Dhimmitude, and Islamic Jew-Hatred: The Sunni-Shiite Continuum (From Tabari to Tabatabai)

Islamic Holy war [jihad] against followers of other religions, such as Jews, is required unless they convert to Islam or pay the poll tax.
    — al Amili (d. 1622), a distinguished theologian under Safavid Shah Abbas I, from his authoritative (and popular) Persian manual of Shiite Islamic Law.¶

[T]he Jews, although they had the same alternatives as the Christians, and they could retain their religion with payment of the jizyah [Koranic poll tax, per verse 9:29], yet they continued in their haughtiness, became harder in their bigotry, and turned to double dealing and deception. They broke their covenants, eagerly waited calamities to befall the Muslims and dealt to them the bitterest deal…[T]he enmity of the Jews…toward the divine religion [Islam] and their sustained arrogance and bigotry, have continued exactly in the same manner even after the Prophet… These unchanged characteristics…confirm what the Mighty Book [the Koran] had indicated.
    — Muhammad Husayn Tabatabai (d. 1981), a revered Iranian Shiite philosopher and the preeminent 20th century Shiite Koranic commentator, from his gloss on Koran 5:82.¶¶

Jihad Doctrine and Practice

Data for 2012 from the National Consortium for the Study of Terrorism and Responses to Terrorism (START) were released December 19, 2013. Gary LaFree, START director and professor of criminology and criminal justice at the University of Maryland, highlighted the report's most salient finding: the "incredible growth" in jihad terror attacks perpetrated by "al-Qaida affiliates." [179] START identified the six most lethal jihad terror groups affiliated with Al-Qaida, and the death tolls these organizations had inflicted during 2012, as follows: the Taliban (more than 2,500 fatalities), Boko Haram (more than 1,200 fatalities), al-Qaida in the Arabian Peninsula (more than 960 fatalities), Tehrik-e Taliban Pakistan (more than 950 fatalities), al-Qaida in Iraq (more than 930 fatalities) and al-Shabaab (more than 700 fatalities). [180] These attacks, as the START report acknowledged, were intrinsic to a broader phenomenon—the emergence of jihad terrorism emanating from the Middle East, South Asia, and North Africa, as the *predominant* form of global terrorism, since the 1990s. [181]

Another macabre tally—updated almost daily—is being kept assiduously in cyberspace: the number of attacks committed by jihad terrorists since the cataclysmic acts of jihad terrorism on September 11, 2001. [182] This grisly compilation is if anything a conservative estimate of jihad-related carnage— murder and severe morbidity—because it doesn't include combat-related statistics per se, or the death toll increases during the days or months after any given attack (as victims die from their injuries). [183] By February 26, 2014, this grim count had reached 22,518. [184]

These data should impress upon us that there is just one historically relevant meaning of jihad despite the surfeit of contemporary apologetics. Dr. Tina Magaard—a Sorbonne-trained linguist specializing in textual analysis—published detailed research findings [185] in 2005 (summarized in 2007) [186] comparing the foundational texts of ten major religions. Magaard concluded from her hard data-driven analyses: [187]

> *The texts in Islam distinguish themselves from the texts of other religions by encouraging violence and aggression against people with other religious beliefs to a larger degree [emphasis added]. There are also straightforward calls for terror. This has long been a taboo in the research into Islam, but it is a fact that we need to deal with.*

For example, in her 2007 essay "Fjendebilleder og voldsforestillinger i islamiske grundtekster" ["Images of enemies and conceptions of violence in Islamic core scriptures"], Magaard observed, [188]

> *There are 36 references in the Koran to expressions derived
> from the root qa-ta-la, which indicates fighting, killing or being
> killed. The expressions derived from the root ja-ha-da, which the
> word jihad stems from, are more ambiguous since they mean "to
> struggle" or "to make an effort" rather than killing. Yet almost
> all of the references derived from this root are found in stories
> that leave no room for doubt regarding the violent nature of
> this struggle. Only a single ja-ha-da reference (29:6) explicitly
> presents the struggle as an inner, spiritual phenomenon, not as an
> outwardly (usually military) phenomenon. But this sole reference
> does not carry much weight against the more than 50 references to
> actual armed struggle in the Koran, and even more in the Hadith.*

Consistent with Magaard's textual analysis, the independent study of Australian
linguist and renowned Arabic to English translator, Paul Stenhouse, claimed the
root of the word jihad appears forty times in the Koran. With four exceptions,
Stenhouse maintained, [189] all the other thirty-six usages in the Koran, and in
subsequent Islamic understanding to both Muslim luminaries—the greatest
jurists and scholars of classical Islam—and to ordinary people, meant and
means, as described by the seminal Arabic lexicographer, E. W. Lane: "He
fought, warred or waged war against unbelievers and the like." [190] A concordant
modern Muslim definition, relevant to both contemporary jihadism and its
shock troop "mujahideen" [holy warriors; see just below], was provided at the
"Fourth International Conference of the Academy of Islamic Research," at Al
Azhar University, Cairo — Sunni Islam's most important religious educational
institution [191] — in 1968, by Muhammad al-Sobki: [192]

> *[T]he words Al Jihad, Al **Mojahadah**, or even "striving against
> enemies" are equivalents and they do not mean especially fighting
> with the atheists . . . they mean fighting in the general sense.*

September 622 C.E. marks a defining event in Islam—the hijra. Muhammad
and a coterie of followers persecuted by fellow Banu Quraysh tribesmen, fled
from Mecca to Yathrib, later known as Medina. The Muslim sources described
Yathrib as having been a Jewish city founded by a Palestinian diaspora population
which had survived the revolt against the Romans. The Jews of the north Arabian
peninsula were highly productive oasis farmers. These Jews were eventually
joined by itinerant Arab tribes from southern Arabia who settled adjacent to them
and transitioned to a sedentary existence. [193]

Following Muhammad's arrival, he re-ordered Medinan society. The Jewish
tribes were isolated, some were then expelled, and the remainder attacked
and exterminated. Muhammad distributed among his followers as "booty" the
vanquished Jews property—plantations, fields, and houses—using this "booty"

to establish a well-equipped jihadist cavalry corps. [194] For example, within a year after the massacre (in 627) of the Jewish tribe the Banu Qurayza, Muhammad, according to a summary of sacralized Muslim sources, waited for some act of aggression on the part of the Jews of Khaybar, whose fertile lands and villages he had destined for his followers to furnish an excuse for an attack. [195]

But, no such opportunity offering, he resolved in the autumn of this year [i.e., 628], on a sudden and unprovoked invasion of their territory. Ali (later, the fourth "Rightly Guided Caliph", and especially revered by Shi'ite Muslims) asked Muhammad why the Jews of Khaybar were being attacked, since they were peaceful farmers, tending their oasis, and was told by Muhammad he must compel them to submit to Islamic Law. The renowned early 20th century scholar of Islam, David Margoliouth, observed aptly: [196]

> *Now the fact that a community was idolatrous, or Jewish, or anything but Mohammedan, warranted a murderous attack upon it.*

Muhammad's subsequent interactions with the Christians of northern Arabia followed a similar pattern, noted by the scholar of Islam's origins, Richard Bell. The "relationship with the Christians ended as that with the Jews (ended)- in war", because Islam as presented by Muhammad was a divine truth, and unless Christians accepted this formulation, which included Muhammad's authority, "conflict was inevitable, and there could have been no real peace while he [Muhammad] lived." [197]

The modern Muslim scholar Ali Dashti's biography of *Muhammad 23 Years: A Study of the Prophetic Career of Mohammad* has also chronicled Muhammad's "changed course" at Medina, where the Muslim prophet begins to "issue orders for war" in multiple and repeated Koranic revelations (Sura [chapter] 9 being composed almost entirely of such war proclamations—permanent injunctions against pagans, Jews, and Christians).[198] Prior to enumerating the numerous assassinations Muhammad ordered, Ali Dashti observes: [199]

> *...Islam was gradually transformed from a purely spiritual mission into a militant and punitive organization whose progress depended on booty from raids and [tax] revenue....The Prophet's steps in the decade after the hejra [emigration from Mecca to Medina] were directed to the end of establishing and consolidating a religion-based state. Some of the deeds done on his command [were] killings of prisoners and political assassinations...*

Thus Muhammad himself waged a series of proto-jihad campaigns to subdue the Jews, Christians and pagans of Arabia. As numerous modern day pronouncements by leading Muslim theologians confirm (see for example, Yusuf Al-Qaradawi's, "The Prophet Muhammad as a Jihad Model"), [200] Muhammad has been the major inspiration for jihadism, past and present.

Jihad was pursued century after century because jihad embodied an ideology and a jurisdiction. Both were formally conceived by Muslim jurisconsults and theologians from the 8th to 9th centuries onward, based on their interpretation of Koranic verses [201] and long chapters in the "hadith," or acts and sayings of the Muslim prophet Muhammad, especially those recorded by al-Bukhari [d. 869] [202] and Muslim [d. 874] [203]

Ibn Khaldun (d. 1406), jurist, renowned philosopher, historian, and sociologist, summarized these consensus opinions from five centuries of prior Muslim jurisprudence with regard to the uniquely Islamic institution of jihad: [204]

> *In the Muslim community, the holy war is a religious duty, because of the universalism of the [Muslim] mission and [the obligation to] convert everybody to Islam either by persuasion or by force... The other religious groups did not have a universal mission, and the holy war was not a religious duty for them, save only for purposes of defense... Islam is under obligation to gain power over other nations.*

Classical Islamic jurists such as Abu Hanifa (d. 767; founder of the Hanafi school of Islamic jurisprudence) [205] formulated the concepts *Dar al Islam* and *Dar al Harb* (Arabic for, "The House of Islam and the House of War"). [206] The great Muslim polymath Al-Tabari's [207] early 10th century "Book of Jihad" [208] includes extracts from Abu Hanifa (and his acolytes) affirming the impunity with which non-combatant "harbis"—women, children, the elderly, the mentally or physically disabled—may be killed. [209]

> *Abu Hanifa and his companions said: "There is no harm in [having] night raids and incursions." They said: "There is no harm if Muslims enter the Territory of War (dar al-harb) to assemble the mangonel [catapults] towards the polytheists' fortresses and to shoot them musing mangonels, even if there are among them a woman, child, elder, idiot (matuh), blind, crippled, or someone with a permanent disability (zamin). There is no harm in shooting polytheists in their fortresses using mangonels even if there are among those whom we have named.*

Armand Abel, the leading 20th century expert on the Muslim conception of Dar al Harb, highlights its salient features: [210]

> *Together with the duty of the "war in the way of God" (or jihad), this universalistic aspiration would lead the Muslims to see the world as being divided fundamentally into two parts. On the*

one hand there was that part of the world where Islam prevailed, where salvation had been announced, where the religion that ought to reign was practiced; this was the Dar al Islam. On the other hand, there was the part which still awaited the establishment of the saving religion and which constituted, by definition, the object of the holy war. This was the Dar al Harb. The latter, in the view of the Muslim jurists, was not populated by people who had a natural right not to practice Islam, but rather by people destined to become Muslims who, through impiousness and rebellion, refused to accept this great benefit. Since they were destined sooner or later to be converted at the approach of the victorious armies of the Prophet's successor, or else killed for their rebelliousness, they were the rebel subjects of the Caliph. Their kings were nothing but odious tyrants who, by opposing the progress of the saving religion together with their armies, were following a Satanic inspiration and rising up against the designs of Providence. And so no respite should be granted them, no truce: perpetual war should be their lot, waged in the course of the winter and summer ghazu. [razzias] If the sovereign of the country thus attacked desired peace, it was possible for him, just like for any other tributary or community, to pay the tribute for himself and for his subjects. Thus the [Byzantine] Empress Irene [d. 803] "purchased peace at the price of her humiliation", according to the formula stated in the dhimma contract itself, by paying 70,000 pounds in gold annually to the Caliph of Baghdad. Many other princes agreed in this way to become tributaries – often after long struggles – and to see their dominions pass from the status of dar al Harb to that of dar al Sulh. In this way, those of their subjects who lived within the boundaries of the territory ruled by the Caliphate were spared the uncertainty **of being exposed arbitrarily, without any guarantee, to the military operations of the summer ghazu and the winter ghazu: indeed, anything within the reach of the Muslim armies as they advanced, being property of impious men and rebels, was legitimately considered their booty; their men, seized by armed soldiers, were mercilessly consigned to the lot specified in the Koranic verse about the sword, and their women and children were treated like things. [emphasis added]**

Yusuf Al-Qaradawi, the widely revered contemporary Muslim cleric, "spiritual" leader of the Muslim Brotherhood, head of the "European Council for Fatwa and Research", and popular Al-Jazeera television personality, reiterated Abel's formulation of Dar al Harb almost exactly in July, 2003, both in conceptual terms, and with regard to Israel, specifically: [211]

It has been determined by Islamic law that the blood and property of people of Dar Al-Harb [the Domain of Disbelief where the battle for the domination of Islam should be waged] is not protected...in modern war, all of society, with all its classes and ethnic groups, is mobilized to participate in the war, to aid its continuation, and to provide it with the material and human fuel required for it to assure the victory of the state fighting its enemies. Every citizen in society must take upon himself a role in the effort to provide for the battle. The entire domestic front, including professionals, laborers, and industrialists, stands behind the fighting army, even if it does not bear arms.

In fact the consensus view of orthodox Islamic jurisprudence regarding jihad, since its formulation during the 8th and 9th centuries, through the current era, is that non-Muslims peacefully going about their lives—from the Khaybar farmers whom Muhammad ordered attacked in 628, [212] to those sitting in the World Trade Center on 9/11/01—are "muba'a", licit, in the Dar al Harb. As described by the great 20th century scholar of Islamic Law, Joseph Schacht, [213]

A non-Muslim who is not protected by a treaty is called harbi, "in a state of war", "enemy alien"; his life and property are completely unprotected by law...

And these innocent non-combatants can be killed, and have always been killed, with impunity simply by virtue of being "harbis" during endless razzias and or full scale jihad campaigns that have occurred continuously since the time of Muhammad, through the present. This is the crux of the specific institutionalized religio-political ideology, i.e., jihad, which makes Islamdom's borders (and the further reaches of todays jihadists) bloody, to paraphrase Samuel Huntington, across the globe. [214] To validate his contention that, "Wherever one looks along the perimeter of Islam, Muslims have problems living peaceably with their neighbors," [215] Huntington adduced these hard data: [216]

The overwhelming majority of fault line conflicts ... have taken place along the boundary looping across Eurasia and Africa that separates Muslims from non-Muslims...Intense antagonisms and violent conflicts are pervasive between local Muslim and non-Muslim peoples...Muslims make up about one-fifth of the world's population, but in the 1990s they have been far more involved in inter-group violence than the people of any other civilization. The evidence is overwhelming. There were, in short, three times as many inter-civilizational conflicts involving Muslims as there were between non-Muslim civilizations...Muslim states also have had a high propensity to resort to violence in international crises,

employing it to resolve 76 crises out of a total of 142 in which
they were involved between 1928 and 1979. ... When they did use
violence, Muslim states used high-intensity violence, resorting to
full-scale war in 41 percent of the cases where violence was used
and engaging in major clashes in another 39 percent of the cases.
While Muslim states resorted to violence in 53.5 percent, violence
was used the United Kingdom in only 1.5 percent, by the United
States in 17.9 percent, and by the Soviet Union in 28.5 percent of
the crises in which they were involved...Muslim bellicosity and
violence are late-twentieth-century facts which neither Muslims
nor non-Muslims can deny.

Ibn Hudayl a 14th century Granadan author of an important treatise on jihad, elucidated the allowable tactics which facilitated the violent, chaotic jihad conquest of the Iberian peninsula, and other parts of Europe: [217]

It is permissible to set fire to the lands of the enemy, his stores of
grain, his beasts of burden – if it is not possible for the Muslims
to take possession of them – as well as to cut down his trees, to
raze his cities, in a word, to do everything that might ruin and
discourage him...[being] suited to hastening the Islamization of
that enemy or to weakening him. Indeed, all this contributes to a
military triumph over him or to forcing him to capitulate.

Again, as recorded in Tabari's early 10th century treatise on jihad, classical jurisprudence supports the views of Ibn Hudayl: [218]

Abu Hanifa (d. 767, founder of the Hanafi school of Islamic
jurisprudence [218a]*) and his companions said: "Abu Bakr's saying,*
'Do not ruin what has been built, do not burn palm trees, and
do not cut down fruit-bearing trees' [is applied] when their
[enemy people] territory has been conquered and controlled [by
*Muslims] and it has fallen into their hands. **They [the Muslims]***
should not do any such actions because it has become a spoil
***of war for the Muslims (emphasis added).** But if the [Muslim]*
army combatants do not have the power to reside in that territory
and they are not able to appoint a leader over it, and they cannot
acquire it so that it becomes theirs, then they should burn their
fortresses, cities, and churches, and destroy their palm trees and
[other] trees and burn them down. And whatever of their animals
and cattle they acquaire and cannot take out [to the Territory of
Islam], they should slaughter and burn them."

These repeated attacks, indistinguishable in motivation from modern acts of jihad terrorism, like the horrific 9/11/01 attacks in New York and Washington, DC, and the Madrid bombings on 3/11/04, or those in London on 7/7/05, were in fact designed to sow terror. [219] The 17th century Muslim historian al-Maqqari explained that the panic created by the Arab horsemen and sailors, at the time of the Muslim expansion in the regions subjected to those raids and landings, facilitated their later conquest, [220]

> *Allah thus instilled such fear among the infidels that they did not dare to go and fight the conquerors; they only approached them as suppliants, to beg for peace.*

Muhammad himself was the ultimate prototype sanctioning jihad terror, as recorded in this canonical hadith: [221]

> *Narrated Abu Huraira: Allah's Apostle said, "I have been sent with the shortest expressions bearing the widest meanings, and **I have been made victorious with terror** (cast in the hearts of the enemy)..."*

According to Islam's seminal early historian, Al-Tabari (d. 923), during Abu Bakr's reign as Caliph, his commander Khalid b. al-Walid's wrote a letter in 634 to a Persian leader in Iraq identified as "Hurmuz," warning of a prototypical expansionist jihad campaign, spearheaded by Muslim warriors enamored of death. [222]

> *Now then. Embrace Islam so that you may be safe, or else make a treaty of protection for yourself and your people, **for I have brought you a people who love death as you love life.** (Emphasis added)*

Contemporary validation of this principle of jihad as described by Ibn Hudayl, and al-Maqqari—rooted in the Koran—(for example, verses 3:151, 8:12, 8:60, and 33:26)—i.e., to terrorize the enemies of the Muslims as a prelude to their conquest—has been provided in the mainstream Pakistani text on jihad warfare by Brigadier S.K. Malik, originally published in Lahore, in 1979. [223] Malik's treatise was endorsed in a laudatory Foreword to the book by his patron, then Pakistani President Zia-ul-Haq, as well as a more extended Preface by Allah Buksh K. Brohi, a former Advocate-General of Pakistan. [224] This text—widely studied in Islamic countries, and available in English, Urdu, and Arabic—has been recovered from the bodies of slain jihadists in Kashmir. [225] Brigadier Malik emphasizes how instilling terror is essential to waging successful jihad campaigns: [226]

> *Terror struck into the hearts of the enemies is not only a means, it is the end in itself. Once a condition of terror into the opponent's heart is obtained, hardly anything is left to be achieved. It is the point where the means and the end meet and merge. Terror is*

> *not a means of imposing decision upon the enemy (sic); it is the decision we wish to impose upon him...*

> *"Jehad," [Jihad] the Quranic concept of total strategy. Demands the preparation and application of total national power and military instrument is one of its elements. As a component of the total strategy, the military strategy aims at striking terror into the hearts of the enemy from the preparatory stage of war...Under ideal conditions, Jehad can produce a direct decision and force its will upon the enemy. Where that does not happen, military strategy should take over and aim at producing the decision from the military stage. Should that chance be missed, terror should be struck into the enemy during the actual fighting.*

> *...the Book [Quran] does not visualize war being waged with "kid gloves." It gives us a distinctive concept of total war. It wants both, the nation and the individual, to be at war "in toto," that is, with all their spiritual, moral, and physical resources. The Holy Quran lays the highest emphasis on the preparation for war. It wants us to prepare ourselves for war to the utmost. The test of utmost preparation lies in our capability to instill terror into the hearts of the enemies.*

"Martyrdom operations" have always been intimately associated with the institution of jihad. Professor Franz Rosenthal, in a magisterial 1946 essay (entitled, "On Suicide in Islam"), observed that Islam's foundational texts sanctioned such acts of jihad martyrdom, and held them in the highest esteem: [227]

> *..death as the result of "suicidal" missions and of the desire of martyrdom occurs not infrequently, since[such] death is considered highly commendable according to Muslim religious concepts.*

Koran 9:111 provides an unequivocal, celebratory invocation of martyrdom during jihad: [228]

> *Verily, Allah has purchased of the believers their lives and their properties; for the price that theirs shall be the Paradise. They fight in Allah's Cause, so they kill (others) and are killed.*

As indicated previously, the Muslim prophet Muhammad is idealized as the eternal model for behaviors that all Muslims should emulate. [229] Nearly six decades ago (in 1956), Arthur Jeffery, a great modern scholar of Islam's origins, reviewed Guillaume's magisterial English translation of Ibn Ishaq's *Sirat Rasul Allah*, [230] the oldest and most important Muslim biography of Muhammad. Jeffery's review included this trenchant observation: [231]

> *Years ago the late Canon Gairdner in Cairo said that the best*
> *answer to the numerous apologetic Lives of Muhammad published*
> *in the interests of Muslim propaganda in the West would be an*
> *unvarnished translation of the earliest Arabic biography of the*
> *prophet.*

W. H. T. (Canon) Gairdner, in 1915, highlighted the dilemma posed by Islam's sacralization of Muhammad's timeless behavioral role model, revealed in such pious Muslim biographical works: [232]

> *As incidents in the life of an Arab conqueror, the tales of*
> *raiding, private assassinations and public executions, perpetual*
> *enlargements of the harem, and so forth, might be historically*
> *explicable and therefore pardonable but it is another matter that*
> *they should be taken as a setting forth of the moral ideal for all*
> *time.*

For example, Muhammad celebrated jihad martyrdom as the supreme act of Islamic devotion in the most important canonical hadith collection: [233]

> *Narrated Anas bin Malik: The Prophet said, "Nobody who dies*
> *and finds good from Allah (in the Hereafter) would wish to come*
> *back to this world even if he were given the whole world and*
> *whatever is in it, except the martyr who, on seeing the superiority*
> *of martyrdom, would like to come back to the world and get killed*
> *again (in Allah's Cause)."*

> *Narrated Abu Huraira: "The Prophet said, 'By Him in Whose*
> *Hands my life is! Were it not for some men amongst the believers*
> *who dislike to be left behind me and whom I cannot provide with*
> *means of conveyance, I would certainly never remain behind any*
> *Sariya' (army-unit) setting out in Allah's Cause. By Him in Whose*
> *Hands my life is! I would love to be martyred in Allah's Cause*
> *and then get resurrected and then get martyred, and then get*
> *resurrected again and then get martyred and then get resurrected*
> *again and then get martyred."*

Yusuf al-Qaradawi's 2001 paean to Muhammad as the "epitome" for *Mujahideen* (holy warriors), and his more detailed 2003 speech (delivered in Stockholm, Sweden) sanctioning jihad martyrdom homicide bombing operations, provide modern validation of both the relevant canonical Islamic doctrine, and the Western scholarly assessments of its meaning (and application) by Rosenthal, Jeffrey, and Gairdner.

[T]he first assignment is to prepare the hero who is willing to put his life in his own hands for Allah's sake, and he who does not care whether he encounters death or death encounters him... He [i.e., a self-immolating bomber] kills the enemy while taking self-risk, similarly to what Muslims did in the past... He wants to scare his enemies, and the religious authorities have permitted this. They said that if he causes the enemy both sorrow and fear of Muslims... he is permitted to risk himself and even get killed. [233a]

What weapon can harm their enemy, can prevent him from sleeping, and can strip him of a sense of security and stability, except for these human bombs - a young man or woman who blows himself or herself up amongst their enemy. This is a weapon the likes of which the enemy cannot obtain...because it is a unique weapon that Allah has placed only in the hands of the men of belief. It is a type of divine justice on the face of the earth... Those who oppose martyrdom operations and claim that they are suicide are making a great mistake. The goals of the one who carries out a martyrdom operation and of the one who commits suicide are completely different. Anyone who analyzes the soul of [these two] will discover the huge difference between them. The [person who commits] suicide kills himself for himself, because he failed in business, love, an examination, or the like. He was too weak to cope with the situation and chose to flee life for death... In contrast, the one who carries out a martyrdom operation does not think of himself. He sacrifices himself for the sake of a higher goal, for which all sacrifices become meaningless. He sells himself to Allah in order to buy Paradise in exchange. Allah said: 'Allah has bought from the believers their souls and their properties for they shall inherit Paradise...While the [person who commits] suicide dies in escape and retreat, the one who carries out a martyrdom operation dies in advance and attack. Unlike the [person who commits] suicide, who has no goal except escape from confrontation, the one who carries out a martyrdom operation has a clear goal, and that is to please Allah. [233b]

America's own first encounters with jihadism—as both a practice, and an ideology—confirmed the doctrines, and their application, described above.

For example, John Paul Jones, in a letter to Prince Potemkin dated June 20, 1788 while Jones commanded Russian naval ships (i.e., before the U.S. had its own navy), wrote about a naval engagement with the Turkish fleet (outside Kimbourn) involving an unsuccessful martyrdom operation planned by the Muslim sailors: [234]

> *...for it was the intention of the Turks to attack us and board us, and if we had been only three versts further the attempt would have been made on the 16ᵗʰ [June 1788] (before the vessel of the Captain Pacha ran aground in advancing before the wind with all his forces to attack us,), God only knows what would have been the result...The Turks had a very large force, and we have been informed by our prisoners that they were resolved to destroy us, even by burning themselves, (in setting fire to their own vessels after having grappled with ours.) [note added by Jones: Before their departure from Constantinople, they swore by the beard of the Sultan to execute this horrible plan...if Providence had not caused its failure from two circumstances which no man could forsee.]*

Two years earlier, Thomas Jefferson and John Adams, then serving as American ambassadors to France and Britain, respectively, met in 1786 in London with the Tripolitan [modern Libyan] ambassador to Britain, Sidi Haji Abdul Rahman Adja. These future American presidents were attempting to negotiate a peace treaty which would spare the United States the ravages of jihad piracy—murder, enslavement (with ransoming for redemption), and expropriation of valuable commercial assets—emanating from the Barbary states (modern Morocco, Algeria, Tunisia, and Libya). During their discussions, they questioned Ambassador Adja as to the source of the unprovoked animus directed at the nascent United States republic. Jefferson and Adams, in their subsequent report to the Continental Congress, recorded the Tripolitan ambassador's justification: [235]

> *[T]hat it was founded on the Laws of their Prophet, that it was written in their Koran, that all nations who should not have acknowledged their authority were sinners, that it was their right and duty to make war upon them wherever they could be found, and to make slaves of all they could take as Prisoners, and that every Mussulman [Muslim] who should be slain in Battle was sure to go to Paradise.*

Thus an aggressive jihad was already being waged against the United States by "martyrdom-seeking" jihadists, almost two hundred years prior to America becoming a dominant international power in the Middle East. Moreover, these jihad depredations targeting America antedated the earliest vestiges of the Zionist movement by a century, and the formal creation of Israel by 162 years—exploding the ahistorical canard that American support for the modern Jewish state is a prerequisite for jihadist attacks on the United States.

A compelling illustration of how well the U.S. Department of State once understood the true nature of jihad as a normative Islamic institution—circa

1880—was provided by Edward A. Van Dyck, then US Consular Clerk at Cairo, Egypt. Van Dyck prepared a detailed report in August, 1880 on the history of the treaty arrangements (so-called "capitulations") between the Muslim Ottoman Empire, European nations, and the much briefer U.S.-Ottoman experience. Van Dyck's report—written specifically as a tool for State Department diplomats— opens with an informed, clear, and remarkably concise explanation of jihad and Islamic law: [236]

> *In all the many works on Mohammedan law no teaching is met with that even hints at those principles of political intercourse between nations, that have been so long known to the peoples of Europe, and which are so universally recognized by them. "Fiqh," as the science of Moslem jurisprudence is called, knows only one category of relation between those who recognize the apostleship of Mohammed and all others who do not, namely Djehad [jihad]; that is to say, strife, or holy war. Inasmuch as the propagation of Islam was to be the aim of all Moslems, perpetual warfare against the unbelievers, in order to convert them, or subject them to the payment of tribute, came to be held by Moslem doctors [legists] as the most sacred duty of the believer. This right to wage war is the only principle of international law which is taught by Mohammedan jurists; ...with the Arabs the term harby [harbi] (warrior) expresses not only an unbeliever but also an enemy; and jehady [jihadi] (striver, warrior) means the believer-militant. From the Moslem point of view, the whole world is divided into two parts—"the House of Islam," and the House of War;" out of this division has arisen the other popular dictum of the Mohammedans that "all kinds of unbelievers from but one people."*

Van Dyck later expands [237] upon this introduction citing al-Quduri (d. 1037), a major scholar (during the Abbasid-Baghdadian Caliphate) in the classical development period of Islamic law, renowned for his *Mukhtasar*, a widely discussed and cited handbook of fiqh (jurisprudence), from the Hanafi (one of the four major Sunni schools of jurisprudence) perspective. Al-Quduri's manual continues to be studied in contemporary Hanafi institutions of traditional Islamic learning, which were of great influence in the Ottoman Empire.[238] Van Dyck's apposite citations from al-Quduri re-emphasize the normative features of jihad (i.e., both those reviewed earlier, and still to be elaborated, subsequently), which remain entirely relevant to modern geo-politics, including "negotiations" with the Islamic Republic of Iran: [239]

> *[B]y the capitulations the Moslem rulers did not mean to bind themselves to lasting peace. The word capitulations corresponds*

*to the Arabic word "sulh," which means a truce, a standstill of arms a reconciliation, by means of which the stranger or enemy preserves a kind of autonomy and does not become wholly subject to the Moslem. Salam means peace, and in everyday life, the greeting "es-Salam alaikum" ("peace be upon you") is addressed by the Moslem to a fellow believer, but never to a Christian or Jew; and according to the Moslem doctors [jurists], war against unbelievers is the duty of the Moslem, and hence is called holy war. This war undertakes the propagation of the Mahommedan faith or at least the subjection of unbelievers to the payment of tribute (djizia [jizya], i.e., ransom). There is no deed more meritorious than that of fighting for religion; thus holy warfare is regarded as an imperative duty ordained by God. Abu-l-Hussain el-Kuduri [Al-Quduri], of the Hanafite school of doctors, who died in the year 428 of the Moslem era [1037 C.E.], commences his treatise on war with unbelievers thus: "War with those that are not of Islam is a work enjoined by God." He then goes on: "When the Moslems go into the enemy's country and surround a city or stronghold to besiege it, they shall invite the dwellers therein to embrace Islam. If they comply, the Moslems shall give up fighting them; but if they refuse, they shall call them to fulfill the tribute." He then continues. "It is laudable to again invite those who have been once invited to Islam, but have refused. If, however, they shall then too refuse, the Moslems shall after having implored Divine aid against them, assail them with instruments of war, burn down their houses, let out their water pools and destroy their crops." From this duty of making war upon unbelievers, the Moslem jurists draw the inference that their rulers are never lastingly bound to peaces and truces made with the enemy, but can break them at pleasure. **Il Hidayah**,[240] a work on Moslem law [also Hanafi], says: "Peace may be granted to unbelievers, but it is only a truce, and may be if advantageous, broken; notice, however, being previously given to the enemy of the rupture." These jurists also hold that Moslem rulers cannot, if they wish, enter into a lasting peace, but can only make temporary truces, to be broken at pleasure by the prince and in the interest of the believers. Kuduri [Quduri], who was already quoted above, says: "If it is seen fit by the Imam (chief, ruler of the Muslims), to make peace with the enemies or with a potion of them, and it is, in the interests of the Moslems, advantageous to do do, that is not wrong. But if he shall make peace with them, for a certain space of time, and should deem it for the good of the Moslems to break the covenant, he shall denounce it to them and renew the war."...*

The history of the relations between the United States and the
Barbary States during the last part of the preceding [18th] and the
first part of the present [19th] century furnishes a good example of
*the practical truth of what has just been said above...**In 1815 the***
United States ended this payment of tribute to a Moslem ruler
by sending a naval force to Algiers. The American negotiators
declared that the United States would never stipulate for paying
tribute under any form whatever, and would not give the Dey
[Muslim ruler] three hours or even a minute for deliberation,
and the second article of the treaty of 1815 distinctly did away
***once and for all with tribute or biennial presents**.*

Emile Tyan (d. 1977) was a major scholar of Islam's Caliphate system noted,
for his monumental works *Le califat en regime sultanien* (1956), and *Sultanat et*
califat (1956). He also wrote a succinct, and thoroughly unapologetic analysis of
jihad for the authoritative *Encyclopaedia of Islam*. Tyan studied the establishment
of Islam's totalitarian Caliphate system of governance by jihad, and the nature of
the uniquely Islamic institution of jihad, itself. The extracts, below, from two of
Tyan's analyses on the Caliphate, and his entry on jihad in the *Encyclopaedia of*
Islam, summarize and validate the discussion herein about jihad, up to this point.

> ... *[O]ne of the basic principles of Islam is that it must be extended*
> *to the whole world by conversion or at the least by submission to*
> *Islamic authority. The caliph has an obligation to promote and*
> *fulfill this universalism, if necessary by the force of arms. This*
> *is the meaning of holy war or jihad. From which it follows that*
> *Islamic sovereignty is at least potentially universal.* [241]

> *The Caliphate conserved its character as a religious institution,*
> *not in the sense of an organism of spiritual power or function, but*
> *quite precisely, in the sense that in the Islamic conception, **the***
> ***Caliphate, as the titulary repository of supreme sovereignty in***
> ***both the religious and civil aspects closely bound up with each***
> ***other, is an institution that constitutes an element of the faith**.*
> *It is a fundamental element of Islam, the pillar on which rests the*
> *whole edifice and which conditions the organization and life of*
> *the Community. **The Islamic faith includes belief in the necessity***
> ***of the Caliphate as the titular organism of the civil and religious***
> ***attributes of sovereignty.**[emphases added]* [242]

> *In [Islamic] law, according to general doctrine and in historical*
> *tradition, the djihad [jihad] consists of military action with the*
> *object of the expansion of Islam and, if need be, of its defense. The*

notion stems from the fundamental principle of the universality of Islam: this religion, along with the temporal power which it implies, ought to embrace to whole universe, if necessary by force.

The principle, however, must be partially combined with another which tolerates the existence, within the Islamic community itself, of the adherents of "the religions with holy books", i.e., Christians, Jews and Madjus [q.v.; (Zoroastrians)]. As far as these latter are concerned the jihad ceases as soon as they agree to submit to the political authority of Islam and to pay the poll tax (jizya [q.v.]) and the land tax (kharadj [q.v.]). As long as the question could still, in fact, be posed, a controversy existed—generally resolved by a negative answer—on the question as to whether the Christians and Jews of the Arabian peninsula were entitled to such treatment as of right. To the non-scriptuaries, in particular the idolaters, this half measure has no application according to the opinion of the majority: their conversion to Islam is obligatory under pain of being put to death or reduced into slavery.

The jihad is a duty. This precept is laid down in all the sources. It is true that there are to be found in the Kuran [Koran] divergent, and even contradictory, texts. These are classified by the doctrine, apart from certain variations of detail, into four successive categories: those which enjoin pardon for offenses and encourage the invitation to Islam by peaceful persuasion; those which enjoin fighting to ward off aggression; those which enjoin the initiative in attack, provided it is not within the four sacred months; and those which enjoin the initiative in attack absolutely, at all times and in all places. In sum, these differences correspond to the stages in the development of Muhammad's thought and to the modifications of policy resulting from particular circumstances; the Meccan period during which Muhammad, in general, confines himself to moral and religious teaching, and the Medina period when, having become the leader of a politico-religious community, he is able to undertake, spontaneously, the struggle against those who do not wish to join this community or submit to his authority. ***The doctrine holds that the later texts abrogate the former contradictory texts (the theory of naskh [q.v.]), to such effect that only those of the last category remain indubitably valid; and, accordingly, the rule on the subject may be formulated in these absolute terms: "the fight (jihad) is obligatory even when they (the unbelievers) have not themselves started it."***

Since the jihad is nothing more than a means to effect conversion to Islam or submission to its authority, there is only occasion to undertake it in circumstances where the people against whom it is directed have first been invited to join Islam. Discussion turned on the question as to whether it was necessary, on this ground, to address a formal invitation to the enemy. The general doctrine holds that since Islam is sufficiently widespread in the world, all peoples are presumed to know that they have been invited to join it. It is observed, however, that it would be desirable to repeat the invitation, except in cases where there is ground for apprehension that the enemy, thus forewarned, would profit from such a delay by better organizing his defenses and, in this way, compromising the successful outcome of the jihad.

Its perpetual character: **The duty of the jihad exists as long as the universal domination of Islam has not been attained.** *"Until the day of the resurrection," and "until the end of the world" say the maxims. Peace with non-Muslim nations is, therefore, a provisional state of affairs only; the chance of circumstances alone can justify it temporarily. Furthermore there can be no question of genuine peace treaties with these nations; only truces, whose duration ought not, in principle, to exceed ten years, are authorized. But even such truces are precarious, inasmuch as they can, before they expire, be repudiated unilaterally should it appear more profitable for Islam to resume the conflict. It is, however, recognized that such repudiation should be brought to the notice of the infidel party, and that he should be afforded sufficient opportunity to be able to disseminate the news of it throughout the whole of his territory.*

The jihad has principally an offensive character; *but it is equally a jihad when it is a case of defending Islam against aggression. This indeed, is the essential purpose of the ribat [q.v.] undertaken by isolated groups or individuals settled on the frontiers of Islam. The ribat is a particularly meritorious act.*

Finally, there is at the present time a thesis, of a wholly apologetic character, according to which Islam relies for its expansion exclusively upon persuasion and other peaceful means, and the jihad is only authorized in cases of "self defense" and of "support owed to a defenseless ally or brother." *Disregarding entirely the previous doctrine and historical tradition, as well as the texts of the Kuran and the sunna [traditions of Muhammad from the hadith and earliest biographies of Islam's prophet] on*

the basis of which it was formulated, but claiming, even so, to
remain within the bounds of strict orthodoxy, this thesis takes into
account only those early texts which state the contrary (v. supra).
[emphases added] [243]

In light of the preceding discussion, it is important to understand that Shiite and Sunni doctrines on jihad are fundamentally the same. [244] Even the so-called requirement for the "hidden" (i.e., during the "occultation" period) Shiite Imam's consent to wage jihad, was already argued away regarding "defensive jihad" by Abu Jaffar al-Tusi (d. 1045) during the 11th century as the Shiites of Iraq were beset by the Sunni Seljuk Turks. [245] This position was reiterated in the 13th century by al-Muhaqqiq al-Hilli (d. 1277). [246] These legists maintained—in a deliberately vague and elastic formulation—that Shiites Muslims could be summoned to jihad by the Imam's so-called "designee(s)"—which came to mean the "fuqaha," or doctors of the (Shiite) Muslim Law. [247]

Ann Lambton claimed that al-Hilli viewed jihad as primarily a defensive obligation, at least within a mid to late 13th century historical context, where "the crucial problem" he confronted "was not the extension of the dar al-Islam, but its defense." [248] However, she conceded that even al-Hilli identified the obligatory nature of jihad against non-Muslims, in the absence of a purely defensive posture, if summoned by the appropriate Shiite religious designee. Thus according to al-Hilli—and in conformity with Sunni jurisprudence—jihad was to be waged against [249]

the ahl-i-kitab until they submitted to the conditions of a dhimma,
and those who had no book, provided that they had been summoned
to accept Islam and had refused..

With the advent, at the outset of the 16th century, of the very aggressive Shiite Safavid theocracy under Shah Ismail I, who claimed direct descent from the Imams, we see "non-fuqaha" rulers declaring unabashed offensive, expansionist jihad throughout this dynasty. [250]

Demonstrating how Safavid Shi'ite jurisprudence was in agreement with the Sunni consensus on the basic nature of *jihad* war, including offensive jihad, here is an excerpt from the *Jami-i-Abbasi* [the popular Persian manual of Shi'a Law] written by al-Amili (d.1622), a distinguished theologian under Shah Abbas I: [251]

Islamic Holy war [jihad] against followers of other religions,
such as Jews, is required unless they convert to Islam or pay the
poll tax.

The 18th century Qajar Shiite theocratic dynasty saw the role of declaring jihad— again, including offensive, expansionist jihad—restored in theory to the Shiite fuqaha. [252] Finally re-emphasizing how such campaigns under the both Safavids and Qajars no longer required endorsement by the Imam, an early 18th century Qajar treatise on jihad states, "It is possible to say that jihad during the Imam's concealment is ***more praiseworthy*** than during his presence." [253]

Given this overview, I will now demonstrate how Shiite doctrine—through the prism of pre-modern and contemporary Shiite religious authorities—comports with Sunni conceptions of not only offensive jihad, but also the targeting of non-combatants, and martyrdom operations.

Ayatollah Khomeini asserted that offensive jihad could be sanctioned by "the Shiite jurist," whom, he claimed possessed "all the authorities of the Imam." [254] Khomeini's formulation of jihad, circa 1942, was unabashed. [255]

> *[T]hose who study jihad will understand why Islam wants to conquer the whole world. All the countries conquered by Islam or to be conquered in the future will be marked for everlasting salvation. For they shall live under [God's law]....Those who know nothing of Islam pretend that Islam counsels against war. Those [who say this] are witless. Islam says: Kill all the unbelievers just as they would kill you all! Does this mean that Muslim should sit back until they are devoured by [the unbelievers]? Islam says: Kill them [the non-Muslims], put them to the sword and scatter [their armies]. Does this mean sitting back until [non-Muslims] overcome us? Islam says: Kill in the service of Allah those who may want to kill you! Does this mean that we should surrender [to the enemy]? Islam says: Whatever good there is exists thanks to the sword and in the shadow of the sword! People cannot be made obedient except with the sword! The sword is the key to paradise, which can be opened only for holy warriors! There are hundreds of other [Koranic] psalms and hadiths [sayings of the prophet] urging Muslims to value war and to fight. Does all that mean that Islam is a religion that prevents men from waging war? I spit upon those foolish souls who make such a claim.*

Ayatollah Ali Khamenei, the current Iranian Supreme Guide, and Khomeini's successor, has also endorsed the principle that offensive jihad may be ordered by a qualified jurist if such a campaign is deemed to be in the Islamic Republic's interest. [256] Mehdi Khalaji adds, with regard to Khamenei's views, [257]

> *In reply to a follower, Khamenei stated that offensive jihad can be ordered by a qualified jurist if it is in the interest of the Islamic Republic. In the transcript of Khamenei's unpublished courses, he advocated the theory that gives legitimacy to the ruling jurist's order for offensive jihad.*

These understandings were in turn shared by the late Ayatollah Montazeri (as described in the Introduction), whose putatively "reformist" ideology was an inspiration for the "Green Movement." [258]

Perhaps most instructive were the writings of Muhammad Husayn Tabatabai (d. 1981), specifically, his glosses on important Koranic verses addressing jihad. A brief biographical introduction to Tabatabai is in order to appreciate the significance of his doctrinal interpretations. Also known as Allamah Tabatabai, he was a prolific writer whose influential Koranic studies, and philosophical works, remain widely read. Tabatabai's **monumental** twenty volume *Al-Mizān fi Tafsir al-Qur'an* ("The measure of balance in the interpretation of the Quran"), is generally regarded as the most important 20th century Shiite Koranic commentary.[259] Jane Dammen McCauliffe, an internationally recognized scholar of Koranic exegesis, is editor of both the six-volume *Encyclopaedia of the Qur'an*, [260] and *The Cambridge Companion to the Qur'an.* [261] Noting Tabatabai's Koranic commentary, "*included with some frequency...excerpts from hadith collections and from previous commentaries, particularly those of al-Ayyashi (d. 932), al-Qummi (d. 939), and al-Tabarsi (d. 1153).,*" McCauliffe concluded that the massive work [262]

> ... *testifies to his [Tabatabai's] broad scholarly background and abiding interest in comparative religion and philosophy. In addition to etymological and grammatical discussions,* ***it combines his own thoughts and elucidations of the passage under consideration with discourses on its moral implications or mystical-philosophical ramifications.*** *[emphasis added]*

Renowned Iranian Professor of Islamic Studies at Georgetown University and prominent contemporary Muslim philosopher, Seyyed Hossein Nasr, translated and wrote the preface to Tabatabai's treatise, *Shi'ite Islam.* [263] Professor Nasr referred to Tabatabai as, "*a man who has devoted his whole life to the study of religion, in whom humility and the power of intellectual analysis are combined,*" a "*celebrated Shi'ite authority,*" who produced the "*monumental Quranic commentary, al-Mizan.*" [264] And Nasr reverently summarized Tabatabai's purported unique combination of scholarship and spirituality, as follows: [265]

> *Allamah Tabatabai represents that central and intellectually dominating class of Shi'ite ulama who have combined interest in jurisprudence and Quranic commentary with philosophy, theosophy, and Sufism and who represent a more universal interpretation of the Shi'ite point of view. Within the class of the traditional ulama, 'Allamah Tabatabai possesses the distinction of being a master of both the Shari'ite and esoteric sciences and at the same time he is an outstanding hakim or traditional Islamic philosopher (or more exactly, "theosopher").*

Allamah Tabatabai, from www.shahed.isaar.ir, May 1, 2012 http://bit.ly/Meh9CO

(Pace the hagiographies of McCauliffe and Nasr, Professor W. Montgomery Watt, in a 1977 review of the Tabatabai-Nasr collaboration, *Shi'ite Islam,* offered this more apt assessment of both Tabatabai and the Islamic apologist, Nasr: *"there is no sign in the present work of any attempt to come to terms with occidental thought. The author [Tabatabai] still lives in the world of traditional Islamic theology, virtually untouched by any 'impact of the West.'...Seyyed Hossein Nasr, a Persian who studied science and philosophy at the Massachusetts Institute of Technology and Harvard, is the most effective apologist for Islam to the West at the present time, as may be seen from his Ideals and Realities of Islam and various other books and articles."*) [265a]

Allameh [Allamah] Tabatabaei University, named in honor of this celebrated Shiite authority and "theosopher," is the largest specialized state social sciences university in Iran and the Middle East, with 17000 students and 500 full-time faculty members. [266] Affirming his continued lofty stature, and relevance, an Iranian national conference was held on May 3, 2012, in Qom, dedicated to "recognizing the interpretative methods and principles used by Allameh [Allamah] Tabatabaee [Tabatabai] in [his] *Al-Mizan* exegesis." [266a]

Below are extracts from Tabatabai's "monumental" Koranic commentary revealing how this learned Shiite paragon of the "mystical-philosophical" implications of the Koran, interpreted Koran 2:193/8:39, and related verses, especially 9:29, pertaining to jihad. Tabatabai's glosses merely reiterated the traditionalist Islamic supremacist *Weltanschauung* which sanctions aggressive jihad to impose an Islamic order on all "unjust" disbelievers in the Muslim creed.

> **Koran:** *"And fight with them until there is no more mischief (disbelief) and the religion be only for Allah." This defines the time-limit of the fighting. Fitnah (translated here as 'disbelief' and 'mischief') means here 'ascribing a partner to Allah and worshipping idols', as was the custom of the polytheists of Mecca, who compelled others to do likewise. This meaning is inferred from the next sentence, and religion be only for Allah. This verse is similar to the verse: "And fight with them until there is no mischief (disbelief), and the religion be only for Allah; but if they desist, then verily Allah sees what they do. And if they turn back, then know that Allah is your Master; The Most Excellent Master and the Most Excellent Helper" (8:39-40). This verse shows that it is obligatory to call them to the right path before the war. If they accept the call, there will be no fighting; but if they reject it then there is no Master except Allah, and He is the most excellent Master and the most excellent Helper; He helps his believing servants. It is known that fighting is prescribed so that the religion be only for Allah. Such a fighting cannot be started until the adversaries are first invited to come onto the right path, i.e. the religion based upon monotheism. Some people wrote that this verse was abrogated by the verse: "Fight those who do not believe in Allah, nor in the latter day, nor do they prohibit what Allah and His Apostle have prohibited, nor follow the religion of truth, from among those who were given the Book, until they pay the jizyah (tributary tax) with their hand while they are in a state of subjection" (9:29). But there is no question of either verse abrogating the other, because they deal with different subjects. The verse under discussion is, as explained earlier, about the Meccan polytheists and does not cover the People of the Book who are referred to in verse 9:29. And the religion be only for Allah means that idol-worship be abolished and the oneness of Allah be accepted. The people of the Book do believe in One Creator. **We know their belief is in reality disbelief** as Allah says that they: do not believe in Allah, nor in the latter day, nor do they prohibit what Allah and His Apostle have prohibited, nor follow the religion of truth. **But Islam is content with their mere profession of monotheism. Fighting with them was ordained not to make them believe in monotheism, but simply so that they might pay tribute to the Muslims, thus raising the true creed above their creed and making Islam victorious over all religions.*** [267]

Islam proceeds by degrees in these three methods. First comes good exhortation and peaceful invitation. If it fails to repulse the unjust people and to remove their corruption and despotism, then the second method is adopted, and that is peaceful boycott, passive resistance and noncooperation with them, withholding all assistance from them. If this too proves ineffective, then the only alternative is the third one, that is, armed confrontation, because Allah is never pleased with injustice; and he who silently agrees with an unjust person, is his partner in injustice. Even when Islam drew sword and took up arms against the unjust people (who had disregarded the divine communications and proofs), it used the force only to remove those who had become like stumbling blocks in the way of the Call of the truth. In other words, it used the arms to repel the enemies' mischief, not to make them enter the fold of Islam. Allah says: And fight with them until there is no more mischief [2:193]. [268]

Tabatabai's exegesis on 9:29 merits particular consideration because this verse is not only the eternal jihad directive against Jews, Christians, (and Zoroastrians), but the ultimate rationale for the discriminatory system of governance imposed upon the survivors of these creeds vanquished by fighting, or those groups of these "real infidels" who submit without a fight. His gloss opens by identifying the specific "People of the Book," i.e., those with "revealed" scriptures, who nonetheless must be subjected by jihad: [269]

These verses speak of battling the People of the Book, namely those who managed to withhold the jizya, *and it recalls matters pertaining to ways in which they deviate from the truth, both in belief and in action.*

As for the words of the Almighty: "Fight those who do not believe in Allah or in the Last Day and who do not consider unlawful what Allah and His Messenger have declared unlawful and who do not apply the religion of truth among those who were given the Scripture," [i.e., Koran 9:29] these 'People of the Book' are the Jews and the Christians to whom many verses in the Holy Quran are dedicated, as well as the Zoroastrians who are mentioned or alluded to by the words of the Almighty [Koran 22:17]: "Indeed, those who have believed and those who practice Judaism and the Sabeans and the Christians and the Zoroastrians and those who associate with Allah - Allah will judge between them on the Day of Resurrection. Indeed Allah is, over all things, Witness," where they are listed among the other representatives of heavenly [inspired] creeds...

Tabatabai then elaborates, at some length, why despite being "People of the Book," they are ultimately considered "real infidels": [269a]

> *The Almighty does not differentiate in His Word between belief in Him and belief in the Last Day. Therefore disbelief in one of these two things constitutes disbelief in God, and disbelief in God constitutes disbelief in these two things together. So the rule about someone who differentiates between God and His messenger, and believes in one without the other, is that he is [considered] an infidel, as it says [Koran 4:150-151]: "Indeed, those who disbelieve in Allah and His messengers and wish to discriminate between Allah and His messengers and say, 'We believe in some and disbelieve in others,' and wish to adopt a way in between; Those are the disbelievers, truly. And We have prepared for the disbelievers a humiliating punishment."*

> **The People of the Book are counted, like [others] who do not believe in the prophethood of Muhammad (peace be upon him), as <u>real infidels</u>,** *even though [in reality] they do have belief in God and in the Last Day.* **The formulation is not that they only deny one of God's wonders, namely the wonder of prophecy, rather the way it is formulated is that they reject belief in God [Himself].** *Therefore [the Quran states that] they do not believe in God and in the Last Day, in the same way as the polytheists who have idols deny God, since they [too] do not see Him as one but instead they see one godhead above [other] multiple gods.* **Even though they establish as a principle [belief in] creation and resurrection [their belief system] does not agree with the truth at all, like their claim that the Messiah is the son of God or that Ezra is the son of God. They resemble in this the words of those infidels who worship statues and idols, namely that among the gods this one is a god who is the father of a god, and that one is a god who is the son of a god**...

> *Therefore is it obvious that belief in God and in the Last Day is banished from the People of the Book. Verily they cannot see the truth of the matter concerning the Oneness of God and the resurrection, even if they acknowledge that the Word has a divine source. It is not that some of them [openly] deny that the Word is divinely inspired by God, praised be He, or that they would deny the resurrection. They actually confirm what the Quran tells about them even though in reality, the Torah as we have it today does not have any information about the resurrection.*

[Let's] now [look at] their second feature [as described] in the text: "who do not consider unlawful what Allah and His messenger have declared unlawful". **This is like what the Jews said to allow things [that are really forbidden] which the Quran enumerates and recalls about them in Surah 2, 4 and others, and what the Christians say to allow wine and pork.** *Surely the prohibition of these two things is established in the laws of Moses, Jesus and Muhammad (peace be upon them), and [also] for them to consume the wealth of the people unjustly.*

What is meant with the [term] "messenger" in the phrase "what Allah and His messenger have declared unlawful" is a messenger from among themselves spoke through his [own] prophecy, like Moses who addressed the Jews, and Jesus who addressed the Christians. **The meaning thus is that none of these communities is upholding the prohibitions that their messengers had imposed on them (while speaking) through prophecy. They [theoretically] acknowledge his validity and therefore [should put] an end to daringly challenging God and His prophet, and playing around with truth and verity.** *As for the prophet Muhammad (peace be upon him) who they can find described in their Scriptures, the Torah and the Gospel, he allows them what is good and forbids them what is bad. He takes away their burden [covenant] and their shackles that were on them.*

Tabatabai elucidates the "purpose" for the permanent designation of the Jews, Christians, and Zoroastrians as genuine infidels: objects of chastisement, the Muslims are to be incited against these reprobates, and violently subject them to an Islamic order, which features, prominently, enforced payment of the blood ransom, jizya. [269b]

So then the purpose for describing them as not forbidding what God and His messenger forbade, is to rebuke and defame them, and to arouse the believers and incite them towards battling them for not submitting to God's and His prophet's prohibitions in their religious practice, and for allowing themselves to fall into Divinely forbidden practices and violating [dishonoring, raping] what is sacrosanct.

However one who contemplates the overall objectives of Islam should not be confused thinking that the purpose of battling the People of the Book until they pay the jizya is for the pleasure of the supporters of Islam... Rather the goal of [our] religion in this [respect] is for the religion of truth [Islam], and the enactment of righteousness, and the word of godliness to triumph over falsehood, iniquity and immorality… **As far as the jizya is concerned, this is a financial donation [i.e., blood ransom!], taken from them and allocated towards upholding their protection [i.e., "protection," from, primarily, the resumption of the jihad against them!] and towards their proper management. An independent government cannot annul this kind of practice, either in an overt or in a concealed manner… they [the Muslims] should battle them [only] in order to bring them [Jews, Christians, Zoroastrians] under the dhimma so that they will no [longer] openly practice any immorality and evil will be contained among them.**

The concluding summary of Tabatabai's gloss on Koran 9:29 enumerates three key points of (re-)emphasis, which all hinge on this overarching principle: Jews, Christians, and Zoroastrians—People of the Book—must be fought, subdued, and humbled because they constitute a chronic danger to an Islamic, Sharia-based society, and its mores. [269c]

> *Firstly, What is meant with the People of the Book not believing in God and in the Last Day is that they do not envelope themselves in the faith [i.e., Islam] that is acceptable for God, and that they do not forbid what God and His messenger forbade, that they are inconsiderate by publicly committing these forbidden things and by doing so they demoralize human society and undermine the current rightful government1. Also, [it means] that they do not profess the religion of truth, and they do not follow the true practice that conforms to creation and with which creation and the universe are consistent.*

> *Secondly, the phrase "who do not believe in God… (until the end of their three characteristics)," comes to explain the wisdom in the commandment to fight them, and from this follows the moral benefit of instigation and incitement to do so.*

> *Thirdly, the intention is to battle all People of the Book, not just some of them, as [would be the case] by taking [the word] "among" in the phrase "among those who were given the Book" as a differentiation.*

> *Considering the word of the Almighty "…until they give the jizya from their hands while they are humbled", Al-Rāghib said in [his book] 'Al-Mufradat': [269d] "Jizya is what is taken from the Ahl adh-Dhimma, and it is called this way because of being*

a reimbursement for sparing their lives" [literally, "blood']. It is a special [obligatory] donation [that works] as a penalty for holding on to unbelief, i.e. as a punishment...

Relying on what Al-Rāghib mentions, this supports what we brought forward before namely that this financial contribution is allocated towards upholding their protection [again, from resumption of the jihad] and saving their lives and towards their proper management. Al-Rāghib also says: "Smallness (or insignificance) versus greatness are opposite terms used to qualify one [concept] or the other. Something can be small in one aspect and great in another." He continues: "There is a saying: 'He is small' (ṣaghura ṣaghiran, [the second word] first with an 'a' and then an 'i') as opposite to great. And another expression: 'He is small and despised' (ṣaghura ṣagharan wa-ṣaghāran, with two times 'a' in both words), referring to [a low level of] gratification. The acceptable kind of [being] humiliated in terms of a religious status is: "...until they give the jizya from their hands while they are humbled"... The "hand": A human limb that aims at power and pleasure. Therefore it says: : "...until they give the jizya from their hands..." which refers to its first meaning, namely 'until they give the jizya which is passed from their hand into your hand', while there is a reference to a second meaning namely 'until they give the jizya because of your power and authority over them', while they are humbled and cannot rise above you nor become haughty towards you.

Regarding their characteristics that necessitate fighting them, as mentioned in the beginning of the verse, followed by them giving the jizya to uphold their protection, it informs [us] that the purpose of humiliating them is their submission to an Islamic lifestyle and to a righteous religious government within an Islamic society. They shall not be equal to Muslims nor stand out against with them as an independent identity, free to express anything their souls feel like, nor to publicize the doctrines and activities invented by their lunacies that corrupt human societies. This all relates to them handing over money from their hands out of a contemptible position.

So the meaning of the verse (and God knows best) is: Fight the People of the Book who do not [truly] believe in God or in the Last Day, with a faith that is acceptable and uncorrupted from being proper, and who do not forbid what is forbidden in Islam namely those [crimes] that, when committed, corrupt human

> *society, and who do not abide by a religion that conforms with the divine creation. Fight them and persist in fighting them until they are humbled among you, and submit to your rule. In this [condition] they shall give a defined financial contribution signifying their humbled position which is allocated towards upholding their position and sparing their lives and towards the necessary expenses for managing their affairs.*

Finally, Tabatabai's gloss on Koran 5:5 adds a related caveat in discussing the possibility of allowing Shiite Muslim men to marry women from among the subjected "People of the Book," which validates the jihad-related concepts of "harbis," and collecting jizya: [269e]

> *the Prophet...said, "Verily the marriage is allowed with only those People of the Book who pay jizya; marriage with others is not lawful"* **The author [Tabatabai] says: It is because without payment of jizya they will be counted among kafir harbi** *[infidels in "lands of war," whose lives and property are licit for the Muslims].*

Grand Ayatollah Sayyid Muhammad Sadiq Husayni Shirazi (d. 2001), was an author and religious leader revered by millions of Twelver Shiite Muslims worldwide. Hagiographies of Shirazi extol his broad ranging contributions in various fields from jurisprudence and theology, to politics, economics, law, sociology, and human rights. [270] Iranian expatriate history professor Reza Afshari, who forthrightly chronicled the human rights abuses in "post-Revolutionary" Iran, from 1979 to 2000, described Shirazi as follows: [271]

> *Perhaps the least political among the Grand Ayatollahs was Sayyid Muhammad Shirazi, who enjoyed a considerable Shiite following. He stayed clear of political involvement during the Khomeini era. However, he became indignant over [Ayatollah Ali] Khamenei's attempt to gain recognition not only as Supreme Leader but also as an eminent marja taqlid (source of emulation), a position reserved only for Grand Ayatollahs. Shirazi seemed to have favored a committee of Grand Ayatollahs to provide leadership for the country.*

Despite his alleged "ecumenism," and "quietist" approach to politics, Shirazi's Islamic law manual simply confirms (*ad nauseum*) the traditionalist Shiite (and overall Islamic) viewpoint on jihad: [272]

> *The jihad against the non-believers—according to its criteria— is "wajib kifai" "collective obligation" or "obligatory as per sufficiency" in that it is not obligatory for the rest of the people*

if sufficient number of individuals take it up; if those who could
execute this duty do not do so, then all those who are able to do
jihad are considered to have committed disobedience... Before the
start of the battle the non-believers of the people of the book are
given the choice between three: 1) Islam, which is to embrace
Islam through declaration of the two shahadah (testimonies of
faith); to testify to the oneness of Allah and to the Prophethood of
the prophet of Islam, Muhammad peace be upon him and his pure
family, and adhering to the laws of Islam.; 2) jizyah, in that they pay
tax for the protection they receive. 3) Combat [note from original:
"The late Imam Shirazi adds a fourth category: or whatever the
Council of the 'fuqaha maraje'(i.e., being both expert in Islamic
law and recognized rulers) deems appropriate."] These options
are also given to the unbelieving who are not people of the book, if
the just religious scholars with knowledge of war issues consider
it to be in the general interest.

This shared, mainstream Sunni and Shiite doctrine on jihad is the validating context in which both Iran's 1979 Constitutional provision on its self-proclaimed "Ideological Army," and the stated *Weltanschauung* of its Lebanese proxy, Hezbollah, must be evaluated. Their aggressive, hegemonic aspirations—animated by the ideology of jihad—are self-evident.

Invoking Koran 8:60, the 1979 Iranian Constitution declares: [273]

In the formation and equipping of the country's defence forces,
due attention must be paid to faith and ideology as the basic
criteria. Accordingly, the Army of the Islamic Republic of Iran
and the Islamic Revolutionary Guard Corps are to be organized
in conformity with this goal, and they will be responsible not only
for guarding and preserving the frontiers of the country, but also
for fulfilling the ideological mission of jihad in God's way; that
is, extending the sovereignty of Allah's law throughout the world
(this is in accordance with the Koranic verse "Prepare against
them whatever force you are able to muster, and strings of horses,
striking fear into the enemy of Allah and your enemy, and others
besides them" [8:60]).

Khomeini's Iran has indeed embraced jihad "as a central pillar of faith and action," demonstrated notably by the unending campaign of vilification and proxy violence (via Hezbollah, in particular) against the "Zionist entity," Israel. This struggle epitomized what Khomeini's Iran viewed as its "sacred struggle to cleanse the region and the world of Muslim and non-Muslim infidel blasphemy." [273a]

Hezbollah's name, "The Party of Allah", derives from Koran 5:56—"And whoever takes Allah and His messenger and those who believe for a guardian, then surely *the party of Allah* are they that shall be triumphant.". In a public statement issued February 15/16, 1986, Hezbollah stressed its indelible links to Iran and Ayatollah Khomeini ("We obey the orders of one leader wise and just…") and conceived of itself as a "nation" linked to Muslims worldwide by "…a strong ideological and political bond, namely Islam". Expressed in the political language of the Koran, Hezbollah's ideology encompasses, triumphantly (as per the slogan adorning the party emblem, "The Party of Allah is Sure to Triumph") at least three major objectives: transforming Lebanon into a Sharia state; destroying Israel; and establishing regional, followed by international Islamic hegemony, i.e., bringing the region, then the world under the Sharia. [274]

> …we do not constitute an organized party in Lebanon. Nor are we a tight political cadre. We are an umma linked to the Muslims of the whole world by the solid doctrinal and religious connection of Islam, whose message God wanted to be fulfilled by the Seal of the Prophets, i.e., Muhammad. This is why whatever touches or strikes Muslims, in Afghanistan, Iraq, the Philippines and everywhere reverberates throughout the Muslim umma of which we are an integral part. Our behavior is dictated to us by legal principles laid down by the light of an overall political conception defined by the leading jurist (wilayat al-faqih) As for our culture, it is based on the Holy Koran, the Sunna and the legal rulings of the faqih who is our source of imitation (marja' al-taqlid). Our culture is crystal clear. It is not complicated and is accessible to all.No one can imagine the importance of our military potential as our military apparatus is not separate from our overall social fabric. Each of us is a fighting soldier. **And when it becomes necessary to carry out the Holy war (Jihad), each of us takes up his assignment in the fight in accordance with the injunctions of the Law, and that in the framework of the mission carried out under the tutelage of the Commanding Jurist.**…our struggle [against Israel] will end only when this entity is obliterated. We recognize no treaty with it, no cease fire, and no peace agreements, whether separate or consolidated.

Hassan Nasrallah, before assuming the leadership of Hezbollah, as its Secretary-General, re-affirmed this vision: [275]

> What is the nature of the regime that Hezbollah wants for Lebanon at present, in light of the state of the country and the numerous sects? The preceding lectures have answered this question. Right now, we do not have a plan for a regime in Lebanon. We believe that we should remove the colonialism and the Israeli

[occupation], and only then can a plan be implemented. **Our plan, to which we, as faithful believers, have no alternative, is to establish an Islamic state under the rule of Islam. Lebanon should not be an Islamic republic on its own, but rather, part of the Greater Islamic Republic, governed by the Master of Time [the Mahdi], and his rightful deputy, the Jurisprudent Ruler, Imam Khomeini.** *[...] [I was asked] about Hezbollah's relations with Iran and with the leadership of the Islamic Revolution in Iran. As far as we are concerned, these relations... I am one of the people working for Hezbollah and its active apparatuses. I would not have remained for a single moment in any apparatus of Hezbollah if I were not absolutely convinced that these apparatuses are connected, through a certain hierarchy, to the Jurisprudent Ruler and Leader, whose decisions are binding. As far as we are concerned, this is axiomatic. Diplomatic and political statements are not what is important in this case. Ayatollah Karroubi cannot simply admit: Yes, Hezbollah are our people in Lebanon. This is inconceivable, both politically and media-wise. Our essential and organic relation with the leadership of the Islamic Revolution in Iran and the Rule of the Jurisprudent is axiomatic, as far as we are concerned. We belong to this path, we make sacrifices for its sake, and we expose ourselves to dangers, because we are convinced that the blood we shed flows for the sake of the Rule of the Jurisprudent. [...]* **Should the Jurisprudent Ruler be the one to appoint the leaders, and bestow legitimacy upon them, in all Muslim countries? Yes, because his jurisprudence is not limited by geographical boundaries. It extends to wherever Muslims may be.**

The killing of non-combatants during jihad campaigns was fully sanctioned according to the prominent 14th, and 18th (to early 19th) century Shiite jurists, respectively, [276] Allameh Helli [Hilli](d. 1325), and Sayyid Ali Tabatabai (d. 1816). [277] Allameh Helli maintained there was a consensus among Shiite legists that if defeating the enemy required attacking and killing children, women, and the elderly, then these actions were to be undertaken. [278] Ali Tabatabai, invoking Muhammad's campaigns against the Medinan Jewish tribe Banu Nadir, and his siege of Taif (as described in Koran sura [chapter] 59, the hadith and Muslim biographies of Islam's prophet [279]), stated: [280]

It is permitted to fight by all means that guarantee victory, such as besieging fortresses, using siege catapults, setting fires [to people's houses and properties], felling trees, flooding residencies, or depriving [enemy civilians] of water and so on, whether it would be necessary or not, although some jurists believe that these measures are permissible only if victory in war depends on using them.

Victory during jihad, Ali Tabatabai added, justified the killing of even Muslim children, women, the elderly, prisoners, and merchants, let alone non-Muslim infidel non-combatants. In the event of such killings, Ali Tabatabai further argued, Muslim governments were not obliged to make payments for blood money (diyah), or "expiation" (kaffarah). [281]

Many influential contemporary Shiite theologians—consistent with the injunctions of the Sharia—argue that the lives of "misguided" non-Muslims are not equivalent to those of Muslims, echoing the traditionalist mindset of their forbears, Allameh Helli and Ali Tabatabai. These shared views continue to rationalize attacks on non-combatants, including the modern phenomenon of homicide bombing "martyrdom" operations. For example, Ayatollah Ahmad Jannati, head of the influential and authoritative Guardian Council, and a close adviser to Ayatollah Ali Khamenei (who also serves on Iran's "Expediency Discernment Council," and "Assembly of Experts"), [282] stated on November 20, 2005: [283]

> *Human beings, apart from Muslims, are animals who roam the earth and engage in corruption. [Note: For an example of Jannati's more specific "ecumenism," vis-a-vis the U.S. and Israel, see extracts from this April 2008 speech [284]]*

Sayyed [Sayyid] Javad Varai, editor of the official quarterly publication of the Assembly of Experts, previously argued, in 2003, that homicide bombings were permissible and virtuous, despite killing non-combatants: [285]

> *First, sometimes all members of the enemy, including women and men, young and old, are involved in the invasion...hence the only way to deprive them of security is [through] isteshhadi [self-sacrifice] operations. Second, it is possible that the enemy's women have been trained to fight along with their men, hence they are the enemy's soldiers and killing them is considered as killing enemy forces, not innocent citizens [namely noncombatant civilians]...Third, when Islam's fighters conduct such operations, the killing of others [civilians] seems to be inevitable...Fourth, even if [Islam's fighters] kill innocent citizens, it would be a legitimate legal retaliation. Is it illegal to reciprocate the actions of an enemy who kills youth and teenagers, women and men, elders and sick people, and considers the killing of children and women as a part of his creed?*

The essential pattern of the jihad war is captured in the classical Muslim historian al-Tabari's recording of the recommendation given by Umar b. al-Khattab (the second "Rightly Guided Caliph") to the commander of the troops he sent to al-Basrah (636 C.E.), during the conquest of Iraq. Umar reportedly said: [286]

> *Summon the people to God; those who respond to your call, accept it from them, but those who refuse must pay the poll tax out of humiliation and lowliness. (Koran 9:29) If they refuse this, it is the sword without leniency. Fear God with regard to what you have been entrusted.*

By the time of al-Tabari's death in 923, jihad wars had expanded the Muslim empire from Portugal to the Indian subcontinent. Subsequent Muslim conquests continued in Asia, as well as Eastern Europe. Under the banner of jihad, the Christian kingdoms of Armenia, Georgia, Byzantium, Bulgaria, Serbia, Bosnia, Herzegovina, Croatia, and Albania, in addition to parts of Poland and Hungary, were also conquered and Islamized by waves of Seljuk, or later Ottoman Turks, as well as Tatars, and Safavid Shiite Iranians. Arab Muslim invaders engaged, additionally, in continuous jihad raids that ravaged and enslaved Sub-Saharan African animist populations, extending to the southern Sudan. When the Ottoman Muslim armies were stopped at the gates of Vienna in 1683, over a millennium of jihad had transpired. These tremendous military successes spawned a triumphant jihad literature. Muslim historians recorded in detail the number of infidels slaughtered, or enslaved and deported, the cities, villages, and infidel religious sites which were sacked and pillaged, and the lands, treasure, and movable goods seized. [287]

This sanctioned, but wanton destruction resulted, specifically in: the merciless slaughter of non-combatants, including women and children; massive destruction of non-Muslim houses of worship and religious shrines—Christian churches, Jewish synagogues, and Zoroastrian, Hindu, and Buddhist temples and idols; and the burning of harvest crops and massive uprooting of agricultural production systems, leading to famine. Christian (Coptic, Armenian, Jacobite, Greek, Slav, etc.), as well as Hebrew sources, and even the scant Zoroastrian, Hindu and Buddhist writings which survived the ravages of the Muslim conquests, independently validate this narrative, and complement the Muslim perspective by providing testimonies of the suffering of the non-Muslim victims of jihad wars. [288]

Shah Tahmasp, the longest reigning Safavid Shiite ruler (r., 1524-1576), waged four prototypical, aggressive jihad campaigns against Christian Georgia—in 1540, 1546, 1551, and 1553 C.E. [289] Safavid era historian Roger Savory has acknowledged that the "launching of these attacks without any necessary provocation on the part of the victims,"—i.e., Christians—was primarily motivated by the ideology of "jihad, or holy war against the infidel." [290] The 16th century chronicle *Ahsanu't-Tawarikh of Hasan-I-Rumlu* was touted by Savory as the most authoritative eyewitness narrative for the reign of Shah Tahmasp, written by a military officer

(Hasan-I-Rumlu) who accompanied the Shah on most of his campaigns, including those in Georgia. [291] What follows are representative extracts from Hasan-I-Rumlu's accounts of the four jihad expeditions Shah Tahmasp waged against the Georgians: [292]

> *First expedition of the Shah against Georgia, 1540 C.E.*
> *This year [1540] the Shah went against the Georgians- hunting on the way to Bargshat and being joined by Chiefs and their forces from all parts. One night the Muslim army poured upon Tiflis, and plundered the city, and took captive women and children. Gulbad the Georgian, one of the chief nobles of Lawasan, took refuge in the Tiflis court, asking for quarter. And he surrendered the fort, and became a Muslim. The Ghazis [jihadists] raided the country. Hish, who was one of the gratest chiefs of Lawasan, threw himself into the fort of Birtis; but the Gabrs [infidels, in this case, Christians] surrendered it, and those who accepted Islam were spared, and the rest were slaughtered. Then the army marched against the mountains of Didku and Georgia, which they took, killing a number of the enemy in the passes of the hills; and the rest were scattered. Then the Shah went to the Kur river, and Lawasan, the Ruler of that land, fled to the hills and forests, and escaped. And the Shah returned to Tabriz.*
>
> *Second expedition of the Shah against Georgia, 1546 C.E.*
> *...the Shah set out for Georgia with a large army, passed Shura-i-gil, and reached Aq Shahr. There, at a time of great cold, he made a night attack on the Gabrs, and covered the snow with their blood, and captured oxen and sheep, and burnt houses.*
>
> *Third expedition of the Shah against Georgia, 1551 C.E.*
> *...the Shah marched with speed from Shaki, and the Ghazis surrounded the hills and dales of the infidels, and leveled every place of refuge, nor did any escape. And the families and possessions of those polytheists were transferred to their slayers, as their lawful heirs. And the young women were taken captive. Then some took refuge in the hills, and in caves, and others in the forts of Malinkot, Arqaru, Darzabad, and in a wondrous church. And the Muslims slew many, and took the fort of Tumuk, and the other forts...the Shah ordered Badr Khan Ustajlu and Ali Sultan Takalu to attack the fort (of Darzabad), which therefore they surrounded. Now it was on a height, near the gate of Tumuk and the source of the river Kur, and in strength it was like the wall of Alexander and the castle of Khaybar. In the middle of the fort they had hollowed out a place ten cubits high, and made a*

*church of four rooms, and a long bench, and had painted its walls
without and within with gold and lapis lazuli and pictures of idols,
and arranged a throne in the second room, and an idol gilt and
covered with precious stones, and with two rubies for the eyes of
the lifeless form, and within the church was a narrow way one
hundred and fifty cubits long to go up, cut into the solid rock. And
they had two hidden kiosks for use in times of trouble, and there
were doors of iron and steel in the outer rooms, and a golden
door in the inner ones. Then the Ghazis fell upon that place, and
climbed above the fort, and slew the men, and took captive their
wives and children. And the Shah and his nobles went to see the
church, and they slew twenty evil priests, and broke the bell of
seventeen maunds weight seven times cast, and destroyed the
doors of iron and gold and sent them to the treasury. And Badr
Khan Ustalju broke four candles, each being sixty maunds of wax.
Thus the Shah got great booty; and in it were two rubies being
the eyes of the idol, each worth fifty tumans. And they leveled
the fort with the ground, so the Georgian Chiefs could go to no
other place...and the Shah put to death Wakhush and Shir Mazan
Ughali, who were Governors of that country.*

<u>*Fourth expedition of the Shah against Georgia, 1553 C.E.*</u>
*At this time it was reported that the Gabrs were rebelling. So
therefore the Shah set out to destroy the land of the infidels.
And all that country was forest. So that the wind could not blow
through the trees. And the infidels scattered, and Lawasan, the son
of Daud, the Governor of the land, fled to a place of refuge. And
the Georgians, being sore afraid, escaped to the hills and caves
and forests, and were besieged in forts. And the Ghazis slew the
men, and took capture their wives and children, and took booty, of
cattle and sheep. Then the army marched on Gori, the capital of
Lawasan, and plundered that land, and took prisoner fair young
women and round-faced boys. Then they reached the fort of
Mazrut, which never yet had been conquered by the Muslims. And
the troops surrounded it, and the Kotwal Parsatan was dismayed,
and left the fort, and yielded it up. Then the Shah set out for
the fort of Aydin...and Lawasan had left his mother there. The
Persians fell upon the defenders, and destroyed them with cannon
and mines, and assaulted and entered the fort and captured the
mother of Lawasan and most of the (defenders). Then the Shah
was told that there was a fort hard by, where the Georgians had
taken refuge. Shah Virdi Sultan Ziyad Ughali was appointed to
take that fort. And he did so; and returned to camp. The army took
many forts, and many prisoners, even more than thirty thousand,*

and much booty; and came to Barda. Then proclamations were
sent around Persia with the glad tidings.

Iskandar Beg Munshi (~1560-1632) was another Muslim historian of the Safavid
era, who composed one of the greatest works of Persian historiography. He
chronicled the origins of the Safavid dynasty, starting with the reigns of Shah
Ismail, and Shah Tahmasp, succeeded by a detailed analysis of the reign of Shah
Abbas I. [293] Iskandar Munshi provided this straightforward summary assessment
of the results of Shah Tahmasp's four mid-16th century jihad campaigns in
Georgia: [294]

> *The governors of all seven districts of Georgia were appointed by*
> *the Shah and became his subjects, contracted to pay the [Koranic]*
> *poll-tax [jizya] and the land tax [kharaj], and were instructed to*
> *have the name and exalted titles of the Shah [Tahmasp] included*
> *in the khutba [ritualistic sermons, especially on Fridays], and*
> *stamped on the coinage. **Thus the infidels of those regions were***
> ***reduced to submission by the sharp swords of the warriors of***
> ***Islam.***

The forcible retreat of Islamic jihadism, beginning with the Ottoman repulsion
at Vienna in 1683, was acutely evident in the aftermath of the Russo-Turkish
War of 1876-1878. [295] Already by 1882, however, Goldziher observed that the
"Muhammadan world," was responding to these historical setbacks, "excited
by a powerful idea." [296] What was this mighty, revitalizing inspiration? The re-
establishment of Islam's Caliphate system, "The spiritual fusion of politically dis-
arrayed Islam into a great unity." [297] Goldziher continued, [298]

> *The external form of this unity is the institution of the indivisible*
> *Caliphate, which is the oldest political structure of Islam. . . .*
> *With regard to Islam, the unification of Muhammadan powers,*
> *and the awakening of the awareness of their unity and solidarity*
> *under a common authority is seen as the sole remedy against the*
> *dangers lurking in the womb of the future. And this unification is*
> *only conceived under the flag of the united Caliphate of Islam. . .*

And Goldziher concluded—over 130 years ago: [299]

> *[T]he idea of Panislamism is a militant idea in their [Muslim]*
> *eyes, as it was a militant idea at the time of the birth of young*
> *Islam. This idea now reigns over Muhammadan public opinion, in*
> *some places with such power that the representatives of European*
> *governments now complain of it.*

Writing in 1916, C. Snouck Hurgronje, the great Dutch Orientalist, confirmed how the jihad doctrine of world conquest, and the re-creation of a supranational Islamic Caliphate remained a potent force among the Muslim masses: [300]

> *..it would be a gross mistake to imagine that the idea of universal conquest may be considered as obliterated...the canonists and the vulgar still live in the illusion of the days of Islam's greatness. The legists continue to ground their appreciation of every actual political condition on the law of the holy war, which war ought never be allowed to cease entirely until all mankind is reduced to the authority of Islam-the heathen by conversion, the adherents of acknowledged Scripture [i.e., Jews and Christians] by submission.*

Hurgronje further noted that although the Muslim rank and file might acknowledge the improbability of that goal "at present" (circa 1916), they were, [301]

> *...comforted and encouraged by the recollection of the lengthy period of humiliation that the Prophet himself had to suffer before Allah bestowed victory upon his arms...*

Thus even at the nadir of Islam's political power, during the World War I era final disintegration of the Ottoman Empire, Hurgronje observed how [302]

> *...the common people are willingly taught by the canonists and feed their hope of better days upon the innumerable legends of the olden time and the equally innumerable apocalyptic prophecies about the future. The political blows that fall upon Islam make less impression...than the senseless stories about the power of the Sultan of Stambul [Istanbul], that would instantly be revealed if he were not surrounded by treacherous servants, and the fantastic tidings of the miracles that Allah works in the Holy Cities of Arabia which are inaccessible to the unfaithful.* **The conception of the Khalifate [Caliphate] still exercises a fascinating influence, regarded in the light of a central point of union against the unfaithful (i.e., non-Muslims).** *[emphasis added]*

Eight years later, in 1924, an article that appeared in the Calcutta Guardian linked the Pan-Islamic Indian Khilafat (Caliphate) Movement to trends that developed, and intensified immediately following the Russo-Turkish War, five decades prior to the eventual advent of the Egyptian Muslim Brotherhood in 1928, and geographically far removed from the latter movement. [303]

> *The Islamic World was aroused to the fact that the area of Islamic independence was steadily narrowing", and the Qur'anic theory that Islam should dominate over every other religion was giving way to the contrary system. It was felt that the only Muslim power*

*which could deal with those of Europe as an equal was Turkey;
and pan-Islamism everywhere inculcated the doctrine that Turkey
should be strengthened and supported. The Sultan was urged to
advance through Persia into India and make common cause with
the Sudanese Mehdi, and restore Egypt to an Islamic Sovereign.*

Thus the prototype modern Sunni jihadist organization, the Muslim Brotherhood,
[304] emerged out of this popular, well-defined historical, and mainstream doctrinal
milieu, a half-century later.

Charles Wendell introduced his elegant 1978 translation of five treatises by Hasan
al-Banna, with perspicacious analyses of the Muslim Brotherhood founder's
Weltanschauung. [305] Wendell stressed not only al-Banna's seamless connection
to the so-called "modernists," [306] Jamal al-Din Afghani, Muhammad Abduh, and
Muhammad Rashid Rida, but to traditional Islam itself. Moreover, Wendell's
concluding observations remain critical to understanding the deep Islamic
religious animus toward Israel—so much in evidence today—that al-Banna and
his movement both inspired, and reflected. [307]

> *One impressive factor that immediately strikes any student of
> the movement [the Muslim Brotherhood] is that it represents a
> continuation of the activist Pan-Islamic doctrine of Jamal al-Din
> al-Afghani and the early Muhammad Abduh. . . . [I]t seems beyond
> dispute that, like Al-Afghani, he [al-Banna] has as his final goal
> a return to the world-state of the Four Orthodox Caliphs (Al-
> Khalafa al-Rashidun) and, this once accomplished, an aggressive
> march forward to conquer the rest of the earth for God and his
> Sacred Law. . . Like most of the Muslim reformers from the early
> nineteenth century on, Al-Banna believed that it was possible to
> pick and choose those aspects of Western civilization he could
> accept as compatible with Islamic doctrine and morality, and
> neatly excise the rest. . . . Hasan, like his heroes like Al-Afghani and
> [Muhammad] Abduh, castigated the clerics for their withdrawal
> from the real world around them. Their fixation on gloss-writing,
> and their abdication of their true responsibilities as spiritual
> guides and models. . . . Hasan's answer to this was essentially
> that of both the fundamentalist Hanbalites and the "Manar"
> ["Al Manar," "The Lighthouse," the title of a publication jointly
> produced by Abduh and Rida] modernists, especially Abduh's
> disciple Muhammad Rashid Rida, whom he admired more than
> Abduh himself: "Back to the Qur'an and the Sunna!" . . .*
>
> **Hasan al-Banna's fundamental conviction that Islam does not
> accept, or even tolerate, a separation of "church" and state, or**

of either from society, is as thoroughly Islamic as it can be. Any attempt to translate his movement into terms reducible to social, political, or religious factors exclusively simply misses the boat. The "totality" created by the Prophet Muhammad in the Medinese state, the first Islamic state, was Hasan's unwavering ideal, and the ideal of all Muslim thinkers before him, including the idle dreamers in the mosque. His ideology then, before it was Egyptian or Arab or whatever, was Islamic to the core. Since it embraced all aspects of human life and thought, it was at least as much religious as anything else. Practically all of his arguments are shored up by frequent quotations from the Qur'an and the Traditions, quite in the style of his medieval forbears. If one considers the public to whom his writings were addressed, it becomes instantly apparent that such arguments must still be the most compelling for the vast bulk of the Muslim populations of today.

The nagging feeling that Islam must, and very quickly at that, catch up with the West, had even by his time filtered down from above to the masses after having been the watchword of the modernizing intellectual for almost a century. There was also the notion that all these Western sciences and techniques were originally adopted from Islamic culture, and were therefore merely "coming home"—a piece of self-conscious back-patting that was already a cliché of most Muslim political writing. . . To this [Islamic] revivalist mentality, nothing could be more hateful than further diminution of the lands traditionally dominated by Islam. I believe that much of the fury and unconcealed hatred of the Zionist state which is expressed by the majority of Arabs will become more comprehensible in light of what the Islamic domain as a concept really means to the Muslims, seen through the lens of Hasan's exposition. Fascists were unable to endow their acts or beliefs with a religious dimension, except for the embarrassing juvenility of the Teutonic shrines reputedly raised in Germany. In the case of the Muslim Brotherhood, however, they had, on the basis of indisputable historical facts and clear religious traditions, a ready-made program for a world crusade that required only actors and a leader. Islam had from the beginning been a proselytizing faith. The error of the Islamic peoples, as Al-Afghani had pointed out forty years before, had been to cease their inexorable forward march, to abnegate their God-ordained destiny.

A late August 1947 interview of Al-Banna by then First Secretary of the American

Embassy in Cairo, Philip W. Ireland, demonstrated the ideological nexus between contemporary Sunni and Shiite jihadism. The August 27, 1947 "Memorandum of Conversation between Shaikh Hassan Al Banna, Supreme Leader of Ikhwan Al Muslimin, and Philip W. Ireland, First Secretary of Embassy," includes Ireland's observation that, [308]

> *He [al-Banna] seemed very proud of the fact that there were chapters of the Ikhwan among the Shiahs of Iraq and Iran...*

Regardless of the veracity of al-Banna's claim that an Iranian Shiite Ikhwan "franchise" actually existed, Iran's own modern Shiite jihadist organization, Fedayeen-e-Islam, was created during 1945, in Tehran, by Sayyed Mojtaba Navvab Safavi. [309] Indeed, whether or not there were formal ties between Egypt's Muslim Brotherhood, and Iran's Fedayeen-e-Islam, [310] Safavi visited Cairo in January, 1954, where he was welcomed by the Ikhwan, and featured as "the main speaker" at two Ikhwan events held during his stay. [310a]

Sayyed Mojtaba Navvab Safavi was born in 1923 to a devoutly religious Shiite family from Tehran, whose original name was Mirlawhi. The family name had been changed to Navvab Safavi ("Deputies of the Safavids"), according to Professor Farhad Kazemi, "to identify with the famous Shiite dynasty of the Safavids, who in the 16th century, made Shi'ism the state religion of Iran." [311]

Between 1946 and 1951, Safavi's Fedayeen-e-Islam formed an alliance with Ayatollah Abul Qasim Kashani. During a major demonstration supporting the Palestinian Arabs, in May, 1948, the Fedayeen-Kashani coalition mustered several thousand active participants. "We are the youth of Iran—the devotees of Islam," the demonstrators proclaimed. Five thousand men volunteered to join the jihad against Palestinian Jewry, and the Fedayeen issued a proclamation which declared, "the pure blood of the brave devotees of Islam is boiling to help the Muslim Palestinian brothers." [312]

Kazemi maintains that the Fedayeen's important political role in Iran was due to four major factors: (I) being a highly successful jihad terror organization whose daring assassinations evoked fear; (II) their espousal of anti-colonialism and Iranian sovereignty, especially oil nationalization; (III) their maintenance of critical ties with the Shiite clergy, including, prominently, Khomeini; (IV) their contacts within the Iranian "bazaar", i.e., marketplace, which took advantage of the "well-established bazaar-mosque nexus," a source of funds, and additional clerical influence. [313]

Not surprisingly, the "overarching principles of the Fedayeen program" invoked traditionalist Shiite Sharia supremacism, seeking "an Islamic state in which the practices of the Sharia would reign supreme." [314] This included: [315]

full application of Islamic law, complete administration of the Islamic judicial system, including qesas ("law of retaliation") and other forms of punishment. The program also demands abolition of all non-Islamic laws and prohibition of all forms of immoral behavior, including gambling, prostitution, consumption of alcoholic beverages, etc. Their ideological handbook discusses all major government institutions and assigns them proper Islamic roles. It expects the parliament to legislate only Islamic laws. For the Fedayeen, clerics have a central leadership role as educators, judges, and moral guides to the people.

The Fedayeen recognize women as principal carriers of virtue and the keystone to an ethical family life. Their legal rights and privileges, however, are restricted, essentially reducing them to no more than second-class citizens. The program also advocates the formation of numerous houses all over the country to facilitate practice of the religious institution of temporary marriage. Significant restrictions, such as the poll tax (jizya), are also placed on recognized religious minorities— Christians, Jews, and Zoroastrians—who are minimally tolerated by the Fedayeen. No such attitude is extended to the Baha'is (q.v.), who are despised and rejected.

In the aftermath of the 1979 Revolution, Kazemi (circa 1999) highlighted these enduring features of the Fedyaeen legacy: [316]

[T]he Coalition of Islamic Associations which grew from the former members and sympathizers of the Fedyaeen, with their well established connections to Ayatollah Khomeini and his lieutenants since 1963 and their role as a major faction in the government of the Islamic Republic... published accounts by Ayatollahs Sayyed ʿAlī Kāmenaʾī [Khamenei] the supreme spiritual leader of the Islamic Republic, and ʿAlī-Akbar Hāšemī Rafsanjānī [Rafsanjani], the powerful chair of the Discretionary Council, all point directly to the important formative impact of Nawwābʾs [Navvabʾs] charismatic appeal in their early careers and anti-government activities.

Finally, Kazemi acknowledged the "important similarities between much of the Fedayeen's basic views," and central "principles and actions of the Islamic Republic of Iran." Khomeini and the Fedayeen "were in accord on issues" including: the role of clerics, morality and ethics, Islamic justice, the rights of women and religious minorities, and attitudes toward foreign powers. [317] Critical Fedayeen goals became [318]

*...enshrined in the core structures and ideological positions of
the Islamic Republic of Iran and are safeguarded by the Coalition
of Islamic Associations and their allies (e.g., Anṣār-e Ḥezb-Allāh
[Hezbollah]) with domination in the legislative, judicial and some
executive branches, including the Revolutionary Guard, and the
Intelligence Ministry*

From Jihad to Dhimmitude

Pooled findings from surveys conducted almost a century after Hurgronje's [319]
1916 observations (i.e., performed between 2006 to 2012), indicate that the vast
preponderance of contemporary Muslims still seek the conjoined goals of re-
establishing a Caliphate, and implementing the Sharia. [320]

For example, polling data released (April 24, 2007) in a rigorously conducted
face-to-face University of Maryland/ WorldPublicOpinion.org interview survey
of 4384 Muslims completed between December 9, 2006 and February 15, 2007-
1000 Moroccans, 1000 Egyptians, 1243 Pakistanis, and 1141 Indonesians-revealed
that **65.2%** of those interviewed-**almost 2/3**, hardly a "fringe minority"—desired
this outcome (i.e., "To unify all Islamic countries into a single Islamic state or
Caliphate"), including 49% of "moderate" Indonesian Muslims. The internal
validity of these data about the present longing for a Caliphate is strongly
suggested by a concordant result: 65.5% of this Muslim sample approved the
proposition "To require a **strict** [emphasis added] application of Shari'a law in
every Islamic country." [321]

A Pew Research Forum report, "The World's Muslims: Religion, Politics and
Society," released April 30, 2013, confirmed the broad appeal of the Sharia,
Islam's religio-political "law," across Islamdom. [322] The data were combined from
surveys conducted between 2008 and 2012, representing, as touted by Pew, "a
total of 39 countries and territories on three continents: Africa, Asia and Europe."
Collectively, the surveys included "more than 38,000 face-to-face interviews in
80-plus languages and dialects, covering every country that has more than 10
million Muslims." [323]

Responses to four related questions on the Sharia comprise the surveys' salient
findings. The questions were, "Do you favor or oppose making sharia law, or
Islamic law, the official law of the land in our country?" and these internally
validating (and equally edifying) queries – "Do you favor or oppose the following:
punishments like whippings and cutting off of hands for crimes like theft and
robbery?"; and "Do you favor or oppose the following: the death penalty for
people who leave the Muslim religion?" [324] Summary data from the nations with
the five largest Muslim populations (as per 2010) surveyed, [325] Indonesia (204

million), Pakistan (178 million), Bengladesh (149 million), Egypt (80 million), and Nigeria (76 million), revealed: [326]

- 72% of Indonesian Muslims, 84% of Pakistani Muslims, 82% of Bengladeshi Muslims, 74% of Egyptian Muslims, and 71% of Nigerian Muslims supported making Sharia the official state law of their respective societies. The population-weighted average from these 5 countries was 77% supportive. (Composite regional data confirmed these individual country trends—84% of South Asian Muslims, 77% of Southeast Asian Muslims, 74% of Middle Eastern/North African Muslims, and 64% of Sub-Saharan African Muslims favored application of the Sharia as official state law.)

- 37% of Indonesian Muslims, 85% of Pakistani Muslims, 50% of Bengladeshi Muslims, 70% of Egyptian Muslims, and 45% of Nigerian Muslims favored Sharia-based mandatory ("hadd") punishments "like whippings and cutting off of hands for crimes like theft and robbery"

- 42% of Indonesian Muslims, 86% of Pakistani Muslims, 54% of Bengladeshi Muslims, 80% of Egyptian Muslims, and 37% of Nigerian Muslims favored the Sharia-based hadd punishment of stoning for adultery

- 16% of Indonesian Muslims, 75% of Pakistani Muslims, 43% of Bengladeshi Muslims, 88% of Egyptian Muslims, and 29% of Nigerian Muslims favored the Sharia-based hadd punishment of execution for "apostasy"

Furthermore, the Pew survey results confirm the abject failure of the U.S. midwifed Iraqi and Afghan "democracies" to fulfill the utopian aspirations of the much ballyhooed "(Bernard) Lewis doctrine." [327] Instead, the negative prognostications, epitomized by Diana West's evocative description "Making the world safe for Sharia," [328] have been realized. Specifically, the Pew data indicated: [329]

- 91% of Iraqi Muslims and 99% of Afghan Muslims supported making Sharia the official state law of their respective societies

- 55% of Iraqi Muslims and 81% of Afghan Muslims favored Sharia-based hadd punishments "like whippings and cutting off of hands for crimes like theft and robbery"

- 57% of Iraqi Muslims and 84% of Afghan Muslims favored the Sharia-based hadd punishment of stoning for adultery

- 42% of Iraqi Muslims and 79% of Afghan Muslims favored the Sharia-based hadd punishment of execution for "apostasy"

Religious piety, as evidenced by frequency of prayer and "Following the Prophet's Example," increased support for Sharia, which was unaffected by age, gender, or educational level. [330] The Pew report fails to elaborate on these strong associations, offering no explanation about *why* increased compliance with prayer and pious conformity with the behavior of Islam's prophet Muhammad might result in broad Muslim approval for mutilating thieves, stoning adulterers to death, or executing those who simply exercise freedom of conscience and forsake Islam. [331]

As noted before, herein, Pew issued a report on June 11, 2013 finding concordant results with regard to the overall popularity of the Sharia in Iran: 83% favored its application. [332]

Ernest Gellner (1925-1995), [333] a renowned Western social anthropologist, whose interests extended to Islamdom, notably his 1981 study *Muslim Society*, [334] contextualized the global Islamic trends revealed by all these data, almost a quarter century ago. Gellner, described by an obituarist (in 1995) as a "defender of positivism, empiricism and rationalism," who, "with cold clarity" and "sternness" critiqued "religious and leftist seekers after umma . . . linguistic philosophy, relativism, psychoanalysis, and post-modernism," [335] wrote in 1991, [336]

> *I think it is fair to say that no secularization has taken place in the world of Islam: that the hold of Islam over its believers is as strong, and in some ways stronger, now than it was 100 years ago. Somehow or other Islam is secularization-resistant, and the striking thing is that this remains true under a whole range of political regimes*. It is true under socially radical regimes which try to fuse Islam with socialist terminology and ideas; it is equally true under traditionalist regimes whose elites belong to the world of Ibn Khaldun [d. 1406, the great Muslim historian and polymath] and come from a ruling tribal network; and it is true of the regimes in between.

Gellner's sobering 1991 assessment, [337] and the ominous contemporary hard polling data that have validated his concerns, [338] contrast starkly with ahistorical drivel from Western Muslim "advocacy" groups, such as the Muslim Association of Britain, which lionizes both the Caliphate, and the corollary implementation of Sharia, as promulgators of "a peaceful and just society." [339]

The prototypical Caliphate under Umar Ibn al-Khattab (d. 644), the second "rightly guided" caliph of Islam, merits summary examination. During his reign, which lasted for a decade (634-644), Syria, Iraq and Egypt were conquered, and Umar was thus responsible for organizing the early Islamic Caliphate. [340]

Alfred von Kremer, the great 19th century German scholar of Islam, described the "central idea" of Umar's regime, as being the furtherance of "...the religious-military development of Islam at the expense of the conquered nations." [341] The predictable and historically verifiable consequence of this guiding principle was a legacy of harsh inequality, intolerance, and injustice towards non-Muslims observed by von Kremer in 1868 (and still evident in Islamic societies to this day, nearly 150 years later): [342]

> *It was the basis of its severe directives regarding Christians and those of other faiths, that they be reduced to the status of pariahs, forbidden from having anything in common with the ruling nation; it was even the basis for his decision to purify the Arabian Peninsula of the unbelievers, when he presented all the inhabitants of the peninsula who had not yet accepted Islam with the choice: to emigrate or deny the religion of their ancestors. The industrious and wealthy Christians of Najran, who maintained their Christian faith, emigrated as a result of this decision from the peninsula, to the land of the Euphrates, and 'Umar also deported the Jews of Khaybar. In this way 'Umar based that fanatical and intolerant approach that was an essential characteristic of Islam, now extant for over a thousand years, until this day [i.e., written in 1868]. It was this spirit, a severe and steely one, that incorporated scorn and contempt for the non-Muslims, that was characteristic of 'Umar, and instilled by 'Umar into Islam; this spirit continued for many centuries, to be Islam's driving force and vital principle....With a strong hand, he held the reins of spiritual and worldly power, commanded with unlimited full authority over the political and religious activities of Muslims, already many millions in number. Under him, the conquest of Syria was completed, Iraq and Persia were conquered as far as the Oxus and the borders of Hindustan, while in the west, Egypt obeyed him...*

The jihad campaigns waged in the era of Umar's Caliphate, consistent with nascent Islamic Law (Sharia), spared neither cities nor monasteries if they resisted. Accordingly, when the Greek garrison of Gaza refused to submit and convert to Islam, all were put to death. In the year 640, sixty Greek soldiers who refused to apostatize became martyrs, while in the same year (i.e., 638) that Caesarea, Tripolis and Tyre fell to the Muslims, hundreds of thousands of Christians converted to Islam, predominantly out of fear. [343]

Muslim and non-Muslim sources record that Umar's soldiers were allowed to break crosses on the heads of Christians during processions and religious litanies, and were permitted, if not encouraged, to tear down newly erected churches and to punish Christians for trivial reasons. Moreover, Umar forbade the employment of Christians in public offices. [344]

The false claims of Islamic toleration during this prototype "rightly guided" Caliphate cannot be substantiated even by relying on the (apocryphal?) "pact" of Umar (Ibn al-Khattab) because this putative decree compelled the Christians (and other non-Muslims) to fulfill self-destructive obligations, including: the prohibition on erecting any new churches, monasteries, or hermitages; and not being allowed to repair any ecclesiastical institutions that fell into ruin, nor to rebuild those that were situated in the Muslim quarters of a town. Muslim traditionists and early historians (such as al-Baladhuri) further maintain that Umar expelled the Jews of the Khaybar oasis, and similarly deported Christians (from Najran) who refused to apostasize and embrace Islam, fulfilling the death bed admonition of Muhammad who purportedly stated: "there shall not remain two religions in the land of Arabia." [345]

Umar imposed limitations upon the non-Muslims aimed at their ultimate destruction by attrition, and he introduced fanatical elements into Islamic culture that became characteristic of the Caliphates which succeeded his. [346] For example, according to the chronicle of the Muslim historian Ibn al-Atham (d. 926-27), under the brief Caliphate of Ali b. Abi Talib (656-61), when one group of apostates in Yemen (Sanaa) adopted Judaism after becoming Muslims, "He [Ali] killed them and burned them with fire after the killing." [347] Indeed, the complete absence of freedom of conscience in these early Islamic Caliphates— while entirely consistent with mid-7th century mores—has remained a constant, ignominious legacy throughout Islamic history, to this day. [348]

Koran 4:59 is the same Koranic injunction cited by Islamic legists from al-Mawardi (d. 1058) to Mawdudi (d. 1979) [349]—as legitimizing the totalitarian Caliphate system. Al-Mawardi, from his seminal treatise *Al-Akham as-Sultaniyyah* [*The Laws of Islamic Governance*], maintained, [350]

> It is the Law . . . which has delegated affairs to those who wield authority over them in matters of the deen [religion]—Allah, may He be exalted, has said: "O you believe, obey Allah and obey the Messenger and those in authority amongst you" (Koran 4:59). Thus He has imposed on us obedience to those in authority, that is those who have the command over us. Hisham ibn 'Urwah has related from Abu Salih from Abu Hurairah that the Messenger of Allah, may Allah bless him and grant him peace, said: "After me the governors will rule over you and those who are corrupt will rule you by their corruptness: listen to them and obey them in everything which is compatible with the truth—if they are correct in their dealings then it will be to your benefit and theirs, and if

*they act incorrectly then that will still be to your benefit (in the
next world) but will be held against them."*

Mawdudi, one of the most important twentieth-century Sunni thinkers, provided
a modern vision of Mawardi's classical formulation which demonstrates its
remarkable consistency across a millennium of time: [351]

*This verse [Koran 4:59] is the cornerstone of the entire religious,
social, and political structure of Islam, and the very first clause
of the constitution of an Islamic state. It lays down the following
principles as permanent guidelines: (1) In the Islamic order of
life, God alone is the focus of loyalty and obedience. . . . (2)
Another basic principle of the Islamic order of life is obedience
to the Prophet. . . . (3) In the Islamic order of life Muslims are
further required to obey fellow Muslims in authority. . . . (4) In an
Islamic order the injunctions of God and the way of the Prophet
constitute the basic law and paramount authority in all matters.
Whenever there is any dispute among Muslims or between the
rulers and the ruled the matter should be referred to the Qur'an
and the Sunnah [traditions], and all concerned should accept
with sincerity whatever judgment results. The basic difference
between a Muslim and a non-Muslim is that whereas the latter
feels free to do as he wishes, the basic characteristic of a Muslim
is that he always looks to God and to His Prophet for guidance,
and where such guidance is available, a Muslim is bound by it.
. . . [T]he Qur'an is not merely a legal code, but also seeks to
instruct, educate, admonish, and exhort. . . . Two things are laid
down. First, that faithful adherence to the above four principles
is a necessary requirement of faith. Anyone who claims to be a
Muslim and yet disregards the principles of Islam involves himself
in gross contradiction. Second, the well-being of Muslims lies in
basing their lives on those principles. This alone can keep them on
the straight path in this life, and will lead to their salvation in the
Next. It is significant that this admonition [Koran 4:59] after the
section which embodies comments about the moral and religious
condition of the Jews. Thus the Muslims were subtly directed to
draw a lesson from the depths to which the Jews had sunk, as a
result of their deviation from the fundamental principles of true
faith just mentioned. Any community that turns its back upon the
Book of God [the Koran] and the guidance of His Prophets, that
wittingly follows rulers and leaders who are heedless of God and
His Prophets, and that obeys its religious and political authorities
blindly without seeking authority for their actions either in the
Book of God or in the practice of the Prophets, will inevitably fall*

into the same evil and corruption as the Israelites.

Conservative author Robert Reilly's contemporary Mutazilite hagiography opens—and closes—with a paean to the twentieth-century Muslim scholar Fazlur Rahman (1919–1988), credited with tracing Islam's purported "intellectual suicide" to the predictably bloody rejection of the violent, autocratic ninth-century Mutazilite movement's so-called rationalism. [352] Unfortunately, Fazlur Rahman's Weltanschauung, expressed, for example, in his 1986 essay "Non-Muslim Minorities in an Islamic State," is profoundly disconcerting. [353] Rahman declines, specifically, to discuss Koran 9:29 and its classical, mainstream exegesis for almost 1,400 years. [354] Moreover, in lieu of such an honest discussion he repeats the dishonest modern Muslim apologetic that, [355]

> *The Muslim jurists in the early centuries of Islam conceived of the jizya as a tax imposed upon the people of the book [i.e., the Bible, originally non-Muslim Jews and Christians, and later expanded to include Zoroastrians, and even "idolatrous" Hindus] in lieu of military service [Note: This is a completely false claim as non-Muslims vanquished by jihad, and living under the sharia were prohibited from bearing arms or defending themselves against Muslims]. . . . Jizya, per se, does not have any insinuation or consequences of a person being a second rate citizen [emphasis added; note. another patently false claim].*

This doctrinally whitewashed and historically deficient apologetic even includes the remarkable (and remarkably mendacious) claim that the well-known twentieth-century Muslim traditionalist ideologue Mawdudi was "on record that in the modern state all citizens should be regarded as equal citizens . . . before the law." [356] Contra Rahman, as per Koran 9:29—the Koranic jihad verse which underpins Islamic law mandates vis-à-vis non-Muslims, but is not discussed at all in Rahman's disingenuous presentation [357]—Mawdudi openly supported dhimmitude for non-Muslims. Thus, Mawdudi's exegesis of Koran 9:29 reaffirmed the classic formulation of dhimmitude [358] in an Islamic state—replete with payment of the debasing, often pauperizing jizya or Koranic poll-tax (etymologically, jizya is "the tax paid in lieu of being slain" [359]) and maintained with full bellicose and discriminatory medieval resonance: [360]

> *The purpose for which the Muslims are required to fight is not as one might think to compel the unbelievers into embracing Islam. Rather, their purpose is to put an end to the sovereignty and supremacy of the unbelievers so that the latter are unable to rule over men. The authority to rule should only be vested in those who follow the true faith; unbelievers who do not follow this true faith should live in a state of subordination. Unbelievers are*

*required to pay jizyah (poll tax) in lieu of the security provided
to them as the Dhimmis of an Islamic state. Jizyah symbolizes
the submission of the unbelievers to the suzerainty of Islam. "To
pay jizyah of their own hands humbled" refers to payment in a
state of submission. "Humbled" also reinforces the idea that
the believers, rather than the unbelievers, should be the rulers
in performance of their duty as Allah's vicegerents. Initially the
rule that jizyah should be realized from all non-Muslims meant
its application to Christians and Jews living in the Islamic
state. Later on the Prophet (peace be upon him) extended it to
Zoroastrians as well, granting them the status of Dhimmis. Guided
by the Prophet's practice the Companions applied this rule to all
non-Muslim religious communities living outside Arabia. Some
nineteenth century Muslim writers and their followers in our own
times never seem to tire of their apologies for jizyah. But Allah's
religion does not require that apologetic explanations be made on
its behalf. The simple fact is that according to Islam, non-Muslims
have been granted freedom to stay outside the Islamic fold and to
cling to their false, man-made ways, if they so wish. They have,
however, absolutely no right to seize the reins of power in any
part of Allah's earth, nor to direct the collective affairs of human
beings according to their own misconceived doctrines. For if they
are given such an opportunity, corruption and mischief will ensue.
In such a situation the believers would be under an obligation
to do their utmost to dislodge them from political power and to
make them live in subservience to the Islamic way of life. . . . One
of the advantages of jizyah is that it reminds the Dhimmis every
year that because they do not embrace Islam, they . . . have to pay
a price—jizyah—for clinging to their errors. . . . The amount so
received should be spent on the administration of that righteous
[Islamic] state.*

Returning to the 11th century jurist al-Mawardi, what was the nature of the system
of governance imposed upon those indigenous non-Muslims conquered by jihad,
whether extolled forthrightly by Mawdudi, or bowdlerized deceitfully by Fazlur
Rahman?

In his The *Laws of Islamic Governance* al-Mawardi, examined the regulations
pertaining to the lands and infidel populations subjugated by jihad. This is the
origin of the system of dhimmitude. The native infidel "dhimmi" (which derives
from both the word for "pact", and also "guilt"—guilty of religious errors)
population had to recognize Islamic ownership of their land, submit to Islamic
law, and accept payment of the Koranic poll tax *(jizya)*, based on Koran 9:29.
Al- Mawardi notes that *"The enemy makes a payment* in *return for peace* and

reconciliation." He then distinguishes two cases: (I) Payment is made immediately and is treated like booty, ***"it does, not however, prevent a jihad being carried out against them** in the **future."*** (II). Payment is made yearly and will *"constitute an ongoing tribute* by *which their security is established."* **Reconciliation and security last as long as the payment is made. If the payment ceases, then the jihad resumes.** A treaty of reconciliation may be renewable, but must not exceed 10 years. [361] This same basic formulation was reiterated during a January 8, 1998 interview by Yusuf al-Qaradawi confirming how jihad continues to regulate the relations between Muslims and non-Muslims to the present day. [362]

The "contract of the *jizya"*, or *"dhimma"* encompassed other obligatory and recommended obligations for the conquered non-Muslim *"dhimmi"* peoples. Collectively, these "obligations" formed the discriminatory system of dhimmitude imposed upon non-Muslims—Jews, Christians, [as well as Zoroastrians, Hindus, and Buddhists]-subjugated by *jihad.* Some of the more salient features of dhimmitude include: the prohibition of arms for the vanquished dhimmis, and of church bells; restrictions concerning the building and restoration of churches, synagogues, and temples; inequality between Muslims and non-Muslims with regard to taxes and penal law; the refusal of dhimmi testimony by Muslim courts; a requirement that Jews, Christians, and other non-Muslims, including Zoroastrians and Hindus, wear special clothes; and the overall humiliation and abasement of non-Muslims. [363] It is important to note that these regulations and attitudes were institutionalized as permanent features of the sacred Islamic law, or Sharia. The writings of the much lionized Sufi theologian and jurist al-Ghazali (d. 1111) highlight how the institution of dhimmitude was simply a normative, and prominent feature of the Sharia: [364]

> *...the dhimmi is obliged not to mention Allah or His Apostle.. .Jews, Christians, and Majians must pay the jizya [poll tax on non-Muslims]...on offering up the jizya, the dhimmi must hang his head while the official takes hold of his beard and hits [the dhimmi] on the protruberant bone beneath his ear [i.e., the mandible]... They are not permitted to ostentatiously display their wine or church bells...their houses may not be higher than the Muslim's, no matter how low that is. The dhimmi may not ride an elegant horse or mule; he may ride a donkey only if the saddler-work] is of wood. He may not walk on the good part of the road. They [the dhimmis] have to wear [an identifying] patch [on their clothing], even women, and even in the [public] baths...[dhimmis] must hold their tongue.*

The practical consequences of such a discriminatory system were summarized in A.S. Tritton's 1930 *The Caliphs and their Non-Muslim Subjects*, a pioneering treatise on the status of the dhimmis: [365]

> *...[C]aliphs destroyed churches to obtain materials for their buildings, and the mob was always ready to pillage churches and monasteries...dhimmis...always lived on sufferance, exposed to the caprices of the ruler and the passions of the mob...in later times..[t]hey were much more liable to suffer from the violence of the crowd, and the popular fanaticism was accompanied by an increasing strictness among the educated. The spiritual isolation of Islam was accomplished. The world was divided into two classes, Muslims and others, and only Islam counted...Indeed the general feeling was that the leavings of the Muslims were good enough for the dhimmis.*

Six other esteemed 20th century scholars of the Sharia's impact on non-Muslims—Hindus and Zoroastrians, as well as Christians and Jews—concurred with Tritton's assessment: Sir Jadunath Sarkar, Antoine Fattal, S.D. Goitein, Ann Lambton, Bat Ye'or, and Mary Boyce.

Sarkar, a pre-eminent historian of Mughal India, wrote the following in 1920 (a decade before Tritton's observations [366] were published) about how centuries of Sharia-imposed dhimmitude affected the indigenous Hindus of the Indian subcontinent: [367]

> *The conversion of the entire population to Islam and the extinction of every form of dissent is the ideal of the Muslim State. If any infidel is suffered to exist in the community, it is as a necessary evil, and for a transitional period only. Political and social disabilities must be imposed on him, and bribes offered to him from the public funds, to hasten the day of his spiritual enlightenment and the addition of his name to the roll of true believers...*
>
> *A non-Muslim therefore cannot be a citizen of the State; he is a member of a depressed class; his status is a modified form of slavery. He lives under a contract (zimma, or "dhimma") with the State: for the life and property grudgingly spared to him by the commander of the faithful he must undergo political and social disabilities, and pay a commutation money. In short, his continued existence in the State after the conquest of his country by the Muslims is conditional upon his person and property made subservient to the cause of Islam.*
>
> *He must pay a tax for his land (kharaj), from which the early Muslims were exempt; he must pay other exactions for the maintenance of the army, in which he cannot enlist even if he offers to render personal service instead of paying the poll-tax; and he must show by humility of dress and behavior that he*

belongs to s subject class. No non-Muslim can wear fine dresses, ride on horseback or carry arms; he must behave respectfully and submissively to every member of the dominant sect.

As the learned Qazi Mughis-ud-din declared, in accordance with the teachings of the books on Canon Law: "The Hindus are designated in the Law as 'payers of tribute' (kharaj-guzar); and when the revenue officer demands silver from them, they should, without question and with all humility and respect, tender gold. **If the officer throws dirt into their mouths, they must without reluctance open their mouths wide to receive it.** *By these acts of degradation are shown the extreme obedience of the zimmi [dhimmi], the glorification of the true faith of Islam, and the abasement of false faiths. God himself orders them to be humiliated , (as He says, 'till they pay jaziya) with the hand and are humbled...The Prophet has commanded us to slay them, plunder them, and make them captive...No other religious authority except the great Imam (Hanifa) whose faith we follow, has sanctioned the imposition of jaziya on Hindus. According to all other theologians, the rule for Hindus is 'Either death or Islam'.*

The zimmi is under certain legal disabilities with regard to testimony in law courts, protection under criminal law, and in marriage...he cannot erect new temples, and has to avoid any offensive publicity in the exercise of his worship...Every device short of massacre in cold blood was resorted to in order to convert heathen subjects. In addition to the poll-tax and public degradation in dress and demeanor imposed on them, the non-Muslims were subjected to various hopes and fears. Rewards in the form of money and public employment were offered to apostates from Hinduism. The leaders of Hindu religion and society were systematically repressed, to deprive the sect of spiritual instruction, and their religious gatherings and processions were forbidden in order to prevent the growth of solidarity and sense of communal strength among them. No new temple was allowed to be built nor any old one to be repaired, so that the total disappearance of Hindu worship was to be merely a question of time. But even this delay, this slow operation of Time, was intolerable to many of the more fiery spirits of Islam, who tried to hasten the abolition of 'infidelity' by anticipating the destructive hand of Time and forcibly pulling down temples.

When a class are publicly depressed and harassed by law and

> *executive caprice alike, they merely content themselves with dragging on an animal existence. With every generous instinct of the soul crushed out of them, the intellectual culture merely adding a keen edge to their sense of humiliation, the Hindus could not be expected to produce the utmost of which they were capable; their lot was to be hewers of wood and drawers of water to their masters, to bring grist to the fiscal mill, to develop a low cunning and flattery as the only means of saving what they could of their own labor. Amidst such social conditions, the human hand and the human spirit cannot achieve their best; the human soul cannot soar to its highest pitch. The barrenness of intellect and meanness of spirit of the Hindu upper classes are the greatest condemnation of Muhammadan rule in India. The Muhammadan political tree judged by its fruit was an utter failure.*

Nearly four decades later, Antoine Fattal, whose 1958 Le Statut Legal de Musulmans en Pays d'Islam remains the benchmark analysis of non-Muslims—especially Christians and Jews—living under the Sharia, observed: [368]

> *The dhimmi, we might say, is a second-class citizen. If they [the ruling Muslims] tolerate him it is a calculated step, whether because they cherish the hope of converting him or for material reasons, because they force him to shoulder virtually the entire burden of taxation. They provide a place for him in the state, but not without reminding him continually of his inferior status. They prevent him from occupying high positions in society, and if by merit or intrigue he manages to climb to such places everything conspires to relegate him once again to obscurity. If the dhimmi acquires an independent legal status or privileges associated with his personal position, if he is permitted even his own courts, it is only because he cannot share with the Faithful [i.e., the Muslims] the advantages of their own justice, which is essentially religious. In no case is the dhimmi the equal of a Muslim. He is condemned to social inequality and forms part of a despised caste: inequality so far as his personal rights are concerned, inequality in taxation, and inequality before the law, since his testimony is neither accepted by the Muslim courts of justice nor even, for the same minor crime, is the punishment the same...No social relationship, no fellowship is possible between Muslims and dhimmis...*

Shlomo Dov [S. D.] Goitein (d. 1985) was a historian of Muslim-Jewish relations whose seminal research findings were widely published, most notably in the monumental five-volume work *A Mediterranean Society: The Jewish Communities of the Arab World as Portrayed in the Documents of the Cairo*

Geniza (1967–1993).[369] Here is what Goitein wrote on the subject of non-Muslim dhimmis under Muslim rule, that is, dhimmitude, circa 1970: [370]

> *[A] great humanist and contemporary of the French Revolution, Wilhelm von Humboldt, defined as the best state one which is least felt and restricts itself to one task only: protection, protection against attack from outside and oppression from within . . . [I]n general, taxation [by the Muslim government] was merciless, and a very large section of the population must have lived permanently at the starvation level. From many Geniza letters [*371] one gets the impression that the poor were concerned more with getting money for the payment of their taxes than for food and clothing, for failure of payment usually induced cruel punishment. . . . [T]he Muslim state was quite the opposite of the ideals propagated by Wilhelm von Humboldt or the principles embedded in the constitution of the United States. An Islamic state was part of or coincided with dar al-Islam, the House of Islam. Its treasury was mal al-muslumin, the money of the Muslims. Christians and Jews were not citizens of the state, not even second class citizens. They were outsiders under the protection of the Muslim state, a status characterized by the term dhimma, for which protection they had to pay a poll tax specific to them. They were also exposed to a great number of discriminatory and humiliating laws. . . . As it lies in the very nature of such restrictions, soon additional humiliations were added, and before the second century of Islam was out, a complete body of legislation in this matter was in existence. . . . **In times and places in which they became too oppressive they lead to the dwindling or even complete extinction of the minorities** [Emphasis added.]*

From 1972 until 1978, the late Ann Lambton (d. 2008) [372] headed the Near and Middle East Department while contributing articles and analyses for *The Cambridge History of Islam*, which she co-edited with Bernard Lewis. Professor Lambton and Bernard Lewis were also both protégés of the famous School of Oriental and Asiatic Studies Islamologist Sir Hamilton Gibb. Ann Lambton wrote the following on the dhimmis, published in 1981: [373]

> *As individuals, the dhimmis possessed no rights. Citizenship was limited to Muslims; and because of the superior status of the Muslim, certain juristic restrictions were imposed on the dhimmi. The evidence of a dhimmi was not accepted in a law court; a Muslim could not inherit from a dhimmi nor a dhimmi from a Muslim; a Muslim could marry a dhimmi woman, but a dhimmi could not marry a Muslim woman; at the frontier a dhimmi*

*merchant paid double the rate of duty on merchandise paid by a Muslim, but only half the rate paid by a harbi; and the blood-wit paid for a dhimmi was, except according to the Hanafis, only half or two-thirds that paid for a Muslim's No dhimmi was permitted to change his faith except for Islam. . . . Various social restrictions were imposed upon the dhimmis such as restrictions of dress. . . . Dhimmis were also forbidden to ride horses . . . and, according to Abu Hanifa valuable mules. The reason for this prohibition was connected with the fact that dhimmis were forbidden to bear arms: the horse was regarded as a "fighter for the faith," and received two shares in the booty if it were of Arab stock whereas its rider received one. Dhimmis were to yield the way to Muslims. They were also forbidden to mark their houses by distinctive signs or to build them higher than those of Muslims. They were not to build new churches, synagogues, or hermitages and not to scandalize Muslims by openly performing their worship or following their distinctive customs such as drinking wine. . . . The humiliating regulations to which [dhimmis] were subject as regards their dress and conduct in public were not, however, nearly so serious as their moral subjection, the imposition of the poll tax, and their legal disabilities. They were, in general, made to feel that they were beyond the pale. Partly as a result of this, the Christian communities dwindled in number, vitality, and morality. . . . **The degradation and demoralization of the [dhimmis] had dire consequences for the Islamic community and reacted unfavorably on Islamic political and social life.** [Emphasis added.]*

Bat Ye'or is an accomplished contemporary scholar [374] of jihad, and the repressive and humiliating system of governance imposed upon the non-Muslim dhimmis subjugated by jihad—dhimmitude, in her parlance. Although she coined the term dhimmitude, Bat Ye'or's characterization of the salient features of this institution is entirely consistent with the views of the seminal scholars from the early and mid 20th century, cited previously. Her extensive analyses of the dhimmi condition for both Jews and Christians published (in English) in1985 and 1996, concluded: [375]

These examples are intended to indicate the general character of a system of oppression, sanctioned by contempt and justified by the principle of inequality between Muslims and dhimmis. . . . Singled out as objects of hatred and contempt by visible signs of discrimination, they were progressively decimated during periods of massacres, forced conversions, and banishments. Sometimes it was the prosperity they had achieved through their labor or ability that aroused jealousy; oppressed and stripped of all their

goods, the dhimmi often emigrated. [I]n many places and at
many periods [through] the nineteenth century, observers have
described the wearing of discriminatory clothing, the rejection of
dhimmi testimony, the prohibitions concerning places of worship
and the riding of animals, as well as fiscal charges—particularly
the protection charges levied by nomad chiefs—and the payment
of the jizya. . . . Not only was the dhimma imposed almost
continuously, for one finds it being applied in the nineteenth-
century Ottoman Empire . . . and in Persia, the Maghreb, and
Yemen in the early twentieth century, but other additional abuses,
not written into the laws, became absorbed into custom, such as the
devshirme [i.e., the periodic levy of non-Muslim children forcibly
converted to Islam, and raised to fight as part of the Ottoman
Muslim slave-soldier janissary corps] the degrading corvées
(as hangmen or gravediggers), the abduction of Jewish orphans
(Yemen), the compulsory removal of footware (Morocco, Yemen),
and other humiliations. . . . The recording in multiple sources of
eye-witness accounts, concerning unvarying regulations affecting
the Peoples of the Book, perpetuated over the centuries from one
end of the dar al- Islam to the other . . . proves sufficiently their
entrenchment in customs.

Bat Ye'or's unique contribution to the study of jihad and dhimmitude has been her ability to accomplish two related tasks: (I) methodically pooling a vast, rich array of primary source data; (II) providing a brilliant synthetic analysis of these data to demonstrate convincingly the transformative power of jihad and dhimmitude, operating as designed, within formerly Christian societies of the Near East and Asia Minor. Mary Boyce, Emeritus Professor of Iranian Studies at the University of London, has confirmed the external validity of Bat Ye'or's analytical approach in her description of how jihad and dhimmitude (without the latter being specifically identified as such) transformed Zoroastrian society in an analogous manner. Boyce has written comprehensive assessments of those Zoroastrian communities which survived the devastating jihad conquests of the mid 7th through early 8th centuries.[376] The Zoroastrians experienced an ongoing, inexorable decline over the next millennium due to constant sociopolitical and economic pressures exerted by their Muslim rulers, and neighbors. This gradual, but continuous process was interspersed with periods of accelerated decline resulting from paroxysms of Muslim fanaticism—pogroms, forced conversions, and expropriations—through the latter half of the 19th century. Boyce describes these complementary phenomena based on an historical analysis, **and her personal observations living in the (central Iranian) Yezd area during the 1960s**: [377]

...in the mid nineteenth century disaster overtook Turkabad, in the

shape of what was perhaps the last massed forcible conversion in Iran. It no longer seems possible to learn anything about the background of this event; but it happened, so it is said, one autumn day when dye-madder - then one of the chief local crops - was being lifted. All the able-bodied men were at work in teams in the fields when a body of Moslems swooped on the village and seized them. They were threatened, not only with death for themselves, but also with the horrors that would befall their women and children, who were being terrorized at the same time in their homes; and by the end of the day of violence most of the village had accepted Islam. To recant after a verbal acknowledgement of Allah and his prophet meant death in those days, and so Turkabad was lost to the old religion. Its fire-temple was razed to the ground, and only a rough, empty enclosure remained where once it had stood.

*A similar fate must have overtaken many Iranian villages in the past, among those which did not willingly embrace Islam; and the question seems less why it happened to Turkabad than why it did not overwhelm all other Zoroastrian settlements. The evidence, scanty though it is, shows, however, that the harassment of the Zoroastrians of Yazd tended to be erratic and capricious, being at times less harsh, or bridled by strong governors; **and in general the advance of Islam across the plain, through relentless, seems to have been more by slow erosion than by furious force. The process was till going on in the 1960s, and one could see, therefore, how it took effect. Either a few Moslems settled on the outskirts of a Zoroastrian village, or one or two Zoroastrian families adopted Islam. Once the dominant faith had made a breach, it pressed in remorselessly, like a rising tide. More Moslems came, and soon a small mosque was built, which attracted yet others. As long as Zoroastrians remained in the majority, their lives were tolerable; but once the Moslems became the more numerous, a petty but pervasive harassment was apt to develop.** This was partly verbal, with taunts about fire-worship, and comments on how few Zoroastrians there were in the world, and how many Moslems, who must therefore posses the truth; and also on how many material advantages lay with Islam. The harassment was often also physical; boys fought, and gangs of youth waylaid and bullied individual Zoroastrians. They also diverted themselves by climbing into the local tower of silence and desecrating it, and they might even break into the fire-temple and seek to pollute or extinguish the sacred flame. Those with criminal leanings found too that a religious minority provided tempting opportunities for theft, pilfering from the open fields,*

and sometimes rape and arson. **Those Zoroastrians who resisted
all these pressures often preferred therefore in the end to sell
out and move to some other place where their co-religionists
were still relatively numerous, and they could live at peace; and
so another village was lot to the old faith.** *Several of the leading
families in Sharifabad and forebears who were driven away by
intense Moslem pressure from Abshahi, once a very devout and
orthodox village on the southern outskirts of Yazd; and a shorter
migration had been made by the family of the centenarian 'Hajji'
Khodabakhsh, who had himself been born in the 1850s and was
still alert and vigorous in 1964. His family, who were very pious,
had left their home in Ahmedabad (just to the north of Turkabad)
when he was a small boy, and had come to settle in Sharifabad to
escape persecution and the threats to their orthodox way of life.
Other Zoroastrians held out there for a few decades longer, but by
the end of the century Ahmedabad was wholly Moslem, as Abshahi
had become in 1961. [Boyce's footnote: The last Zoroastrian
family left Abshahi in 1961, after the rape and subsequent suicide
of one of their daughters.] It was noticeable that the villages
which were left to the Zoroastrians were in the main those with
poor supplies of water, where farming conditions were hard.*

Canonical Islamic Jew-Hatred:
Doctrine and Practice

Important scholars of Islamic antisemitism, i.e., Jew-hatred— from Hartwig
Hirschfeld in the mid 1880s, Georges Vajda in the late 1930s, S.D. Goitein in
1971, and Haggai Ben-Shammai in 1988 — have demonstrated: [378]

- Clear historical evidence of specific Islamic antisemitism, from
the Geniza record of the high Middle Ages — including the
coinage of a unique Hebrew word to characterize such Muslim
Jew hatred, *sin'uth* (published in full by Goitein as of 1971).

- The content of foundational Muslim sources detailing the
sacralized rationale for Islam's anti-Jewish bigotry, including,
notably—Hartwig Hirschfeld's mid-1880s essay series describing
Muhammad's subjugation of the Jews of Medina, based upon
the earliest pious Muslim biographies of Muhammad.; George
Vajda's elegant, comprehensive 1937 analysis focusing primarily
on the Jew-hating motifs in the hadith (the putative words and
deeds of the Muslim prophet Muhammad, as recorded by pious

transmitters).; Haggai Ben-Shammai's concise 1988 study of
key examples of Jew-hatred in the Koran, and Koranic exegesis.

The material in this section will introduce evidence compiled from their seminal
analyses, complemented by additional studies. Most importantly, Islam's central
Jew-hating motifs from its foundational texts, consistent with the classical and
modern exegeses of these archetypes by authoritative Muslim theologians, will
be adduced. These canonical Islamic text sources—the Koran, hadith, and sira—
and their standard interpretations, elucidate how Islam's primal anti-Jewish
animus operates in tandem with Islam's institutions of jihad war and dhimmitude,
analyzed earlier, to sanction the annihilationist Muslim Jew-hatred directed at the
Jews of Israel, in particular, by the Shiite Islamic Republic of Iran.

The less familiar terms hadith, and sira merit a brief introduction.

Hadith, which means "story" ("narrative"), refers to any report of what the Muslim
prophet Muhammad said or did, or his tacit assent to something said or done in
his presence. (Hadith is also used as the technical term for the "science" of such
"Traditions"). As a result of a lengthy process which continued for centuries after
Muhammad's death (in 632), the hadith emerged for Muslims as second in authority
to the Koran itself. Sunna, which means "path," refers to a normative custom of
Muhammad or of the early Islamic community. The hadith "justify and confirm"
the Sunna. Within the first century of Islam's advent, this aphorism was coined,
which highlighted the importance of the Sunna (and, by extension, the hadith):
"The Sunna can dispense with the Koran but not the Koran with the Sunna."
The hadith compiled by al-Bukhari (d. 870) and Muslim b. al-Hajjaj (d. 875)
are considered, respectively, to be the most important authoritative collections.
The titles Sahih ("sound") or Jami, indicating their comprehensiveness, signify
the high esteem in which they are held. Their comprehensive content includes
information regarding religious duties, law and everyday practice (down to the
most mundane, or intimate details), in addition to a considerable amount of
biographical and other material. Four other compilations, called Sunan works,
which indicates that they are limited to matters of religious and social practice,
and law, also became authoritative. Abu Dawud (d. 888), al-Tirmidhi (d. 892), Ibn
Maja (d. 896), and al-Nasi (d. 915) compiled these works. By the beginning of
the 12th century, Ibn Maja's collection became the last of these compilations of
hadith to be recognized as "canonical." [379]

Sira, which can mean "epistle," "pamphlet," or "manifesto," also means
"biography," "the life and times of ." Ibn Ishaq of Medina (d. 767-770) composed
the earliest full-length biography of Muhammad, *Sirat Rasul Allah* (*Biography
of the Prophet of Allah*), nearly 150 years after the Muslim prophet's death.
However, as has been observed, little written standard text by Ishaq survives;
we are dependent, primarily upon Ibn Hisham's (d. 834) selections from Ishaq's

work. The combined efforts of Ibn Ishaq and Ibn Hisham produced a biography that placed Muhammad in the tradition of the earlier prophets, with Ibn Hisham (possibly) focusing the perspective on ancient Arabia. Two other important early Muslim biographies of Muhammad were composed by al-Wakidi (d. 822), and his student and secretary, Ibn Sa'd (d. 845). The accounts by al-Wakidi (*Kitab al-Maghaz*) and Ibn Sa'd (*Kitab al-Tabakat al-Kabir*) concentrate on the life and times of Muhammad, only, in particular the many battles, razzias (raids), and even political assassinations he led or sanctioned. [380]

Demonizing Israel and Jews via motifs in the Koran, hadith, and sira, Hezbollah views the jihad against the "Zionist entity" as an annihilationist war intrinsic to broader conflicts: the struggle between the Islamic world and the non-Muslim world, and the historical struggle between Islam and Judaism. [381]

Hezbollah's, most senior clerical authority, the late Husayn Fadlalah, stated: [382]

> *We find in the Koran that the Jews are the most aggressive towards the Muslims ... because of their aggressive resistance to the unity of the faith.*

Fadlallah repeatedly referred to anti-Jewish archetypes in the Koran, hadith, and sira: the corrupt, treacherous, and aggressive nature of the Jews; their reputation as killers of prophets who spread corruption on earth; and the notion that the Jews engaged in conspiratorial efforts against Muhammad. [383]

Wall Street Journal Editorial Features Editor Robert Pollock interviewed Fadlallah less than 4-months before the Grand Ayatollah's death. [384] Pollock utterly ignored Fadlallah's theological Jew-hatred, but did note the Shiite cleric was possessed of a "disarming twinkle in his eyes," and closed his "Dialogue" with Fadlallah as follows: [385]

> *The interview is over. We pose for pictures and the Ayatollah presents me with an English translation of one of his books: "Islam: The Religion of Dialogue." He signs it for me in Arabic: "With my affection and prayers*

When Fadlallah died in early July, 2010, the Associated Press affirmed the Grand Ayatollah's mainstream influence, notably with the leaders of the U.S. "ally" regime of al-Maliki in Iraq: [386]

> *Among his followers are many of Iraq's Shiite leaders, including al-Maliki. In Iraq, a prominent leader in al-Maliki's Dawa Party, Ali al-Adeeb, said Fadlallah's death was a major loss to the Islamic world and that it "will be hard to replace him."*

Hassan Nasrallah — current secretary general of Hezbollah, and a protégé of Iran's Ayatollah Ali Khamenei— has reiterated the antisemitic views of Fadlallah with particular vehemence. Invoking motifs from Islam's foundational texts, Nasrallah has characterized Jews as the "grandsons of apes and pigs" (consistent with Koran 5:60) and as "Allah's most cowardly and greedy creatures."(see Koran 2:96, 4:53, and 59: 13-14) [387] He elaborates these themes into an annihilationist animus against all Jews, not merely Israelis: [388]

> *Anyone who reads the Koran and the holy writings of the monotheistic religions sees what they did to the prophets, and what acts of madness and slaughter the Jews carried out throughout history. ...Anyone who reads these texts cannot think of co-existence with them, of peace with them, or about accepting their presence, not only in Palestine of 1948 but even in a small village in Palestine, because they are a cancer which is liable to spread again at any moment. ... There is no solution to the conflict in this region except with the disappearance of Israel. If we searched the entire world for a person more cowardly, despicable, weak, and feeble in psyche, mind, ideology, and religion, we would not find anyone like the Jew. Notice, I do not say the Israeli. ... [I]f they [the Jews] all gather in Israel, it will save us the trouble of going after them worldwide.*

These antisemitic interpretations of Fadlallah, and even to a considerable extent, his vociferous colleague, Nasrallah, were validated (once again) by the modern doyen of Shiite Koranic exegesis, and "theosopher," Allameh Tabatabai. [389]

Tabatabai provides this general description of the Koranic portrayal of the Jews, beginning at Koran 2:40 to 2:44, and continuing for over a hundred verses thereafter: [390]

> **Now begins the rebuking of the Jews that continues for more than a hundred verses**. *Allah reminds them of the bounties bestowed, of the honors given; contrasting it with their ingratitude and disobedience; showing how at every juncture they paid the favours of Allah with disregard of their covenant, open rebellion against divine commands and even with polytheism. **The series reminds them of twelve events of their history — ... all of which shows how they were chosen to receive the especial favors of Allah. But their ingratitude runs parallel to it. They repeatedly broke the covenants made with Allah, committed capital sins, heinous crimes and shameful deeds; more despicable was their spiritual poverty and moral bankruptcy — in open defiance to their book and total disregard to reason. It was all because their hearts were hardened, their souls lost and their endeavors worthless.***

Tabatabai's gloss on Koran 2:75 emphasizes the Jews alleged hostility to Islam's prophet, and his new creed: [391]

> *The pagan tribes of Aws and Khazraj lived with the Jews of Medina, and they knew that the latter followed a divine religion and a revealed book. Thus it was not too much to expect them to believe in the latest in the series of divine religions and books. This was the basis of their hope that the Jews would accept the Apostle of Allah as the true prophet, and would strengthen the cause of religion, and actively participate in the propagation of truth. But* **no sooner did the Prophet migrate to Medina than the Jews showed their latent hostility. The hope was shattered and the expectation turned to disappointment.** *That is why Allah addresses the believers, saying: "Do you then hope that they would believe in you?" Concealment of truth and alteration of divine words was their deep-rooted life pattern. Why wonder if they go back on what they used to say before the advent of Islam?*

Tabatabai also offers a traditionalist gloss on Koran 2:61, 2:88-2:93, and 3:112-3:116, which accuse the Jews of "prophet-killing," "disbelief" in, and "disobedience" to, Allah, engendering His wrath, "hatching conspiracies" against Islam and the Muslim prophet Muhammad, and therefore, deserving permanent abasement, which was indeed "stamped" upon them. [392]

> *[2:61] Their disobedience and perennial excesses caused them to reject the signs of Allah and kill the prophets... Needless to say that murder, and especially of the prophets, and rejection of the signs of Allah cannot be termed as mere disobedience. It should be the other way round. But if we take the disobedience to mean disclosing the secrets then it would be perfectly right to say that they killed the prophets, because they (disobeyed them and) did not keep their secrets and thus delivered them into the hands of their enemies who killed them.*
>
> *[2:89-2:93] They knew that Muhammad was the awaited Prophet, because all the attributes and particulars mentioned in their books fitted on him perfectly. And yet they denied his truth... [T]hey returned doubly enraged. It may also mean that they invited double wrath of Allah upon themselves — the first because they disbelieved in Torah and the second because they disbelieved in the Quran. The verse says that they were partisans of the Prophet long before he was born; they prayed to Allah for victory by his name and his Book. When the Prophet was sent and the Quran was revealed, they very well recognized that he was the Prophet in*

*whose name they used to pray for victory, and whose coming they
awaited. But they were overwhelmed by envy and arrogance. No
sooner did the Prophet begin his call then they denied his truth,
and forgot all that they used to tell about the awaited prophet.
It was not surprising as they had earlier disbelieved in Torah
too. Thus they committed disbelief after disbelief, and invited the
wrath of Allah upon themselves, not once but twice... "We believe
in that which was revealed to us". If this claim of yours is correct
then why did you kill the prophets of Allah? And why did you
disbelieve in Musa [Moses] by taking the calf for a god? And why
did you say, "We hear and disobey", when We took a promise
from you and lifted the mountain over you?... "Evil is that which
your belief bids you . . .": It is a derisive expression ridiculing
them for their killings of the prophets, their disbelief in Musa and
their arrogance in committing sin after sin and then claiming that
they were the true believers. The verse tauntingly asks them: Is
this what your belief bids you?*

*[3:112-3:116] The verses, as you see, now revert to the original
theme,* **describing the behavior of the People of the Book — and
particularly the Jews** *—exposing their disbelief in the Divine
Revelation, their going astray and their hindering the believers
from the way of Allah...* **Abasement is stamped on them as a
design is stamped on a coin, or it encompasses them as a tent
encompasses a man. Anyhow, they are either branded with,
or overwhelmed by abasement and humiliation — except
when they get a protection or guarantee from Allah and a
protection or guarantee from men. The word "protection" is
repeated when referring to Allah and then to men, because the
connotation differs from one place to the other. Protection***
**392a given by Allah is His decree and command, either creative
or legislative; and that provided by men is their decision and
action. Abasement is stamped on them; it means that Allah has
ordained a law affirming their abasement. This meaning is
supported by the proviso "wherever they are found". Obviously,
it means that wherever the believers find them and subjugate
them; this proviso is obviously more appropriate to legislative
abasement, one of whose effects is the payment of the jizya. The
meaning of the verse therefore is as follows: They are abased
and humiliated, according to the law of Islamic Sharia...** *"those
who disbelieve" refers to the other groups of the People of the
Book which did not respond to the call of the Prophet;* **those were
the people who used to hatch conspiracies against Islam and had
left no stone unturned in extinguishing the light of the truth...**

Obviously it describes the Jews' behavior with the Muslims

In his gloss on Koran 3:181-185/189, Tabatabai reiterates these interpretations, (again) labeling the Jews as "prophet killers" who acted "knowingly and intentionally." He also repeats the accusations of their "upsetting the Muslims affairs, rejecting the evidence of messenger-ship, and hiding what they had been enjoined to make known."[393]

Koran 5:64 is an overt, ancient Koranic warning of "Jewish conspiracism." Tabatabai, adding a deliberate and transparent pejorative reference to the Jews of modern Israel, and their alleged promulgation of "ethnic supremacism," glosses this verse as follows:[394]

> *"whenever they kindle a fire for war Allah puts it out": To kindle a fire is to inflame it, and to put it out is to extinguish it. The meaning is clear. There is another possibility that the clause: "whenever they kindle a fire," explains the preceding clause: "and We put enmity and hatred . . ." Thus the meaning will be as follows: Whenever they kindled a fire of war against the Prophet and the believers, Allah puts it out by reviving their internal discords and differences.* **The context points to the divine decree that their endeavors in kindling the fire of war against the divine religion and against the Muslims (because of their belief in Allah and His signs) are bound to fail.** *However, it does not cover those* **wars, which the Jews might wage against the Muslims, not for religious motive, but because of politics, or because of ideas of racial or national superiority.**

Tabatabai's gloss on Koran 5:71 continues his rhetorical assault on the stubborn, vain, and ultimately (and deservedly!) self-destructive behaviors of the Jews, because of their inherent—"Jewishness": [395]

> *This blindness and deafness have been caused by their delusion that there would be no affliction; and apparently that delusion had emanated from their vanity and conceit that they had a special status before Allah because they were from the seed of Israel, and they were sons and beloveds of Allah. Therefore, no evil would fall to them no matter what they did and what they indulged in. The meaning of the verse then is as follows – and Allah knows better: They, because of their vanity that they enjoyed the prestige of* **Jewishness**, *thought that they would not be afflicted by any evil, and would not be put on trial no matter what they did; this thought and delusion blinded their eyes – so they cannot see the truth – and deafened their ears – so they cannot listen to their Prophets' [i.e., Muhammad's] call which would have benefited them. This*

interpretation favors what we have said earlier that these verses are a sort of proof of the verse: Surely those who believe and those who are Jews . . . It shows in short that names and titles are not to avail anyone anything. Look at these Jews who thought that they had a special prestige because they were Jews; yet this delusion did not do them any good, rather it made them blind and deaf and led them to perils of destruction and tribulation when they called the Prophets of Allah liars and murdered them.

Koran 5:78, a Koranic curse upon the Jews, is glossed by Tabatabai in this straightforward manner: [396]

It adversely alludes to the Jews who were cursed by their own prophets, and it was because they exceeded the limit, and continued in this transgression generation after generation. The words: "They used not to forbid . . . evil was that which they did," explain that transgression.

Koran 5:82, arguably the central Koranic verse defining Islam's eternal attitudes towards Jews and Judaism, is glossed by Tabatabai, thusly: [397]

*[T]he Jews, although they had the same alternatives as the Christians, and they could retain their religion with payment of the jizyah [Koranic poll tax, per verse 9:29], yet they continued in their haughtiness, became harder in their bigotry, and turned to double dealing and deception. They broke their covenants, eagerly waited calamities to befall the Muslims and dealt to them the bitterest deal...[T]he enmity of the Jews...toward the divine religion [Islam] and their sustained arrogance and bigotry, have continued exactly in the same manner even after the Prophet... **These unchanged characteristics...confirm what the Mighty Book [the Koran] had indicated.***

Ayatollah Khomeini's own references to Islam's antisemitic canon (as exemplified, below), comport with the interpretations of Fadlallah, Nasrallah, and Tabatabai. [398]

Islam is prepared to subordinate individuals to the collective interest of society and has rooted out numerous groups that were a source of corruption and harm to human society. Since the Jews of Bani Qurayza were a troublesome group, causing corruption in Muslim society and damaging Islam and the Islamic state, the Most Noble Messenger eliminated them.

From the very beginning, the historical movement of Islam has had to contend with the Jews, for it was they who first established anti-Islamic propaganda and engaged in various stratagems, and as you can see, this activity continues down to the present.

Let us return to Tabatabai's Koranic exegeses, his gloss on Koran 5:82, in particular. Does Tabatabai's exegesis represent an anomalous interpretation, born of a *sui generis* "revolutionary" antisemitic fervor that ushered in, and still pervades, Khomeini (and post-Khomeini)-era Iran? As I will demonstrate, Tabatabai's gloss on 5:82 is consistent not only with the contemporary interpretation proffered by Sunni Islam's most respected religious teaching institution, but the exegeses of Sunni Islam's most authoritative, classical Koranic commentators.

Since its founding in 973 C.E., Al Azhar University (and its mosque) have represented a pinnacle of Islamic religious education, which evolved into the *de facto* Vatican of Sunni Islam. [399] Ahmad Al-Tayeb, as current Grand Imam of Al-Azhar, is the Sunni Muslim Papal equivalent. During an interview with Al-Tayeb, which aired on Channel 1, Egyptian TV, October 25, 2013, the Al-Azhar Grand Imam gave a brief explanation of the ongoing relevance of Koran 5:82, which has been invoked—"successfully"—to inspire Muslim hatred of Jews since the advent of Islam: [400]

> *A verse in the Koran explains the Muslims' relations with the Jews and the polytheists. The second part of the verse describes the Muslims' relations with the Christians, and the third part of the verse explains why the Christians are the closest and most friendly to the Muslims. This is an historical perspective, which has not changed to this day. See how we suffer today from global Zionism and Judaism, whereas our peaceful coexistence with the Christians has withstood the test of history.* ***Since the inception of Islam 1,400 years ago, we have been suffering from Jewish and Zionist interference in Muslim affairs. This is a cause of great distress for the Muslims. The Koran said it and history has proven it****: "You shall find the strongest among men in enmity to the believers to be the Jews and the polytheists." This is the first part. The second part is: "You shall find the closest in love to the believers to be those who say: 'We are Christians'." The third part explains why the Christians are "the closest in love to the believers," while the Jews and the polytheists are the exact opposite.*

Grand Imam Al-Tayaeb's assessment is upheld by a continuum of authoritative Koranic exegeses that span over a thousand years, till now. The classical Koranic commentaries on Koran 5:82 by al-Tabari (d. 923), Zamakashari (d. 1143), Baydawi (d. 1316), and Ibn Kathir demonstrate a uniformity of opinion regarding the animus of the Jews toward the Muslims, which is repeatedly linked to the curse of Koran 2:61 (i.e., for killing prophets, and transgressing against the will of Allah, repeated at verses including 2:90-91, 3:112, 3:181, and 4:155): [401]

> *[Tabari]: In my (Tabari's) opinion, (the Christians) are not like the Jews who always scheme in order to murder the emissaries and the prophets, and who oppose Allah in his positive and negative commandments, and who corrupt His scripture which He revealed in His books.*

> *[Zamakshari]: Here Allah portrays the Jews as being unyielding and as acknowledging the truth only grudgingly. . . . On account of their vehement enmity against the believers, Allah places the Jews together with the idolaters; indeed, going even further, he shows them to be at the head, since they are mentioned before the idolaters. Allah does the same in his words: "And thou shalt find them (the Jews) the eagerest of men for life—even more so than the idolaters. Each of them wishes he could be given a life of a thousand years; but the grant of life would not save him from chastisement—for God sees well all that they do!" (sura 2:96/90). The Jews are surely like this, and even worse! From the Prophet (the following is related): "If a Muslim is alone with two Jews, they will try to kill him.". . . The Jews focused their hostility to the Muslims in the most overt and intense manner . . .*

> *[Baydawi]: [B]ecause of [the Jews'] intense obstinacy, multifaceted disbelief, and their addiction to following their whims, their adherence to the blind following of their tradition, their distancing themselves from the truth, and their unrelenting denial of, and hostility toward, the prophets . . . [the Christians] . . . easiness to deal with, the softness of their hearts, their dismissal of gain in this world, and their serious concern with learning and good deeds . . . their acceptance of the truth as soon as they understand it; or, because of their humility as opposed to the arrogance of the Jews.*

> *[Ibn Kathir]: Allah said, "Verily you will find the strongest among men in enmity to the believers the Jews and those who commit Shirk [i.e., the polytheists, or idolaters]." This describes the Jews, since their disbelief is that of rebellion, defiance, opposing the truth, belittling other people, and degrading the scholars. This is why the Jews—may Allah's continued curses descend on them until the Day of Resurrection—killed many of their Prophets and tried to kill the Messenger of Allah several times, as well*

*as performing magic spells against him and poisoning him. They
also incited their likes among the polytheists against the Prophet.*

Maulana Muhammad Shafi (1898-1976), a former grand mufti of India (prior to
the August, 1947 partition), was the author of *Maariful Qur'an*, which remains
the best-known Koranic commentary in Urdu. [402] Mufti Shafi's **modern gloss on
Koran 5:82 in *Maariful Qur'an* confirms its classical exegesis**, noting that the
vast preponderance of Jews felt an unremitting malice toward the Muslims, and
a lust for the "material pleasures of mortal life"—the rare exceptions to this rule
(for example, Abdullah ibn Salam), became Muslims! [403]

The ex-Mufti of Jerusalem, pre-eminent Muslim leader of his era, and founder
of the jihadist Palestinian Muslim movement, Hajj Amin el-Husseini, issued a
1937 proclamation seeking to galvanize the global Muslim *umma* (community)
for a jihad to annihilate Palestinian Jewry, and abort a modern re-establishment of
the pre-Islamic nation of Israel on any portion of the Jews' ancestral homeland.
[404] As I documented in a recent monograph, *The Mufti's Islamic Jew-Hatred*, el-
Husseini ends his own litany of Jew-hating motifs from the Koran in the 1937
proclamation with this same verse, Koran 5:82. [405]

Current Al-Azhar Grand Imam al-Tayeb's invocation of Koranic Jew-hatred
(especially, 5:82) represents a modern historical continuum from Hajj Amin
el-Husseini, and more directly his immediate predecessor, the late Sheikh
Muhammad Sayyid Tantawi—Grand Imam of Al-Azhar from 1996, till his death
in March, 2010. [406] Extensive and fully representative extracts from Tantawi's
magnum opus—a 700 page tract glorifying Islam's output of doctrinal Jew-hatred
from the Koran, the most important Koranic commentaries, the hadith, and sira—
are included in my *The Legacy of Islamic Antisemitism*. Originally his Al-Azhar
University Ph.D. thesis, Tantawi provided this summary Koranic depiction of the
Jews in the treatise: [407]

> *[The] Koran describes the Jews with their own particular
> degenerate characteristics, i.e. killing the prophets of Allah
> [Koran 2:61/ 3:112], corrupting His words by putting them in
> the wrong places, consuming the people's wealth frivolously,
> refusal to distance themselves from the evil they do, and other
> ugly characteristics caused by their deep-rooted lasciviousness...
> only a minority of the Jews keep their word...[A]ll Jews are not
> the same. The good ones become Muslims [Koran 3:113], [408] the
> bad ones do not.*

Not surprisingly, the Koran's "sacralized" characterizations imbue Tantawi's
conclusions about how Muslims should view—and treat— contemporary Jews: [409]

> *the Jews always remain maleficent deniers....they should desist*

> *from their negative denial...some Jews went way overboard in*
> *their denying hostility, so gentle persuasion can do no good with*
> *them, so use force with them and treat them in the way you see as*
> *effective in ridding them of their evil. One may go so far as to ban*
> *their religion, their persons, their wealth, and their villages.*

These examples of how the most authoritative Muslim theologians and scholars—
Sunni and Shiite, modern and ancient—interpret Koran 5:82 (and other related
Koranic verses on the Jews), validate Camilla Adang's summary 1999 observation.
Adang, a mainstream, contemporary Islamologist, wrote, plainly: [410]

> ***Islamic polemics against Judaism and its adherents is a***
> ***phenomenon as old as Islam itself, and the Quran is its very***
> ***first source.***

The crux of the Koranic "polemics against Judaism," to paraphrase Adang, is
a central antisemitic motif in the Koran which decrees an eternal curse upon
the Jews (Koran 2:61, reiterated at 2:90, 3:112, and elsewhere) for slaying the
prophets and transgressing against the will of Allah. [411] It should be noted that
Koran 3:112 is featured before the pre-amble to Hamas' foundational covenant. [412]
This central motif is coupled to Koranic verses 5:60 and 5:78, which describe the
Jews transformation into apes and swine (5:60) or simply apes, (i.e., verses 2:65
and 7:166), having been " ... cursed by the tongue of David, and Jesus, Mary's
son (5:78)." Muhammad himself repeats this Koranic curse in a canonical hadith
(in Sunan Abu Dawud): [413]

> *He [Muhammad] then recited the verse [5:78]: "curses were*
> *pronounced on those among the children of Israel who rejected*
> *Faith, by the tongue of David and of Jesus the son of Mary."*

The related verse 5:64 accuses the Jews of being "spreaders of war and corruption"
— a sort of ancient Koranic antecedent of *The Protocols of the Elders of Zion*[414]
— a verse invoked not only by Hezbollah leaders Fadlallah and Nasrallah,[414a]
but "moderate" Palestinian Authority President Mahmoud Abbas. He cited Koran
5:64 during a January 2007 speech which urged Palestinian Muslims to end their
internecine strife and "aim their rifles at Israel." [415]

Indeed the Koran's overall discussion of the Jews is marked by a litany of their
sins and punishments, as if part of a divine indictment, conviction, and punishment
process. Two examples of such Koranic litanies, were compiled independently
(and from very different perspectives) by historian Saul S. Friedman, [416] and
the contemporary Al-Azhar University theologian Atiyyah Saqr. [417] Friedman
enumerated the following: [418]

> *[Sins and punishments]: the Jews wronged themselves (16:118) by*

*losing faith (7:168) and breaking their covenant (5:13). The Jews
are a nation that has passed away (2:134; repeated in 2:141).
Twice Allah sent his instruments (the Assyrians/or Babylonians,
and Romans) to punish this perverse people (17:4–5)—their
dispersal over the earth is proof of Allah's rejection (7:168). The
Jews are further warned about both their arrogant claim that they
remain Allah's chosen people (62:6), and continued disobedience
and "corruption" (5:32–33).*

*[Additional sins]: the Jews are typified as an "envious" people
(2:109), whose hearts are as hardened as rocks (2:74). They are
further accused of confounding the truth (2:42), deliberately
perverting scripture (2:75), and being liars (2:78). Ill-informed
people of little faith (2:89), they pursue vague and wishful
fancies (2:111). Other sins have contributed to their being
stamped (see 2:61/3:112 above) with "wretchedness/ abasement
and humiliation," including—usury (2:275), sorcery (2:102),
hedonism (2:96), and idol worship (2:53).*

*[More (and repeat) sins, still]: the Jews' idol worship is again
mentioned (4:51), then linked and followed by charges of other
(often repeat) iniquities—the "tremendous calumny" against
Mary (4:156), as well as usury and cheating (4:161). Most Jews
are accused of being "evil-livers"/"transgressors"/"ungodly"
(3:110), who, deceived by their own lies (3:24), try to turn Muslims
from Islam (3:99). Jews are blind and deaf to the truth (5:71), and
what they have not forgotten they have perverted—they mislead
(3:69), confound the truth (3:71), twist tongues (3:79), and cheat
Gentiles without remorse (3:75). Muslims are advised not to
take the clannish Jews as friends (5:51), and to beware of the
inveterate hatred that Jews bear towards them (5:82).*

On March 22, 2004, Sheikh Saqr, former head of the Al-Azhar Fatwa Committee, was asked the following question in an online chat room: "What, according to the Koran, are the Jews' main characteristics and qualities?" Sheikh Saqr answered by highlighting 20 negative, inveterate traits of the Jews as described by the Koran: fabricating (Koran 3:75; 5:64); listening to lies (5:41); disobeying Allah (5:13); disputing and quarreling (2:247); hiding the truth and supporting deception (3:78); rebelling against the prophets and rejecting their guidance (2:55); hypocrisy (2:44); selfishness (2:87); wishing evil on people (2:105); feeling pain at others' happiness and feeling happiness at others' afflictions (2:120); arrogance and haughtiness (5:18); utilitarianism and opportunism (4:161); rudeness and vulgarity (4:46); murder of innocents, especially prophets (2:61; 3:112); mercilessness and heartlessness (2:74); breaking promises (2:100); rushing to sin and transgress

(5:79); cowardice and greed (59:13; 2:96); miserliness (4:53); and distorting divine revelation (2:79). [419]

The Jews' ultimate sin and punishment are made clear: They are the devil's minions (4:60) cursed by Allah, their faces will be obliterated (4:47), and if they do not accept the true faith of Islam — the Jews who understand their faith become Muslims (3:113) — they will be made into apes (2:65/ 7:166), or apes and swine (5:60), and burn in the Hellfires (4:55, 5:29, 98:6, and 58:14-19). [420]

Haggai Ben-Shammai's 1988 essay "Jew Hatred in the Islamic Tradition and Koranic Exegesis," [421] remains a benchmark modern academic analysis of these motifs, which riveted on two key examples of Jew-hatred in the Koran (and Koranic exegesis): the "curse against the Jews" (in Koran 2:61, etc.), and Koranic verses (most notably, 5:82) rationalizing why Jews were to be held in greater contempt than Christians. [422] Ben-Shammai highlighted the centrality of the Jews' "abasement and humiliation," and being "laden with God's anger" in the corpus of Muslim exegetic literature on Qur'an 2:61, including the hadith and Koranic commentaries. Despite the literal reference of 2:61 to the Israelites in the wilderness during their exodus from Egypt, he noted, [423]

> *to all of the Muslim exegetes, without exception, it was absolutely clear that the reference was to the Jews of their day. The Arabic word translated as "pitched upon them" also means, literally, that the "abasement and poverty" were decreed for them forever. The "abasement" is the payment of the poll tax [jizya] and the humiliating ceremony involved. As for the "poverty," this insured their remaining impoverished forever. There are traditions which attribute this interpretation to Muhammad himself.*

The terrifying rage decreed upon the Jews forever is connected in the hadith and exegeses to Koran 1:7, where Muslims ask Allah to guide them rightly, not in the path of those who provoke and must bear His wrath. Authoritative exegeses on Koran 1:7 spanning the late 7th through early 21st centuries, concur, from Ibn Abbas (d. 687), Muqatil ibn Sulayman (d. 767), Tabari (d. 923), and Qurtubi (d. 1273), through Maulana Mufti Muhammad Shafi (d. 1976), and the analyses written by 43 Muslim and non-Muslim mainstream academic experts in the 2006 publication, *The Qur'an: An Encyclopedia.* [424] For example the consensus gloss from this latter standard academic reference, states: [425]

> *...[T]he phrase in the daily prescribed prayers" Guide us to the straight path, to the path of those you have blessed, not of those who incurred [Your] wrath, nor of the misguided (al-Fatiha, 1:5-7.)...mention two groups of people but do not say who they are. The Prophet [Muhammad] interpreted those who incurred God's wrath as the Jews and the misguided as the Christians.*

The Jews, we are told [i.e., in both the Koran, and hadith] killed many of their prophets, and through their character and materialistic tendencies have contributed much to moral corruption, social upheaval and sedition in the world...[T]hey were readily misled and incurred both God's wrath and ignominy.

(Pious Muslims repeat Koran 1:7 up to 17 times a day, as part of the five daily prayer sessions, consistent with this admonition, recorded by Ibn Kathir: *"[R]eciting the Opening of the Book [the Fatiha, verses Koran 1:1 to 1:7], during the prayer by the Imam and those praying behind him is required in every prayer, and in every Ra'kah [unit of prayer]"*) [426]

This verse (Koran 1:7) is in turn linked to Koranic verses 5:60 and 5:78, which describe the Jews' transformation into apes and swine (5:60), having been "cursed by the tongue of David, and Jesus, Mary's son" (5:78). Ben-Shammai explains the primary reason for this "fearful decree," which resulted in the Jews being "so terribly cursed": [427]

> *[F]rom time immemorial the Jews rejected God's signs, the wonders performed by the prophets. They did not accept the prophecy of Jesus whom the Koran counts among the prophets. But this is all part of the Jews' nature: they are by their very nature deceitful and treacherous.*

Indeed according to the sira of both Ibn Ishaq and Ibn Sa'd, just before subduing the Medinan Jewish tribe Banu Qurayza, and orchestrating the mass execution of their adult males, Muhammad himself invoked Koran 5:60, addressing these Jews, with hateful disparagement, as "You brothers of monkeys" (Ibn Sa'd's account adds, "and pigs"). [428] Muhammad also repeats the Koranic curse (of verse 5:78) upon the Jews in a canonical hadith, "He [Muhammad] then recited the verse [5:78]: '...curses were pronounced on those among the children of Israel who rejected Faith, by the tongue of David and of Jesus the son of Mary'." [429]

Although the Jews initially longed for Muhammad to triumph over the pagan Arabs, "Would that Allah send this prophet of whom our Book says that his coming is assured" (according to a tradition cited by Ben-Shammai), realizing that Muhammad was not one of them, Ben-Shammai observes, quoting from Koran 5:64, [430]

> *they then denied him out of jealousy of the Arabs, though they knew in truth he is the prophet. Furthermore, this Jewish trait brought them to grave heresy. They thought that they would succeed not only in leading humankind astray but also in fooling God . . . (5:64). "The Jews have said, God's hand is tied. . . . As often as they light a fire for war, God will extinguish it." Exegetes*

cite traditions which prove that the Jews always hated the true prophets and put them to death. Therefore they always failed in their wars and their Temple was destroyed time and again.

Ben-Shammai's analysis of Koran 5:82 links this verse to Koran 3:54-56, and in turn to the tradition, "The Christians are to be above the Jews until the day of Judgment, for there is no land where the Christians are not above the Jews, neither in the east nor the west. The Jews are degraded in all the lands." [431]

He emphasizes that in the traditions, [432]

the Christians have a clear priority over the Jews. If we posit that the early tradition reflects the historical development of early Islam and that the political, economic, and social reality was apt to produce this preference, there is no doubt that these traditions reflect this reality.

Ben-Shammai, arguing for prolonged historical continuity, "As has been stated, this tradition (i.e., of more intense Muslim-Jewish hatred) has remained alive to this very day," [433] refers to the travelogue accounts of Edward William Lane, which record Lane's observations of Egyptian society, originally published in 1835.[434] But Ben-Shammai fails to discuss a remarkable essay by the polymath Arabic writer al-Jahiz (d. 869), [435] composed a millennium earlier, which bolsters his argument **by illustrating the anti-Jewish attitudes already prevalent within an important early (i.e., mid-9th century), Islamic society—the seat of the Abbasid-Baghdadian Caliphate**.

Al-Jahiz's essay—an anti-Christian polemic believed to have been commissioned by the Abbasid caliph al-Mutawakkil (d. 861), who inaugurated a literary campaign against the Christians—explores the reasons why the Muslim masses prefer the Christians to the Jews. This empirical preference (although decried by the author) is acknowledged by al-Jahiz from the outset: [436]

I shall begin to enumerate the causes which made the Christians more liked by the masses than the Magians [Zoroastrians], and made men consider them more sincere than the Jews, more endeared, less treacherous, less unbelieving, and less deserving of punishment. For all this there are manifold and evident causes.

Al-Jahiz offers two primary explanations for this abiding hostility of the Muslim rank and file toward the Jews. First was the "rancorous" relationship between the early Muslim community, exiles from Mecca, and their Jewish neighbors in Medina: [437]

When the [Muslim] Emigrants [from Mecca] became the

> *neighbors of the Jews [in Medina] . . .the Jews began to envy*
> *the Muslims the blessings of their new faith, and the union which*
> *resulted after dissension. They proceeded to undermine the belief*
> *of our [i.e., the Muslim] masses, and to lead them astray. They*
> *aided our enemies and those envious of us. From mere misleading*
> *speech and stinging words they plunged into an open declaration*
> *of enmity, so that the Muslims mobilized their forces, exerting*
> *themselves morally and materially to banish the Jews and destroy*
> *them. Their strife became long-drawn and widespread, so that it*
> *worked itself up into a rage, and created yet greater animosity*
> *and more intensified rancor. The Christians, however, because of*
> *their remoteness from Mecca and Medina, did not have to put up*
> *with religious controversies, and did not have occasion to stir up*
> *trouble, and be involved in war. That was the first cause of our*
> *dislike of the Jews, and our partiality toward the Christians.*

However, al-Jahiz then identifies as "the most potent cause" of this particular animus toward the Jews, Koran 5:82, and its interpretation by the contemporary (i.e., mid-ninth-century) Muslim masses. [438] It is also worth noting that al-Jahiz (described as a "skeptic," who harbored "indifferent views toward religion in general") [439] included these sociological observations that reveal the interface between Islamic religious and indigenous (and indigenous ethnic/racial discriminatory attitudes toward) Jews expressed a millennium before any secular Western European antisemitic ideologies would be exported to the Muslim Near East: [440]

> *Our people [the Muslims] observing thus the occupations of the*
> *Jews and the Christians concluded that the religion of the Jews*
> *must compare unfavorably as do their professions, and that their*
> *unbelief must be the foulest of all, since they are the filthiest of all*
> *nations. Why the Christians, ugly as they are, are physically less*
> *repulsive than the Jews may be explained by the fact that the Jews,*
> *by not intermarrying, have intensified the offensiveness of their*
> *features. Exotic elements have not mingled with them; neither*
> *have males of alien races had intercourse with their women, nor*
> *have their men cohabited with females of a foreign stock. The*
> *Jewish race therefore has been denied high mental qualities,*
> *sound physique, and superior lactation. The same results obtain*
> *when horses, camels, donkeys, and pigeons are inbred.*

Al-Jahiz's contention that the Muslims harbored greater enmity toward the Jews than the Christians is supported by the independent observations of another Arab author active during the beginning of the ninth century in Iraq, the Sufi theologian al-Harith al-Muhasibi (d. 857). He maintained that because the Jews stubbornly denied Muhammad's truth, they were "in the eyes of the Muslims worse than the Christians." [441]

The impact upon Jews of such distinctly antisemitic attitudes by Muslims in the specific context of the Arab Muslim world during the high Middle Ages (circa 950-1250 C.E.) is evident in S.D. Goitein's seminal analyses of the primary source Geniza documentary record. Goitein's research caused him to employ the term antisemitism, [442]

> ...in order to differentiate animosity against Jews from the discrimination practiced by Islam against non-Muslims in general. Our scrutiny of the Geniza material has proved the existence of 'antisemitism' in the time and the area considered here...

Goitein cites as one important concrete proof of his assertion that a unique strain of Islamic Jew hatred was extant at this time (i.e., up to a millennium ago)— exploding the common assumption of its absence—the fact that letters from the Cairo Geniza material, [443]

> ...have a special word for it and, most significantly, one not found in the Bible or in Talmudic literature (nor registered in any Hebrew dictionary), but one much used and obviously coined in the Geniza period. It is sin'ūth, "hatred," a Jew-baiter being called sōnē, "a hater."

Incidents of such Muslim Jew hatred documented by Goitein in the Geniza come from northern Syria (Salamiyya and al-Mar'arra), Morocco (Fez), and Egypt (Alexandria), with references to the latter being particularly frequent. [444]

One thousand years after al-Jahiz and al-Muhasibi recorded their observations, Lane's 19th century testimony on the difference between the attitude of Egyptian Muslims toward the Jews and the Christians, again highlights the specific influence of Koran 5:82: [445]

> They [the Jews] are held in the utmost contempt and abhorrence by the Muslims in general, and they are said to bear a more inveterate hatred than any other people to the Muslims and the Muslim religion. It is said, in the Koran [quoting 5:82] "Thou shalt surely find the most violent all men to those who have believed to be the Jews . . . "

Lane further notes: [446]

> It is a common saying among the Muslims in this country, "Such one hates me with the hate of the Jews." We cannot wonder, then, that the Jews are detested far more than are the Christians. Not

long ago, they used often to be jostled in the streets of Cairo, and sometimes beaten for merely passing on the right hand of a Muslim. At present, they are less oppressed: but still they scarcely ever dare to utter a word of abuse when reviled or beaten unjustly by the meanest Arab or Turk; for many a Jew has been put to death upon a false and malicious accusation of uttering disrespectful words against the Koran or the Prophet. It is common to hear an Arab abuse his jaded ass, and, after applying to him various opprobrious epithets, end by calling the beast a Jew.

The missionary Gregory Wortabet's mid-19th century account from Jerusalem (published in 1856) confirms Lane's reference about the apparent commonality of Muslims equating their domesticated asses (donkeys) with Jews, accompanied by "opprobrious epithets"—and often abuse—of either, or both. Wortabet cites another Jew-hating motif from canonical Islam's repertoire, the alleged poisoning of Muhammad by a Khaybar Jewess, as a possible rationale for such chronic Muslim attitudes toward Jews. His anecdote also documents the pejorative reference to Jews as "hogs" (pigs), in accord with Koran 5:60. [447]

*The Jew is still an object of scorn, and nowhere is the name of "Yahoodi (Jew)" more looked down upon than here in the city of his fathers. One day, as I was passing the Damascus gate, I saw an Arab hurrying on his donkey amid imprecations such as the following: "Emshi ya Ibn-el-Yahoodi (Walk, thou son of a Jew)! Yulaan abuk ya Ibn-el-Yahoodi (Cursed be thy father, thou son of a Jew)!" I need not give any more illustrations of the manner in which the man went on. The reader will observe, that the man did not curse the donkey, but the Jew, the father of the donkey. Walking up to him, I said, "Why do you curse the Jew? What harm has he done you?" "El Yahoodi khanzeer (the Jew is a hog)!" answered the man. "How do you make that out?" I said. "Is not the Jew as good as you or I?" "Ogh!" ejaculated the man, his eyes twinkling with fierce rage, and his brow knitting. By this time he was getting out of my hearing. I was pursuing my walk, when he turned round, and said, "El Yahoodi khanzeer! Khanzeer el Yahoodi! (The Jew is a hog! A hog is a Jew!)" Now I must tell the reader, that, in the Mahomedan vocabulary, there is no word lower than a hog, that animal being in their estimation the most defiled of animals; and good Mahomedans are prohibited by the Koran from eating it. **The Jew, in their estimation, is the vilest of the human family, and is the object of their pious hatred, perhaps from the recollection that a Jewess of Khaibar first undermined the health of the prophet by infusing poison into his food.** [emphasis added] Hence a hog and a Jew are esteemed*

> *alike in the eye of a Moslem, both being the lowest of their kind;
> and now the reader will better understand the meaning of the
> man's words, "El Yahoodi khanzeer!"*

Moshe Perlmann, an eminent scholar of Islam's Medieval era anti-Jewish polemical literature, made this rueful summary observation in 1964: [448]

> *The Koran, of course became a mine of anti-Jewish passages.
> The hadith did not lag behind. Popular preachers used and
> embellished such material.*

Tabari's classical interpretations of Koran 5:82 and 2:61, as well as his discussion of the related verse 9:29 mandating the Jews payment of the jizya (Koranic poll-tax), represent both antisemitic and more general anti-dhimmi views that became and remain intrinsic to Islam to this day. Here is Tabari's discussion of 2:61 and its relationship to verse 9:29, which emphasizes the purposely debasing nature of the Koranic poll tax: [449]

> *"Abasement and poverty were imposed and laid down upon
> them," as when someone says "the imam imposed the poll tax
> (jizya) on free non-Muslim subjects," or "The man imposed land
> tax on his slave," meaning thereby that he obliged him [to pay]
> it, or, "The commander imposed a sortie on his troops," meaning
> he made it their duty. ... God commanded His believing servants
> not to give them [i.e., the non-Muslim people of the scripture]
> security — as long as they continued to disbelieve in Him and
> his Messenger — unless they paid the poll tax to them; God said:
> "Fight those who believe not in God and the Last Day and do not
> forbid what God and His Messenger have forbidden — such men
> as practice not the religion of truth [Islam], being of those who
> have been given the Book [Bible] — until they pay the poll tax,
> being humble." (Koran 9:29)*

> *The dhimmis posture during the collection of the jizya "[should be
> lowering themselves] by walking on their hands ... reluctantly."*

> *His words "and abasement and poverty were imposed upon
> them," "These are the Jews of the Children of Israel. ... Are they
> the Copts of Egypt?" ... What have the Copts of Egypt to do with
> this? No, by God, they are not; but they are the Jews, the Children
> of Israel. ... By "and slain the prophets unrightfully," He means
> that they used to kill the Messengers of God without God's leave,
> denying their messages and rejecting their prophethood.*

The Koranic curse (verses 2:61/3:112) upon the Jews for (primarily) rejecting, even slaying Allah's prophets, including Isa/Jesus (or at least his "body double," 4:157-4:158), is updated with perfect archetypal logic in the canonical hadith. Following the Muslims' initial conquest of the Jewish farming oasis of Khaybar, one of the vanquished Jewesses reportedly served Muhammad poisoned mutton (or goat), which resulted ultimately in his protracted agonizing death. [450] Verbatim canonical hadith which chronicle Muhammad's alleged poisoning by a Khaybar Jewess, are reproduced below: [451]

> *Ibn Abbas replied, "That indicated the death of Allah's Apostle which Allah informed him of." Umar said, "I do not understand of it except what you understand." Narrated Aisha: The Prophet in his ailment in which he died, used to say, "O Aisha! I still feel the pain caused by the food I ate at Khaibar, and at this time, I feel as if my aorta is being cut from that poison."*

> *Anas reported that a Jewess came to Allah's Messenger (may peace be upon him) with poisoned mutton and he took of that what had been brought to him (Allah's Messenger). (When the effect of this poison were felt by him) he called for her and asked her about that, whereupon she said: "I had determined to kill you." Thereupon he said: "Allah will never give you the power to do it." He (the narrator) said that they (the Companions of the Holy Prophet) said: "Should we not kill her?" Thereupon he said: "No." He (Anas) said: "I felt (the affects of this poison) on the uvula of Allah's Messenger."*

> *Narrated Abu Huraira: When Khaibar was conquered, a (cooked) sheep containing poison, was given as a present to Allah's Apostle.*

> *Narrated Abu Huraira: When Khaibar was conquered, Allah's Apostle was presented with a poisoned (roasted) sheep. Allah's Apostle said, "Collect for me all the Jews present in this area." (When they were gathered) Allah's Apostle said to them, "I am going to ask you about something; will you tell me the truth?" They replied, "Yes, O Abal-Qasim!" Allah's Apostle said to them, "Who is your father?" They said, "Our father is so-and-so." Allah's Apostle said, "You have told a lie. for your father is so-and-so," They said, "No doubt, you have said the truth and done the correct thing." He again said to them, "If I ask you about something; will you tell me the truth?" They replied, "Yes, O Abal-Qasim! And if we should tell a lie you will know it as you have known it regarding our father," Allah's Apostle then asked, "Who are the people of the (Hell) Fire?" They replied, "We will remain in the (Hell) Fire for a while and then you (Muslims) will*

*replace us in it" Allah's Apostle said to them. "You will abide in it
with ignominy. By Allah, we shall never replace you in it at all."
Then he asked them again, "If I ask you something, will you tell
me the truth?" They replied, "Yes." He asked. "Have you put the
poison in this roasted sheep?" They replied, "Yes," He asked,
"What made you do that?" They replied, "We intended to learn if
you were a liar in which case we would be relieved from you, and
if you were a prophet then it would not harm you."*

Additional narrative regarding Muhammad's poisoning is provided by the sira
accounts of Ibn Ishaq, and Ibn Sa'd. Ibn Ishaq's report concludes that Muhammad
ultimately died from this poisoning episode, and notes his death was considered
an act of "martyrdom": [452]

*When the apostle had rested Zaynab b. al-Harith, the wife of
Sallam b. Mishkam prepared for him a roast lamb, having first
inquired what joint he preferred. When she learned that it was the
shoulder she put a lot of poison in it and poisoned the whole lamb.
Then she brought it in and placed it before him. He took hold of
the shoulder and chewed a morsel of it, but he did not swallow it.
Bishr b. al-Bara b. Ma'rur who was with him took some of it as
the apostle had done, but he swallowed it, while the apostle spat
it out, saying, "This bone tells me that it is poisoned." Then he
called for the woman and she confessed, and when he asked her
what had induced her to do this she answered: "You know what
you have done to my people. I said to myself, If he is a king I shall
ease myself of him and if he is a prophet he will be informed (of
what I have done)." So the apostle let her off. Bishr died from
what he had eaten. Marwan b. Uthman b. Abu Sa'id b. al-Mu'alla
told me: "The apostle had said in his illness of which he was
to die when Umm Bishr d. al-Bara' came to visit him, 'O Umm
Bishr, this is the time in which I feel a deadly pain from what I ate
with your brother at Khaybar.'" The Muslims considered that the
apostle died as a martyr in addition to the prophetic office with
which God had honored him.*

Ibn Sa'd (in his *Kitab Al-Tabaqat Al- Kabir*) focuses on the putative Jewish
conspiracy behind Muhammad's poisoning, while insisting adamantly that the
Khaybar Jewess perpetrator was put to death: [453]

*The Jews discussed about poisons and became united in one poison. She
[a Khaybar Jewess, Zaynab Bint al-Harith] poisoned the goat putting
more poison in the forelegs. . . . The Apostle of Allah took the foreleg, a
piece of which he put into his mouth. . . . The Apostle of Allah sent for*

Zaynab Bint al-Harith [and] . . . handed her over to the heirs of Bishr Ibn al-Barra [who the Jewess had also poisoned, leading to his rapid death] who put her to death. **This is the approved version** *[emphasis added]. . . . The Apostle of Allah lived after this three years, till in consequence of his pain he passed away. During his illness he used to say: "I did not cease to find the effect of the poisoned morsel I took at Khaybar."*

It is worth recounting, as depicted in the Muslim sources, the events that antedated Muhammad's reputed poisoning at Khaybar. [454]

Muhammad's failures or incomplete successes were consistently recompensed by murderous attacks on the Jews. The Muslim prophet-warrior developed a penchant for assassinating individual Jews and destroying Jewish communities by expropriation and expulsion (Banu Quaynuqa and B. Nadir), or massacring their men and enslaving their women and children (Banu Qurayza). [455]

Just before subduing the Medinan Jewish tribe Banu Qurayza and orchestrating the mass execution of their adult males, Muhammad invoked perhaps the most striking Koranic motif for the Jews debasement: He addressed these Jews, with hateful disparagement, as "You brothers of apes." [456] A consensus Muslim account of the massacre of the Qurayza has emerged as conveyed by the canonical hadith, sira, as well as classical Muslim jurists and historians. [457] This narrative is summarized as follows: Alleged to have aided the forces of Muhammad's enemies in violation of a prior pact, the Qurayza were subsequently isolated and besieged. Twice the Qurayza made offers to surrender, and depart from their stronghold, leaving behind their land and property. Initially they requested to take one camel load of possessions per person, but when Muhammad refused this request, the Qurayza asked to be allowed to depart without any property, taking with them only their families. However, Muhammad insisted that the Qurayza surrender unconditionally and subject themselves to his judgment. Compelled to surrender, the Qurayza were lead to Medina. The men with their hands pinioned behind their backs, were put in a court, while the women and children were said to have been put into a separate court. A third (and final) appeal for leniency for the Qurayza was made to Muhammad by their tribal allies the Aus. Muhammad again declined, and instead he appointed as arbiter Sa'd Mu'adh from the Aus, who soon rendered his concise verdict: the men were to be put to death, the women and children sold into slavery, the spoils to be divided among the Muslims.

Muhammad ratified the judgment stating that Sa'd's decree was a decree of God pronounced from above the Seven Heavens. Thus some 600 to 900 men from the Qurayza were lead on Muhammad's order to the Market of Medina. Trenches were dug and the men were beheaded, and their decapitated corpses buried in the trenches while Muhammad watched in attendance. Male youths who had not reached puberty were spared. Women and children were sold into slavery, a number of them being distributed as gifts among Muhammad's companions. According to Muhammad's biographer Ibn Ishaq, Muhammad chose one of the Qurayza women (Rayhana) for himself. The Qurayza's property and other possessions (including weapons) were also divided up as additional "booty" among the Muslims. The following details have been chronicled consistently by Muslim sources: the arbiter (Sa'd Mu'adh) was appointed by Muhammad himself; Muhammad observed in person the horrific executions; Muhammad claimed as a wife a woman (Rayhana) previously married to one of the slaughtered Qurayza tribesmen; the substantial material benefits (i.e., property; receipts from the sale of the enslaved) which accrued to the Muslims as a result of the massacre; the extinction of the Qurayza.

Abu Yusuf (d. 798), the prominent Hanafi jurist who advised Abbasid Caliph Harun al-Rashid (d. 809), made the following observations about the Qurayza massacre in his writings on *jihad*: [458]

> *Whenever the Muslims besiege an enemy stronghold, establish a treaty with the besieged who agree to surrender on certain conditions that will be decided by a delegate, and this man decides that their soldiers are to be executed and their women and children taken prisoner, this decision is lawful. This was the decision of **Sa'ad b. Mu'adh in connection with the Banu Qurayza**...it is up to the imam to decide what treatment is to be meted out to them and he will choose that which is preferable for religion and for Islam. If he esteems that the execution of the fighting men and the enslavement of their women and children is better for Islam and its followers, then he will act thus, **emulating the example of Sa'ad b. Mu'adh**.*

As noted by M.J. Kister, [459] al-Mawardi (d. 1058 C.E.), another eminent Muslim jurist from Baghdad, characterized the slaughter of the Qurayza as a religious duty incumbent on Muhammad. Professor Kister quotes al-Mawardi as follows: "...it was not permitted (for Muhammad) to forgive (in a case of) God's injunction incumbent upon them; he could only forgive (transgressions) in matters concerning his own person." The notion that this slaughter was sanctioned by God as revealed to Muhammad was, according to Kister, reflective of "...the current (as of 1986) Sunni view about the slaughter of the Banu Qurayza." [460]

Gairdner, also relying exclusively upon Muslim sources characterizing the slaughter of the Qurayza, highlights the pivotal role that Muhammad himself played in orchestrating the overall events: [461]

> *The umpire who gave the fatal decision (Sa'ad) was extravagantly praised by Muhammad. Yet his action was wholly and admittedly*

due to his lust for personal vengeance on a tribe which had occasioned him a painful wound. In the agony of its treatment he cried out- "O God, let not my soul go forth ere thou has cooled my eye from the Bani Quraiza". This was the arbiter to whose word the fate of that tribe was given over. His sentiments were well-known to Muhammad, who appointed him. It is perfectly clear from that that their slaughter had been decreed. What makes it clearer still is the assertion of another biographer that Muhammad had refused to treat with the Bani Quraiza at all until they had "come down to receive the judgment of the Apostle of God". Accordingly "they came down"; in other words put themselves in his power. And only then was the arbitration of Sa'ad proposed and accepted- but not accepted until it had been forced on him by Muhammad; for Sa'ad first declined and tried to make Muhammad take the responsibility, but was told "qad amarak Allahu takhuma fihim" "Allah has commanded you to give sentence in their case". From every point of view therefore the evidence is simply crushing that Muhammad was the ultimate author of this massacre.

In the immediate aftermath of the massacre, the Muslims benefited substantially from the Qurayza's assets which they seized as booty. The land and property acquired helped the Muslims gain their economic independence. The military strength of the Muslim community of Medina grew due to the weapons obtained, and the fact that captured women and children taken as slaves were sold for horses and more weapons, facilitating enlargement of the Muslim armed forces for further conquests. Conversely, the Jewish tribe of the Qurayza ceased to exist.

Subsequently, in the case of the Khaybar Jews, Muhammad had the male leadership killed and plundered their riches. The terrorized Khaybar survivors, industrious Jewish farmers, became prototype subjugated dhimmis whose productivity was extracted by the Muslims as a form of permanent booty. (According to the Muslim sources, even this tenuous vassalage was arbitrarily terminated within a decade of Muhammad's death when Caliph Umar expelled the Jews of Khaybar.) [462]

Thus Maimonides (d. 1203), the renowned Talmudist, philosopher, astronomer, and physician, as noted by historian Salo Baron, emphasizes the bellicose "madness" of Muhammad and his quest for political control. Muhammad's mindset and the actions it engendered had immediate and long term tragic consequences for Jews — from his massacring up to 24,000 Jews to their chronic oppression as described in the Islamic sources by Muslims themselves. [463]

Muhammad's brutal conquest and subjugation of the Medinan and Khaybar Jews and their subsequent expulsion by one of his companions, the (second) "Rightly

Guided" Caliph Umar, epitomize permanent archetypal behavior patterns Islamic Law deemed appropriate to Muslim interactions with Jews. [464] Hartwig Hirschfeld's detailed mid-1880s analysis of the sira accounts of Muhammad's interactions with the Jews includes this rather understated summary of the "mutual disappointment" that characterized their relationship, and the predictably disastrous results for the Jews: [465]

> *The Jews, for their part, were singularly disappointed in their expectations. The way in which Muhammad understood revelation, his ignorance and his clumsiness in religious questions in no way encouraged them to greet him as their Messiah. He tried at first to win them over to his teachings by sweetness and persuasion; they replied by posing once again the questions that they had already asked him; his answers, filled with gross errors, provoked their laughter and mockery. From this, of course, resulted a deep hostility between Muhammad and the Jews, whose only crime was to pass a severe judgment on the enterprise of this Arab who styled himself "God's prophet" and to find his conduct ridiculous, his knowledge false, and his regulations thoughtless. This judgment, which was well founded, was nevertheless politically incorrect [une faute politique], and the consequences thereof inevitably would prove to be disastrous for a minority that lacked direction or cohesion.*

Georges Vajda's 1937 essay "Juifs et Musulmans selon Le Hadit" ("Jews and Muslims according to the Hadith")—a magisterial seventy-page analysis, replete with 202 accompanying notes—remains the definitive study of Jews and their relations with Muhammad and the Muslims, as depicted in the hadith.[466] Vajda's meticulously documented research conclusions were not understated.

In the everyday, corporeal world, Vajda observes, "distrust must reign" in Muslims' relations with Jews, because, [467]

> *the Jews . . . are rebels to the solicitations of Islam and keep their religious traditions in a way liable to lead Muslims into error. Even when Islam knowingly borrows from Judaism, these borrowings are presented as amendments of the corresponding Jewish customs, unless they expressly forge traditions that aim to efface the true origin of the rite in question, by transposing it either into Arab paganism or into "Israelite" or pre-Israelite antiquity . . . especially beware of asking them for information of a religious kind.*

But it is the Jews' stubborn malevolence, Vajda adds, that is their defining worldly characteristic: [468]

*Jews are represented in the darkest colors [i.e., in the hadith].
Convinced by the clear testimony of their books that Muhammad
was the true prophet, they refused to convert, out of envy, jealousy
and national particularism, even out of private interest. They
have falsified their sacred books and do not apply the laws of
God; nevertheless, they pursued Muhammad with their raillery
and their oaths, and harassed him with questions, an enterprise
that turned to their own confusion and merely corroborated the
authenticity of the supernatural science of the prophet. From
words they moved to action: sorcery, poisoning, assassination
held no scruples for them.*

Vajda concludes that these archetypes, in turn, justify Muslim animus toward the
Jews, and the admonition to at best "subject [the Jews] to Muslim domination," as
dhimmis, treated "with contempt," under certain "humiliating arrangements." [469]

Meir Bar-Asher's 2013 analysis on Shiite doctrine regarding Judaism and Jews
underscores the extensive overlap between Sunni and Shiite conceptions [470] —
the former being highlighted in the discussion of dhimmitude, and Islamic Jew-
hatred, to this point. Bar-Asher notes,[471]

*Given that both Sunni and Shiite Islam are based largely on the
same religious sources, we can expect to see similarities between
them with regards to the focus of their theological and juridical
attitude to Jews and their religion.*

He adds indeed, "the two great branches of Islam share many common points
in their attitude toward Judaism," that includes, "notably," pejorative "aspects
of Jews and their religion," which "holds true for the past as well as for recent
periods." [472] Bar-Asher summarizes, "the main negative aspects, the reasons for
God's disappointment with the Jews according to the Koran and the Hadith,"—
understandings shared between Sunnis and Shiites—as follows: [473]

*...the Jews falsified their Scripture, deviated from the monotheistic
faith as shown, for example, by the worship of the golden calf,
and attributed a son to God, as do the Christians, according to
Koran 9 :30 "The Jews said, 'Uzayr is the son of God,' and the
Christians said, 'The messiah is the son of God...' ". Further,
they are accused of assassinating the prophets and breaking the
Alliance with God. These reasons, among others, lead to the
Koranic assertion trusting Jews and Christians is forbidden and
avoiding all alliances and contracts with them is an obligation.*

An additional shared [473a] antisemitic motif not included in Bar-Asher's opening
summary, but described later by the author, is Islam's replacement theology

pertaining to Judaism and Jews. [473b]

> *The idea of the people of Israel as prototype of the Shiites
> is expressed in exegetic traditions attributed to the imams
> Muhammad al-Baqir and Ja'far al-Sadiq. In their commentaries
> on Koranic verse 2:47/(2:40): "O sons of Israel! Remember the
> bounties I bestowed upon you! I preferred you over all others,"
> the first Imamite Koranic commentaries attributed to the Imam al-
> Sadiq the idea that...**the true chosen people referred to is none
> other than the family of the Prophet Muhammad, that is, the
> Shiite Imams...***

> *Another illustration of this identification of the family of
> Muhammad, that is, the Shiites, with the people of Israel is
> found in the same work [i.e., al-Majlisi's Bihar al-anwar], The
> Prophet is said to have declared, "I am 'Abd Allah and my name
> is Ahmad, and I am also the son of 'Abd Allah and my name is
> Israel. All that God ordained for Israel, he also ordained for me
> and wherever there is reference to Israel he also referred to me."
> **The implication of this identification of Muhammad with Israel/
> Jacob is that the Prophet and his descendants are seen to be the
> continuation of the Israelites of the Bible.***

Noting what he characterizes as the "the majority trend that emerges from Koranic exegeses, the literature of the Hadith, and juridical writings" amongst the Shiite theologians and jurists, Bar-Asher ascribes to them "a certain zeal in the rejection of Jews and Christians." [474] Bar-Asher concludes there is a greater severity in the Shiite position on the impurity ("najis") of Jews and Christians (and I must add, Zoroastrians [475]).

> *According to these sources, Jews and Christians should be
> considered as infidels and consequently as impure. Shiites, as
> Sunnis in fact, justify this position by broadening the meaning of
> the term shirk (associationism, polytheism, idolatry). **Nonetheless,
> the Shiite position on this question seems much harsher.*** [476]

The third chapter will elaborate on the consequences of the application of Shiite najis regulations for Iranian Jews, validating Bar-Asher's general observation about "harshness."

Georges Vajda's research on the hadith further demonstrates how Sunni Muslim eschatology emphasizes the Jews supreme hostility toward Islam. Jews are described as adherents of the Dajjâl—the Muslim equivalent of the Antichrist—and, as per another tradition, the Dajjâl is in fact Jewish. [477] Armand Abel, the renowned Belgian scholar of Islam, includes this summary characterization of the Dajjâl (from his official entry, "al-Dajdjal," in the Encyclopedia of Islam): [478]

> *A giant, false prophet, king of the Jews, representations of him*
> *vary according to the degree of literary information available*
> *or the predominating prejudices… Abd al-Kahir al-Baghdadi [479]*
> *regards him as the ultimate term of comparison to describe false*
> *doctrine and going astray…he [the Dajjal] would perish at the*
> *hands of Jesus [i.e., Isa, the Muslim Jesus [480]] who, in that way,*
> *would be converted to Islam after killing pigs, scattering wine and*
> *taking his place for prayer at the [Meccan] Kaba.*

- The "Muslim Jesus" hadith variant which takes place in Jerusalem, is described by James Robson. [481]

> *[M]ost of the Arabs will be in Jerusalem when Jesus will descend.*
> *The imam will give place to him, but Jesus will tell him to lead the*
> *prayers. Afterwards, Jesus will order the door to be opened, and*
> *the Dajjal will be seen there with 70,000 armed Jews. The Dajjal*
> *will begin to melt, but Jesus will pursue and catch him and kill*
> *him at the east gate of Ludd. God will rout the Jews who will find*
> *that even the places where they shelter will shout out where they*
> *are hiding.*

At his appearance, other traditions state that the Dajjâl will be accompanied by seventy thousand Jews from Isfahan wrapped in their robes and armed with polished sabers, their heads covered with a sort of veil. When the Dajjâl is defeated, his Jewish companions will be slaughtered—everything will deliver them up except for the so-called gharkad tree. Thus, according to several canonical hadith if a Jew seeks refuge under a tree or a stone, these objects will be able to speak to tell a Muslim: "There is a Jew behind me; come and kill him!" [482] Here are examples of these hadith: [483]

> *Anas b. Malik reported that Allah's Messenger said: "The Dajjal*
> *would be followed by seventy thousand Jews of Isfahan wearing*
> *Persian shawls."*
>
> *Narrated Abu Huraira: Allah's Apostle said, "The Hour will not*
> *be established until you fight with the Jews, and the stone behind*
> *which a Jew will be hiding will say. "O Muslim! There is a Jew*
> *hiding behind me, so kill him."*
>
> *Abu Huraira reported Allah's Messenger (may peace be upon him)*
> *as saying: "The last hour would not come unless the Muslims will*
> *fight against the Jews and the Muslims would kill them until the*
> *Jews would hide themselves behind a stone or a tree and a stone*

*or a tree would say: Muslim, or the servant of Allah, there is a Jew
behind me; come and kill him; but the tree Gharqad would not
say, for it is the tree of the Jews."*

Apropos of their longstanding Islamic relevance, Ibn Kathir's 14th century
commentary on Koran 4:155-159, which discusses Isa's (the Muslim Jesus') role
in defeating the *Dajjal*, and his Jewish minions, invokes these same apocalyptic
canonical hadith of Jew annihilation. [484]

Vajda also emphasizes how the notion of jihad "ransom" extends even into Islamic
eschatology: [485]

*Not only are the Jews vanquished in the eschatological war, but
they will serve as ransom for the Muslims in the fires of hell. The
sins of certain Muslims will weigh on them like mountains, but
on the day of resurrection, these sins will be lifted and laid upon
the Jews.*

This Judeo-centric Sunni eschatology resonates broadly, with an authoritative
imprimatur, across Islamdom, in the modern era, and even within the Muslim
diaspora. [486] For example, Hajj Amin El-Husseini concluded his compendious
1937 discourse on Islam's canonical Jew-hatred by reproducing the hadith (*Sahih
Bukhari, Volume 4, Book 52, Number 177*; *Sahih Muslim, Book 041, Number
6985*) [487] about how the destruction of the Jews is requisite for ushering in the
messianic times. Fifty years later Article 7 of Hamas' foundational 1988 charter
re-stated the same canonical, apocalyptic hadith of Jew annihilation, which closed
Hajj Amin el-Husseini's 1937 declaration: [488]

*...the Islamic Resistance Movement aspires to realize the promise
of Allah, no matter how long it takes. The Prophet, Allah's prayer
and peace be upon him, says: "The hour of judgment shall not
come until the Muslims fight the Jews and kill them, so that the
Jews hide behind trees and stones, and each tree and stone will
say: 'Oh Muslim, oh servant of Allah, there is a Jew behind me,
come and kill him,' except for the Gharqad tree, for it is the tree of
the Jews." (Sahih Muslim, Book 41, Number 6985)*

The current Palestinian Authority Grand Mufti of Jerusalem, Muhammad Hussein
repeated this   canonical tradition during a January 9, 2012 sermon. [489] Most
recently, during a May 10, 2013 sermon at Sunni Islam's Vatican equivalent, Al-
Azhar University, and its mosque, Muhammad Al-Mahdi, a senior scholar and
head of the Sharia association at Al-Azhar also proclaimed the same end of times
Jew-annihilating hadith (and Koran 5:82, as well). [490]

Cook's extensive 2002 study of Islam's apocalyptic literature, devotes a chapter to classical Shiite eschatology. [491] He emphasizes the broad divergence ("the chasm is wide") between the Shiite and Sunni portrayals of the apocalyptic "Mahdi" figure, beginning with his alleged superhuman, versus human qualities. [492] While the Shiite Mahdi is "superhuman and prophet-like (if not a prophet himself)," Sunni apocalyptic, in contrast, "emphasizes his humanity, his reluctance and his fallibility (and sometimes even his personal bodily defects)," qualities absent from the Shiite descriptions. [493] Accordingly, Cook observes, [494]

> *The triumph of the Mahdi is not a triumph of all Shi'is, though they frequently portray it as such...the Sunni [Mahdi] both suffers the tribulations and actively triumphs over his foes. The Mahdi in the Shi'i view, together with his band of 313, is a self-sufficient unit that can take on any enemy and win.*

Cook also stresses (repeatedly) the more benign character of Shiite apocalyptic, vis-à-vis the Jews, in his discussions of both the Muslim Jesus, and the Dajjal. [495]

> *His [i.e., the Muslim Jesus, Isa's] job, first and foremost, is to assist the Mahdi in the conversion of the Jews and the Christians to Islam. Unlike in Sunni apocalyptic, there is no massacre of the Jews at this point and no polemical attacks, which is a tendency that holds true throughout Shi'i apocalyptic. At places where in the former there is a massacre of the Jews, in the latter the Sunnis themselves take their place—a rather ironic slap in the face.*

> *Nowhere in the Shi'i apocalyptic is it said specifically that the Dajjal is Jewish (though he is said to come from Yahudiya and his followers are Jewish), which is a significant difference from the Sunni material. Indeed, in one of the most obnoxious elements of the Dajjal story, where the Jews are massacred after the Dajjal is killed by Jesus, the people who are massacred in fact are the Sunnis themselves.*

However, in a footnote, Cook concedes, "anti-Jewish traditions do occur, though," citing [496] (although not translating) the following material from al-Majlisi's monumental compilation of Shiite traditions, *Bihar al-anwar* ("Oceans of Light"), which is translated below:

> *"Muḥammad b. 'Ali, on the authority of Mufaḍḍal b. Ṣalih al-Asadi, on the authority of Muḥammad b. Marwan, on the authority of Abu 'Abdallah, peace be upon him, said: "The Messenger of Allah, may Allah bless him and his family, said: 'Whoever hates us, Ahl Al-Bayt [i.e., the Prophet's family], Allah will resurrect him [on the Day of Judgment] as a Jew.' It was said [to him]: 'Oh, Messenger of Allah, even though he uttered the Two Shahadas?'*

He said: 'Yes, he is protected by these two utterances from having his blood spilled and from [being required to] pay the poll tax in a state of humiliation.' Then he reiterated: 'Whoever hates us, Ahl Al-Bayt, Allah will resurrect him as a Jew.' It was said [to him]: 'And how is that, Oh Messenger of Allah?' He said: 'If the Dajjal [Anti-Christ] comes during his lifetime, he will follow him.'"

I [the author, al-Majlisi] say: We have already mentioned in the chapter [containing] the words of the Imam [Ja'far] Al-Sadiq [the 6th Imam] about [the Twelfth Imam, known as] Al-Qa'im, [the 12th Imam] peace be upon him, that he [Al-Qa'im] will kill the Dajjal.

Furthermore, Mehdi Khalaji's January, 2008 monograph, "Apocalyptic Politics," also citing Majlisi, elucidates these "functions" to be performed by the Muslim Jesus in the Shiite apocalyptic traditions: [497]

[The Muslim] Jesus will appear when the Mahdi rises. According to the tradition[s], Jesus will: perform jihad under the Mahdi's commandership and kill [the] Dajjal...invite people to Islam, killing Christians and destroying churches; and also die before the Mahdi.

Ze'ev Maghen has argued trenchantly—but with great cogency—against the popular notion that contemporary Iran is somehow gripped with a Shiite apocalyptic fervor of imminent geo-strategic consequence. [498] Maghen's 2008 study acknowledged then "charismatic" Iranian President Ahmadinejad's "messianic words and deeds," including "refurbishment" projects, i.e., of the Qom mosque housing the Well of Jamkaran, an alleged site where the 12th Imam will reappear, and highway broadening to service the Mahdi and his retinue on their way to Tehran, as well as purported allusions to communications Ahmadinejad had received from the Hidden Imam, etc. [499] However, Maghen's analysis thoroughly rejected the prevalent contention "by pundits and even many serious Iran-*shenasan* (Iran specialists)," that Ahmadinejad and his coterie of "dangerous dreamers," represented, [500]

...the tip of a gargantuan chiliastic iceberg subsuming important groups within the government apparatus as well as large sections of the military and even the populace, all of whom are wittingly or unwittingly implementing policies inspired by the radical, messianist-oriented wing of the Shi'ite clerical class. The clandestine Hojjatiyyeh society, one of whose key figures, Ayatollah Muhammad Taqi Mesbah-e-Yazdi, is also considered to be Ahmadinejad's personal marja' (Source of Emulation, i.e. religious guide), is often specifically referenced in this connection, and is lumped together with a more general trend or tendency

whose purvey ors are referred to as ta'jiliyan or "hasteners [of the End]."

Maghen added that, [501]

> *Ahmadinejad's verbal antics over the past two years, combined with the increasingly tense situation surrounding the nuclear issue, have led to a seemingly endless medley of repetitious clichés in the press and, unfortunately, even in academia regarding the Islamic Republic's "apocalyptic" philosophy and the influence thereof on the country's short—and long-term strategic objectives.*

He then observed that even the doyen of Islamic studies, Bernard Lewis, "jumped on the bandwagon" insistent that Iran was a seething "hotbed of eschatological excitement." [502] Observing that "for Shiite Muslims, the long awaited return of the Hidden Imam" concludes with "the final victory of the forces of good over evil, however these may be defined," Lewis made the following calamitous "prediction," in an August 8, 2006 Wall Street Journal essay: [503]

> **Mr. Ahmadinejad and his followers clearly believe that this time is now, and that the terminal struggle has already begun and is indeed well advanced. It may even have a date, indicated by several references by the Iranian president to giving his final answer to the U.S. about nuclear development by Aug. 22 [2006].** *This was at first reported as "by the end of August," but Mr. Ahmadinejad's statement was more precise. What is the significance of Aug. 22? This year, Aug. 22 corresponds, in the Islamic calendar, to the 27th day of the month of Rajab of the year 1427. This, by tradition, is the night when many Muslims commemorate the night flight of the prophet Muhammad on the winged horse Buraq, first to "the farthest mosque," usually identified with Jerusalem, and then to heaven and back (c.f., Koran XVII.1).* **This might well be deemed an appropriate date for the apocalyptic ending of Israel and if necessary of the world.**

Commenting on Lewis' 2006 prognostication, Maghen wrote, acidly [504]

> **Lewis went so far as to predict the probable date of an Iranian nuclear strike on Israel**—*based on its concurrence with the holiday of Muhammad's Night Journey and Ascension (which is rarely celebrated among Shi'ites)*—**a date which came and went.**

The crux of Maghen's argument is that dating from shortly after its advent—across a continuum of over a millennium, through the present—"orthodox" Shi'ism has developed and implemented "an impressive expertise in repressing the messianic aspirations of its adherents." [505] Mainstream, conservative Shiite clerics even succeeded in repressing Mahdism—brutally, via executions and massacres, when required—during both the expansionist jihad-waging Safavid, and Qajar dynasties. [506] Maghen argues further that the Khomeini "revolution" marked "the logical conclusion of the multi-stage process of de-messianization." [507] He maintains, [508]

> *all of those centuries of impressive Shi'ite clerical achievement, now culminating in 1979 in the glorious realization of the primeval Shi'ite dream of reuniting sacerdotum and imperium in a bona fide Islamic Republic—all of this was and continues to be based on one essential, indispensible prerequisite: that the Mahdi stay far away.*

Maghen contrasts this Shiite trend, with the parallel development of Mahdism in Sunni Islam. [509]

> *It is no coincidence that for over a millenium now the Sunni world, which ad opted the concept of the Mahdi from the Shi'a early on, has had to contend with considerably more messianic pretenders than the Twelver Shi'ites. No year better illustrates this ironic phenomenon than 1979: While the experience of leading Islamic history's most glorious revolution did not induce Khomeini to declare himself (or anyone else of consequence to declare him) the Mahdi, across the gulf in Saudi Arabia a young Sunni zealot named Juhayman—who had a chip on his shoulder but, unlike Khomeini, no achievements to his credit—took over Mecca's sacred precinct with some 250 armed cohorts and declared his brother-in-law Qahtan the Muslim messiah. Shi'ism, contrary to popular belief, is the antithesis and nemesis of messianism.*

Maghen also explodes the uninformed, if oft-repeated canards about the "cult of Hojjatiyyeh," and its reputed clerical affiliate, and Ahmadinejad "spiritual" mentor, Ayatollah Yazdi. [510]

> *Far from being composed of radical messianists who seek to usher in the apocalyptic millenium, the Anjoman-e-Hojjatiyyeh, founded in the mid-twentieth century by Shaykh Mahmud-e-Halabi, was and remains an ultra-conservative association devoted to the suppression of a particular latter-day messianic movement that claims that the Hidden Imam is already here: the Baha'i. It advocates, in perfectly traditional, orthodox Twelver fashion, the pious and passive practice of "awaiting" the Savior (entezar), but specifically discourages and condemns as heretical any active effort to hasten his arrival.*

Ayatollah Mesbah-e-Yazdi, the reputed senior figure of the now underground Hojjatiyyeh and supposed marja' of President Ahmadinejad—the cleric with whom Iran's purported messianic fervor is most commonly associated these days—vociferously denies any connection with the clandestine society, and even were his past affiliation somehow proven, this would, again, show him to be nothing other than vehemently anti-mahdist.

*Indeed, on the rare occasions when Mesbah e-Yazdi discusses subjects related to eschatology—such as in a speech delivered in 2004 at the Jamkaran Mosque itself and entitled "The Explanation of the Concept of 'Anticipating Deliverance'" (tabyin-e-mafhum-e-entezar-e-faraj)—he goes out of his way to reinterpret the yearning for the Imam's advent in mundane, psycho-socio political terms. Its meaning for our generation, he urges, involves preserving hope and avoiding despair; relying on God to strengthen Muslims individually and collectively against their enemies; implementing the laws and performing the rituals of the Sharia; and supporting the institution of the Guardianship of the Jurist. **In the Islamic Republic, such sentiments are as mainstream as it gets, and there is not a hint of activist messianism in them.***

In his closing discussion, Maghen concedes that during the past century, "changes, even profound ones, in the Shi'ite doctrinal worldview," have occurred, citing as an example, how the traditionally understood 7th century fatalist martyrdom of Husayn (commemorated each year during Ashura [511]), "has been for the most part replaced with the more politicized perception of Husayn as defiant rebel." [512] He then adds, "the metamorphosis of the figure of the Hidden Imam into a rallying point for apocalypticism among clerics and government officials is not an impossible eventuality." [513] Despite this caveat, Maghen concludes, [514]

But there is, as yet—contrary to the clichéd asseverations of anti-regime activists—no sign of such a transformation.

Perhaps apropos to Maghen's (albeit minor) caveat, David Cook's 2005 study of the modern genre of Muslim apocalyptic writings—which rivets on Sunni eschatology—notes the "amazing extent" to which contemporary apocalyptists, [515]

...are willing to go in the effort to find a scenario acceptable to them, even digging into their opponents apocalyptic and messianic expectations in order to corrupt these.

Cook then reiterates the centrality of the "Jewish Dajjal" motif to the "Arab-Israeli conflict" (with the unmentioned corollary destruction of the Jews), in this corpus of eschatological literature. [516]

> [The] identification of the Jews' expected messiah with the
> Antichrist is so firmly rooted in Muslim apocalyptic that it even
> appears in certain conservative works, as well as appearing in
> all radical ones. This identification enables them to see the Arab-
> Israeli conflict in its entirety as an apocalyptic event and one in
> which the Arabs are destined to be victorious, despite the present
> gloomy situation. Of course, for many of these authors, the Arab-
> Israeli conflict is simply part of a greater conflict between Islam
> and the West, which must also be resolved in favor of the former
> before the end of the world.

Finally, recent polling data [517] indicate that these traditionalist Sunni Islamic
eschatological views—espoused, in the modern era, across a continuum of
75 years, by the ex-Grand Mufti of Jerusalem, Hajj Amin el-Husseini, current
Grand Mufti of Jerusalem, Muhammad Hussein, head of the Sharia association
at Al-Azhar University, Muhammad Al-Mahdi, and Hamas—resonate with the
Palestinian Muslim population. American pollster Stanley Greenberg performed
what was described as an "intensive, face-to-face survey in Arabic of 1,010
Palestinian adults in the West Bank and the Gaza Strip." [518] As reported in July,
2011 these data revealed that **seventy-three percent** of Palestinian Muslims
agreed with the dictates of the apocalyptic hadith (*Sahih Muslim, Book 41,
Number 6985*; included in el-Husseini's 1937 declaration, the 1988 Hamas
Covenant, Muhammad Hussein's January, 2012 sermon, and Al Azhar senior
cleric Muhammad Al-Mahdi's May, 2013 sermon) calling for the annihilation of
the Jews, to bring on the messianic age. [519]

One last significant, and unabashedly conspiratorial, Jew-hating theme, is
associated with "the birth pangs" of Islam. As put forth in early Sunni Muslim
historiography (for example, by Tabari), Abdullah Ibn Saba, was an alleged
renegade Yemenite Jew, and founder of the heterodox Shiite sect. [520] Sean
Anthony's extensive modern analysis of Abdullah Ibn Saba adds another
pejorative characteristic conferred upon this ostensible Yemenite Jew in the
Muslim literature: his mother was black. Anthony notes that a "favorite derisive
handle for him," was "son of the Black woman." [521]

According to Sunni dogma, Abdullah Ibn Saba is held responsible — identified as
a Jew (and black) — for promoting the Shiite heresy and fomenting the rebellion
and internal strife associated with this primary breach in Islam's "political
innocence," culminating in the assassination of the third Rightly Guided Caliph
Uthman, and the bitter, lasting legacy of Sunni-Shiite sectarian strife. [522]

Here are key extracts from Tabari's account: [523]

'Abd Allah b. Saba' was a Yemenite Jew. . . . He later converted to Islam in the time of [Caliph] Uthman. Then he traveled through the lands of the Muslims trying to lead them into error. . . . [For example] in Egypt he promulgated to the people the [heterodox] doctrine of the Return [of Muhammad as Messiah]. So the Egyptians discussed this idea. Then, after that, he said that there were one thousand prophets, each of whom had an agent; and that Ali was Muhammad's agent. Then he said, Muhammad was the Seal of the Prophets and Ali was the Seal of the Agents. Also, he asked: "Who is more evil than those who denied Muhammad's designation of Ali as his agent-successor, pounced upon this successor- designate of Ali's messenger and seized (illegitimately) the rulership of the Muslim community?" [In answer to this question as it were,] he told the Egyptians that Uthman had seized power illegitimately while Ali was, in fact, the agent-successor of Allah's messenger. "Rebel against this illegitimate rule, provoke it, and challenge your rulers . . ." [said 'Abd Allah b. Saba'].

Over a millennium later, the momentous international gathering of Muslim religious authorities, sponsored by Sunni Islam's Vatican, Al-Azhar University, the Fourth Conference of the Academy of Islamic Research, September, 1968, included Al-Azhar Professor Muhammad El-Sayyed Husein Al-Dahabi's paper, which declared, [524]

Among the leading figures of heresy and sectarianism was Abdullah ibn Saba the Jew, who feigned to be a Muslim, disguising his unbelief, making a show of supporting the Prophet's offspring (Alu-l-Bait), so as to deceive Muslims and to propagate among them his heretical and noxious views... [T]he earliest heresiarch, Abdullah ibn Saba, who was the foremost leader of sedition and heterodoxy. He, with his adherents, ... feigned to be devout Muslim, and went to all lengths in their deceitfulness, by simulating to be the most fervent supporters of the offspring of the Prophet, so as to corrupt the beliefs of Muslims.

Circa 2008, a Hudson Institute Center for Religious Freedom review of Saudi Arabian textbooks, ("Update: Saudi Arabia's Curriculum of Intolerance"), demonstrated that this traditionalist, mainstream example of Sunni Islam's conspiratorial Jew-hatred was still being inculcated amongst Muslim youth: [525]

The cause of the discord: The Jews conspired against Islam and its people. A sly, wicked person who sinfully and deceitfully professed Islam infiltrated (the Muslims). He was 'Abd Allah b. Saba' (from the Jews of Yemen) began spewing his malice and

> *venom against the third of the Rightly-Guided Caliphs, 'Uthman (may God be pleased with him), and falsely accused him."*
> *(Tawhid: Literature, Science, and Qur'an Memorization Section, Twelfth Grade. Kingdom of Saudi Arabia. Ministry of Education. Education Development, 1428-1429; 2007-2008, p. 78.)*

But what is the Shiite position on Abdullah Ibn Saba? Is this literature "silent" on the subject, for example, conceding the discussion to Sunni polemicists? In fact authoritative Shiite authors claimed he was guilty of perverting and warping the message of Caliph Ali's true (Shiite) followers. Mainstream Shiites thus designated Abdullah Ibn Saba an archetypal avatar of extreme, heretical beliefs, notably, the profession of Ali's divinity. [526] This profession was an egregious heresy for which Caliph Ali purportedly had Ibn Saba burned alive, as described in a Shiite hadith: [527]

> *Muhammad b. Qūlawayh al-Qummī—Sa'd b. 'Abd Allāh b. Abī Khalaf al-Qummī—Muhammad b. 'Uthmān al-'Abdī—Yūnus b. 'Abd al-Rahmān—'Abd Allāh b. Sinān—his father (Sinān b. Tarīf)—Abū Ja'far (Muhammad al-Bāqir) said: "'Abd Allāh b. Saba' made a claim to prophecy while asserting that the Commander of the Faithful ('Alī) is God. This reached the Commander of the Faithful, and he called for him and questioned him. (Ibn Saba') reaffirmed this and said, 'Yes, you are he! It was cast into my heart that you indeed are God, and I am a prophet.' The Commander of the Faithful said to him, 'Woe to you, for Satan mocks you! Turn away from this, lest your mother be bereaved of you, and repent!' (Ibn Saba') refused. **('Alī) imprisoned him and urged him to repent for three days, but he did not repent. Then 'Alī burned him alive with fire and said, 'Satan led him astray with false imaginings He would come to him and cast such things into his heart.'"***

Caliph Ali is also claimed to have denounced Ibn Saba's blackness, allegedly declaring, [528]

What do I have to do with the vile, black man?

How was the system of dhimmitude—redolent with the motifs of Islamic Jew-hatred just discussed—applied to Jews, specifically? (I will illustrate its application in Iran, at some length, in chapter three).

Contemporary observations regarding the application of the system of dhimmitude upon the Jews in their indigenous homeland were made by the Polish Jew Gedaliah of Siemiatyce (d. 1716). Braving numerous perils, Gedaliah journeyed to Jerusalem in 1700. He recorded these appalling conditions for Jews (and

Christians) in his book, *Pray for the Peace of Jerusalem*—consistent with a millennium of such oppressions since the jihad conquest of historical Palestine by Caliph Umar, between 634 to 638 C.E. What Gedaliah witnessed compelled him to return to Europe in order to raise funds for the Jews of Jerusalem. [529]

> *We [Jews] were obliged to give a large sum of money to the Muslim authorities in Jerusalem in order to be allowed to build a new synagogue. Although the old synagogue was small and we only wanted to enlarge it very slightly, it was forbidden under Islamic law to modify the least part. . . .* **In addition to the expenses in bribes destined to win the favor of the Muslims, each male was obliged to pay an annual poll tax of two pieces of gold to the sultan.** *The rich man was not obliged to give more, but the poor man could not give less. Every year, generally during the festival of the Passover, an official from Constantinople would arrive in Jerusalem.* **He who did not have the means to pay the tax was thrown into prison and the Jewish community was obliged to redeem him. The official remained in Jerusalem for about two months and consequently, during that period, the poor people would hide wherever they could, but if ever they were caught, they would be redeemed by community funds. The official sent his soldiers throughout the streets to control the papers of the passers-by, for a certificate was provided to those who had already paid the tax. If anyone was found without his certificate, he had to present himself before the official with the required sum, otherwise he was imprisoned until such time as he could be redeemed.**
>
> *The Christians are also obliged to pay the poll-tax…during the week, the paupers dared not show themselves outside…in their wickedness, the [Muslim]soldiers would go to the synagogues, waiting by the doors, requesting the certificate of payment from the congregants who emerged…*
>
> **No Jew or Christian is allowed to ride a horse,** *but a donkey is permitted, for [in the eyes of Muslims] Christians and Jews are inferior beings…The Muslims do not allow any member of another faith—unless he converts to their religion—entry to the Temple [Mount] area, for they claim that no other religion is sufficiently pure to enter this holy spot.* **They never weary of claiming that, although God had originally chosen the people of Israel, He had since abandoned them on account of their iniquity in order to choose the Muslims**…

> *In the Land of Israel, no member of any other religion besides Islam may wear the color green, even if it is a thread [of cotton] like that with which we decorate our prayer shawls. If a Muslim perceives it, that could bring trouble. Similarly, it is not permitted to wear a green or white turban. On the Sabbath, however, we wear white turbans, on the crown of which we place a piece of cloth of another color as a distinguishing mark. The Christians are not allowed to wear a turban, but they wear a hat instead, as is customary in Poland.* **Moreover, the Muslim law requires that each religious denomination wear its specific garment so that each people may be distinguished from another. This distinction also applies to footwear. Indeed, the Jews wear shoes of a dark blue color, whereas Christians wear red shoes. No one can use green, for this color is worn solely by Muslims.** *The latter are very hostile toward Jews and inflict upon them vexations in the streets of the city...the common folk persecute the Jews, for we are forbidden to defend ourselves against the Turks or the Arabs.* **If an Arab strikes a Jew, he [the Jew] must appease him but dare not rebuke him, for fear that he may be struck even harder, which they [the Arabs] do without the slightest scruple.** *This is the way the Oriental Jews react, for they are accustomed to this treatment, whereas the European Jews, who are not yet accustomed to suffer being assaulted by the Arabs, insult them in return.*
>
> *Even the Christians are subjected to these vexations.* **If a Jew offends a Muslim, the latter strikes him a brutal blow with his shoe in order to demean him, without anyone's being able to prevent him from doing it.** *The Christians fall victim to the same treatment and they suffer as much as the Jews, except that the former are very rich by reason of the subsidies that they receive from abroad, and they use this money to bribe the Arabs.* **As for the Jews, they do not possess much money with which to oil the palms of the Muslims, and consequently they are subject to much greater suffering.**

Two particularly humiliating "vocations" that were imposed upon Jews by their Muslim overlords in Yemen, and Morocco — where Jews formed the only substantive non-Muslim dhimmi populations — merit elaboration.

Moroccan Jews were confined to ghettos in the major cities, such as Fez (since the 13th century) called mellah(s) (salty earth) which derives from the fact it was here that they were forced to salt the decapitated heads of executed rebels for public exposition. [530] This brutally imposed humiliating practice — which could be enforced even on the Jewish Sabbath — persisted through the late 19th century, as described by Eliezer Bashan: [531]

> *In the 1870's, Jews were forced to salt the decapitated heads of rebels on the Sabbath. For example, Berber tribes frequently revolted against Sultan Muhammad XVIII. In order to force them to accept his authority, he would engage in punitive military campaigns. Among the tribes were the Musa, located south of Marrakesh. In 1872, the Sultan succeeded in quelling their revolt and forty-eight of their captives were condemned to death. In October 1872, on the order of the Sultan, they were dispatched to Rabat for beheading. Their decapitated heads were to be exposed on the gates of the town for three days. Since the heads were to be sent to Fez, Jewish ritual slaughterers [of livestock] were forced to salt them and hang them for exposure on the Sabbath. Despite threats by the governor of Rabat, the Jews refused to do so. He then ordered soldiers to enter the homes of those who refused and drag them outside. After they were flogged, the Jews complied and performed the task and the heads of the rebels were exposed in public.*

Yemenite Jews had to remove human feces and other waste matter (urine which failed to evaporate, etc.) from Muslim areas, initially in Sanaa, and later in other communities such as Shibam, Yarim, and Dhamar. Decrees requiring this obligation were issued in the late 18th or early 19th century, and re-introduced in 1913. [532] Yehuda Nini reproduces an 1874 letter written by a Yemenite Jew to the Alliance Israelite in Paris, lamenting the practice: [533]

> *...it is 86 years since our forefathers suffered the cruel decree and great shame to the nation of Israel from the east to sundown...for in the days of our fathers, 86 years ago, there arose a judge known as Qadi, and said unto the king and his ministers who lived in that time that the Lord, Blessed be He, had only created the Jews out of love of the other nations, to do their work and be enslaved by them at their will, and to do the most contemptible and lowly of tasks. And of them all...the greatest contamination of all, to clear their privies and streets and pathways of the filthy dung and the great filth in that place and to collect all that is left of the dung, may your Honor pardon the expression.*

And when the Jews were perceived as having exceeded the rightful bounds of this subjected relationship, as in mythically "tolerant" Muslim Spain, [534] the results were predictably tragic. The Granadan Jewish viziers Samuel Ibn Naghrela, and his son Joseph, who protected the Jewish community, were both assassinated between 1056 to 1066, and in the aftermath, the Jewish population was annihilated by the local Muslims. It is estimated that up to four thousand Jews perished in the pogrom by Muslims that accompanied the 1066 assassination. [535] This figure equals or exceeds the number of Jews reportedly killed by the Crusaders during their pillage of the Rhineland, some thirty years later, at the outset of the First Crusade. [536]

A contemporary chronicle written by sultan Abd Allah (who became Sultan of Granada in 1073) confirms that a breach in the system of dhimmitude precipitated the outburst of anti-Jewish violence by the Muslims of Granada: [536a]

> *Both the common people and the nobles were disgusted by the cunning of the Jews, the notorious changes they had brought in the order of things, and the positions they occupied in violation of their pact [i.e., the dhimma]. Allah decreed their destruction on Saturday 10 Safar 459 (December 31, 1066). . . . The Jew [Joseph Ibn Naghrela] fled into the interior of the palace, but the mob pursued him there, seized him, and killed him. They then put every Jew in the city to the sword and took vast quantities of their property.*

The inciting "rationale" for this Granadan pogrom was reiterated in the bitter anti-Jewish ode of Abu Ishaq, a well-known Muslim jurist and poet of the times, who wrote: [537]

> *Bring them down to their place and return them to the most abject station. They used to roam around us in tatters covered with contempt, humiliation, and scorn. They used to rummage amongst the dung heaps for a bit of a filthy rag to serve as a shroud for a man to be buried in...Do not consider that killing them is treachery. Nay, it would be treachery to leave them scoffing.*

Abu Ishaq's rhetorical incitement to violence also included the line, [538]

> *Many a pious Muslim is in awe of the vilest infidel ape*

Moshe Perlmann, in his analysis of the Muslim anti-Jewish polemic of 11th century Granada, notes, [539]

> **[Abu Ishaq] Elbiri used the epithet "ape" (qird) profusely when referring to Jews. Such indeed was the parlance.**

Saad ad Daula's late 13th century plight demonstrates the impact of violent anti-dhimmi agitation, and Islam's indigenous, conspiratorial Jew-hatred. The Mongol conquest of Baghdad in 1258 under Hulagu Khan (d. 1265) destroyed Muslim suzerainty and the domination of Islam as a state religion, rendering it "a religion among all others." [540] Mongol rule thus eliminated the system of dhimmitude, and, in contrast to Islamic chauvinism, writes historian Walter Fischel,[541]

> *the principle of tolerance for all faiths, maintained by the Il Khans [Mongol rulers], (depriving) the [Islamic] concept of the "Protected People" the ahl adh-Dhimma [dhimmi system] . . . of its former importance; with it fell the extremely varied professional restrictions into which it had expanded, . . .primarily those regarding the admission of Jews and Christians to government posts.*

The thirteenth-century Christian chronicler Bar Hebraeus recorded this telling observation: [542]

> *With the Mongols there is neither slave nor free man, neither believer nor pagan, neither Christian nor Jew; but they regard all men as belonging to one and the same stock.*

And the Iraqi Ghazi b. al-Wasiti (fl. 1292), author of a contemporary Muslim treatise on the dhimmis, noted: [543]

> *A firman of the Il Khan [Hulagu] had appeared to the effect that everyone should have the right to profane his faith openly and his religious connection; and that the members of one religious body should not oppose those of another.*

Fischel concludes: [544]

> *For Christians and Jews, the two groups chiefly affected by the ahl adh-Dhimma policy, current until then, this change in constitutional and religious principles implied a considerable amelioration of their position; whereas for the Muslims it meant they had sunk to a depth hitherto unknown in their history.*

The brief rise and calamitous fall of Saad ad-Daula—which mirrored the experience of his Jewish co-religionists—took place during this Mongol epoch. Saad ad-Daula was a Jewish physician who successfully reformed the Mongol revenue and taxation system for Iraq. In recognition of these services, he was appointed by the Mongol emperor Arghun (who reigned from 1284 to 1291) to the position of administrative vizier (in 1289) over Arghun's empire. According to Bar Hebraeus, [545]

> *The king of kings [Arghun] ordered that Saad ad-Daula, the Jew, hitherto the Governor of Baghdad, should be appointed Chief of the administrative officials. . . throughout all provinces of the Empire.*

Despite being a successful and responsible administrator (which even the Muslim sources confirm), [545a] the appointment of a Jew as the vizier of a heathen ruler over a predominantly Muslim region predictably aroused the wrath of the Muslim masses. This reaction was expressed through and exacerbated by "all kinds of[Muslim] diatribes, satirical poems, and libels." [546] Ibn al-Fuwati (d. 1323), a contemporary Muslim historian from Baghdad, recorded this particularly revealing example that emphasized traditional anti-Jewish motifs from the Koran: [547]

> *In the year 689/1291 a document was prepared which contained libels against Saad ad-Daula, together with verses from the Qur'an and the history of the prophets, that stated the Jews to be a people whom Allah hath debased.*

Another contemporary Muslim source, the chronicler and poet Wassaf, [548] according to Fischel, "empties the vials of hatred on the Jew Saad ad-Daula and brings the most implausible accusations against him." [549] **These accusations included the claims that Saad had advised Arghun to cut down trees in Baghdad (dating from the days of the conquered Muslim Abbasid dynasty) and build a fleet to attack Mecca and convert the cuboidal Ka'ba (the holiest place and structure in Islam) to a heathen temple.** [550] **Wassaf's account also quotes satirical verses to demonstrate the extent of public dissatisfaction with what he terms "Jewish Domination,"** adding to the existing line, "Turn Jews, for heaven itself hath turned a Jew," his own: [551]

> *Yet wait and ye shall hear their torments cry And see them fall and perish presently.*

When Arghun took ill, influential Mongol dukes inimical to Saad ad-Daula for purely political reasons shifted the "blame" for Arghun's terminal illness to the Jewish physician-vizier. Saadand his supporters were arrested and a large number of them, executed (1291). Saad ad- Daula's murder precipitated a broad attack on Jewry throughout the Il Khan Empire, beginning in the Baghdad Jewish ghetto, where, according to Bar Hebraeus and Wassaf, despite Jewish resistance, [552]

> *when the report of the murder of the Jew was heard, the Arabs armed themselves and went to the quarter of the Jews, because the Jews were all living together in one quarter in Baghdad . . . in Baghdad more than a hundred of the noble and wealthy Jews were slain, and their property plundered*

Wassaf and Ibn al-Fuwati further reveal that such attacks spread well beyond Baghdad: [553]

> *Throughout the lands of Islam, the Jewish people were oppressed and their goods plundered . . . there was no town left in Iraq in*

which the Jews were not served with that which had happened to
them in Baghdad, until a part of them embraced Islam, although
they later turned back again.

Bar Hebraeus was moved to depict the calamity for the Jews in these poignant words: [554]

The trials and wrath which were stirred up against the Jews at
this time neither tongue can utter nor the pen write down.

Walter Fischel concludes that "a tremendous wave of suffering and persecution must have overwhelmed the entire Jewry of Iraq and Persia," while noting "[t]he Muslims, however, gave expression to their joy at the end of Jewish domination in many verses filled with enmity against the Jews." [555] One such celebratory verse, by the poet Zaynu'd-Din Ali b. Sa'id, opens with the debasing reference to the Jews as apes: [556]

*His name we praise who rules the firmament. **These apish Jews***
are done away and shent [ruined or destroyed].

The verse continues by reiterating antisemitic Koranic motifs of the Jews as "wretched dupes of error and despair," "foulest race," "hatefulest," dispatched to "hell" in "molten torments," doomed "without reprieve"—while celebrating their wanton spoliation and slaughter. [557]

Throughout the lands they're shamed and desolate.
God hath dispersed their dominant accord,
And they are melted by the burnished sword.
Grim captains made them drink Death's cup of ill,
Until their skulls the blood-bathed streets did fill,
And from their dwellings seized the wealth
they'd gained, ...

Two centuries later, the Moroccan cleric al-Maghili (d. 1505), referring to the Jews as "brothers of apes" (just as Muhammad, the sacralized prototype, had addressed the Banu Qurayza), who repeatedly blasphemed the Muslim prophet, and whose overall conduct reflected their hatred of Muslims, fomented, and then personally lead, a Muslim pogrom (in ~ 1490) against the Jews of the southern Moroccan oasis of Touat, plundering and killing them en masse, and destroying their synagogue in neighboring Tamantit. [558] An important Muslim theologian whose writings influenced Moroccan religious attitudes towards Jews into the 20th century, al-Maghili also declared in verse, "Love of the Prophet, requires hatred of the Jews." [559]

Mordechai Hakohen (1856-1929) was a Libyan Talmudic scholar and auto-didact anthropologist who composed an ethnographic study of North African Jewry in the early 20th century. Hakohen describes the overall impact on the Jews of the Muslim jihad conquest and rule of North Africa, thusly: [560]

> *They [also] pressed the Jews to enter the covenant of the Muslim religion. Many Jews bravely chose death. Some of them accepted under the threat of force, but only outwardly...Others left the region, abandoning their wealth and property and scattering to the ends of the earth. Many stood by their faith, but bore an iron yoke on their necks. They lowered themselves to the dust before the Muslims, lords of the land, and accepted a life of woe — carrying no weapons, never mounting an animal in the presence of a Muslim, not wearing a red headdress, and following other laws that signaled their degradation.*

What follows is a preliminary, incomplete sampling of pogroms and mass murderous violence against Jews living under Islamic rule, across space and time, all resulting from the combined effects of jihadism, general anti-dhimmi, and/or specifically antisemitic motifs in Islam: [561] 6,000 Jews massacred in Fez in 1033; hundreds of Jews slaughtered in Muslim Cordoba between 1010 and 1015; 4,000 Jews killed in Muslim riots in Grenada in 1066, wiping out the entire community; the Berber Muslim Almohad depredations of Jews (and Christians) in Spain and North Africa between 1130 and 1232, which killed tens of thousands, while forcibly converting thousands more, and subjecting the forced Jewish converts to Islam to a Muslim Inquisition; the murderous persecutions of the Jews of Egypt by al-Hakim during the early 11th century, one of which was timed for Passover in 1012; Jews in Alexandria and Cairo being pogromed and plundered in 1047, 1168, 1265, and 1324; and Sultan Baybars in the 13th century blaming Jews for starting a plague, and subjecting them to extortion, massacre, and expulsion; [562] the 1291 pogroms in Baghdad and its environs, which killed (at least) hundreds of Jews; the 1465 pogrom against the Jews of Fez; the late 15th century pogrom against the Jews of the Southern Moroccan oasis town of Touat; the 1679 pogroms against, and then expulsion of 10,000 Jews from Sanaa, Yemen to the unlivable, hot and dry Plain of Tihama, from which only 1,000 returned alive, in 1680, 90% having died from exposure; recurring Muslim anti-Jewish violence — including pogroms and forced conversions — throughout the 17th, 18th and 19th centuries, which rendered areas of Iran (for example, Tabriz) Judenrein; the 1834 pogrom in Safed where raging Muslim mobs killed and grievously wounded hundreds of Jews; the 1888 massacres of Jews in Isfahan and Shiraz, Iran; the 1910 pogrom in Shiraz; the pillage and destruction of the Casablanca, Morocco ghetto in 1907; the pillage of the ghetto of Fez Morocco in 1912; the late August, 1929, anti-Jewish pogrom in Hebron, [563] fomented by Hajj Amin el-Husseini, then Mufti of Jerusalem, and his minions (via statements such as, "..he who kills a Jew is assured a place in the next world" [564]), that caused the slaughter of some 70 Jews, including at least a dozen women and 3 children under the age of five; the government sanctioned anti-Jewish pogroms by Muslims in Turkish Eastern Thrace during June-July, 1934 which ethnically cleansed at least 3000 Jews; and the series of pogroms, expropriations, and finally mass expulsions of some 900,000 Jews from Arab Muslim nations, beginning in 1941 in Baghdad (the murderous "Farhud," during which 600 Jews were murdered, and at least 12,000 pillaged) — eventually involving cities and towns in Egypt, Morocco, Libya, Syria, Aden, Bahrain, and culminating in 1967 in Tunisia — that accompanied the planning and creation of a Jewish state, Israel, on a portion of the Jews' ancestral homeland.

The rise of Jewish nationalism, Zionism, has posed a predictable, if completely unacceptable challenge to the Islamic order, jihad-imposed chronic dhimmitude for Jews, of unprecedented, even apocalyptic magnitude. As Bat Ye'or has explained, [565]

> ...because divine will dooms Jews to wandering and misery, the Jewish state appears to Muslims as an unbearable affront and a sin against Allah. Therefore it must be destroyed by Jihad.

Saul S. Friedman, also citing the emergence of Zionism (as an ideology anathema to the Islamic system of dhimmitude for Jews), concluded that this modern movement, and the creation of the Jewish State of Israel has, not surprisingly, unleashed a torrent of annihilationist Islamic antisemitism, "the brew of thirteen centuries of intolerance": [566]

> Since 1896, the development of modern, political Zionism has placed new tension on, and even destroyed, the traditional master-serf relationship that existed between Arab and Jew in the Middle East. An Arab world that could not tolerate the presence of a single, "arrogant" Jewish vizier in its history was now confronted by a modern state staffed with self-confident Jewish ministers.

Nowhere is this concatenation of doctrinal motifs, and historical events, more evident than present day Iran. The "Islamic Republic of Iran," a modern Shiite theocracy, has re-animated five centuries of religio-political desiderata: jihadism, dhimmitude, and Shiite Islamic Jew-hatred.

3

THE *DHIMMI* CONDITION FOR IRANIAN JEWRY UNDER SHIITE THEOCRATIC RULE: A HALF-MILLENNIAL PAST AS PROLOGUE

Living in the midst of a fanatical and hostile population, Jews in Persia are reduced to the last extremity of degradation. Nearly all trades are forbidden to them; everything they touch is considered defiled...There is very little justice in Persia for anybody—for the Jews there is none at all. Every possible exaction is practiced on them; nobody takes their part; and they live in appalling poverty, while their moral and physical degradation is beyond description.

— CLAUDE ANET, 1905 observations, recorded in his eyewitness travelogue, *Through Persia in a Motor-Car*

A 16ᵗʰ century European portrait of the founder of the Safavid dynasty, Shah Ismail I (1487-1524), now housed at the Ulfizi Gallery, Florence, Italy. http://bit.ly/1ezGE8g

At the outset of the 16ᵗʰ century, Iran's Safavid rulers formally established Shiite Islam as the state religion, while permitting a clerical hierarchy nearly unlimited control and influence over all aspects of public life.[567] The profound influence of the Shiite clerical elite, continued for almost four centuries, although interrupted, between 1722-1795 (during a period precipitated by [Sunni] Afghan invasion [starting in 1719], and the subsequent attempt to re-cast Twelver Shi'ism as simply another Sunni school of Islamic Law, under Nadir Shah),[568] through the later Qajar period (1795-1925), as characterized by E.G. Browne:[569]

> *The Mujtahids [an eminent, very learned Muslim jurist/scholar who is qualified to interpret the law] and Mulla [a scholar, not of Mujtahid stature] are a great force in Persia and concern*

themselves with every department of human activity from the minutest detail of personal purification to the largest issues of politics.

These Shiiite clerics emphasized the notion of the ritual uncleanliness (*najis*) of Jews, in particular, but also Christians, Zoroastrians, and others, as the cornerstone of inter-confessional relationships toward non-Muslims.[570] The impact of this *najis* conception was already apparent to European visitors to Persia during the reign of the first Safavid Shah, Ismail I (1502-1524). The Portuguese traveler Tome Pires observed (between 1512-1515), "Sheikh Ismail…never spares the life of any Jew,"[571] while another European travelogue notes, "…the great hatred (Ismail I) bears against the Jews…"[572] During the reign of Shah Tahmasp I (d. 1576), the British merchant and traveler Anthony Jenkinson (a Christian), when finally granted an audience with the Shah,[573]

…was required to wear 'basmackes' (a kind of over-shoes), because being a giaour [infidel], it was thought he would contaminate the imperial precincts…when he was dismissed from the Shah's presence, [Jenkinson stated] 'after me followed a man with a basanet of sand, sifting all the way that I had gone within the said palace'- as though covering something unclean.

Two examples of the restrictive codes for Jews conceived and applied during the Safavid period (1501-1725) are presented below,[574] in Table 1, and Table 2. Their persistent application into the Qajar period, which includes the modern era (1795-1925), is confirmed by the observations of the mid-19th century traveler Benjamin in Table 3,[575] and a listing of the 1892 Hamadan edict conditions in Table 4.[576]

Table 1. <u>Behavior Code of Abul Hassan Lari (1622)</u>

1. Houses that are too high (higher than a Muslim's) must be lowered.

2. Jews may not circulate freely among the Believers

3. In their stores, Jews must sit on low stools, in order they not see the purchaser's face.

4. Jews must wear a specially constructed hat of eleven colors.

5. Around this hat they must sew a yellow ribbon, three meters long.

6. Women must tie many little bells on their sandals

7. Jewish women must also wear a black chador

8. When a Jew speaks to a Muslim, he must humbly lower his head.

Table 2. The *Jam'i Abbasi* of al-Amili, Instituted by Shah Abbas I (1588-1629) and Administered in Some Measure Until 1925

1. Jews are not permitted to dress like Muslims

2. A Jew must exhibit a yellow or red "badge of dishonor" on his chest

3. A Jew is not permitted to ride on a horse

4. When riding on an ass, he must hang both legs on one side

5. He is not entitled to bear arms.

6. On the street and in the market, he must pass stealthily from a corner or from the side

7. Jewish women are not permitted to cover their faces

8. The Jew is restricted from establishing boundaries of private property.

9. A Jew who becomes a Muslim, is forbidden to return to Judaism.

10. Upon disclosure of a disagreement between Jew and Muslim, the Jew's argument has no merit.

11. In Muslim cities, the Jew is forbidden to build a synagogue

12. A Jew is not entitled to have his house built higher than a Muslim's

Table 3. Listing by Israel Joseph Benjamin (1818-1864) of the "Oppressions" Suffered by Persian Jews, During the Mid-19th Century

1. Throughout Persia the Jews are obliged to live in a part of town separated from the other inhabitants; for they are considered as unclean creatures, who bring contamination with their intercourse and presence.

2. They have no right to carry on trade in stuff goods.

3. Even in the streets of their own quarter of the town they are not allowed to keep open any shop. They may only sell there spices and drugs, or carry on the trade of a jeweler, in which they have attained great perfection.

4. Under the pretext of their being unclean, they are treated with the greatest severity, and should they enter a street, inhabited by Mussulmans, they are pelted

by the boys and mob with stones and dirt.

5. For the same reason they are forbidden to go out when it rains; for it is said the rain would wash dirt off them, which would sully the feet of the Mussulmans.

6. If a Jew is recognized as such in the streets, he is subjected to the greatest of insults. The passers-by spit in his face, and sometimes beat him so unmercifully and is obliged to be carried home.

7. If a Persian kills a Jew, and the family of the deceased can bring forward two Mussulmans as witnesses to the fact, the murderer is punished by a fine of 12 tumauns (600 piastres); but if two such witnesses cannot be produced, the crime remains unpunished, even thought it has been publicly committed, and is well known.

8. The flesh of the animals slaughtered according to Hebrew custom, but as Trefe declared, must not be sold to any Mussulmans. The slaughterers are compelled to bury the meat, for even the Christians do not venture to buy it, fearing the mockery and insult of the Persians.

9. If a Jew enters a shop to buy anything, he is forbidden to inspect the goods, but must stand at respectful distance and ask the price. Should his hand incautiously touch the goods, he must take them at any price the seller chooses for them.

10. Sometimes the Persians intrude into the dwellings of the Jews and take possession of whatever pleases them. Should the owner make the least opposition in defense of his property, he incurs the danger of atoning for it with his life.

11. Upon the least dispute between a Jew and a Persian, the former is immediately dragged before the Achund [Muslim cleric] and, if the complainant can bring forward two witnesses, the Jew is condemned to pay a heavy fine. If he is too poor to pay this penalty in money, he must pay it in his person. He is stripped to the waist, bound to a stake, and receives forty blows with a stick. Should the sufferer utter the least cry of pain during this proceeding, the blows already given are not counted, and the punishment is begun afresh.

12. In the same manner, the Jewish children, when they get into a quarrel with those of the Mussulmans, are immediately lead before the Achund [Muslim cleric], and punished with blows.

13. A Jew who travels in Persia is taxed in every inn and every caravanserai he enters. If he hesitates to satisfy any demands that may happen to be made on him, they fall upon him, and maltreat him until he yields to their terms.

14. If, as already mentioned, a Jew shows himself in the street during the three days of Katel (feast of the mourning for the death of the Persian founder of the

religion of Ali) he is sure to be murdered.

15. Daily and hourly new suspicions are raised against the Jews, in order to obtain excuses for fresh extortion; the desire of gain is always the chief incitement to fanaticism.

Table 4. Conditions Imposed Upon the Jews of Hamadan, 1892

1. The Jews are forbidden to leave their houses when it rains or snows [to prevent the impurity of the Jews being transmitted to the Shiite Muslims]

2. Jewish women are obliged to expose their faces in public [like prostitutes].

3. They must cover themselves with a two colored izar (an izar is a big piece of amterial with which eastern women are obliged to cover themselves when leaving their houses].

4. The men must not wear fine clothes, the only material being permitted them being a blue cotton fabric.

5. They are forbidden to wear matching shoes.

6. Every Jew is obliged to wear a piece of red cloth on his chest.

7. A Jew must never overtake a Muslim on a public street.

8. He is forbidden to talk loudly to a Muslim.

9. A Jewish creditor of a Muslim must claim his debt in a quavering and respectful manner.

10. If a Muslim insults a Jew, the latter must drop his head and remain silent.

11. A Jew who buys meat must wrap and conceal it carefully from Muslims.

12. It is forbidden to build fine edifices.

13. It is forbidden for him to have a house higher than that of his Muslim neighbor.

14. Neither must he use plaster for whitewashing.

15. The entrance of his house must be low.

16. The Jew cannot put on his coat; he must be satisfied to carry it rolled under his arm.

17. It is forbidden for him to cut his beard, or even to trim it slightly with scissors.

18. It is forbidden for Jews to leave the town or enjoy the fresh air of the countryside.

19. It is forbidden for Jewish doctors to ride on horseback [this right was generally forbidden to all non-Muslims, except doctors].

20. A Jew suspected of drinking spirits must not appear in the street; if he does he should be put to death immediately.

21. Weddings must be celebrated in the greatest secrecy.

22. Jews must not consume good fruit.

A letter (dated October, 27, 1892) by S. Somekh of The Alliance Israelite Universelle, regarding the Hamadan edict, provides this context: [577.]

> *The latter [i.e., the Jews] have a choice between automatic acceptance, conversion to Islam, or their annihilation. Some who live from hand to mouth have consented to these humiliating and cruel conditions through fear, without offering resistance; thirty of the most prominent members of the community were surprised in the telegraph office, where they had gone to telegraph their grievances to Teheran. They were compelled to embrace the Muslim faith to escape from certain death. But the majority is in hiding and does not dare to venture into the streets...*

The latter part of the reign of Shah Abbas I (1588-1629) was marked by progressively increasing measures of anti-Jewish persecution, from the strict imposition of dress regulations, to the confiscation (and destruction) of Hebrew books and writings, culminating in the forced conversion of the Jews of Isfahan, the center of Persian Jewry. [578] Walter Fischel elaborates on the exploits of two renegade Jewish converts to Islam, Abul Hasan Lari (of Lar), and Simon Tob Mumin of Isfahan. Lari was instrumental in having the Shiite authorities enforce restrictive headdress and badging regulations as visible signs of discrimination and humiliation. Lari succeeded in having these regulations applied to Jews as confirmed by the accounts of European travelers to Iran. For example, Jean de Thevénot (1633-1667) commented that Jews were required, [579]

> *To wear a little square piece of stuff two or three fingers broad... it had to be sewn to their labor gown and it matters not what that piece be of, provided that the color be different from that of the clothes to which it is sewed.*

And when the British physician John Fryer visited Lar in 1676, he noted that,

"...the Jews are only recognizable by the upper garment marked with a patch of different color." [580]

However the renegade Abul Hasan Lari's "mission" **foreshadowed more severe hardships imposed upon the Jews because of** *their image as sorcerers and practitioners of black magic,* **which was** *"as deeply embedded in the minds of the [Muslim] masses as it had been in medieval Europe."* **[emphasis added]** [581] The consequences of these bigoted superstitions were predictable: [582]

> *It was therefore easy to arouse their [the Muslim masses] fears and suspicions at the slightest provocation, and to accuse them [the Jews] of possessing cabalistic Hebrew writings, amulets, talismans, (segulot, goralot, and refu'ot), which they [the Jews] were using against the Islamic authorities. Encouraged by another Jewish renegade, Siman Tob Mumin from Isfahan, who denounced his co-religionists to the authorities, the Grand Vizier was quick in ordering the confiscation of all Hebrew cabalistic writings and having them thrown into the river.*

These punitive measures in turn forebode additional persecutions which culminated in the Jews of Isfahan being forcibly converted to Islam toward the end of Abbas I's rule. Moreover, even when Isfahan's Jews allowed living to return to Judaism under Shah Safi, they continued to live under the permanent threat posed by the "law of apostasy," till the late 19th century. [583]

> *One of the most dangerous measures which threatened the very existence of the Jewish community in Isfahan and elsewhere was the so-called "law of apostasy" promulgated at the end of Abbas I's rule and renewed in the reign of Abbas II. According to this law, any Jew or Christian becoming a Muslim could claim the property of his relatives, however distant. This decree, making the transfer of goods and property a reward for those who became apostates from their former religion, became a great threat to the very survival of the Jews. **While the Christian population in Isfahan protested, through the intervention of the Pope, and the Christian powers in Europe, against the injustice of this edict, there did not arise a defender of the rights of Jews in Persia.** [emphasis added] Although the calamity which this law implied was lessened by the small number of Jewish apostates who made use of this inducement, it was a steady threat to the existence of Jewish community life and brought about untold hardship. It was only in the 19th century that leaders of European Jewry such as Sir Moses Montefiore and Adolph Cremieux took up the fight for their brethren in Persia against this discriminatory law.*

Apart from this legal discrimination, the Jews of Isfahan were particularly singled out for persecution and forced conversion in the seventeenth century. **It is reported that they were forced to profess Islam publicly; that many of their rabbis were executed, and that only under Shah Safi (1629-1642), the successor of Abbas I, were the Jews of Isfahan, after seven years of Marrano life, permitted to return publicly to their Jewish religion**... [emphasis added]

After a relatively brief respite under Shah Saf'i (1629-1642), the severe persecutions wrought by his successor Shah Abbas II (1642-1666), nearly extinguished the Iranian Jewish community outright, as Fischel, explains: [584]

Determined to purify the Persian soil from the "uncleanliness" caused by the presence of non-believers (Jews and Christians in Isfahan) a group of fanatical Shi'ites obtained a decree from the young Shah Abbas II in 1656 which gave the Grand Vizier, I'timad ad-Daula, full power to force the Jews to become Muslims. In consequence, a wave of persecution swept over Isfahan and the other Jewish communities, a tragedy which can only be compared with the persecution of the Jews in Spain in the fifteenth century **[more appositely, the 13th century Muslim Almohad persecutions]** [585]

[the important eyewitness Jewish chronicles, the Kitab i Anusi]... describe in great detail how the Jews were compelled to abandon their religion, how they were drawn out of their quarters on Friday evening into the hills around the city and, after torture, 350 Jews are said to have been forced to [convert] to Islam. Their synagogues were closed and the Jews were lead to the Mosque, where they had to proclaim publicly the Muslim confession of faith, after which a Mullah, a Shi'a religious leader, instructed the newly-converted Muslims in the Qur'an and Islamic tradition and practice. These newly-converted Muslims had to break with the Jewish past, to allow their daughters to be married to Muslims, and to have their new Muslim names registered in a special Divan [council]. To test publicly their complete break with the Jewish tradition, some were even forced to eat a portion of camel meat boiled in milk. After their forced conversion, they were called New Muslims, Jadid al-Islam. They were then, of course, freed from the payment of the poll tax and from wearing a special headgear or badge.

The resistance of the Jews developed the phenomenon of

"Marranos", Anusim, and for years they lived a dual religious life by remaining secretly Jews while confessing Islam officially

Fischel also refers to the fact that contemporary Christians sources "confirm... with an astounding and tragic unanimity" the historical details of the Judaeo-Persian chronicle regarding the plight of the Jews of Isfahan (and Persia, more generally). [586] For example, the Armenian chronicler Arakel of Tabriz, included a chapter entitled, "History of the Hebrews of the City of Isfahan and of all Hebrews in the Territory of the Kings of Persia-the Case of Their Conversion to Islam." Arakel describes the escalating brutality employed to convert the hapless Jewish population to Islam—deportation, deliberately harsh exposure to the elements, starvation, imprisonment, and beatings. According to his account, the forced conversion of a rabbi marked a turning point in this ugly sequence of events: [587]

> *...after many words and promises, the Hakham's [rabbi's] sentence was pronounced. "If he does not embrace the Muslim faith, his stomach will be split open and he will be paraded through the town attached to a came; his property and his family would be consigned to pillage." The sentence given, a camel was brought, on which he was seated, the executioners came and bared his stomach, then they beat him with a naked sword, saying that either he apostatized or his stomach would be split open. Fear of death as well as affection for those close to him having lead him to weaken, he was made to pronounce his belief in the Muslim faith, and he was incorporated into the religion of Muhammad, which was cause of untold joy to the [Muslim] Persians... Those [Jews following their rabbi's forced conversion] who resisted were kept in prison; then they were brought back to the tribunal two or three times, even more often, and were urged to apostatize. By these actions, all the prisoners were lead to the religion of Muhammad; in the space of a month, three hundred and fifty men became Muslims. Ever since then, half the Jews having adopted the religion of the Persians, their nation lost what the Persians gained by their ascendancy over them: they were not even allowed to exist any longer, for every day they were dragged by force before the ehtim al-dawla [ranking Muslim official] and there they were forced to become Persians. The Persians put so much determination into their violence, aimed at conversion, that all Jews living in Isfahan... about three hundred families, adopted the religion of Muhammad.*

Additional confirmation is provided by eyewitness accounts from Carmelite priests [an enclosed Catholic order founded in the 12th century by Saint Bertold (d. after 1185) on Mount Carmel, Israel], residing in Isfahan: [588]

The Jews have been forced to become Muhammadans, and in order to 'purify' the city of Isfahan they are obliging all the Armenians who were near the city to go and live outside..." [February 24, 1657]

I cannot say all, but shall only tell you that the King of Persia has thrown off the mask, and let the venom he has in his heart be seen. He has ordered that all the Jews in his realm should become Muslims, to the number of 100,000. [May 12, 1657]

Everything is done by one of his (Abbas II's) ministers called Itimad-ud-Dauleh, who is very hostile to Catholics and Christians, whom he expelled from Isfahan. Armenians in Julfa and the Hebrews he has forced to become Muslims, and many of the Armenians at the present day are becoming Muslims, especially the sons, in order to inherit their father's property; because they have made an accursed law, by which all Christians who become Muslims inherit everything." [August 20, 1660]

Alexander de Rhodes (1591-1660), a Jesuit missionary, who spent the final decade of his life in Persia (dying in Isfahan), included a chapter in a book on these experiences, entitled, "The Jews in Persia compelled to become Muhammadans and the Christians delivered from the fear of a like evil". He describes the plight of the Jews during this time, as follows: [589]

The Jews had spread themselves all over Persia in far greater numbers than might be supposed, and were leading a most peaceable existence without any suspicion of the terrible misfortune which was hanging over their heads. It came as an unexpected blow and threw them into dreadful consternation when, all of a sudden, an edict from the King was issued and published in every place in Persia commanding them, on pain of death, to abjure the Jewish religion and profess, thenceforth, that of Muhammad.

The terror and consternation recorded in Scripture (Esther iii and iv), which the ancestors of this unhappy nation suffered long ago, when Haman, their cruel enemy, caused the fatal decree obtained from the King against them to be proclaimed throughout this same kingdom, may be taken as a picture of the fear and anguish experienced by these, their descendants, at the first news of this edict.

Portrait of Allamah al-Majlisi, opaque watercolor on paper
~1670-80, http://bit.ly/1ffepSM

Mohammad Baqer Majlisi (d. 1699), the highest institutionalized clerical officer under both Shah Sulayman (1666-1694) and Shah Husayn (1694-1722), [590] is recognized as the most influential cleric of the Safavid Shiite theocracy in Persia. By design, he wrote many works in Persian to disseminate key aspects of the Shiite ethos among ordinary persons.

Dwight M. Donaldson's landmark (and very sympathetic) 1933 study of Shi'ism, included this panegyric on al-Majlisi: [591]

> *Mulla Muhammad Bakir-i-Majlisi was the last and the greatest theologian of the Safavid period. Thorough and diligent as a scholar, he has the distinction also of having perceived that*

the masses should be reached in their own language. While his monumental work on the traditions is in Arabic, the Bilharu'l Anwar [Bihar al anwar] ("Oceans of Light"), he managed to put the bulk of that vast amount of material about the Prophet and the Imams into a series of readable manuals in Persian. **His remarkable success in thus making the sources of the Shi'ah faith intelligible to the people of Persia in their own language has made him undoubtedly the most influential of all the Shi'ah theologians.** *He died in 1699.*

A 2005 analysis by Rainer Brunner observed, [592]

Already contemporary Western travelers at the end of the seventeenth century noticed the extraordinary position of this scholar and gave some descriptions of his power

Brunner concluded: [593]

al-Majlisi's influence in the political sphere may be compared only with that of [Ayatollah] Khomeini in the twentieth century.

In his magnum opus *Bihar al-anwar* ("Oceans of Light"), Majlisi clarifies the two aspects of the People of the Book's ostensible "impurity." The first concerns "spiritual impurity" (*najasa ma'nawiyya*) caused by **"their essential nastiness, and the corruption of their beliefs"** (*khubth batinihim wa-su'i it'tiqadihim*). The second aspect flows logically from the first: the concrete, physical impurity, frequently called "juridical impurity" (*najasa shar'iyya* [Sharia]), that is, an impurity defined by legal prescriptions. [594] Majlisi's treatise, "*Lightning Bolts Against the Jews*", was written in Persian, and despite its title, was actually an overall guideline to anti-*dhimmi* regulations for all non-Muslims within the Shiite theocracy. [594a] Al-Majlisi, in this treatise, describes the standard humiliating requisites for non-Muslims living under the Sharia, first and foremost, the blood ransom *jizya* poll tax, based on Koran 9:29. He then enumerates six other restrictions relating to worship, housing, dress, transportation, and weapons (specifically, i.e., to render the *dhimmis* defenseless), before outlining the unique Shiite impurity or "najis" regulations, as per their "juridical impurity." It is these latter najis prohibitions which lead Anthropology Professor Laurence Loeb (who studied and lived within the Jewish community of Southern Iran in the early 1970s) to observe, "Fear of pollution by Jews led to great excesses and peculiar behavior by Muslims." [595] According to al-Majlisi, [596]

And, that they should not enter the pool while a Muslim is bathing at the public baths...It is also incumbent upon Muslims that they should not accept from them victuals with which they had come into contact, such as distillates , which cannot be purified.   In something can be purified, such as clothes, if they are dry, they can be accepted, they are clean. But if they [the dhimmis] had come into contact with those cloths in moisture they should be rinsed with water after being obtained. As for hide, or that which has been made of hide such as shoes and boots, and meat, whose religious cleanliness and lawfulness are conditional on the animal's being slaughtered [according to the Sharia], these may not be taken from them. Similarly, liquids that have been preserved in skins, such as oils, grape syrup, [fruit] juices, myrobalan [an astringent fruit extract used in tanning], and the like, if they have been put in skin containers or water skins, these should [also] not be accepted from them...It would also be better if the ruler of the Muslims would establish that all infidels could not move out of their homes on days when it rains or snows because they would make Muslims impure. [emphasis added]

Daniel Tsadik's 2007 study of Iranian Jewry during the 19th, through early 20th centuries, cites important Shiite treatises—Sayyid Muhammad Ali Khurasani Tabai's 1876 Najasat-i Ayniyah-yi-Kuffar ("The Real Impurity of the Infidels"), and Sheikh Muhammad Shariatmadar-Astrabadi's Najasat-i Ahl-i-Kitab ("The Impurity of the People of the Book"), published in 1908—as re-affirming that infidel Jews and Christians were *najis*. [597] These publications validate Tsadik's observation that, "the nineteenth [and early twentieth] century's most prominent jurists usually declared non-Muslims, specifically Jews, to be impure." [598]

Ignaz Goldziher believed that Shi'ism manifested this greater doctrinal intolerance toward non-Muslims, relative to Sunni Islam, because of the Shiites "literalist" conception of *najis*. [599]

On examining the legal documents, we find that the Shi'i legal position toward other faiths is much harsher and stiffer than that taken by Sunni Muslims. Their law reveals a heightened intolerance to people of other beliefs...Of the severe rule in the Qur'an (9:28) that 'unbelievers are unclean', Sunni Islam has accepted an interpretation that is as good as a repeal. Shi'i law, on the other hand, has maintained the literal sense of the rule; it declares the bodily substance of the unbeliever to be ritually unclean, and lists the touching of an unbeliever among the ten things that produce najasa, *[najis] ritual impurity.*

The enduring, applied nature of the fanatical *najis* regulation prohibiting *dhimmis* from being outdoors during rain and/or snow, is well established. For examples, see (Table 3, above) item 5 of Benjamin's list of "oppressions", and item 1 of Hamadan's 1892 (Table 4, above) anti-Jewish regulations, as well as this account provided by the missionary Napier Malcolm who lived in the Yezd area at the close of the 19th century: [600]

> *They [the strict Shi'as] make a distinction between wet and dry; only a few years ago it was dangerous for an Armenian Christian to leave his suburb and go into the bazaars in Isfahan on a wet [rainy] day. "A wet dog is worse than a dry dog."*

Moreover, the late Persian Jewish scholar Sarah (Sorour) Soroudi related this family anecdote: [601]

> *In his youth, early in the 20th century, my late father was eyewitness to the implementation of this regulation. A group of elder Jewish leaders in Kashan had to approach the head clergy of the town (a Shi'i community from early Islamic times, long before the Safavids, and known for its religious fervor) to discuss a matter of great urgency to the community. It was a rainy day and they had to send a Muslim messenger to ask for special permission to leave the ghetto. Permission granted, they reached the house of the clergy but, because of the rain, they were not allowed to stand even in the hallway. They remained outside, drenched, and talked to the mullah who stood inside next to the window.*
>
> *As late as 1923, the Jews of Iran counted this regulation as one of the anti-Jewish restrictions still practiced in the country.*

And this disconcerting 20th century anecdote from an informant living in Shiraz, was recounted by Loeb: [602]

> *When I was a boy, I went with my father to the house of a non-Jew on business. When we were on our way, it started to rain. We stopped near a man who had apparently fallen and was bleeding. As we started to help him, a Muslim akhond (theologian) stopped and asked me who I was and what I was doing. Upon discovering that I was a Jew, he reached for a stick to hit me for defiling him by being near him in the rain. My father ran to him and begged the akhond [Shiite Muslim cleric] to hit him instead.*

Far worse, the dehumanizing character of these popularized "impurity" regulations appears to have fomented recurring Muslim anti-Jewish violence, including pogroms and forced conversions, throughout the 17th, 18th and 19th centuries, as opposed to merely unpleasant, "odd behaviors" by individual Muslims towards Jews. Indeed, the oppression of Persian Jewry continued unabated, perhaps even intensifying, during both Safavid successors of Shah Abbas II, Shah Sulayman (1666-1694), and Shah Husayn (1694-1722).[603] Fischel highlights the prominent role played by the conception of *najis* in this sustained anti-*dhimmi* persecution: [604]

> *Day by day accounts of eyewitnesses establish beyond doubt how the notion of the ritual uncleanliness of the non-Muslims raged wildly all over the country, affecting Christians and Jews alike, and how the times of Shah Abbas II seem to have been revived.*

The Chronicle of the Carmelites includes these observations from 1678 and 1702, the 1678 entry recounting a particularly gruesome event: [605]

> *As all were apprehensive of a great barrenness of the soil from a protracted drought, a general dearness of corn being already experienced, everyone began to pour out prayers to God, each in the fashion of his own religion to implore the gift and succor of rain. But certain zealots of the Muhammadan faith, anxious as they had been unable to obtain anything from God by the rites and prayers enjoined on their own sect, lest some possibly more fortunate result should happen to be attributed to the votive offerings of another religion, complained to the king that the Jews and the Armenians by the unbounded license of their tenets had contrived the harm of the Muhammadan faith, and brought to naught the national religious rites with alien sacrileges. So the Shah [Suliaman], not in possession of his wits, admitting as a serious crime what he had heard exaggerated by the pretended sincerity of the false accusers, orders on the tenth day of the month of May (1678) those of the Jews, whose flight could be forestalled, to be seized and, with a hasty sentence of his furious temper, that the abdomens of their principal men should be ripped open-which was at once put into execution. **The bellies of the Rabbi or priest of the Hebrews and of two of their chief men having been slit open, they perished: and their corpses, thrown out into the great royal square, called the Maidan, lay for a week unburied, while for a burial permit a tax of four Tumans was being levied for each. Then for the rest if them (the Jews) fetters and chains were waived on payment of a fine of 600 Tumans (one Tuman is 15 scudi, or piastres). But the Armenians, who were involed with the same accusation and were in peril of being generally slaughtered, having a certain grandee to protect them with the king, obtained pardon by paying some hundreds of Tumans as the price of their remaining unharmed.** [emphasis added]*

> *...by the arbitrariness of the now reigning Shah Sultan Husain, whom the flattery of certain of his officials in giving him the*

*surname 'Din Parwar' [fosterer of the religion], i.e., 'zealous
promoter of religious law', has instigated, all races, subjects
of his dominions, are obliged to profess the Muhammadan
religion; [emphasis added] after having begun this by the forced
circumcision of the Gabrs [Zoroastrians] of the ancient Persian
belief, still remaining worshippers of the perpetual fire, who lived
in a very populous suburb above Julfa; passing on to wanting
to do the same to all the Christians of Julfa, some four or five
years back the decree for which would already have been issued
had it not been for its execution being prevented by the king's
grandmother who is the owner and overlord of Julfa: yielding
therefore to such powerful patronage for the time being, they
attacked the somewhat more remote villages, little short of a
hundred, by exactions of an intolerable grievousness, in order to
compel them to find escape from these by having recourse to the
immunity of Islam...*

The overthrow of the Safavid dynasty was accompanied by an initial period of
anarchy and rebellion.[606] A contemporary Jewish chronicler of these struggles,
Babai ibn Farhad, lamented, "At a time when the Muhammadans fight amongst
each other, how much less safe were the Jews".[607] However, beyond this early
stage of instability, Fischel maintains, [608]

*Only the downfall of the Safavid dynasty, through the successful
invasion of the Afghans and the subsequent rise of a new
[relatively] tolerant ruler, Nadir Shah (1734-1747), saved the
Jews of Isfahan and the Jews of Persia as a whole from complete
annihilation.*

The advent of the Qajar dynasty in 1795 marked a return to Shi'ite theocratic
orthodoxy. Thus, according to Fischel, [609]

*Since the religious and political foundations of the Qajar dynasty
were but a continuation of those of the Safavids, the 'law of
apostasy' and the notion of the ritual uncleanliness of the Jews
remained the basis of the attitude toward the Jews.*

*The Jew being ritually unclean, had to be differentiated from
the believer externally in every possible way. This became the
decisive factor making the life of the Jews in the 19th century
an uninterrupted sequence of persecution and oppression. They
could not appear in public, much less perform their religious
ceremonies, without being treated with scorn and contempt by the
Muslim inhabitants of Persia.*

The early 19th century British historian of Persia, Sir John Malcom, who also sojourned there on several diplomatic missions, wrote that, [610]

> *The Jews in Persia, who are not numerous, cannot appear in public, much less perform their religious ceremonies with out being treated with contempt and scorn by the Mahomedans... [I]n Persia they [the Jews] live despised and in poverty*

European travelers confirm that the *najis* conception was applied to Jews with fanatical rigidity throughout 19th century Persia. Rabbi David d'Beth Hillel, who traveled in Persia during the reign of Shah Fath Ali (1797-1834), provided these characterizations, based on personal experience: [611]

> *They [the Shiites] do not eat with anyone of another nation, even touching their bread and liquids or fresh fruits; they consider it as defiled and will never eat it...[It is their belief] that all the other nations are unclean, that no one who believes in Mohammad ought to be well acquainted with them and ought not to touch their victuals- and only to be acquainted with them in trade... [Arriving one night at a village near Bashaka] nobody would receive me into their houses for any money I offered them, saying that the house would be defiled by my coming in, because they knew me to be a Jew and the same night was a very cold one and abundance of snow had fallen and it was impossible to sleep in the street. After many supplications, I gave half a rupee to be allowed to sleep in a stable among their cattle.*

There are many confirmatory 19th century reports of the strict application of *najis* regulations towards Jews. Table 3 (above) includes Benjamin's listing of mid-19th century "oppressions" related to *najis*. James Fraser noted that Jews were forbidden from using the public baths, [612] and Henry A. Stern further described how in the holy Shi'ite city of Qom, [613]

> *...the few [Jews] who are allowed to reside here come from Koshan [Kashan, in Isfahan province], Isfahan, and the ostentatious vocation which they pursue is peddling; but as the pious living in the religious atmosphere of so many descendants of the Prophet would be shocked at the idea of touching anything that has passed the hands of a defiled and impure Jew, they have had recourse to a more profitable traffic, the sale of spirituous liquors.*

In the late 19th century Napier Malcolm reported, [614] "It is more easy to get the Mussulmans to eat food with the Parsis than with the Jews, whose religion ranks higher than Zoroastrianism in the popular regard.", and Reverend Isaac Adams observed,[615] "Christians and Jews are not subject to decapitation as they are considered unclean by the Mohammedans and not sufficiently worthy of this privilege."

Regardless, Soroudi comments, [616]

> *The impurity of the non-Muslim and his belongings, however, never deterred Shi'ah Muslims from plundering Jewish or Zoroastrian quarters on the smallest pretext or as a result of clerical or official instigation.*

Rabbi d'Beth Hillel also described incidences of violent persecutions, including murder and forced conversions, directed at Persian Jews in Urmia and Shiraz: [617]

> *[From Urmia, 1826] A Mohammedan child being missing, the Persians accused the Jews of having murdered him in order to use his blood for the coming Passover (which was, however, a full five months away). Consequently, they rounded up all the Jews and removed them to prison, with the exception of their chief [Rabbi], he being a very old man and much respected...His children, however, were taken prisoner. One of the Jews was hewn in two in the gate of the town and the others were nearly beaten to death."*

> *"[Forced conversions in Shiraz]...some years ago a number of Jews turned Mohammedan owing to great oppression from the Mohammedans. They are not, however, connected with them in marriage, but with their own people, and it is the same in many parts of Persia where Jews have become Mohammedan by reason of great oppression.*

The missionary Asahel Grant further reported, [618]

> *During my residence in Ooroomiah, [Urmia] a Jew was publicly burned to death in the city by order of the governor, on an allegation of that pretended crime! [i.e., a blood libel] Naphtha was freely poured over him, the torch was applied, and the miserable man was instantly enveloped in flame!*

Fischel offers these observations based on the narrative of d'Beth Hillel, and additional eyewitness accounts, which describe the rendering of Tabriz, **Judenrein**, and the forced conversion of the Jews of Meshed to Islam: [619]

> *Due to the persecution of their Moslem neighbors, many once flourishing communities entirely disappeared. Maragha, for example, ceased to be the seat of a Jewish community around 1800, when the Jews were driven out on account of a blood libel. Similarly, Tabriz, where over 50 Jewish families are supposed to*

have lived, became Judenrein towards the end of the 18ᵗʰ century through similar circumstances.

The peak of the forced elimination of Jewish communities occurred under Shah Mahmud (1834-48), during whose rule the Jewish population in Meshed, in eastern Persia, was forcibly converted, an event which not only remained unchallenged by Persian authorities, but also remained unknown and unnoticed by European Jews

Reverend Joseph Wolff provided this contemporary travelogue account of the mid-19ᵗʰ century events in Meshed, including the practice of crypto-Judaism: [620]

The occasion was as follows: A poor woman had a sore hand. A Mussulman physician advised her to kill a dog and put her hand in the blood of it. She did so; when suddenly the whole population rose and said that they had done it in derision of their prophet. Thirty-five Jews were killed in a few minutes; the rest, struck with terror, became Mohammedans. They are now more zealous Jews in secret than ever, but call themselves Anusim, the Compelled Ones.

And Fischel wrote a modern analysis of the Meshed pogrom and forced conversions in 1949, which highlighted these details: [621]

The [Jewish] woman [see Wolff's account above] hired a Persian boy to catch a dog in the street and then kill it in her courtyard. Following a dispute about payment, the boy ran off in a rage. A rumor that the Jews had killed a dog on the holiest of holy days [the day of mourning for Husain, the grandson of Muhammad] and had even called it Husain to insult the Mohammedans. When this rumor reached the thousands assembled in mourning at the Mosque of the Imam Riza, hundreds of the devout, together with Shaikhs, Mullahs, Sayyids, and other spiritual leaders, rushed to the Jewish quarter. There they plundered, robbed, and burned. Soon the synagogue and the scrolls of the Law stood in flames; many scores of Jews were wounded and some thirty-five were left dead in the streets. The mob would have destroyed the entire Jewish quarter had not a group of priests given their word that the survivors would be converted to Islam. For the remaining Jews the only chance of survival was to recite the Moslem confession of faith. This they did, and on the following day they were officially accepted into Islam...They were now called, 'Jadid al-Islam', or 'neo-Moslem'. With this acceptance of Islam, the convert was immediately freed from all his previous restrictions; he was no

*longer required to wear a special hat or have his hair dressed in
a special way or wear any particular Jewish badge on his clothes,
nor was he required to pay the poll-tax (jizya). His 'uncleanliness'
was gone- he was now a Moslem among Moslems...The mosque
became the legal meeting place of the Jedidim. There, they were
under the supervision of the chief priest,* **the Mujtahid, who
exercised the dual role of instructor in Mohammedanism and
inquisitor for Islam** *[emphasis added]. He acted as the official
head of the Jews as well as their supreme judicial authority.
Demanding the diligent study of the Koran and the traditional
books, he forbade ritual slaughtering, circumcision on the 8th day,
ordered mixed marriages between Jedidim and Moslems, and
was empowered to grant permission for burial. In 1839, then, the
Jewish community in Meshed officially ceased to exist. Yet this
forced conversion could not extinguish Judaism in the hearts of
the Jedidim; the hope that they might one day return to their own
religion remained alive in them.*

During the nearly 50 year reign (1848-1896) of Nasr ad-Din Shah, reform efforts to
improve the plight of non-Muslims, in particular Jews, were opposed strenuously
and effectively by the Shi'ite clerical hierarchy. Accordingly, [622]

*...Under Nasr ad-Din Jews continued to suffer, not only in
consequence of the deep-rooted hatred against them and the
conception of ritual uncleanliness, but also as a result of legal
discrimination of a most severe nature. Thus the entire community
of Jews was held responsible for crimes and misdemeanors
committed by its individual members; the oath of a Jew was not
received in a court of justice; a Jew converted to the Muslim
religion could claim to be the sole inheritor of family property,
to the exclusion of all relatives who had not changed their
religion, thereby causing the greatest possible distress to those
Jews who preferred death to apostasy. In many towns the Jew was
prohibited from keeping a shop in the bazaars, while in addition
to the legal taxes the local authorities levied arbitrary exactions
on the Jews. Although the Jew had the nominal right of appeal to
a superior court of justice he did not exercise that right because of
the fear of vengeance of the lower tribunal. The life of a Jew was
not protected by law, inasmuch as the murderer of a Jew could
purchase immunity by payment of a fine.*

Loeb maintains that the Jews were also victimized by tax farming throughout
the 19th century, which reduced them, [623] "...to virtual serfdom." C.J. Wills, an
English physician who traveled widely in Iran from 1866-1881 while working

for the Indo-European Telegraph Department, illustrates this abusive practice in a contemporary late 19th century account: [624]

> *The principle is very simple. The Jews of a province are assessed at a tax of a certain amount. Someone pays this amount to the local governor together with a bribe; and the wretched Jews are immediately placed under his authority for the financial year. It is a simple speculation. If times are good, the farmer of the Jews makes a good profit; if they are bad he gains nothing, or may fail to extract from them as much as he has paid out of pocket- in that case, woe betide them. During the Persian famine the Jews suffered great straits before the receipt of subsidies sent from Europe by their co-religionists. The farmer of the Jewish colony in a great Persian city (of course a Persian Mohammedan) having seized their goods and clothes, proceeded, in the cold of Persian winter, to remove the doors and windows of their hovels and to wantonly burn them. The farmer was losing money, and sought thus to enforce what he considered his rights. No Persian pitied the unfortunates; they were Jews and so beyond the pale of pity. Every street boy raises his hand against the wretched Hebrew; he is beaten and buffeted in the streets, spat upon in the bazaar. The only person he can appeal to is the farmer of the Jews. From him, he will obtain a certain amount of protection if he be actually robbed of money or goods; not from the farmer's sense of justice, but because the complainant, were his wrongs unredressed, might be unable to pay his share of the tax.*

Wills also provides these acerbic descriptions of two of the most egregious forms of degradation, both public and private, suffered by the Jews throughout the 19th century: [625]

> *At every public festival—even at the royal salaam [salute], before the King's face—the Jews are collected, and a number of them are flung into the hauz or tank, that King and mob may be amused by seeing them crawl out half-drowned and covered with mud. The same kindly ceremony is witnessed whenever a provincial governor holds high festival: there are fireworks and Jews.*
>
> *When a Jew marries, a rabble of the Mahommedan ruffians of the town invite themselves to the ceremony, and, after a scene of riot and intoxication, not infrequently beat their host and his relations and insult the women of the community; only leaving the Jewish quarter when they have slept off the drink they have swallowed at their unwilling host's expense.*

Despite a number of direct, hopeful meetings between the Shah and prominent European Jews and Jewish organizations throughout Western Europe in 1873, Fischel concludes, [626]

> *The intervention of European Jewry in favor of their Persian brothers did not bring about the hoped-for improvement and scarcely lessened the persecution and suffering of the Jews after the return of the Shah from Europe.*
>
> *After his visit to Europe Nasr ad-Din issued a number of decrees and firmans which brought about some social and administrative changes in favor of the Jews, but the government was apparently too weak to prevent the recurrence of public outbreaks against the Jews. Even the law which provided that a Jew who turned Muslim had the right to claim the entire property of his family, although abolished in Teheran in 1883, was still in force in some provinces in the Persian empire as a result of the opposition of the clergy. In 1888, a massacre of the Jews occurred in Isfahan and Shiraz, which brought about intervention and investigation of the British consulate.*

Adler and Margalith's compilation of American diplomatic actions (and related correspondence) affecting the Jews, independently confirms Fischel's conclusions. In their introduction to the prevailing conditions for Persian Jews through the end of the 19th century, Adler and Margalith observe, [627]

> *[F]or centuries, the Persian Jews had been kept at such a low condition as to have become inarticulate. They did not dare to complain against the ruling authorities for fear of aggravating a condition already bad enough. As late as 1894 the Jews of Persia had to wear a patch on their clothes to signify their origin. Jews who, as a result of continuous persecution, changed their religion and were converted to Mohammedanism or Christianity, soon discovered that their situation did not improve because of their conversion. And it is because of the continued discrimination against Jewish converts that the Jewish question in Persia first appeared in the United States diplomatic correspondence.*

Demonstrating that even Jewish converts to Islam did not escape persecution, they cite the correspondence between an American medical missionary (Dr. Holmes), stationed in Hamadan, and John Tyler, U.S. vice-consul general at Tehran. [628]

> *[T]he occasional interventions of the American missionaries and the promises they extracted from the Persian officials could not change a condition inherently unfavorable to Jews. The lawless*

> *spirit of the people, the failure of the ruling authorities to control the situation, and the cupidity of the populace, all combined to make the Jews the most available outlet for the lowest passions of men. Again it must be pointed out that those Jews who had forsaken the religion of their fathers with the hope of securing safety for themselves and their property failed utterly to achieve their aims. In a letter to Mr. Tyler, dated September 25, 1896, Dr. Holmes refers to the condition of the Moslem converts as follows:*

> *"The fact that the man charged with the crime was a Moslem and had forsaken the religion of his fathers makes no difference at all in the eyes of the people who are after loot and not justice. There has been much pressure brought upon the Jews in the past to make Moslems of them. But it seems they have to bear the curse of their nationality and responsibility even for those who have turned away from their faith."*

> *Dr. Holmes refers here specifically to a case that happened at Hamadan when personal enemies trumped up charges against a Jew, who after the disturbances of 1892, had entered the Moslem faith. At the trial, a large crowd of Moslems appeared and threatened the Ameer [local Muslim authority] that unless the accused was put to death, the whole Jewish community would be massacred. The innocent Moslem Jew was executed, and his home and those of his neighbors were broken into, pillaged, and burnt.*

U.S. vice-consul general John Tyler's own terse assessment of the plight of Persian Jews (*not* written from the perspective of one with "philo-semitic" sentiments), was recorded in correspondence dated October 7, 1896: [629]

> *Ever since the establishment of the Mohammedan faith in Persia the dominant class has always manifested a bitter spirit of animosity toward them [the Jews]...In Hamadan the conflict between the civil and priestly [Muslim] powers has given the disorderly class occasion to commit every kind of excess at the expense of the Jews, in which they have had the connivance if not the actual support of the priests [Muslim clerics]; and the central government, when they have made a show of authority, have rarely punished the ringleaders of disorder or stamped out the elements of disaffection, consequently they are always ready to break forth when the conditions are favorable.*

Such persecutions extended to Tehran, the Persian capital. U.S. Minister to Persia, Alexander McDonald wrote to U.S. Secretary of State, John Sherman, in a letter dated May 17, 1897, [630]

[Y]esterday, I interposed unofficially in behalf of the Jews of this city [Tehran], who, by concerted action, were subjected to riot and mob violence by the Mohammedans.

Despite a series of equivocations (and some statements which reflect cognitive dissonance), Tsadik's analysis of Iranian Jews during the 19th century is remarkably consistent with the earlier accounts of Fischel and Loeb, at whom, he nevertheless, levels rather incoherent "criticism." For example, Fischel commented aptly (in a 1950 essay), "the peculiar economic status of the [Iranian] Jews was a result of their centuries-long oppressions and persecution." [631] Apparently concerned Fischel's statement lacked appropriate "nuance," Tsadik weighed in, "Even if this comment is partly accurate, it assumes, to some extent, a static situation." [632] But (one page) prior to leveling this criticism, Tsadik, quoting 19th century eyewitness accounts, wrote, [633]

Given their low status, Jews were permitted to pursue vocations that were shunned by Muslims as socially despised, or regarded as immoral. The Jews were "expected to undertake dirty work of every kind." "When anything very filthy is to be done a Jews is sent for." "Jews are saved, all over Persia, to perform the most loathsome and degrading offices." Examples include dyeing, which sometimes involved strong odors, doing scavenger work, and cleaning excrement pits. Some Jews were also singers, musicians, and dancers—all activities regarded as worthy of only dissolute persons.

And just (one page) after his critique of Fischel, Tsadik, noted further the perils associated with the Jews' very limited professional avenues to "social mobility": [634]

Examination of Iranian Jews' professions not only indicates their economic basis, but also reflects their usually socially inferior status within the larger Muslim society...Jews were frequently reduced to vocations religiously illicit for Muslims, socially despised, or regarded as immoral...

Some Jewish movement from socially debased functions to new professions and economic spheres usually controlled by Muslims economically, and this may have resulted in increased levels of mistreatment and persecution. Although Jews comprised a statistically insignificant portion of Iranian society, their relatively high presence in some major cities enhanced their visibility—for better or worse—in the eyes of the Muslim majority.

Tsadik acknowledges "steps toward change...were wavering and hesitant." [635] There was no "transformation" of the Jews status because it "was resisted by indigenous elements," **prominently**, "members of the ulama [clerics]," who[636]

> *rejected improvement of the Jews' situation and in fact called to reinforce their secondary status under Islam for religious, social, economic, and political reasons. The government found itself maneuvering between **foreign pressure to improve the Jews' condition** and **pressure from local Shi'i elements calling for the preservation of old indigenous practices and the Islamic worldview**. The Jews' political status improved to a limited extent, but their religious and social status generally remained the same.*

However, Tsadik later concedes,[637]

> *[T]his erratic and restricted amelioration process did not satisfy the Jews, nor was it clear enough for them to discern. To the Jews, their situation may have seemed, if anything, to be changing for the worse.*

He then argues against conferring the "sole" blame for the anti-Jewish religious incitement upon the Shiite clerics noting, "it was not **only** the ulama who abused the Jews; other elements, such as certain government officials were also heavily involved."[638] Tsadik then proceeds from this straw man argument of the Shiite clerics as "sole" causative agents to demonstrate, albeit inadvertently, how mainstream Shiite anti-Jewish doctrine, as inculcated by the preponderance of Shiite clerics, were indeed the major ostensible (and chronic) contributors to the Jews' plight.[639]

> *Apparently, **a handful actively assisted the Jews**. To blame all the ulama for the situation of the Jews would be incorrect. **With regard to those ulama who did incite against the Jews—and there seem to have been many of them—there can be no doubt that their activity should be partly attributed to certain <u>deeply rooted mainstream Shi'i religious concepts</u> that dated back to earlier centuries**...*

Tsadik reinforces this salient point in both his own previous elucidation of the nexus between Shi'ism's canonical Jew-hatred, and najis-punctuated dhimmitude (i.e., chapter 2, "Shi'i Legal Attitudes Toward the Jews"), and the study's final observations from its concluding chapter 5. Riveting on the quintessence of Shi'isms's combined theological and juridical doctrines pertaining to Jews, Tsadik identifies as "most important" the[640]

> *impurity laws, which penetrate deep into the Shi'i public psyche, as well as the inheritance and jizyah laws. The need to humiliate the Jews, in accordance with the saghar [see earlier discussion of*

Allamah Tabatabai's gloss on Koran 9:29 [641] component of the dhimmah regulations, seems to have been ubiquitous.

He then summarizes other key features of this debasing and hateful dogma—consistent with the previous discussions herein of Sunni and Shiite Islam's shared motifs of canonical Islamic Jew-hatred—which were manifested in the legal and social status of Iranian Jews. [642]

Both the inheritance and the jizyah laws imposed significant economic hardships on the Jews, while other dhimmah regulations debased them socially and distinguished them from the Muslim majority. Overall, these laws and this worldview regarded Jews as second-class subjects. Although they occasionally received protection [i.e., typically via foreign consuls intervening on their behalf with Iran's rulers], the Jews were subjected to limitations and an inferior status. More than anything, the dhimmah regulations and the laws applicable to the Jews usually reflect a basic inequality between Jew and Shi'i, and generally between the religious minorities and the Shi'i majority.

Shi'i attitudes toward the Jews and Judaism were expressed not only in the realm of laws but also in written and live polemics criticizing the Jews and Judaism. Based on earlier Shi'i and Sunni literature, late eighteenth- and nineteenth-century Shi'i polemicists regarded the Jews as deviating fro the right path and adhering to false notions. The Jews displayed the trait of stubborn obstinacy toward their own major prophet, frequently rebelling against Moses as attested in the Torah. They opposed other prophets, and in fact, killed some prophets sent to guide them. According to this line, the Jews rejected the Truth, and persistently denied God's prophets and indubitable proofs. They went further and devised an oral law that was an illegitimate innovation, whereas their code could at best have predicted the emergence of Muhammad and the twlve Shi'i imams and the supremacy of Islam. The Torah was essentially repealed (naskh; [abrogated]) in the face of later and more complete revelations...[T]he version of the Torah sanctified by contemporary Jews and Christians is not even the one originally revealed. For various reasons, the original text of the Torah and its meaning were not preserved for posterity; the Torah was altered and erroneously understood. The Jews misunderstood their Torah and therefore misinterpreted God's will; with the passage of time they introduced devant rituals and customs as well as flawed beliefs.

The status of the Torah as an abrogated and altered text influenced or implied the status of the Torah's followers. Even if the Jews had once been God's beloved ones, they had lost this standing a long time ago. Together with the Shi'i dhimmah, and other laws and legal concepts that pertained to the Jews, these views embodied the Imami Shi'i [Twelver Shiite] view of Judaism and the Jews during the late eighteenth and nineteenth century. According to Shi'i law and doctrine—which, broadly speaking, was shared by Sunni Islam—the Jews were regarded as on a lower level than that of Muslims.

Tsadik's concluding chapter fittingly (if somewhat redundantly) entitled, "Reassertion of the Dhimmah," identifies the Shiite clergy as being at the "forefront" of those "social groups" most assiduously enforcing the system of dhimmitude upon the Jews: [643]

At the forefront of such social groups were some members of the Shi'i clergy. Throughout the period under discussion, these ulama gradually became more assertive and more involved in religious, political, and socio-economic matters. One of these was the status of religious minorities...they strove to apply the traditional Muslim dhimmah concepts, according to which Jews were immutably inferior to Muslims. Employing Islamic phraseology, some of the ulama vindicated and furthered the regulation and subordination of religious minorities to Islamic law...Their involvement with the Jews' lives was yet another avenue through which they could intervene in, and exert influence on, social affairs. More specifically, calling for the implementation of Islam could stabilize or enhance their prestige, power, and influence in society. At times, their incitement against the Jews was a means of challenging the authorities, thus hoping for an increased following. Other social elements occasionally assisted those ulama who called for the imposition of the dhimmah laws on the Jews. The unquantified Muslim "mob" or "roughs" participated in anti-Jewish activity to gain possible booty, whereas some merchants sought to deal an economic blow to their Jewish competitors...[F]earing agitation, rancor, and upheaval, the government had to take local practices and Muslim concepts into account.

All these observations about the plight of Iranian Jewry, must be considered against the backdrop of their insignificant demographic presence at the outset of the 20th century. Although noting, "their percentage in some of the major cities was occasionally higher than in Iran as a whole," [644] Tsadik, relying upon Alliance Israélite Universelle 1903-1904 census tabulations, concluded, [645]

This, then, leaves us with the likely figure of at least 40,000 Jews at the start of the twentieth century. The population of Iran at that time is estimated at about ten million. If these figures are correct, the Jews represented at least **0.4 percent of the total population. Numerically, the Jews were thus a relatively negligible component of Iranian society.**

The reigns of Muzafar ad-Din Shah (1896-1907; following the assassination of Nasr ad-Din) , Shah Muhammad (1907-1909), and Shah Ahmad (1909-1925), included a nascent constitutional movement, which again aroused hopes for the elimination of religious oppression against Persian Jews and other non-Muslims. However, [646]

... neither the Jews nor the Armenian Christians or Parsee Zoroastrian minorities were yet permitted to send a deputy of their own group to parliament. At first the Jews were compelled to agree to be represented by a Muslim...Unfortunately, three months after the convening of Parliament Shah Muzaffar ad-din died, and under Shah Muhammad (1907-1909) the constitutional movement very quickly disappointed the high hopes which the liberal elements of the Muslims and the Jews in Persia had entertained. Anti-Jewish riots became common, particularly in Kermanshah in 1909...

Jean Schopfer, nom de plume Claude Anet (d. 1931), was a tennis player who reached two singles finals at the Amateur French Championships, winning in 1892 and losing in 1893. Schopfer/ Anet's *Through Persia in a Motor-Car,* [647] published in English translation during 1907, chronicled his ~1905 first hand observations of the chronic plight of Iran's Jews under Iran's Qajar dynasty Shiite theocracy, despite the alleged "Constitutional movement" era reforms. Anet's blunt travelogue noted the continued application of Shiite Islam's "najis" or impurity regulations, and the Jews overall vulnerable, and degraded status. [648]

Living in the midst of a fanatical and hostile population, Jews in Persia are reduced to the last extremity of degradation. Nearly all trades are forbidden to them; everything they touch is considered defiled. They cannot even live in the house of a Mussulman. There is very little justice in Persia for anybody—for the Jews there is none at all. Every possible exaction is practiced on them; nobody takes their part; and they live in appalling poverty, while their moral and physical degradation is beyond description.

Apropos of Fischel's observation about the "commonality" of anti-Jewish riots, David Littman has provided the full translation of an Alliance Israélite Universelle report of the 1910 Shiraz pogrom which was precipitated by two false accusations against the Jewish community: desecrating copies of the Qur'an by placing them in cesspools (latrines); and the ritual murder of a child. [649]

> *(M. Nataf, October 31, 1910)* **What happened yesterday in the Jewish quarter exceeds, in its horror and barbarity, anything that the most fertile imagination can conceive. In the space of a few hours, in less time than it would take to describe it, 6,000 men, women, children and the elderly were stripped of everything they possessed.** *[emphasis added]*

> *In relating the dreadful incidents which occurred yesterday, the sequence of events will be followed wherever possible... First a few retrospective details: about three weeks ago, some scavengers were busy cleaning out the cesspools of a Jewish house when they brought to light an old book, a few pages of which were unsoiled and which was recognized as a Koran...*

> *On the first day of the festival of Succoth, some Jews were returning home from synagogue in the morning when they noticed at the entrance of their house a veiled Muslim woman holding a parcel under her arm. As soon as she saw them approaching, she hurriedly threw her parcel into the cesspool... then she ran away. The parcel was hastily pulled out. Once again, it was a Koran. It was placed in a safe place and I was informed. This time, I considered it necessary at least to acquaint the high priest of the city, Mirza Ibrahim, with the facts. I was not sure, in effect, that other Korans had not been thrown, likewise as the first ones, into Jewish houses without the knowledge of their inhabitants, and it was prudent for this dignitary to be informed, in case one of these books should be discovered and seized on as a pretext to molest the Jews. Mirza Ibrahim promised me his kindly assistance, should the occasion arise, and advised me to mention the incident as little as possible.*

> *On the eve of the next to last day of the festival, at around 10 o'clock in the evening, the house of the community's two chief rabbis was invaded by a gang of people without authorization. They were accompanied by a bazaar merchant who pretended that one of his children, a girl of four, had disappeared in this afternoon and was indubitably in the Jewish quarter, where she had been confined or killed in order to have her blood. The unfortunate rabbis, terrorized to a degree that may be imagined, swore that they were not aware that a Muslim child had strayed into the Jewish quarter and protested against such a monstrous*

accusation. The loutis ("good for nothings") withdrew after threatening to put the Jewish quarter to fire and sword if the little girl had not been found by noon the next day. On the morrow, I was informed that, on the previous day, the body of a child, assumed to be that of the little Muslim girl, missing six days beforehand, had been found one kilometer away from the city behind an old abandoned palace, one hundred meters from the Jewish cemetery; it was rumored abroad that Jews had killed her and that any Jew who ventured out of the quarter would be well and truly chastised...

I heard these details at the school where I was at the time, and there first perceived the clamor of the crowd, which was gradually gathering in front of the government palace and which, collecting around the body of the alleged little Muslim girl found close to the Jewish cemetery **(it was subsequently established that the body was that of a little Jewish boy buried eight days ago and disinterred, for the requirements of the cause, being completely putrefied and absolutely unrecognizable)** *[emphasis added] was accusing the Jews of having committed this heinous crime, for which it demanded vengeance.*

Then Cawan-el-Mulk, the temporary governor, having ordered his troopers to disperse the frenzied mob, they headed for the Jewish quarter, where they arrived at the same time as the soldiers sent by Nasr-ed-Dowlet. These latter, as if they were obeying an order, were the first to fling themselves at the Jewish houses, thereby giving the signal to plunder. **The carnage and destruction which then occurred for six to seven hours is beyond the capacity to describe…Not a single one of the Jewish quarter's 260 houses was spared.** *[emphasis added] Soldiery, loutis, sayyids [descendants of the prophet and/or Muslim dignitaries], even women and children, driven and excited, less by religious fanaticism than by a frenetic need to plunder and appropriate the Jews' possessions, engaged in a tremendous rush for the spoils. At one point, about a hundred men from the Kashgaïs tribe, who were in town to sell some livestock, joined the first assailants, thereby completing the work of destruction.*

The thieves formed a chain in the street. They passed along the line, carpets, bundles of goods, bales of merchandise…, anything, in a word, which was saleable. Anything which didn't have a commercial value or which, on account of its weight or size, could not be carried off was, in a fury of vandalism, destroyed and broken. The doors and windows of the houses were torn off their hinges and carried away or smashed to pieces. The rooms and cellars were literally ploughed up to see whether the substratum wasn't concealing some wealth.

But these fanatics weren't satisfied to rob the Jews of their possessions. They engaged in all sorts of violence against their persons. As soon as their quarter was stormed, the Jews fled in all directions, some to the houses of Muslim friends, others to the British Consulate, on to the terraces, and even into mosques. A few remained to try and defend their property. They paid for it with their lives or a serious injury. Twelve of them were killed in this way in the mêlée. Another fifteen were stabbed or hit with bludgeons or bullets from rifles or revolvers; they are in an alarming condition. A further forty sustained light injuries. An unlucky woman was wearing gold rings in her ears. A soldier ordered her to surrender them. She made haste to comply and had taken off one of the rings and was trying to remove the other when the impatient fanatic found it more expeditious to tear off the ear lobe together with the ring. Another woman was wearing around her neck a big silk braid to which was attached a small silver case containing some amulets. A louti tried to snatch it from her and, seeing that the braid held, cut it with his knife, making at the same time a deep gash in the flesh of the unfortunate Jewess. How many more such atrocious scenes have occurred, of which I have not yet heard!

In short the outcome of yesterday's events is as follows: 12 people dead and about 50 more or less seriously injured, whilst the five to six thousand people comprising Shiraz community now possess nothing in the world but the few atatters they were wearing when their quarter was invaded. *[emphasis added]*

What is striking, and appears strange, about these sad circumstances is the inertia of the local authorities, who seem to have done only one thing—encourage the soldiers, in conjunction with the populace, to attack and plunder the Jewish quarter...

Early this morning, I went to the Jewish quarter. How can I describe the scene of pitiful distress and frightful desolation which I witnessed? The streets, which, 48 hours previously, were full of the bustle of life and the most intense activity, now give the poignant impression of a city in mourning, a place ravaged by some cataclysm, a heart-rending valley of tears. Women, men and old folk are rolling in the dust, beating their chests and demanding justice. Others, plunged into a state of genuine stupor, appear to be unconscious and in the throes of an awful nightmare which won't end...

Reza Pahlavi's spectacular rise to power in 1925 was accompanied by dramatic reforms, including secularization and westernization efforts, as well as a revitalization of Iran's pre-Islamic spiritual and cultural heritage. This profound sociopolitical transformation had very positive consequences for Iranian Jewry. Walter Fischel's analysis from the late 1940s (published in 1950), along with Laurence Loeb's complementary insights three decades later, underscore the impact of the Pahlavis' (i.e., Reza Shah and Mohammad Reza Shah) reforms: [650]

(Fischel) In breaking the power of the Shia clergy, which for centuries had stood in the way of progress, he [Reza Shah] shaped a modernized and secularized state, freed almost entirely from the fetters of a once fanatical and powerful clergy...The rebirth of the Persian state and the manifold reforms implied therein tended also to create conditions more favorable to Jews. It enabled them to enjoy, along with the other citizens of Persia, that freedom and liberty which they had long been denied.

(Loeb) The Pahlavi period...has been the most favorable era for Persian Jews since Parthian rule [175 B.C. to 226 C.E.]... the 'Law of Apostasy' was abrogated about 1930. While Reza Shah did prohibit political Zionism and condoned the execution of the popular liberal Jewish reformer Hayyim Effendi, his rule was on the whole, an era of new opportunities for the Persian Jew. Hostile outbreaks against the Jews have been prevented by the government. Jews are no longer legally barred from any profession. They are required to serve in the army and pay the same taxes as Muslims. The elimination of the face-veil removed a source of insult to Jewish women, who had been previously required have their faces uncovered; now all women are supposed to appear unveiled in public...Secular educations were available to Jewish girls as well as to boys, and, for the first time, Jews could become government-licensed teachers...Since the ascendance of Mohammad Reza Shah (Aryamehr) in 1941, the situation has further improved...Not only has the number of poor been reduced, but a new bourgeoisie is emerging...For the first time Jews are spending their money on cars, carpets, houses, travel, and clothing. Teheran has attracted provincial Jews in large numbers and has become the center of Iranian Jewish life...The Pahlavi era has seen vastly improved communications between

Iranian Jewry and the rest of the world. Hundreds of boys and girls attend college and boarding school in the United States and Europe. Israeli emissaries come for periods of two years to teach in the Jewish schools...A small Jewish publication industry has arisen since 1925...Books on Jewish history, Zionism, the Hebrew language and classroom texts have since been published...On March 15, 1950, Iran extended de facto recognition to Israel. Relations with Israel are good and trade is growing.

But Loeb, who finished his anthropological field work in southern Iran during the waning years of Pahlavi rule, concluded on this cautionary, prescient note, in 1976, emphasizing the Jews tenuous status: [651]

*Despite the favorable attitude of the government and the relative prosperity of the Jewish community, all Iranian Jews acknowledge the precarious nature of the present situation. There are still sporadic outbreaks against them because the Muslim clergy constantly berates Jews, inciting the masses who make no effort to hide their animosity towards the Jew. Most Jews express the belief that it is only the personal strength and goodwill of the Shah that protects them: that plus God's intervention! "**If either should fail**..." [emphasis added].*

Farideh Goldin (born 1953), an Iranian Jewess, published her memoir, *Wedding Song*, in 2003. Goldin's moving, elegantly written narrative chronicles (primarily) her coming of age experiences in the Shiraz, Iran Jewish ghetto, interspersed with reflections on the germane prior anecdotal experiences of her grandparents, and parents, from the first half of the 20th century. Her compelling autobiography also describes the inexorable disintegration of the Pahlavi state during the 1970s, and its deleterious impact on Jews, which Goldin forthrightly connects to the open resurgence of Shiite Islamic antisemitism, and the documented legacy of Shiite religious fanaticism. [652] Goldin, for example, provides an illuminating discussion about the association between paroxysms of Shiite anti-Jewish violence, and the Ashura commemorations, and re-enactments: [653]

Again and again across many generations, the Moslem clerics had initiated attacks on the Jews as holy wars [jihads]. The ghetto had been decimated time after time. Our elders retold the stories of horror, remembering times when pogroms had been carried on through the ghetto. Lost in their deep sorrows, highly emotional Moslem men recreated in the Jewish ghettos the story of a war lost long ago. Wanting to avenge the dead, the mourners carried on a jihad, a holy war against the Jews, to imitate Imam Ali who had shed blood for the advancement of Islam. The killing, they

*believed, would bring personal salvation and global peace. It
would expedite the resurrection of the messiah, the twelfth Imam,
who would reappear when all nations accepted Allah as the only
God and Mohammed as the final prophet to replace all before him.*

*During the Moslem holy month of Moharam, my family was
especially careful. "Don't wear colorful clothes," my grandmother
reminded us. It was a month of mourning, of wearing black. None
of us wanted to provoke hostility by any implications of happiness.
The men came home early every night, bringing their work home
if they could, although there was not much business at such times,
since most of their customers were Moslems preoccupied with
their rituals of grief.*

Understandably, these recurrent episodes begot a mentality of chronic trepidation. [654]

*Fear permeated our lives. I didn't know then that the frequent
attacks on the mahaleh [ghetto] had not only instilled terror in
my grandmother's generation and those before them who had
witnessed such rampages, but also on those of us who heard the
horror stories connected with the raids.*

An experience related by her father captures the chronic, grinding oppression Jews
suffered, including not only individual (as opposed to mass) Muslim violence, but
the application of najis regulations. [655]

*Baba's [her father's] mistrust of the Moslem's had a valid
foundation. Not only had he witnessed the raid against the
mahaleh as a child, but he had also seen his father beaten bloody
as they walked home from the synagogue one Shabbat [Saturday]
morning. The ghetto alleyways being muddy, they had decided
to walk on the street although **it was forbidden for Jews to be
outside the ghetto on rainy days**. My grandfather, the chief rabbi
of the community...looked pathetic and humiliated—his caftan
[front buttoned overcoat] torn, his kippa [skullcap] a toy for
the thugs, his long white beard smeared with blood and mud.
My father had been too young and too frightened to protect him
agains strong and angry young men. Baba had seen unprovoked
violence against the Jews, who were hated for being meek and
poor, yet despised when wealthy and strong.*

When she was in high school, Goldin could already see frank evidence of an
anti-Pahlavi Islamic revival, epitomized by Muslims who "started to wear Islamic
garbs and openly shunned me for my religion." [656] During the fall of 1974, her
last year at Pahlavi University, Goldin detected a burgeoning trend towards re-

Islamization, concordant Islamic Jew-hatred, and anti-Westernism. [657]

> *I felt a shifting mood among my Moslem friends. In this American-style university, many women put aside their latest Western clothing, covered their hair, and discarded their French make-up; men grew stubble and exchanged their American jeans for black pants and dress shirts without ties.* **Adherence to strict Islamic teachings, and, as a consequence, hatred against the Jews and the West, bonded the young and strengthened their resolve against the rule of the Shah.** *The sword of Islam became the weapon that would eventually destroy the Peacock Throne.*

Goldin left Iran in July, 1975, and ultimately completed her B.A. at Old Dominion University. She returned to Iran for the last time, during the summer of 1976, and recounted these anecdotes, complemented by her astute observations. [658]

> *My [Jewish] friend [Taraneh] and I walked down the street, stopped by a café, and asked for Pepsi. The waiter spat on the floor. Didn't we know it was made by the Bahais? he asked. He didn't sell anything made by the Jews or Bahais—such filthy people! He looked at us suspiciously as if trying to figure out if either one of us were a non-Moslem.*
>
> **Anti-Western and antisemitic sentiments weren't unusual in a religious section of town,** *but they were surprising in the heart of shopping and entertainment areas, where restaurants relied on money spent the Westernized segment of the community, where most shopkeepers were Jewish. I wondered if it was possible that the Shah's government had lost its tight grip on the people, enabling them to openly display a hatred that had been just underneath the surface when they were afraid of SAVAK, the Shah's secret service listening to their every single word. As Jews, we had always avoided involvement in political issues, but political was quickly becoming personal in our lives.*
>
> *When I returned home from visiting Taraneh, I tried to convince my father to sell everything and move. I told him that a revolution hid in the wind, promising to churn the hatred of the Jews deep within the Iranian psyche. I pleaded, "Sell the farm, the house, get your money out of the bank, take the family to Israel or America before it's too late."* **My Moslem friends had changed during the last few years, I added, electrified with the anticipation of a holy man who was going to lead them to create a just country according to the laws of Islam, where they thought every Moslem was going to live in financial equality and freedom. There would**

be no room for the Jews under this government.

After her visit, Goldin permanently re-located to the U.S., later in 1976, and her immediate family escaped to Israel in 1979. [659]

> *When my family heard chants of "Allah-O-Akbar, death to America, down with the Shah," they trembled. As any procession went through our neighborhood, men banged on the doors with their fists and a few threw rocks at the windows. "Come out dirty Jews. You are next!" they shouted. The revolutionaries attacked the Bahai section of town one week, mowing down residents with machine guns. The killers promised that the Jews would be next. Not being a citizen yet, I could not obtain American visas for my family. My father found out about two El-Al planes landing in Mehrabad airport in Tehran to help evacuate the Iranian Jews. My four-year-old sister left the country on my mother's lap, in one of those planes, jammed with frightened and crying Jews. Most of them had never left their cities of birth and had never been on a plane before. They sat in the aisles or two or three to a chair, their luggage abandoned on the tarmac to make room for bodies, and in the darkness, the plane took off without the use of the tower, its own lights off.*

The so-called "Khomeini revolution", which deposed Mohammad Reza Shah, was in reality a mere return to oppressive Shiite theocratic rule, the predominant form of Persian/Iranian governance since 1501. Conditions for all non-Muslim religious minorities, particularly Bahais and Jews, rapidly deteriorated. David Littman recounts the Jews immediate plight: [660]

> *In the months preceding the Shah's departure on 16 January 1979, the religious minorities...were already beginning to feel insecure...Twenty thousand Jews left the country before the triumphant return of the Ayatollah Khomeini on 1 February... On 16 March, the honorary president of the Iranian Jewish community, Habib Elghanian, a wealthy businessman, was arrested and charged by an Islamic revolutionary tribunal with "corruption" and "contacts with Israel and Zionism"; he was shot on 8 May.*

And Littman concluded this 1979 essay with the following appeal: [661]

> *It is to be hoped that the new regime will not revert to the pre-Pahlavi attitudes of the Shī'a clergy, but will prefer a path of equality for all of its citizens, thus demonstrating in practice the "tolerant" attitude of Islam so frequently proclaimed.*

Littman's essay also alludes to the emigration of 20,000 Iranian Jews just prior to Khomeini's assumption of power. [662] The demographic decline of Iranian Jewry since the creation of Israel has been dramatic even including the relatively "halcyon days" before 1978/1979: from nearly 120,000 in 1948 to roughly 70,000 in 1978, [663] then dropping precipitously to less than 8800, at present. [664]

The writings and speeches of the most influential religious ideologues of this restored Shi'ite theocracy—including Khomeini himself—make apparent their seamless connection to the oppressive doctrines of their forbears in the Safavid and Qajar dynasties. For example, Sultanhussein Tabandeh, the Iranian Shi'ite leader of the Ne'ematullahi Sultanalishahi Sufi Order, wrote an "Islamic perspective" on the Universal Declaration of Human Rights. [665] According to Professor Eliz Sanasarian's important study of religious minorities in the Islamic Republic, Tabandeh's tract became "…the core ideological work upon which the Iranian government…based its non-Muslim policy." [666] Tabandeh [667] begins his discussion by lauding as a champion "…of the oppressed" Shah Ismail I (1501-1524), the repressive and bigoted founder of the Safavid dynasty, who "…bore hatred against the Jews and ordered their eyes to be gouged out if they happened to be found in his vicinity." [668] It is critical to understand that Tabandeh's key views on non-Muslims, summarized below, were implemented "…almost verbatim in the Islamic Republic of Iran." [669] In essence, Tabandeh simply reaffirms the sacralized inequality of non-Muslims relative to Muslims, under the Sharia: [670]

> *Thus if [a] Muslim commits adultery his punishment is 100 lashes, the shaving of his head, and one year of banishment. But if the man is not a Muslim and commits adultery with a Muslim woman his penalty is execution…Similarly if a Muslim deliberately murders another Muslim he falls under the law of retaliation and must by law be put to death by the next of kin. But if a non-Muslim who dies at the hand of a Muslim has by lifelong habit been a non-Muslim, the penalty of death is not valid. Instead the Muslim murderer must pay a fine and be punished with the lash.*

> *Since Islam regards non-Muslims as on a lower level of belief and conviction, if a Muslim kills a non-Muslim…then his punishment must not be the retaliatory death, since the faith and conviction he possesses is loftier than that of the man slain…Again, the penalties of a non-Muslim guilty of fornication with a Muslim woman are augmented because, in addition to the crime against morality, social duty and religion, he has committed sacrilege, in that he has disgraced a Muslim and thereby cast scorn upon the Muslims in general, and so must be executed.*

> *Islam and its peoples must be above the infidels, and never permit*

non-Muslims to acquire lordship over them. Since the marriage of a Muslim woman to an infidel husband (in accordance with the verse quoted: 'Men are guardians form women') means her subordination to an infidel, that fact makes the marriage void, because it does not obey the conditions laid down to make a contract valid. As the Sura ("The Woman to be Examined", [i.e., sura 60, specifically verse 60:10]) says: "Turn them not back to infidels: for they are not lawful unto infidels nor are infidels lawful unto them (i.e., in wedlock)."

And Sanasarian emphasizes the centrality of this notion of Islam's superiority to all other faiths: [671]

...even the so-called moderate elements [in the Islamic Republic] believed in its truth. Mehdi Barzagan, an engineer by training and religiously devout by family line and personal practice, became the prime minister of the Provisional Government in 1979. He believed that man must have one of the monotheistic religions in order to battle selfishness, materialism, and communism. Yet the choice was not a difficult one. [Barzagan stated] "Among monotheist religions, Zoroastrianism is obsolete, Judaism has bred materialism, and Christianity is dictated by its church. Islam is the only way out". In this line of thinking, there is no recognition of Hindusim, Buddhism, Bahaism, or other religions

The conception of *najis* or ritual uncleanliness of the non-Muslim has also been reaffirmed. Ayatollah Khomeini stated explicitly, "Non-Muslims of any religion or creed are *najis*." [672]

Khomeini elaborated his views on *najis* and non-Muslims, with a specific reference to Jews, as follows: [673]

*Eleven things are unclean: urine, excrement, sperm, blood, a dog, a pig, bones, **a non-Muslim man and woman** [emphasis added], wine, beer, perspiration of a camel that eats filth...The whole body of a non-Muslim is unclean, even his hair, his nails, and all the secretions of his body...A child below the age of puberty is unclean if his parents and grandparents are not Muslims; but if he has a Muslim for a forebear, then he is clean...The body, saliva, nasal secretions, and perspiration of a non-Muslim man or woman who converts to Islam automatically become pure. As for the garments, if they were in contact with the sweat of the body before conversion, they will remain unclean...It is not strictly prohibited for a Muslim to work in an establishment run by a Muslim who employs Jews, if the products do not aid Israel*

*in one way or another. How ever it is shameful [for a Muslim] to
be under the orders of a Jewish departmental head.*

Ayatollah Khomeini's pronouncements on najis, aside, what were the recorded views of modern icons of Shiite "quietism," often much ballyhooed, as well, for their purported "reformism?"

Allamah Tabatabai, 20th century Shi'ism's towering "Theosopher" figure, and greatest Koranic exegete, [674] appeared quite at ease with the classical conceptualization of najis in his gloss on Koran 9:28, but other than a passing reference to "moisture," offered none of the familiar litanies of specific juridical examples. [675]

> *Anything that is found dirty is called najis (impure). We say:
> A najis man, a najis woman, najis people, because najis is a
> (verbal) noun. And when we use this phrase in combination with
> the [word] rajis (filthy), one says rajis najis (dirty and filthy), with
> an 'i' after the 'n'...The argument that the Almighty brings forth
> to prevent them [non-Muslims] from entering the mosque is that
> they are impure (najis), referring to a type of uncleanliness that
> they possess, as it also refers to a type of cleanliness and purity
> that the Sacred Mosque possesses. And there are [also] quite
> different reasons behind this law, such as avoiding encountering
> them in [connection to] moisture, and so on...*

As discussed previously, Ayatollah Montazeri, the "Green Movement's" purported ideological inspiration, despite political disagreements with Khomeini, shared Khomeini's traditionalist views on juridical impurity, and provided an extensive litany of specific juridical illustrations, and guidelines. [676] Montazeri also adamantly upheld the doctrine of "spiritual impurity," insisting it was designed to promote "hatred" of non-Muslims, so that Shiite Muslims would remain impervious to "corrupt" non-Islamic ideas. [677]

The late Hezbollah spiritual authority, and avatar of canonical Islam's most virulent Jew-hating archetypes, Grand Ayatollah Husayn Fadlallah (extolled for his willingness to "dialogue," and the "disarming twinkle in his eyes," by the Wall Street Journal Editorial Features Editor Robert Pollock), [678] proffered unexpectedly ecumenical sounding views on najis: [679]

> *Concerning the question of purity, several of our modern (Shiite)
> scholars are inclined to consider the ahl al-kitab ["People of the
> Book"] as pure, though they consider the other associationist
> infidels as impure. This is also our opinion.*

Bar-Asher's analysis elucidates the most likely doctrinal explanation for

Fadlallah's tone on najis, which diametrically opposed the renowned modern
Twelver Shiite authority's unabashed (and popular Shiite consensus) antisemitic
pronouncements: [680]

> [T]he doctrine of takiya serves as the background to Fadlallah's
> concept. Wishing to be seen as a non-sectarian scholar interested
> in Islam as a whole and not only in his Lebanese Shiite community,
> he was led to obscure the differences between Sunnism and
> Shi'ism, minimizing the disagreements between the two camps
> and accenting their common denominator... In other words, this
> tendency to hide the true Shiite positions—whether motivated by
> fear of the reaction of the Sunni rival or a desire to resemble it—is
> a manifest illustration of the practice of takiya.

The doctrine of takiya, [681] notwithstanding, another revered exemplar of modern
Shiite "quietism," Iranian Grand Ayatollah Sayyid Muhammad Sadiq Husayni
Shirazi, [682] considered interpretations on najis such as Fadlallah's, fundamentally
erroneous, highlighting: [683]

> [T]wo technical defects in several of the permissive traditions:
> (a) the weakness of the chain of transmitters of the Hadith (sanad
> da'if); (b) the origin of some of those traditions from isolated
> transmitters (akhbar al-ahad).

Shirazi's doctrinally sound, authoritative discussion on najis from his Islamic
law manual was an unequivocal re-statement of the traditionalist understandings,
replete with a detailed, illustrative example "scenario" about the marriage of a
Shiite Muslim woman to a non-Muslim man: [684]

> The unbeliever (Kafir) is najis. The unbeliever is he who denies
> the existence of God, or associates a partner for Him, or denies
> the prophethood of the Seal of the Prophets Muhammad peace
> be upon him and his pure family. Furthermore [an unbeliever
> is] anyone who denies any one of indispensable aspects of the
> religion [i.e., Islam] such as the [obligatory] prayers and fasting,
> which the Muslims consider as part of the religion, provided that
> he knows these are indispensable aspects of the religion, and
> provided that his denial leads to the denial of the prophet. This is
> also applicable if one denies the resurrection and the great sins
> such as adultery and drinking of wine. All of the Kafir's body
> is najis, including hair, fingernail, and moisture, on the basis
> of an obligatory precaution. If the father of the non-adolescent
> child, and his grandfather, mother and grandmother were all
> unbelievers, then the child would follow them in being najis too.

Q: A Muslim woman has married a kitabi [Jew, Christian, Zoroastrian] or a polytheist {Hindu, Buddhist, Animist] man. What is the ruling regarding this marriage? If she is to divorce her husband or leave him, does she need to observe the iddah or the divorce waiting period, or is it sufficient to observe istibra which is to wait for the start of her next menstruation period? What is the ruling regarding her children with respect to the issue of being mahram to her? A: 1. **The marriage is invalid.**; *2. She must observe iddah for divorce, as a precaution, for shubhah intercourse.; 3. If she was ignorant of the ruling, her children are deemed to be children of shubhah and they are mahram [to her], and other rulings of children who are of legitimate birth apply to them. [accompanying note: shubhah literally means 'erroneous', and this status concerns any action or transaction that involves a possible or unintended prohibited (haram) act. Amongst the other scenarios, shubhah marriage is when a Muslim woman marries a non-Muslim man; such a marriage is not permissible, and they must separate immediately, and the marriage and intercourse between the Muslim woman and the non-Muslim man is referred to as shubhah. The children from such a marriage are referred to as shubhah children – they are not referred to as illegitimate children, but they are not referred to as legitimate either.*

The final contemporary Shiite "quietist-reformist" whose opinions on najis warrant illustration is Grand Ayatollah Ali Sistani (b. 1930). Hagiographic assessments of Sistani abound, transcending the ideological "right-left" chattering class, and policymaking divide.

Writing in March, 2005, liberal *New York Times* columnist Thomas L. Friedman, opined: [685]

> *As we approach the season of the Nobel Peace Prize, I would like to nominate the spiritual leader of Iraq's Shiites, Grand Ayatollah Ali al-Sistani, for this year's medal. I'm serious.*

Less than a year later (i.e., in February, 2006), mainstream conservative bastion, *The National Review Online*, echoed this sentiment: [686]

> *In a better world, Sistani would have a Nobel Peace Prize.*

Fouad Ajami, Director of Middle East Studies at John Hopkins University for three decades (1980-2011), and present Co-Chair of the Hoover Institution's "Working Group on Islamism and The International Order," during a June, 2007 interview, gushed, [687]

Grand Ayatollah Ali Sistani living in a simple house, a rented house; he owns no property, by the way, and a man of exquisite moderation, a man who abhors violence, a man who believes in liberty, a man who believes in Democracy, a man who rarely speaks in public. He has his pronouncements; he has his agents speak for him. On every issue that came up in the last so many years, whether within Iraq or in the Muslim world, he has been forthright in his defense of liberty, in his defense of peace, in his defense of modernity.

Neoconservative "Iran expert," Reuel Marc Gerecht, wrote in October 2010 that Sistani was, [688]

the most revered Shiite thinker in the world, and one who tried desperately and selflessly to keep his country from descending into internecine savagery...

L. Paul Bremer, the U.S. diplomat who oversaw the initial reconstruction of post-Saddam Hussein Iraq for 14-months, beginning in May, 2003, provided a more sobering and realistic perspective on Sistani: [689]

Ayatollah Sistani operated on a different rational plane than we Westerners. From his austere quarters in Najaf, Sistani viewed Iraq and the wider world through the perspective of Shia Islamic theology, as well as hardnosed politics. He had issued thousands of fatwas on a bewildering range of issues, even on how and when the faithful should drink water. And despite his cloistered image, the Grand Ayatollah was determined to influence the political process...

Bremer's memoir of his experiences in Iraq confirms that he never met in person with Sistani, despite numerous indirect exchanges. [690] Sistani insisted, in Bremer's words, [691]

he [Sistani] would forfeit some of his credibility among the [Shiite] faithful were he to cooperate openly with Coalition officials

I wrote a brief February, 2004 essay which placed Sistani's refusal to meet directly with Ambassador Bremer in a doctrinal context readily discernible to the "Shiite faithful," if not the good infidel Ambassador. [692]

Thus far, the influential Iraqi Shiite cleric, the Grand Ayatollah Ayatollah Ali al-Husseini al-Sistani, has refused to meet with the U.S. Civilian Administrator in Iraq, Ambassador L. Paul Bremer. At al-Sistani's website, the Grand Ayatollah summarizes his views on "najis," or sources of "pollution." These items would pollute Muslims simply by touching them, and they include non-Muslims themselves. While the Grand Ayatollah's writings equivocate regarding which non-Muslims are "officially" najis, al-Sistani's failure to meet with Ambassador Bremer may reflect his true, unstated sentiments. Clearly, al-Sistani and Ambassador Bremer are engaged in a political dispute over the timing and conduct of elections in Iraq. However, the Grand Ayatollah's refusal to even meet with the U.S. Civilian Administrator (in stark contrast to al-Sistani's meetings with the Muslim UN Representative Lakhdar Brahimi) suggests that a more profound dynamic may be operative: the Ayatollah may fear becoming "polluted" by a non-Muslim.

Below are Sistani's views on najis—specifically enumerated—which remain posted online at his website. [693]

107. An infidel, i.e., a person who does not believe in Allah and His Oneness, is najis. Similarly, Ghulat who believe in any of the holy twelve Imams as God, or that they are incarnations of God, and Khawarij and Nawasib who express enmity towards th e holy Imams, are also najis. And similar is the case of those who deny Prophethood, or any of the necessary laws of Islam, like, namaz and fasting, which are believed by the Muslims as a part of Islam, and which they also know as such. As regards the people of the Book (i.e. the Jews and the Christians) who do not accept the Prophethood of Prophet Muhammad bin Abdullah (Peace be upon him and his progeny), they are commonly considered najis, but it is not improbable that they are Pak. However, it is better to avoid them.

108. The entire body of a Kafir, including his hair and nails, and all liquid substances of his body, are najis.

109. If the parents, paternal grandmother and paternal grandfather of a minor child are all kafir, that child is najis, except when he is intelligent enough, and professes Islam. When, even one person from his parents or grandparents is a Muslim, the child is Pak.

110. A person about whom it is not known whether he is a Muslim or not, and if no signs exist to establish him as a Muslim, he will be considered Pak. But he will not have the privileges of a Muslim, like, he cannot marry a Muslim woman, nor can he be buried in a Muslim cemetery.

111. Any person who abuses any of the twelve holy Imams on account of enmity, is najis.

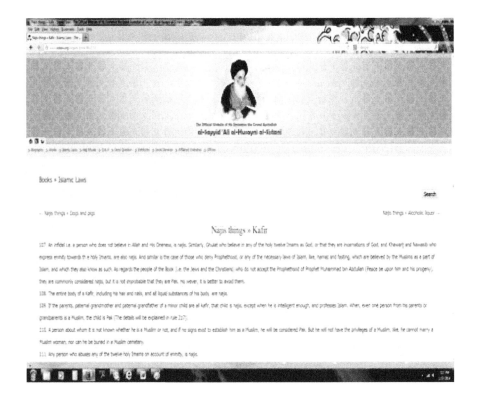

Conservative political scientist and former University President John Agresto, wrote a poignant, and sympathetic, yet brutally honest memoir of the 9-months (September 2003 to June 2004) he spent in Iraq working as then Ambassador Paul Bremer's senior advisor to the Iraqi Ministry of Higher Education and Scientific Research. [694] Agresto, who had indirect dealings with Sistani, remained "more skeptical of the Ayatollah al-Sistani and his partisans than so many of my colleagues in the Coalition." [695] He highlights one astonishing fact about Sistani that has received scant attention, let alone comment, in light of legitimate concerns over undue Iranian influence on Iraqi affairs: [696]

The Ayatollah Sistani is…Iranian by birth, Iranian by religious training--he still retains his Iranian citizenship in preference to accepting Iraqi citizenship.

But Agresto's more immediate and tangible concerns with Sistani derived from the Ayatollah's deeply rooted Islamic religious bigotry, and his illiberal, theocratic vision of the governance of Iraqi society.[697]

> *I do not believe that parties that demand that all public legislation be based on Islamic law as interpreted by Shiite imams are liberal. I do not believe that a religious leader who refused even once to meet with Ambassador Bremer, or any American, but would gladly meet with every anti-American antagonist and criminal, from Muqtada al-Sadr to Ahmed Chalabi, is a "moderate" I do not believe that the same Sistani who condemned the interim Iraqi Constitution because it protected the rights of the Kurds and secured property rights to Jews should be thought of as terribly tolerant. Indeed, the very first time I heard, in all my months there, an Antisemitic diatribe was from the Grand Ayatollah.*

Agresto lamented that comforting, if corrosive delusions about Sistani and "Iraqi democracy" persist, oblivious to concrete, readily discernible evidence. [698]

> *We insisted that the Ayatollah Sistani was surely a "moderate" and a friend to civil and religious liberty despite all the hard evidence to the contrary. Let me repeat my previous observations and predictions: The Ayatollah Sistani is an Islamist bent on establishing a theocracy not far removed from that found in Iran. He is an open antisemite and a not-too-subtle anti-Christian. He threw his support behind democratic elections because they were the handy vehicles for imposing religious authority all over Iraq...[W]e only see what we want to see, not what's visible.*

Sistani's views on najis were—and remain—quite visible, if not to the willfully blind.

Eliz Sanasarian documented a striking example of the practical impact of renewed *najis* consciousness in contemporary Iran: [699]

> *In the case of the Coca-Cola plant, for example, the owner (an Armenian) fled the country, the factory was confiscated, and Armenian workers were fired. Several years later, the family members were allowed to oversee the daily operations of the plant, and Armenians were allowed to work at the clerical level; however, the production workers remained Muslim. Armenian workers were never rehired on the grounds that non-Muslims should not touch the bottles or their contents, which may be consumed by Muslims.*

Khomeini's views were the most influential in shaping the ideology of the revitalized Shiite theocracy, and his attitudes towards Jews (both before and after he assumed power) were particularly negative. Khomeini's speeches and writings invoked a panoply of *Judenhass* motifs, including orthodox interpretations of sacralized Muslim texts (for e.g., describing the destruction of the Banu Qurayza), [700] and the Shiite conception of *najis*. More ominously, Khomeini's rhetoric blurred the distinction between Jews and Israelis, reiterated paranoid conspiracy theories about Jews (both within Persia/Iran, and beyond), and endorsed the annihilation of the Jewish State. Sanasarian highlights these disturbing predilections: [700a]

> *The Jews and Israelis were interchangeable entities who had penetrated all facets of life. Iran was being "trampled upon under Jewish boots". The Jews had conspired to kill the Qajar king Naser al-Din Shah and had a historically grand design to rule through a new monarchy and a new government (the Pahlavi dynasty): "Gentlemen, be frightened. They are such monsters". In a vitriolic attack on Mohammad Reza Shah's celebration of 2500 years of Persian monarchy in 1971, Khomeini declared that Israeli technicians had planned the celebrations and they were behind the exuberant expenses and overspending. Objecting to the sale of oil to Israel, he said: "We should not ignore that the Jews want to take over Islamic countries"...In an address to the Syrian foreign minister after the Revolution Khomeini lamented: "If Muslims got together and each poured one bucket of water on Israel, a flood would wash away Israel."*

Not surprisingly, popular Farsi translations of the Koran published in Iran make explicit the well- established gloss on Koran 1:7 ("The Way of those on whom You have bestowed Your Grace, not (the way) of those who earned Your Anger, nor of those who went astray"), discussed

earlier, [701] that the Jews are those who "earned" Allah's wrath, by inserting the word "Johood," adjacent to the words "earned Your Anger." [702]

Sanasarian provided one particularly disturbing example of this Islamic state-sanctioned Jew hatred, involving the malevolent indoctrination of young adult candidates for national teacher training programs. Affirming as objective, factual history the hadith account (for eg., *Sahih Bukhari, Volume 3, Book 47, Number 786*) of Muhammad's supposed poisoning by a Jewish woman from ancient Khaybar, she notes, [703]

> *Even worse, the subject became one of the questions in the ideological test for the Teachers' Training College where students were given a multiple-choice question in order to identify the instigator of the martyrdom of the Prophet Muhammad, the "correct" answer being "a Jewess."*

Reza Afshari's seminal analysis of human rights in contemporary Iran summarizes the predictable consequences for Jews of the Khomeini "revolution": [704]

> *As antisemitism found official expression...and the anti-Israeli state propaganda became shriller, Iranian Jews felt quite uncertain about their future under the theocracy. Early in 1979, the execution of Habib Elqaniyan, a wealthy, self-made businessman, a symbol of success for many Iranian Jews, hastened emigration. The departure of the chief rabbi for Europe in the summer of 1980 underlined the fact that the hardships that awaited the remaining Jewish Iranians would far surpass those of other protected minorities*

Beyond the well publicized execution of Habib Elganian in May 1979, an excess of Jews compared to other "recognized religious minorities" were imprisoned, and by 1982, nine more Jews had been executed. [705]

Afshari also captures the crushing psychosocial impact on Iran's remaining Jews of restored Shiite theocratic rule—the recrudescence of a fully servile *dhimmi* mentality: [706]

> *The Jewish leaders had to go so far as to openly denounce the policies of the State of Israel. It was disquieting to read a news item that reported the Jewish representative in the Majlis criticizing, in carefully chosen words...actions of his co-religionists in Israel, especially when upon the conclusion of his remarks the other (Shiite) deputies burst into the chant "Death to Israel!" The contemporary state violating the human rights of its citizens left behind a trail of pathological behaviors [emphasis added]... Equally baffling, if not placed against the Jewish community's predicament, was the statement by the Jewish leaders concerning the arrests of thirteen Jews charged with espionage for Israel in June 1999. "The Islamic Republic of Iran has demonstrated to the world that it has treated the Jewish community and other religious minorities well; the Iranian Jewish community has enjoyed constitutional rights of citizenship, and the arrest and charges against a number of Iranian Jews has nothing to do with their religion." The bureaucratic side of the state needed such a statement, and the Jewish leaders in Tehran had no choice but to oblige.*

The Jewish dhimmi behaviors Afshari witnessed resulted from a purposeful, chronic conditioning of non-Muslims, brought under Islamic hegemony by jihad. Eighteenth century Moroccan Sufi "master" Ibn Ajiba's Koranic commentary provides a remarkably candid assessment of this deliberate psychological (and spiritual) transformation process. Describing the Koranic poll tax (as per Koran 9:29) of submission for non-Muslims, Ibn Ajiba makes clear the ultimate goal of its imposition was to achieve what he called the death of the "soul," through the dhimmi's execution of their own humanity: [707]

> *[The dhimmi] is commanded to put his soul, good fortune and desires to death. Above all he should kill the love of life, leadership and honor. [The dhimmi] is to invert the longings of his soul, he is to load it down more heavily than it can bear until it is completely submissive. Thereafter nothing will be unbearable for him. He will be indifferent to subjugation or might. Poverty and wealth will be the same to him; praise and insult will be the same; preventing and yielding will be the same; lost and found will be the same. Then, when all things are the same, it [the soul] will be submissive and yield willingly what it should give.*

Jovan Cvijic, the early 20th century sociologist and geographer, in his detailed psychosocial analysis of the Serbian and other Christian *dhimmis* under Turkish Muslim rule, depicted how the fear of recurrent violence accentuated their submission, engendering prototypical *dhimmi* adaptive behaviors: [707a]

> *[they became]...accustomed to belonging to an inferior, servile class, whose duty it is to make themselves acceptable to the master, to humble themselves before him and to please him. These people become close-mouthed, secretive, cunning; they lose all confidence in others; they grow used to hypocrisy and meanness because these are necessary in order for them to live and to avoid violent punishments.*

> *The direct influence of oppression and violence is manifested in almost all the Christians as feelings of fear and apprehension. Whenever Moslem brigands or evil-doers made their appearance somewhere, entire districts used to live in terror, often for months on end. There are regions where the Christian population has lived under a reign of fear from birth until death. In certain parts of Macedonia, they don't tell you how they fought against the Turks or against the Albanians, but rather about the way that they managed to flee from them, or the ruse that they used to escape them. In Macedonia I heard people say: "Even in our dreams we flee from the Turks and the Albanians." It is true that for about twenty years a certain number of them have regained their composure, but the deep-seated feeling has not changed among the masses of people. Even after the liberation in 1912 one could tell that a large number of Christians had not yet become aware of*

their new status: fear could still be read on their faces.

Afshari's blunt description of the same phenomenon among contemporary Iranian Jews labels such behaviors a "pathological", if understandable response to their "predicament." The apotheosis of Iranian Jewish dhimmitude is perhaps Parviz Yeshaya. A staunch anti-Zionist, Yeshaya who until recently headed the Jewish Committee in Tehran, was one of the first Jews to support Ayatollah Khomeini, and has called for the destruction of the state of Israel. [708]

And public *dhimmi* behaviors were again evident in the summer of 2006. During the conflagration on the Israeli-Lebanon border—initiated by the Iranian regime's jihadist proxy organization, Hezbollah—Jews from the southern Iranian city of Shiraz were prominently displayed on state-run television participating in a regime-sponsored pro-Hezbollah rally.[709]

As described earlier, [710] Hezbollah is viscerally opposed to Judaism and the existence of Israel, stressing the eternal conflict between the Jews and Islam. Eradicating Israel represents an early stage of Hezbollah's Pan-Islamic ambitions, and its jihad against the rest of the non-Muslim world.

Support for Hezbollah abroad—which seeks the destruction of Israel, the Middle East's lone state liberated from the system of dhimmitude—is mirrored by contemporary Iran's treatment of its own Jews (and other non-Muslim populations) since 1979. Dhimmitude has been formally re-imposed, and in the case of Jews, complemented by state-supported antisemitism, irrespective of any given regimes "moderation."

Law Professor Ann Mayer's discussion of the Iranian Constitution reveals how this document, subservient to Shari'a norms (Article 4)—in her words, a "Sharia-based system"—subjects non-Muslim minorities to legalized discriminations. [711] Article 144, for example, effectively excludes non-Muslims from the Iranian military, Mayer notes, [712] "...just as *dhimmis* were [excluded] in pre-modern Iran." Article 14 states, in part, [713]

> *The government of the Islamic Republic of Iran and all Muslims are duty-bound to treat non-Muslims **in conformity with ethical norms and the principles of Islamic justice** [emphasis added] and equity, and to respect their human rights [hoquq-e ensani]. This principle applies to all who refrain from engaging in conspiracy or activity against Islam and the Islamic Republic of Iran.*

But the application of "Islamic justice"—Shari'a law—severely limits non-Muslim rights *vis a vis* universal modern standards. Mayer concludes, [714]

> *Far from granting non-Muslims protections for the rights to*

which they are entitled under international law, the constitution reinforces the principle that all rights are subject to Shari'a qualifications. In addition, Article 14 provides that the human rights that non-Muslims enjoy, which one may assume will be very limited to begin with, are to be forfeited if the non-Muslims become involved in activity against the Islamic Republic, a vague standard affording a broad range of potential justifications for curbing their rights. It is interesting that this article provides special grounds for depriving non-Muslims of human rights, even though there is already a general provision in Article 26 that enables the government to curb the activities of groups, including "minority religious associations," if they are contrary to the principles of Islam or the Islamic Republic." Article 14 seems to contemplate even more extensive deprivations of human rights than those involved in the curbs placed on the freedom of association by Article 26. Taken together, they betoken a suspicion on the part of the drafters of the constitution that non-Muslims are likely to be disposed to oppose Iran's Islamic Republic. Of course, given the Islamic bias in the system, such opposition would only be natural.

Other discriminatory liabilities implicit in Iran's legal code are exploited fully, worsening the plight of Iran's Jews. These include: the imposition of collective punishment on a Jewish community for an individual act; a "contract of silence" regarding anti-Jewish discrimination and persecution; and an unrelenting campaign of virulent antisemitism openly expressed by the Iranian media, and religious and political hierarchy. Pooya Dayanim, an Iranian Jewish attorney, recently summarized these phenomena: [715]

This reluctance to criticize, or even the eagerness to support the Islamic Regime, however, is not evidence of informal intimidation of the Jewish Community by government officials, but is also, and more significantly, a result of an obligatory contractual agreement between the minority community and the Islamic Republic. The silence, therefore, of the Iranian Jewish community inside Iran concerning discrimination and persecution is in itself evidence of the dangerous and precarious situation the community finds itself in and which it is unable to denounce without breaking its contractual agreement as a religious minority living in a Muslim land.

This contractual agreement under Sharia, Islamic Law presupposes complete loyalty to the Islamic Regime, in exchange for which the minority community receives second-class, limited privileges in practicing its religion. If the terms of this contract are breached, supposedly even by individual members of the community, the limited privileges of the entire community can be suspended or revoked or the minority community (in this instance the Jewish community) can even face deportation from the country. Under these circumstances the Iranian Jewish Community must avoid any statements that could be interpreted as critical of the regime and forces the government-imposed or government-tolerated leaders of the Iranian Jewish Community to turn in or turn against those individual members of the community who are brave enough to dare to speak out about the true condition of Jews in Iran.

After the arrest of 13 Jews in Shiraz and Isfahan in March of 1999 on trumped up charges of spying for Israel and the United States, the Iranian Jewish Community leaders inside Iran (Parviz Yeshaya, Manouchehr Eliasi and Maurice Motamed) not only did not inform anyone on the outside world about the situation but became enforcers of silence asking Iranian Jewish leaders outside of Iran to remain silent as well. It was only in July of 1999 that the case was revealed to the world in an exclusive interview granted the BBC by an Iranian Jewish leader based in the United States [home to 65,000 Iranian Jews compared to the ~ 20,000 that still remain in Iran (that inflated 1999 estimate is now down < 8800, circa 2012)] who feared that the imprisoned Jews faced immediate execution and decided to break his silence and save their lives. However, even during the trial, during which the Iranian Jewish Community knew they had the support of the international media and governments worldwide, statements from the official Iranian Jewish community were very measured, generally limiting themselves to faith that the accused would be treated fairly.

While the Islamic Republic does not guarantee the right of free speech and protest to any of its citizens, the situation, because of the Islamic Law, is considerably worse for the Jews. If an Iranian Muslim criticizes the Islamic Republic, he himself can be punished; if a Jew does it, under the laws of the Islamic Republic his actions may legally affect the well being of the entire Jewish community. Given, moreover, the suspicion in which Jews are generally held because of actual or perceived connections to Israel, the level of intimidation, especially regarding anyone who could be thought to speak for the community in general is extreme. Iranian Jewish leaders in the United States who have been brave enough to speak out have repeatedly been threatened by Iranian agents that their life and the life of their loved ones are in danger because of their decision to speak out and that they should stay silent.

Ayatollah Khamenei, Iran's supreme leader....in March 2001, denied the Holocaust and called the survivors of the death camps "...a bunch of hooligans who emigrated to Palestine." On May 18, 2001, in a televised speech, Khamenei directly attacked the Jews, calling Jews the enemies of the prophet Mohammad and threatened the Jews with expulsion and expropriation of their property, citing a similar action taken by the prophet Mohammad against the three Jewish tribes in Medina, [during] which they were annihilated. This attack, placed in the context in which the Jews of Iran were still feeling shock of the Shiraz show trials reveals the true feelings of the Islamic Regime toward the Jews of Iran.

A large part of the Antisemitic campaign waged by the government takes place in Farsi [so as] to not raise [the] attention of the non-Farsi speaking world. For example, when some specifically Antisemitic articles appear in Farsi newspapers with wide distribution, the articles are omitted from their international edition and from the website of those newspapers. It is clear that the Iranian authorities do not wish to highlight their Antisemitic activities and want to present Iran as a shining example of religious tolerance. When Maurice Motamed, the sole Jewish MP in Iran's Parliament, was interviewed by the Forward in his trip to the United States [during early 2003] for example, there were Iranian diplomats present and the interview took place at the residence of Iran's Ambassador to the UN to make sure that he does not say anything that the regime finds unproductive to its PR efforts.

The threat of retaliation against the entire community is an ever present factor in the minds of Iranian Jews and all community leaders. The Islamic Republic reminds Iranian Jews of their uncertain fate and future from time to time in speeches that are delivered by the leaders of the regime...There is good reason to believe, therefore, that there is an effective mechanism of intimidation operating against the Iranian Jewish Community, and their refusal to report incidents of severe discrimination and persecution is in itself evidence of the dangerous situation that Jews in Iran live under.

Additional forms of legal and extra-legal discrimination adversely affect criminal proceedings for Jews, and limit their employment and educational opportunities. [716] Even private religious education and observance are hindered, or abused by Iranian authorities to spy upon and threaten Jewish communities, despite continued Western media claims that "...Jews face no restrictions on their religious practice." [717] Dayanim elaborates on what amounts to a nearly full recrudescence of the system of dhimmitude. [718]

> *(Legal disabilities) The Jews suffer from official inferior status under Iranian Law and are not protected by police or the courts. The amount of financial compensation a Jew can receive from a Muslim in case of murder or accidental death of a relative is equal to one-eighth of that which would be paid if the victim was a Muslim. In practice this means that a life of a Jew in Iran has very little value. In addition, since Iranian courts routinely refuse to accept the testimony of a Jew against a Muslim, most cases of this sort are not even prosecuted and the police do not even investigate such claims. As a result of their legally inferior status, Jews find themselves outside the protection of the courts and police. This is not simply a perception on their part, but rather, sadly, a harsh reality. In none of the cases of the murder of Jews in Iran has a perpetrator ever been found, much less prosecuted.*

> *(Limitations on employment/business opportunites) Ayatollah Khomeini's edicts concerning the Jews, published in his book Tozieh Almasael (Explanation of Problems), state clearly that while there is no Islamic law prohibiting a situation in which a Muslim may work under a Jew, this is a shameful situation for a Muslim to be in. These edicts still carry the force of law in Iran, and as a result, Jews have been barred from any position in which they would be superior to Muslims. Jews are excluded from most government positions. Virtually all government entities (most sectors in Iran are government-owned) have a "Muslim only" policy and they print this requirement in their job notices in newspapers. This formal exclusion of Jews from large areas of employment is badly damaging to the Jews. Most private companies, thanks to the anti-Semitic media campaign in Iran, do not hire Jews either. Most Jews are forced into self-employment, but due to general public prejudice, few buy anything from them. The US State Department Religious Freedom Report of 2001 confirms that Jewish businesses have been targets of vandalism and boycotts.*

> *(Limitations on educational opportunities) All Jewish university*

students must pass a course on Islamic ideology. In general, the professors in these courses are, by definition, very dedicated to their ideology and many Jewish Students that I have interviewed have reported that attending such a course has been a humiliating experience, in which their religion has been ridiculed and trivialized. Jewish students who protest are expelled and blocked from entering the University. Jewish students have also reported that instructors have arbitrarily failed them to block their educational goals. Parents of Jewish elementary and secondary school students, I interviewed in Vienna (processing center for Iranian Jewish refugees) in July of 2002, report frequent verbal and even physical abuse of their children by allegedly anti-Semitic teachers. Iranian "Jewish" schools are forced to stay open on the Jewish Sabbath. Principals of "Jewish" schools in Iran by law must be Muslim and are generally selected based on their Islamic credential.

(Restrictions on private religious practice) Judaism is one of the recognized minority religions in Iran. Jews, therefore, are allowed to conduct religious services and give religious education to their children. The privileges of religious education, can, however, be suspended if it is thought by the authorities that such an education may prevent Jewish children from converting to Islam. Many informed observers believe that one reason that Jewish rabbis and teachers were arrested in Shiraz was the fact that they were instructing in the spirit of Orthodox Judaism. The US State Department Religious Freedom Report for 2001 notes that the Jewish community, and its religious, cultural and social organizations, are closely monitored by the Ministry of Islamic Culture and Guidance and the Ministry of Intelligence and Security. The form that this monitoring has taken is either sending agents to synagogues posing as Jews, or forcing Jewish communal leaders to inform on the activities of the Jewish community. This situation has created an atmosphere of terror and mistrust in the Jewish community. Many Jews who flee Iran relate that they told no one of their plans to emigrate, not even friends or relatives in fear of an unknown collaborator informing authorities of their plans.

During mid-May, 2006 public allegations were made that Iran's government was going to mandate that non-Muslims wear identifying clothing. [719] The *Canadian National Post* subsequently retracted its May 19, 2006 report about a putative Iranian Law requiring non-Muslim minorities—Jews, Christians, and Zoroastrians—to wear color-coded strips of cloth attached to their garments, to distinguish them from Muslims. [720] However, journalist and author Amir Taheri, who wrote the original article describing the alleged law, stood by his report, issuing this clarification: [721]

> *Regarding the dress code story it seems that my column was used as the basis for a number of reports that somehow jumped the gun. As far as my article is concerned I stand by it. The law has been passed by the Islamic Majlis and will now be submitted to the Council of Guardians. A committee has been appointed to work out the modalities of implementation. Many ideas are being discussed with regard to implementation, including special markers, known as zonnars, for followers of Judaism, Christianity and Zoroastrianism, the only faiths other than Islam that are recognized as such. The zonnar was in use throughout the Muslim world until the early 20th century and marked out the dhimmis, or protected [Note: again, "protected" from the resumption of the jihad against them] religious minorities. I have been informed of the ideas under discussion thanks to my sources in Tehran, including three members of the Majlis who had tried to block the bill since it was first drafted in 2004. I do not know which of these ideas or any will be eventually adopted. We will know once the committee appointed to discuss them presents its report, perhaps in September* (2006).[722] Interestingly, the Islamic Republic authorities refuse to issue an official statement categorically rejecting the concept of dhimmitude and the need for marking out religious minorities. I raised the issue not as a news story, because news of the new law was already several days old, but as an opinion column to alert the outside world to this most disturbing development.*

Possible overzealous reporting by *The National Post* aside, the plausibility of such a law being implemented should not have been dismissed based on the living legacy of Shiite religious persecution of non-Muslims in Iran since the founding of the Shiite theocracy in (then) Persia under Shah Ismail, at the very outset of the 16th century. The stipulations of Al-Majlisi (d. 1699)— the most influential Shiite cleric of the Safavid theocracy in Persia—from his late 17th century treatise on non-Muslims, are consistent with the requirements purportedly under discussion by the contemporary the Iranian Parliament (although, the "color-coding" differs): [723]

> *...it is appropriate that the ruler of the Muslims imposed upon them clothing that would distinguish then from Muslims so that they would not resemble Muslims. It is customary for Jews to wear yellow clothes while Christians wear black and dark blue ones. Christians [also] wear a girdle on their waists, and Jews sew a*

piece of silk of a different color on the front part of their clothes.

Loeb's analysis of Jewish dhimmitude in Shiite Iran, documents the social impact of *najis* regulations—across a continuum of 350 years—**punctuated** by the forced donning of a [724]

> *...badge of shame [as] an identifying symbol which marked someone as a najis Jew and thus to be avoided. From the reign of Abbas I [1587-1629] until the 1920s, all Jews were required to display the badge [emphases added]*

Following a relatively brief hiatus under Pahlavi reign (1925-1979), the Khomeini-inspired Shiite theocracy in Iran has been accompanied, as discussed earlier, by a revival of *najis* regulations. Thus, if formal badging requirements for non-Muslims were now to be implemented, these measures would simply mark the further retrogression of Iran's non-Muslim religious minorities, completing in full their descent to a pre-1925 status. The non-sequitur reaction of Jewish advocacy groups, [725] and world leaders [726] invoked comparisons to Nazi requirements that Jews wear a yellow Star of David on their clothing. Rabbi Marvin Hier, the dean of the Simon Wiesenthal Center proclaimed, [727] "This is reminiscent of the Holocaust...Iran is moving closer and closer to the ideology of the Nazis.", while The American Jewish Committee maintained, [728] "...the story, with its chilling echoes of the Shoah, is another heinous example of the Iranian regime's contempt for human rights." Australian Prime Minister John Howard, speaking in Ottawa after a meeting with Canadian Prime Minister Stephen Harper, stated, [729]

> *It obviously echoes the most horrible period of genocide in the world's history and the markings of Jewish people with a mark on their clothing by the Nazis...*

His host, Prime Minister Harper remarked, [730] "I think it boggles the mind that any regime on the face of the earth would want to do anything that could remind people of Nazi Germany." And US State Department spokesman Sean McCormack stated from Washington, DC, [731] "I think it has clear echoes of Germany under Hitler."

These uninformed comments confirmed the profound historical ignorance of sanctioned Islamic practices and doctrines such as *najis*, the *dhimmi* condition, discriminatory badging, etc., and their implementation for centuries in Iran.

Irrespective of the overwrought "badging proposal" allegations, Iran's undeniable persecution of its vestigial remnant Jewish dhimmi population continued apace.

The U.S. Department of State's 2012 International Religious Freedom Report on Iran acknowledged bluntly that, "Antisemitism remained a problem"—indeed an official Iranian government policy: [732]

> *the Jewish community experienced official discrimination.*
> *Government officials continued to make antisemitic statements,*
> *organize events designed to deny the Holocaust, and sanction*
> *antisemitic propaganda. Such propaganda involved official*
> *statements, media outlets, publications, and books.*

The report further noted that, "many Jews sought to limit their contact with or support for the state of Israel due to fear of reprisal, and "Anti-American and anti-Israeli demonstrations included the denunciation of Jews," specifically, not merely of "Israel" and "Zionism." [733]

One particularly ghoulish, murderous incident was alluded to by the State Department, and elaborated upon elsewhere. The brutal slaying occurred on Monday, November 26, 2012, in the Iranian city of Isfahan, home to a mere 100 remaining Jewish families. [734] Muslim neighbors, in what her family insisted was a religiously motivated crime related to a property dispute, attacked, and murdered Tuba N. She and her family had been harassed for years in an ongoing effort to drive them from their home, and seize the property for the adjoining mosque. Alleged "religious radicals" had "even expropriated part of the house and attached it to the mosque's courtyard." Seeking redress, the Jewish family, assisted by a local attorney, appealed to the courts despite lethal threats. While her husband was in Tehran on a business trip, Muslim assailants "broke into her [Tuba N.'s] home, tied up her two sisters who were living with her, and repeatedly stabbed her to death." [735] The *Times of Israel* report added these grisly details about the murder, and the subsequent behavior of local authorities: [736]

> *Afterward, her attackers allegedly butchered her body and cut off*
> *her hands, a sister who witnessed the event told her relatives in*
> *the U.S....Iranian authorities were said to have not returned the*
> *woman's dismembered body to her family and have tried to cover*
> *up the case.*

A subsequent report identified the 57-year-old Jewish woman victim as Toobah Nehdaran, and disputed the claim local Iranian authorities had withheld Nehdaran's body from the family, but confirmed the gruesome nature of her killing: [737]

> *Our investigation indicates that the victim's body was surrendered*
> *to the family and the local rabbis, who had requested it on Nov.*
> *29.... People who have seen the body talk of mutilation as a result*
> *of multiple stabbings following the strangulation of the victim.*

Hoping to raise public awareness of the murder, an ad-hoc group of Iranian-Jewish activists in Los Angeles, New York and Washington, D.C., created the Jewbareh Committee—named after the ancient Jewish ghetto in Isfahan where Toobah Nehdaran was killed. The committee dismissed "robbery" as a plausible motive, "because the victim's family was poor and living in a dilapidated home in one of the poorest areas of Isfahan." [738] Consistent with Farideh Goldin's account of the history of similar depredations by Muslims against the Jews of the Shiraz ghetto, during the Ashura commemorations, [739] Jewbareh Committee members surmised, [740]

> *Nehdaran's murder may have been premeditated because it took place during the Islamic month of Muharram, a holy time for religious Shiite Muslims, when they publicly mourn the killing of their prophet Hussein through large public rallies, as well as a time when religious fanatics have, for centuries, killed non-Muslims in Iran.*

Barely over a month after Toobah Nadharan's brutal killing, 24 year-old Iranian Jew, Daniel Magrufta was murdered (in late December, 2012). His Muslim girlfriend—reportedly the daughter of an Iranian Revolutionary Guard member—was held on suspicion of committing the murder, but released without being indicted. Iranian investigators allegedly praised the Muslim woman suspect, stating, "if you were involved in killing a Jew, you did a good deed." [741]

Finally, this pathognomonic anecdote was recorded by political scientist Eliz Sanasarian, an Iranian expatriate, of Armenian descent. It is a depressing, *res ipsa loquitur* demonstration of the inveterate nature of Shiite Iranian Jew-hatred, a "cultural prejudice," which persists even within the "secular," highly-educated diaspora. [742]

> *A group of [Iranian] émigré medical doctors used to meet and socialize on a regular basis in a major city in the United States. Among them only one couple were Jewish; the rest were Iranian Shiite Muslims, none of whom practiced any aspect of the religion or attended mosque. At a social occasion, out of the blue, a group of them began a conversation about "johooda [a reference to the Jews]" and their conspiracies, deceits, and lies. A friend of the author [Sanasarian], present in the gathering, turned to the Jewish couple: "How can you stand this? Say something!" "No," responded the couple, "we are used to it. Don't say anything." My friend, unable to hold back, reminded the chatterers that they had Jews in their midst. They changed their tune immediately; addressing the Jewish couple, one of them sighed: "Khoda margam bedeh [God strike me dead—a colloquial expression]. We hope you don't think we were talking about you. We are speaking in generalities which we know you'll agree with us." The Jewish couple remained silent and my friend walked out of the party in disgust.*

Since 1979, the restored Iranian theocracy—in parallel with returning their small remnant Jewish community to a state of obsequious dhimmitude—has always focused its obsessive, canonical Islamic Jew-hatred on the autonomous Jewish state of Israel. Additional pillars of this continuous campaign of annihilationist antisemitism are Holocaust denial [743]—re-affirmed vociferously by current Supreme Leader Ayatollah Khamenei [743a]—and the development of a nuclear weapons program intended expressly for Israel's eradication. [744]

Iran's steadfast pursuit of nuclear weapons may have even accelerated under the "progressive" regime of Muhammed Khatami, [745] who denounced U.S. and European Union demands that Iran sign an agreement to terminate such efforts, transparently and verifiably.[746] An early 2002 report warned: [747]

> *Nearly five years after his first election, Khatami has enacted few if any tangible reforms. Indeed, while many younger Iranians do enjoy some additional flexibility in dress, freedoms have actually declined under the Khatami administration. Khatami has accomplished one important task, though. With a gentle face, soft rhetoric, and numerous trips abroad, Khatami has succeeded in softening the image of the Islamic Republic. No longer is Iran associated with waves of 14-year-olds running across minefields, nor do many Western academics and commentators dwell on Iran's export of terror, so long as Tehran keeps its assassination squads away from Europe. However, the fundamentals of the regime' behavior have not changed. Indeed, under Khatami, Iran has accelerated not only its drive for a nuclear capability, but also actively increased its pursuit of chemical and biological weapons, as well as long-range ballistic missiles*

Previously, the "Al-Quds Day", December 14, 2001 sermon of former Iranian President Ali Akhbar Hashemi Rafsanjani made clear the purpose of such weapons. During this "pious" address, Rafsanjani, who was also deemed a "moderate" while President, argued that nuclear weapons could solve the "Israel problem," because, as he observed, "...the use of a nuclear bomb in Israel will leave nothing on the ground, whereas it will only damage the world of Islam." [748] Indeed, Rafsanjani was merely reiterating motifs of Jew hatred and jihad martyrdom expressed continuously by his spiritual inspiration, Ayatollah Khomeini. Between 1963 and 1980, for example, Khomeini made these statements: [749]

> *(1963) Israel does not want the Koran to survive in this country. . . It is destroying us. It is destroying you and the nation. It wants to take possession of the economy. It wants to demolish our trade and agriculture. It wants to grab the wealth of the country. [Iran]*

> *(1977) The Jews have grasped the world with both hands and*

are devouring it with an insatiable appetite, they are devouring America and have now turned their attention to Iran and still they are not satisfied.

(1980) We do not worship Iran, we worship Allah. For patriotism is another name for paganism. I say let this land [Iran] burn. I say let this land go up in smoke, provided Islam emerges triumphant in the rest of the world.

For recent Iranian President Mahmoud Ahmadinejad, the destruction of Israel was an openly avowed policy. Despite an international outcry of condemnation following Ahmadinejad's statements in late October, 2005 that Israel "…should be wiped off the map." [750], and, "…very soon this stain of disgrace will be purged from the center of the Islamic world," [751] he continued to express such annihilationist sentiments throughout 2006, while simultaneously referring to the "myth of the Holocaust," [752] and even sponsoring a December, 2006 Holocaust deniers "conference" in Tehran. [753] Ahmadinejad also maintained he has "…a connection with God," [754] and his genocidal pronouncements have been endorsed by the upper echelons of Iran's national security establishment. [755] The conclusion (circa 2006) that Israel's eradication had become "Iran's principal foreign policy objective," [756] did not seem unwarranted.

Expressions of this annihilationist intent—confirming it is a (perhaps *the*) central pillar of the Iranian regime's *Weltanschauung*—have not waned over the intervening eight years. Bookending current "moderate" President Rouhani's statement at an Iranian Al Quds (Jerusalem) Day demonstration (August, 2013), in support of the jihad against Israel—"The Zionist regime has been a wound on the body of the Islamic world for years and the wound should be removed" [757]—were iterations of this recurring metaphor that Israel was a "cancerous" nidus, with obvious implications about "curative removal," by Iranian Majlis (Parliament) Speaker Ali Larijani, and Supreme Leader, Ayatollah Ali Khamenei. Speaker Larijani, addressing an audience in the Tunisian capital of Tunis, on Friday, February 7, 2014, reiterated that Israel was the "cancer" of the region. [758] Two years earlier, during a (Friday) February 3, 2012 sermon, Khamenei intoned explicitly that Israel was a "cancerous tumor that should be cut, and will be cut." [759] This statement was conjoined to a defiant proclamation that Iran was forging ahead with its nuclear program. [760] Speaking to an audience of tens of thousands of volunteer Basij militiamen, on November 20, 2013—just a few days before the "P5 +1" agreement was announced, November 24, 2013—Khamenei declared: [760a]

Zionist officials cannot be called humans, they are like animals, some of them. The Israeli regime is doomed to failure and annihilation.

Mohammad Hassan Rahimian, Ayatollah Khamenei's representative in the

Iranian Martyr Foundation, made a November, 2006 pronouncement redolent with both eschatological, and corporeal world (specifically, Koranic, i.e., verse 5:82), annihilationist Islamic Jew-hatred. [761]

> *The Jew is the most obstinate enemy of the devout. [Koran 5:82]...*
> *And the main war will determine the destiny of mankind.... The*
> *reappearance of the twelfth Imam will lead to a war between*
> *Israel and the Shia.*

During a January 2010 interview, Rahimian clearly articulated the purpose of Iran's ballistic missile program, particularly if brandishing nuclear warheads: [762]

> *We have manufactured missiles that allow us, when necessary, to*
> *replace (sic) Israel in its entirety with a big holocaust.*

Ze'ev Maghen, as previously discussed, has argued strenuously that apocalyptic messianism was not a "potent force" animating either past, or contemporary Shiite Iranian foreign policy. [763] However, Maghen also acknowledged that the present era Islamic republic represents fulfillment "of the primeval Shiite dream of reuniting sacerdotum and imperium." [764] Now fully empowered and possessed of *"an endemic antisemitism inculcated by centuries of religious indoctrination,"* [765] Maghen observed that although the Islamic Republic was capable of pragmatism, it "nevertheless partakes of no small degree of irrationality" in its attitude toward Israel. [766] Maghen concluded his 2008 essay with an ominous warning: [767]

> *Iran's consistent demonization and dehumanization of the*
> *population of the Jewish state is preparing the moral ground*
> *in Muslim minds for nothing less than that population's mass*
> *extermination. Here is the realm in which sober cost-benefit*
> *analyses—and even the unforgiving logic of Mutually Assured*
> *Destruction—may well break down. In the framework of a serious*
> *escalation, a phenomenon more common than ever these days in*
> *the Middle East, their own vitriolic rhetoric could conceivably*
> *run away with the leaders of the Islamic Republic, and an Iranian*
> *nuclear warhead find its way to Tel Aviv. Such an eventuality*
> *would lead in turn to a regional and probably worldwide nuclear*
> *holocaust. Regimes need not be messianic in order to carry out*
> *horrific acts.*

This parlous dynamic remains the status quo, six years later, if anything, exacerbated by the absurdly destabilizing "P5 + 1" agreement, which has emboldened Iran, and further isolated Israel.

CONCLUSIONS

The history of failure in war can be summed up in two words...
"Too Late":...Too late in comprehending the deadly purpose of
a potential enemy; too late in realizing the mortal danger; too
late in preparedness; too late in uniting all possible forces for
resistance; too late in standing with one's friends.
— **GENERAL DOUGLAS MACARTHUR,** September 16, 1940 [C1]

As righteousness tendeth to life: so he that pursueth evil pursueth
it to his own death.
— **PROVERBS** 11:19 [C2]

Whittaker Chambers' passing 1947 allusion to the congruence between Islamic and Communist totalitarianism, was accurate—answering the initial query posed in the Preface. This conclusion flows logically and dispassionately from the answers provided to all the other questions raised in the Preface, and subsequently addressed in Chapters 1-3. The discussions about Sharia and jihad—their doctrinal bases, and historical application across a continuum of more than 13 centuries, through the present—provide the strongest proof of the validity of Chambers' analogy.

Chambers' assessment was shared, furthermore, by a diverse array of respected modern Western intellectuals—philosophers, sociologists, two major 20th century Islamologists, and even one of the preeminent 20th century Muslim intellectuals, Sayyid Abul Ala Mawdudi.

Jules Monnerot's, 1949 *Sociologie du Communisme*, was translated into English and published as *Sociology and Psychology of Communism*, in 1953. [768] Monnerot elaborated at length upon a brief, but remarkably prescient observation by Bertrand Russell from his *The Practice and Theory of Bolshevism*, published already in 1920. [769] Russell compared emerging Bolshevism to Islam, noting their shared fanaticism, impervious to reason. Despite his vaunted anti-Christian polemics, Russell further maintained that Christianity and Buddhism each possessed a spiritualism that contrasted starkly with the unspiritual aims shared by Islam and Communism—global conquest of mankind, and its subjugation to a single ruling order. [770]

Bolshevism combines the characteristics of the French Revolution
with those of the rise of Islam... Those who accept Bolshevism

become impervious to scientific evidence, and commit intellectual suicide. Even if all the doctrines of Bolshevism were true, this would still be the case, since no unbiased examination of them is tolerated...Among religions, Bolshevism is to be reckoned with Mohammedanism [Islam] rather than with Christianity and Buddhism. Christianity and Buddhism are primarily personal religions, with mystical doctrines and a love of contemplation. Mohammedanism and Bolshevism are practical, social, unspiritual, concerned to win the empire of this world.

G. K. Chesterton shared the atheist philosopher Bertrand Russell's views, and prescience, also comparing nascent Bolshevism and Islam, in 1921, albeit from the radically different perspective of a devout Catholic thinker. Chesterton emphasized how the ideologies of both the Muslim creed and Bolshevism were antithetical to the Western Judeo-Christian ethos that produced constitutions protecting individual freedom: [771]

Now a man preaching what he thinks is a platitude is far more intolerant than a man preaching what he admits is a paradox. It was exactly because it seemed self-evident, to Moslems as to Bolshevists, that their simple creed was suited to everybody, that they wished in that particular sweeping fashion to impose it on everybody. . . . Those who complain of our creeds as elaborate often forget that the elaborate Western creeds have produced the elaborate Western constitutions; and that they are elaborate because they are emancipated.

But it was Monnerot who made very explicit connections between pre-modern Islamic and 20th century Communist totalitarianism. The title of his first book chapter (and entire first section of the full work) labeled Communism as "The Twentieth Century Islam." [772] He elucidates these two primary shared characteristics of Islam and Communism: "conversion"—followed by subversion—from within, and the fusion of "religion" and state. [773]

*Communism takes the field both as a **secular religion** [emphasis in original] and as a **universal State** [emphasis in original]; it is therefore...**comparable to Islam** [emphasis added]...Soviet Russia (to use the name it gives itself, although it is a mis-description of the regime) is not the first empire in which the temporal and public power goes hand in hand with a shadowy power which works outside the imperial frontiers to undermine the social structure of neighboring States.*

Monnerot's compendious analysis supplements these apposite examples from Islam's enduring legacy of jihad—the exploits of Sunni Muslims Mahmud of

Ghazni, Togrul [Tughril] Beg, Alp Arslan—with additional jihad campaigns waged by the Fatimids of Egypt, and **notably, the Shiite Persian Safavids,** whose efforts featured collaboration by Sufis. [774]

> *The Islamic East affords several examples of a like duality and duplicity. The Egyptian Fatimids, and later the Persian Safavids, were the animators and propagators, from the heart of their own States, of an active and organizing legend, an historical myth, calculated to make fanatics and obtain their total devotion, designed to create in neighboring States an underworld of ruthless gangsters. The eponymous ancestor of the Safavids was a saint from whom they magically derived the religious authority in whose name they operated. They were Shi'is of Arabian origin, and the militant order they founded was dedicated to propaganda and 'nucleation' throughout the whole of Persia and Asia Minor. It recruited 'militants' and 'adherents' and 'sympathizers'. These were the Sufis.*

A half century later, the renowned French scholar of Islam, and ex-Communist, Maxime Rodinson (d. 2004), re-affirmed the essential validity of Monnerot's comparison. Rodinson, during a September 28, 2001 interview with *Le Figaro*, acknowledged that while still a Communist, he had taken umbrage with Monnerot's assessment. [775] But having long since renounced the Communist Party, Rodinson (circa September, 2001) conceded that there were "striking similarities" [776] between Communism and Islam, noting that like Communism, contemporary "Islamic fundamentalism" [777] promulgated [778]

> *...an ideology that claims to explain everything, drawing on a vision of the world that is fiercely paranoid [and] conspiratorial.*

Bernard Lewis is still the doyen of living Western Islamic scholars, idolized by conservative and neoconservative publications and think tanks, in particular. [779] These Lewis acolytes remain oblivious to the fact that in his 1954 essay "Communism and Islam," their doyen expounded upon the quintessence of totalitarian Islam, and how it was antithetical in nature to Western democracy, while sharing important features of Communist totalitarianism — most notably, manichean division of the world, requiring its global domination via jihad: [780]

> *I turn now from the accidental to the essential factors, to those deriving from the very nature of Islamic society, tradition, and thought. The first of these is the authoritarianism, perhaps **we may even say the totalitarianism, of the Islamic political tradition...** [T]he political history of Islam is one of almost unrelieved autocracy. ... [I]t was authoritarian, often arbitrary, sometimes tyrannical...[N]othing but the sovereign power, to which the*

*subject owed complete and unwavering obedience as a religious duty imposed by the Holy Law [Sharia]... Quite obviously, the Ulama [religious leaders] of Islam are very different from the Communist Party. Nevertheless, on closer examination, we find certain uncomfortable resemblances. **Both groups profess a totalitarian doctrine, with complete and final answers to all questions on heaven and earth**; the answers are different in every respect, alike only in their finality and completeness, and in the contrast they offer with the eternal questioning of Western man. **Both groups offer to their members and followers the agreeable sensation of belonging to a community of believers, who are always right, as against an outer world of unbelievers, who are always wrong. Both offer an exhilarating feeling of mission, of purpose, of being engaged in a collective adventure to accelerate the historically inevitable victory of the true faith over the infidel evil-doers. The traditional Islamic division of the world into the House of Islam and the House of War, two necessarily opposed groups, of which- the first has the collective obligation of perpetual struggle against the second, also has obvious parallels in the Communist view of world affairs. There again, the content of belief is utterly different, but the aggressive fanaticism of the believer is the same. The humorist who summed up the Communist creed as "There is no God and Karl Marx is his Prophet" was laying his finger on a real affinity. The call to a Communist Jihad, a Holy War for the faith — a new faith, but against the self-same Western Christian enemy***

Finally, Mawdudi independently confirmed all these observations by Western intellectuals and scholars from the perspective of a seminal 20th century Muslim thinker candidly acknowledging the shared, intrinsically totalitarian natures of both Islamic and Communist (or Fascist) states: [781]

> *A state of this sort [i.e., an Islamic state] cannot evidently restrict the scope of its activities. Its approach is universal and all-embracing. Its sphere of activity is coextensive with the whole of human life. It seeks to mould every aspect of life and activity in consonance with its moral norms and programme of social reform. In such a state no one can regard any field of his affairs as personal and private. Considered from this aspect the Islamic state bears a kind of resemblance to the Fascist and Communist states.*

The Islamic Republic of Iran melds Islam's totalitarian religious zealotry—a living embodiment of aggressive jihadism and Sharia supremacism—to Shi'ism's najis-inspired Jew-hatred. Having forcibly returned its indigenous vestigial remnant Jewish population (i.e., the small minority of those who have not fled!) to a state of obsequious dhimmitude, this toxic amalgam of belligerent, if "sacralized" Islamic ideologies animates Iran's obsession to destroy the autonomous Jewish State of Israel, the initial goal of its larger hegemonic aspirations. Moreover, the Islamic Republic's "pious" adherence to a jihad martyrdom mentality renders deterrence of its expressed nuclear annihilationist designs on Israel, a dubious proposition. Regardless, Iran's jihadist proxies, in particular, Lebanese Hezbollah, with its demonstrated jihad martyrdom pedigree, [782] and now possessing an estimated 100,000 rockets, [783] could operate with impunity under an Iranian nuclear umbrella.

Deciding to cancel a planned visit to her Iranian homeland, Jewish refugee Farideh Goldin, born (1953) and raised in the Shiraz, Iran Jewish ghetto, made these plaintive observations, in a 2006 essay: [784]

> *Visiting Iran for the last time in the summer of 1976, I vowed never to return. But during the past few years, the temptation slowly crept into me, like a long-abandoned addiction... My husband has never visited the country of my birth. We had planned to spend a year in Iran after he finished his medical internship... [A] medical conference in Mashad [Iran] seemed to be my best chance to introduce my husband to my first homeland. I made the decision to go with much trepidation, however. I am a woman; I am Jewish; I am a writer; each category subjected me to discrimination and suspicion... That was October 21, 2005. Barely a week later, Iran was in the headlines. Its president, Mahmoud Ahmadinejad, called for the destruction of the state of Israel: every man, woman and child; artist, farmer scientist, grocer; the young girl whose parents walked from Yemen; my friend who was carried out of Syria in her father's arms, screaming from hunger; the young man from Ethiopia who left everything behind; ...—and yes, my mother, father and sister too. What are they to this fanatic leader but a small price to pay on the road to heavenly redemption? ...How could I go back to Iran? I mourn for my parents' loss of dignity, for all the Iranian Jewish refugees still numb with the political earthquake that tumbled their lives. **The hands of evil are strong and long, seeking them still—not with daggers and clubs, as when my parents and grandparents lived in the dark ghettos of Iran, when Jew-haters, encouraged by fanatical mullahs, rampaged through their meager belongings—but now with missiles and atomic bombs.***

All the potentially catastrophic dynamics Goldin characterized with such eloquence—and despair—persist, and now, after the destabilizing "P5 + 1" interim agreement, have advanced to a more imminent stage. Under these dire circumstances, Norman Podhoretz recently elucidated why military pre-emption remains the only concrete option to slow down Iran's relentless pursuit of nuclear weapons. [785] Mr. Podhoretz reiterated the salient points that a nuclear Iran is not only an existential threat to Israel, but its hegemonic aspirations—driven by a jihad martyrdom mentality that may not be deterrable—will cause potentially catastrophic geopolitical chaos throughout the region, and beyond. I close with his pellucid words, hoping against hope they will be heeded: [786]

> *Given how very unlikely it is that President Obama, despite his all-options-on-the-table protestations to the contrary, would ever take military action, the only hope rests with Israel. If, then, Israel fails to strike now, Iran will get the bomb. And when it does, the Israelis will be forced to decide whether to wait for a nuclear attack and then to retaliate out of the rubble, or to pre-empt with a nuclear strike of their own. But the Iranians will be faced with the same dilemma. Under these unprecedentedly hair-trigger circumstances, it will take no time before one of them tries to beat the other to the punch.*
>
> *And so my counsel to proponents of the new consensus is to consider the unspeakable horrors that would then be visited not just on Israel and Iran but on the entire region and beyond. The destruction would be far worse than any imaginable consequences of an Israeli conventional strike today when there is still a chance to put at least a temporary halt, and conceivably even a permanent one, to the relentless Iranian quest for the bomb.*

REFERENCES

Author's Note

[n1.] D.M. Donaldson, *The Shiite Religion. A History of Islam in Persia and Iran*, 1933, London, pp. 303-304. http://bit.ly/M2cWCh

[n2.] W. Madelung, "Shi'a," in *The Encyclopaedia of Islam*, 1997, Edited by C.E. Bosworth, E. Van Donzel, W.P. Heinrichs, and G. Lecomte, Leiden, E.J. Brill, Vol. IX, pp. 420-424.

[n3.] S.H. Nasr, "Ithna Ashariyya" [i.e., a discussion of Twelver Shi'ism], in *The Encyclopaedia of Islam*, 1997, Edited by C.E. Bosworth, E. Van Donzel, B. Lewis, and Ch. Pellat, Leiden, E.J. Brill, Vol. IV, pp. 277-279.

Author's Original Preface

[p1.] "Text of Iran-Powers Nuclear Deal, Obama and Zarif Statements About Iran's Nuclear Activities" *Al Jazeerah*, November 23, 2013 http://bit.ly/18AJEFv

[p2.] Ariel Ben Solomon, "Rouhani says nuclear program 'forever' as Iran marks anniversary of Islamic Revolution," *Reuters*, February 11, 2014 http://bit.ly/MHtyzK; For discussion of Shiite theocratic rule before and after the Pahlavi Dynasty, see Chapter Three, "The Dhimmi Condition for Iranian Jewry Under Shiite Theocratic Rule: A Half-Millennial Past as Prologue," herein.

[p3.] Ben Solomon, "Rouhani says nuclear program 'forever' as Iran marks anniversary of Islamic Revolution"

[p4.] Ibid.

[p5.] Oren Dorrell, "Nuclear talks with Iran headed for collision in Austria," *USA Today*, February 17, 2014 http://usat.ly/1e33PYK

[p6.] "Iran says it won't scrap any nuclear facility," *Associated Press*, February 18, 2014 http://fxn.ws/1c1nyby

[p7.] Jay Solomon, "Iran Nuclear Talks Turn to Missiles," *The Wall Street Journal*, February 18, 2014 http://on.wsj.com/1gV3EDm

[p8.] Adam Kredo, "Iranian Oil Exports Soar as Sanctions Collapse," *The Washington Free Beacon*, February 14, 2014 http://bit.ly/1jhk0Xd

[p9.] "Iran's Supreme Leader Khamenei: I Am Not Optimistic about Nuclear Talks; US Will Continue to Be an Enemy," The Middle East Media Research Institute, Clip No. 4154, February 17, 2014 http://bit.ly/O8ZdeZ

[p10.] "Rouhani: Iranian Nation Aspiring Liberation of Holy Quds," *Fars News Agency*, February 19, 2014 http://bit.ly/OaY32u

[p11.] Richard Falk, "Trusting Khomeini, " *The New York Times*, February 16, 1979. http://bit.ly/1coIBJM

[p12.] Maxime Rodinson, "The Western Image and Western Studies of Islam," in *The Legacy of Islam*, edited by Joseph Schacht, with C.E. Bosworth, 1974, London, p. 59.

[p13.] Ibid.

[p14.] Elliott Abrams, "A Misleading Cold War Analogy—Don't count on containing Iran," *The Weekly Standard*, February 17, 2014, Vol. 19, No. 22 http://tws.io/1aNr2Dm

[p15.] Ibid.

[p16.] Ibid.

[p17.] Ibid.

[p18.] Ibid.

[p19.] Ibid.

[p20.] Robert Conquest, *The Dragons of Expectation—Reality and Delusion in the Course of History*, 2005, New York/London, p. 135.

[p21.] Ronald Reagan, "Remarks at the Annual Convention of the National Association of Evangelicals in Orlando, Florida," March 8, 1983 http://bit.ly/1hqbwfj

[p22.] Andrew Bostom, "Whittaker Chambers, Communism, and Islam," in Andrew Bostom, *Sharia Versus Freedom*, 2012, Amherst, N.Y., p. 500.

[p23.] Ibid.

[p24.] Abrams, "A Misleading Cold War Analogy—Don't count on containing Iran"

[p25.] Ibid.

Chapter 1

Introduction: The "Trusting Khomeini" Syndrome, Redux?

§ Richard Falk, "Trusting Khomeini," *New York Times*, February 16, 1979. http://bit.ly/1coIBJM

§§ For the text of the speech, see Khomeini, *Sahifeh-ye Nour*, vol. 15, Tehran: Entesharat-e vezarat-e farhang va ershad-e eslami, 1378, p. 107, as quoted (in English) and referenced by Mehdi Khalaji in his 2011 essay, "Shiite Jurisprudence, Political Expediency, and Nuclear Weapons," pp. 13-26 [in, Michael Eisenstadt and Mehdi Khalaji, *Nuclear Fatwa—Religion and Politics in Iran's Proliferation Strategy*, Policy Focus #115, September 2011, http://bit.ly/19k2YVA], note 1, p. 25.

[1.] "Text of Iran-Powers Nuclear Deal, Obama and Zarif Statements About Iran's Nuclear Activities" *Al Jazeerah*, November 23, 2013 http://bit.ly/18AJEFv Note: This *Al Jazeerah* posting also included—"Statement By President Obama On First Step Agreement On Iran's Nuclear Program" http://1.usa.gov/1gNG0YL, "Iranian FM: Iran to Continue Nuclear Activities" (no separate hyperlink available), and Parisa Hafezi and Justyna Pawlak, "Six powers clinch breakthrough deal curbing Iran's nuclear activity" http://reut.rs/1gIefnl; See also, "Pres. Rouhani: Deal with P5+1 'recognized Iran's nuclear rights'", *Russia Today*,

November 24, 2013, http://bit.ly/18AL8zr ; Herb Keinon, "Netanyahu says Iran nuclear deal is 'historic mistake' ", *The Jerusalem Post*, November 24, 2013 http://bit.ly/1bSkxMq; and "Iranian President Hassan Rohani: Iran's Enrichment Activities Will Proceed Similar to the Past", *The Middle East Media Research Institute*, Clip #4050, broadcast November 24, 2013, with audio translation http://bit.ly/1cCunQ9

[2.] "Iranian Political Analyst Mohammad Sadeq Al-Hosseini: 'If Not for the Geneva Deal, Obama Would Have Had to Kiss Nasrallah's and Khamenei's Hands to Prevent the Annihilation of Israel'" *Middle East Media Research Institute*, December 11, 2013, Clip No. 4073 (transcript) http://bit.ly/1gDDcQS; For hagiographic media portrayals of the alleged moderation of Khatami and Mohajerani, see the BBC's, "Profile: Mohammad Khatami," June 6, 2001, http://bbc.in/18ZErVz, and PBS's report by Tara Mahtafar, "Mr. Mohajerani goes to Washington," October 20, 2009, http://to.pbs.org/1jlYYKU; Elsewhere, see Khatami's October 24, 2000, remark (via Khabar TV), **"If we abide by real legal laws, we should mobilize the whole Islamic world for a sharp confrontation with the Zionist regime…if we abide by the Koran, all of us should mobilize to kill."** (from, Joshua Teitelbaum, Michael Segall, "The Iranian Leadership's Continuing Declarations of Intent to Destroy Israel" http://bit.ly/1bT10bk, *Jerusalem Center for Public Affairs*, 2012, p. 6), and then Minister of Culture and Islamic Guidance Mohajerani's May, 1999 statement regarding press "freedom of speech," which he argued must be subservient to its *de facto* abrogation by the Sharia: **"the press have freedom of expression, except when it is detrimental to the fundamental principles of Islam."** (from, "As Fragile as a Crystal Glass—Press Freedom in Iran," http://bit.ly/1kmpeCM, Section IV, "The Iranian Legal Framework and International Law," http://bit.ly/1i4po2c, *Human Rights Watch*, October, 1999); For relevant discussion of the "Treaty of Hudaybiyya[h]" armistice, see (below) the classical interpretation of the great jurist and scholar Averroes (d 1198), followed by the historical/ juridical analyses of two important 20th century scholars of Islamic Law/ jihadism, Antoine Fattal, and Bassam Tibi, from Andrew Bostom, *The Legacy of Jihad*, Amherst, NY, 2005/2008, pp. 155,96, 98-99, and also, "Educating Charles Krauthammer on Hamas' Ten Year "Truce" Offer," *www.AndrewBostom.org/blog*, May 8, 2009 http://bit.ly/1klRLIP. Dr. Krauthammer (see his Charles Krauthammer, "The Hamas 'Peace' Gambit", *Townhall.com*, May 8, 2009 http://bit.ly/1dRIsLH), in uniformity with media "pundits" across the political spectrum, clearly did not comprehend the Islamic religio-political concepts underlying such truces.

> Averroes (Ibn Rushd) [d. 1198]—"Among those who profess that the Imam is entitled to *conclude a truce when he considers it in the interest [of the Muslims]* are Malik (founder of the Maliki school of Sunni Islamic Law), Shāfiī (founder of the Shafi'ite school of Sunni Islamic Law), and Abū Hanifah (founder of the Hanafi school of Sunni Islamic Law). Shafii maintains that a truce may not be concluded for a period longer than that of the truce which the Prophet concluded with the unbelievers in the year of Hudaybiyyah… *Therefore, says Shafii, a truce may never exceed the period for which the Prophet concluded truce in the case of Hudaybiyyah. Still, there is controversy about the duration of this period. According to some it amounts to four years, but according to others three **or ten years**. Shafii opts for the latter.*"

> Antoine Fattal (1958)— "Connected with the notion of jihad is the distinction between dar al-harb (territory or "house" of war) and dar al-islam (house of Islam). The latter includes all territories subject to Moslem authority. It is in a state of perpetual war with the dar al-harb. The inhabitants of the dar al-harb are harbis, who are not answerable to the Islamic authority and whose persons and goods are mubah, that is, at the mercy of Believers. However, when Muslims

are in a subordinate state, *they can negotiate a truce with the Harbis lasting no more than ten years, which they are obliged to revoke unilaterally as soon as they regain the upper hand, following the example of the Prophet after Hudaibiyya.*"

Bassam Tibi (1996)— "Islamic wars are not hurub (the plural of harb) but rather futuhat, acts of "opening" the world to Islam and expressing Islamic jihad. Relations between dar al-Islam, the home of peace, and dar al-harb, the world of unbelievers, nevertheless take place in a state of war, according to the Qur'an and to the authoritative commentaries of Islamic jurists. Unbelievers who stand in the way, creating obstacles for the da'wa, are blamed for this state of war, for the da'wa can be pursued peacefully if others submit to it. In other words, those who resist Islam cause wars and are responsible for them. *Only when Muslim power is weak is 'temporary truce' (hudna) allowed.*"

3. *Sahih Bukhari Volume 4, Book 52, Numbers 267-269*; *Sahih Bukhari*, Translator: M. Muhsin Khan; Edited by: Mika'il al-Almany; 1st online edition October 2, 2009 http://bit.ly/16GJkUY; Khan's translations are also (largely) reproduced here: http://bit.ly/GAsiLN

Sahih Bukhari Volume 4, Book 52, Number 267—Narrated Abu Huraira: The Prophet said, "Khosrau [Sassanid Zoroastrian ruler] will be ruined, and there will be no Khosrau after him, and Caesar [Byzantine Christian ruler] will surely be ruined and there will be no Caesar after him, and you will spend their treasures in Allah's Cause." He called, "War is deceit."; *Volume 4, Book 52, Number 268*: Narrated Abu Huraira: Allah's Apostle called,: "War is deceit."; *Volume 4, Book 52, Number 269*: Narrated Jabir bin 'Abdullah: The Prophet said, "War is deceit." http://bit.ly/1fpsj1o

4. "Takiya" [Taqiy(y)a], from *The Shorter Encyclopaedia of Islam*, Edited by H.A.R. Gibb and J.H. Kramers, Leiden/New Delhi, 1953/2008, pp. 795-796:

Muhammad himself avoided the Passion motive in religion—in dogmatics by docetism (**Koran 4:157**) [i.e., the heretical early Christian belief that Christ only seemed to have a human body and to suffer and die on the cross, repeated at Koran 4:157] in his own life by the Hidjira [Muhammad's emigration from Mecca to Medina] and further by allowing in case of need the denial of the faith (Koran 16:106), friendship with unbelievers (**Koran 3:128**) and the eating of forbidden foods (**Koran 6:119, 5:3**). This point of view is general in Islam...Tabari [Al-Tabari (838-923), born in Tabaristan, died in Baghdad; historian, theologian, and jurisconsult; author of a monumental commentary on the Koran, and a universal history, *Annals*, and *Kitab al-Jihad* (*Book of the Holy War*)] says on **Koran 16:106**. "If anyone is compelled and professes unbelief with his tongue, while his heart contradicts him, to escape his enemies, no blame falls on him, because Allah takes his servants as their hearts believe."...In Shi'i [Shiite] biographies concealment is a regular feature; we are told, and not at all in an apologetic way, that the hero broke the laws of religion like the prohibition of wine under compulsions...[T] following sayings of Ali [d. 661, cousin and son-in-law of Muhammad, and the fourth "Rightly Guided Caliph," revered by Shia as the threefold imam, warrior, and saint of Islam] in juxtaposition:... **"He among you who is most honored before Allah is the most fearful (of Allah)," that is "he who uses the takiya most,"**; and it is also said, **"The kitman [synonymous with takiya] is our jihad."**

Sami Mukaram, a former Islamic studies professor at the American University of Beirut, wrote the contemporary treatise on takiya, *At-Taqiyya fi 'l-Islam* ("Dissimulation in Islam") published in 2004. Confirming the *Shorter Encylcopaedia of Islam* summary discussion (above) from 50 years before, Mukaram highlighted the ongoing mainstream nature, pervasiveness, and centrality of takiya, in particular, as an Islamic political tool:

> Taqiyya [takiya] is of fundamental importance in Islam. Practically every Islamic sect agrees to it and practices it … We can go so far as to say that the practice of taqiyya is mainstream in Islam, and that those few sects not practicing it diverge from the mainstream … Taqiyya is very prevalent in Islamic politics, especially in the modern era (*At-Taqiyya fi 'l-Islam*, London, Mu'assisat at-Turath ad-Druzi, 2004, p. 7, cited in, Raymond Ibrahim, "How Taqiyya Alters Islam's Rules of War", *Middle East Quarterly* Winter, 2010, pp. 3-13, extract translated by Ibrahim http://bit.ly/1cXqNnj)

Orientalist par excellence Ignaz Goldziher* made the following observations about takiya in the Shiite traditions, specifically:

> Ali [the 4th, "Rightly Guided" Caliph, revered by Shiites] is shown at the conversion of a Greek philosopher explaining the details of taqiyya. After he has presented him with the basic dogmas of Shia Islam, he issues an extensive admonition: "I instruct you in your faith to use taqiyya (he quotes sura 3:28). I permit you to say that our enemies are better, if fear drives you to that. I permit you to publicly reject us .You may neglect obligatory prayers if their performance would bring you harm. Preferring our enemies to us if you are afraid cannot help them or hurt us. We suffer no disadvantage if you reject us out of fear. For you are only saying that, and temporarily, and are keeping faith inwardly, so that you may save your life and spare for the following months and years those of the faithful and brothers whom you know, until the affliction is gone and the wretched situation dissipates. This is preferable to exposing yourself to destruction and cutting off all possibility of working for the faith and the salvation of your brothers. Therefore, do not fail to make use of the taqiyya I commend to you, for you could shed your own blood and that of your brothers, expose your and their well-being to ruin and deliver yourself and them into the hands of the enemies of the religion. God has commanded you to bring luster to his faith and its faithful. If you act against my command, you will be damaging yourself and your brothers more than the *nawasib* [term used by the Shiites for persons whom they claim abhor the Ahlul Bayt, the family of Muhammad], and the infidels do."

> We see from this admonition that taqiyya if first and foremost advanced in the interest of the security of allies, whose welfare could be put at risk by the bravery and martyr's courage of an individual. Therefore, taqiyya appears mostly in connection with the *hukuk al-ikhwan*, the "interests of the brothers." Imam Ali b. Muhammed [Alī ibn Muhammad ibn 'Alī. , the tenth imam, fl. 9th century]was asked, "Who is the most complete person in good characteristics?" He answered, "He who most carefully uses taqiyya. gaining his brothers most good." (Ignaz Goldziher, "Das Prinzip der takijja im Islam" *Zeitschrift der Deutschen Morgenländischen Gesellschaft*, 1906, S. 213–226; from pp. 219-220, translation by Professor James L. Hodge; * Goldziher [1860–1921], the preeminent Hungarian scholar of Islam, has been widely acclaimed as one of the most profound and original European scholars from an era that produced seminal investigators. The English translations of his major works published between

1967 and 2006, include: *Muslim Studies, A Short History of Classical Arabic Literature, The Zahiris, Introduction to Islamic Theology and Law,* and *Schools of Koranic Commentators.*)

And Etan Kohlberg's 1975 analysis of takiya emphasized the critical bearing this doctrine had on the Shi'ite way of life:

> …[W]itness the numerous claims in Imami literature that many professed Sunnis had in fact been Shi'is practising taqiyya. **The disappearance of the twelfth Imam (in 874) is explained as an act of taqiyya designed to save him from harm until his return as Mahdi. There even exists a special legal term, dar al-taqiyya, denoting the areas where taqiyya is obligatory.** The notion of taqiyya likewise had important implications for various facets of Shi'i hadith. In early Shi'i circles, for instance, great stress was laid on the principle that genuine Shi'i traditions should be concealed from strangers (kitman, taqiyya) and be propagated (*idhdi'a*) only among the faithful. The principle of taqiyya was not restricted to the hostile outside world, but was sometimes applied to relationships among the Shi'is themselves. (Etan Kohlberg, "Some Imāmī-shī'ī Views on Taqiyya," *Journal of the American Oriental Society,* 1975, Vol. 95, No. 3, pp. 395-402; p. 397 http://bit.ly/19XzIAZ)

More than a century earlier, Orientalist, and French chargé d'affaires in Tehran (from 1855-1858), Joseph Arthur de Gobineau, made these observations about the doctrine and practice of kitman (takiya), based upon his first hand experiences:

> [I]t is not a good idea to expose one's faith to the insult of disbelievers…The possessor of truth must not expose his person, his worldy goods or esteem to the aberration, to the folly, the perversity of those whom it has pleased God to lead into and to keep in error. As long as he is sensible and walks the right path he is precious to God; his health and prosperity are of consequence to the world. Never could speaking lightly bring advantage; for God knows what he wants, and if it suits him that the infidel or the wayward believer discover the true path, he needs help from no one to bring about the miracle. Silence must therefore be considered useful, as well as knowing that speaking and exposing the believer and perhaps even the religion, is ill-advised and at times may even amount to impiety. However there are cases where silence is no longer sufficient, where it could pass for an admission. In that case there is no hesitation. One should not only renounce one's real opinion but its imperative that one misleads one's adversary by all manner of ruse. One makes all the professions of faith that may please him, performs all the most senseless of rites, distorts one's own books, exhausts all the possibilities of deception. In this way one acquires the multiple satisfaction and merit of having safeguarded oneself and one's loved ones, of not having exposed a venerable faith to horrid contact with the infidel, and finally of having imposed on the former [the infidel] the spiritual shame and wretchedness he deserves by tricking him and confirming him in his error… Kitman ennobles him who practises it. The believer raises himself to a perpetual state of superiority over the person he deceives, be it a minister or a powerful king, no matter; for he who uses kitman against him he is above all a poor wretch to whom one closes the true path and who suspects nothing; ragged and starving you stand, outwardly quaking in your boots before deceived might, yet thine eyes are filled with light; thou treadst in brightness before thy foes. You ridicule an unintelligent being; you disarm a dangerous beast. What multifarious delights!

(*Comte de Gobineau and Orientlaism—Selected eastern writings*, translated by Daniel O'Donoghue, edited by Geoffrey Nash, 2009, New York, pp. 119-120.)

Finally, as per the consensus view of Sunni and Shi'ite Islam's most authoritative Koranic commentators, classical and modern alike, Koran 3:28 is the keystone verse sanctioning Muslim deception towards non-Muslims, as elaborated further in the doctrine of takiya/ kitman. What follows are the glosses on Koran 3:28, in chronological order, across a millennium, by: al-Tabari (d. 923; see above); Ibn Kathir (d. 1373), one of the best-known historians and traditionalists of Syria during the reign of the Bahri Mamluks, who also compiled an important Koranic commentary; al-Suyuti (d. 1505) recognized as a brilliant jurist, historian, and biographer, among whose many scholarly contributions are about twenty works of Koranic studies, including seminal Koranic commentaries; Maulana Muhammad Shafi (d.1976), former grand mufti of India (prior to the August, 1947 partition), author of *Maariful Qur'an*, which remains the best-known Koranic commentary in Urdu, who wrote more than three hundred books, and in addition to these literary works, broadcasted tafsir of the Koran on Radio Pakistan for a number of years; and most aptly, Muhammad Husayn Tabatabai (d. 1981), the pre-eminent 20th century Shi'ite Koranic commentator, and renowned Muslim philosopher-educator.

> **(Tabari)** If you [Muslims] are under their [non-Muslims'] authority, fearing for yourselves, behave loyally to them with your tongue while harboring inner animosity for them … [know that] God has forbidden believers from being friendly or on intimate terms with the infidels rather than other believers—except when infidels are above them [in authority]. Should that be the case, let them act friendly towards them while preserving their religion. (Abu Ja'far Muhammad at-Tabari, *Jami' al-Bayan 'an ta'wil ayi'l-Qur'an al-Ma'ruf: Tafsir at-Tabari*, Beirut: Dar Ihya' at-Turath al-'Arabi, 2001, vol. 3, p. 267, translated in Ibrahim, "How Taqiyya Alters Islam's Rules of War", http://bit.ly/1cXqNnj)

> **(Ibn Kathir)** [B]elievers who in some areas or times fear for their safety from the disbelievers...such believers are allowed to show friendship to the disbelievers outwardly, but never inwardly. For instance, Al-Bukhari [d. 869, author of the most important of the six canonical hadith collections] recorded that Abu Darda said, "We smile in the face of some people although our hearts curse them." Al-Bukhari said that Al-Hasan said, "The Tuqyah [takiya] is allowed until the Day of Resurrection." (*Tafsir Ibn Kathir*, English translation produced by a group of scholars under the supervision of Shaykh Safiur-Rahman Al-Mubarakpuri, Vol. 2, 2000, Riyadh, p 142)

> **(al-Suyuti)** The believers should not take unbelievers as friends and protectors rather than the believers. Anyone who does that and befriends unbelievers has nothing whatsoever to do with the din [religion] of Allah—unless it is because you are afraid of them, unless it is dissimulation out of fear of them so that the befriending takes place with the tongue alone and not the heart. (*Tafsir al-Jalalayn*, 2008, translated by Aisha Bewley, London, pp. 122-124)

> **(Shafi)** [F]riendship which binds a Muslim in very close ties with non-Muslims is not permissible under any condition...politeness and friendly treatment is... permissible when the purpose is to entertain a guest, convey Islamic teachings to non-Muslims or to stay safe against being hurt or harmed by them. (*Ma'ariful Qur'an*, 2009, Vol. 2, Karachi, p. 58)

> **(Tabatabai)** The verse [3:28] clearly allows taqiyyah, as is shown by the

traditions of the Imāms of *Ahlu 'l-bayt* [the family of Muhammad; Shias believe they consist of Muhammad, Fatima, and Muhammad's "successors," Ali, Hasan and Husayn]... The Qur'ān and the sunnah both agree that taqiyyah is permissible in places. Also, reason supports it. **The main purpose of the religion and the Apostle is to keep the truth alive; and sometimes this purpose can be achieved by practicing taqiyyah, by keeping good relations with the enemies of the religion, while discarding taqiyyah would serve no purpose at all.** It is a reality which no reasonable man can deny... The tafsīr *as-Sāfī* [Koranic commentary, in this case, written by 17th century Shi'ite scholar Mohsen Fayz Kashani (d. 1679)], quotes under the words: except (when) you guard yourselves against (them) . . ., from al-Ihtijāj, that the Commander of the faithful (a.s.) said, inter alia, in a tradition: "and He ordered you to practice taqiyyah in your religion; because **Allāh says: Be careful, and be careful again, not to expose yourself to perdition, and not to neglect taqiyyah which I have ordered you (to practise); otherwise, you will cause shedding of your blood and the blood of your brethren (as well); will expose your bounties as well as theirs to ruin; and will cause their humiliation at the hands of the enemies of the religion of Allāh, while Allāh has ordered you to exalt them.**" as-Sādiq (d. 765, sixth Shi'ite imam and jurist) **said: "The Apostle of Allāh used to say: 'He has no religion who does not have taqiyyah;' then he used to say: 'Allāh says: except (when) you guard yourselves against them for fear from them."** (al-'Ayyāshī, fl. ? 2nd half of the 9th century, the Shi'ite commentator and traditionalist) **al-Bāqir** (d. 733, fifth Shi'ite imam and jurist) **said: "taqiyyah is (allowed) in every matter about which a man falls in predicament; and Allāh has made it lawful to him."** (al-Kāfī; a Shiite hadith collection compiled by Muhammad Ya'qūb Kulaynī [d. 941]) The author says: There are very many traditions from the Imāms of Ahlu 'l-bayt — probably reaching the limit of mutawātir ['that which comes successively'; it can denote a Prophetic tradition, hadith, or, in general, any report], with multiple chains of transmission] containing the permission of taqiyyah; and you have already seen how the Qur'ānic verses [notably Koran 3:28] incontestably prove it. (Sayyid Muhammad Husayn at-Tabataba'i, *Al-Mizan fe Tafsir al-Quran*, translated by Sayyid Saeed Akhtar Rizvi, 1982, Vol. 3, Tehran, pp. 221-222, 234-235, http:// bit.ly/1cIpQf6)

Koranic translations from: Taqi al-Din Hilali; Muhammad Muhsin Khan. *Interpretation of the meanings of the noble Qur'ān in the English language: a summarized version of At [i.e. al.]-Tabarī, Al-Qurtubī, and Ibn Kathīr with comments from Sahīh Al-Bukhārī*, 23rd revised, edition, Riyadh, Saudi Arabia, 1998.; and A J Arberry. *The Koran interpreted: a translation*, New York, N.Y., 1996,1955.

Koran 4:157 [Hilali-Khan] And because of their saying (in boast), "We killed Messiah Isa (Jesus), son of Maryam (Mary), the Messenger of Allah," - but they killed him not, nor crucified him, but the resemblance of Isa (Jesus) was put over another man (and they killed that man), and those who differ therein are full of doubts. They have no (certain) knowledge, they follow nothing but conjecture. For surely; they killed him not [i.e. Isa (Jesus), son of Maryam (Mary)]:; [Arberry] and for their saying, "We slew the Messiah, Jesus son of Mary, the Messenger of God" – yet they did not slay him, neither crucified him, only a likeness of that was shown to them. Those who are at variance concerning him surely are in doubt regarding him; they have no knowledge of him, except the following of surmise; and they slew him not of a certainty -- no indeed; http://bit.ly/1cWb0VX

Koran 3:28 [Hilali-Khan] Let not the believers take the disbelievers as Auliya (supporters, helpers, etc.) instead of the believers, and whoever does that will never be helped by Allah in any way, except if you indeed fear a danger from them. And Allah warns you against Himself (His Punishment) and to Allah is the final return.; [Arberry] Let not the believers take the unbelievers for friends, rather than the believers -- for whoso does that belongs not to God in anything -- unless you have a fear of them. God warns you that You beware of Him, and unto God is the homecoming. http://bit.ly/1gKqfVw

Koran 6:119 [Hilali-Khan] And why should you not eat of that (meat) on which Allah's Name has been pronounced (at the time of slaughtering the animal), while He has explained to you in detail what is forbidden to you, except under compulsion of necessity? And surely many do lead (mankind) astray by their own desires through lack of knowledge. Certainly your Lord knows best the transgressors.; [Arberry] How is it with you, that you do not eat of that over which God's Name has been mentioned, seeing that He has distinguished for you that He has forbidden you, unless you are constrained to it? But surely, many lead astray by their caprices, without any knowledge; thy Lord knows very well the transgressors. http://bit.ly/Jabtbx

Koran 5:3 [Hilali-Khan] Forbidden to you (for food) are: Al-Maytatah (the dead animals - cattle-beast not slaughtered), blood, the flesh of swine, and the meat of that which has been slaughtered as a sacrifice for others than Allah, or has been slaughtered for idols, etc., or on which Allah's Name has not been mentioned while slaughtering, and that which has been killed by strangling, or by a violent blow, or by a headlong fall, or by the goring of horns - and that which has been (partly) eaten by a wild animal - unless you are able to slaughter it (before its death) and that which is sacrificed (slaughtered) on AnNusub (stone altars). (Forbidden) also is to use arrows seeking luck or decision, (all) that is Fisqun (disobedience of Allah and sin). This day, those who disbelieved have given up all hope of your religion, so fear them not, but fear Me. This day, I have perfected your religion for you, completed My Favour upon you, and have chosen for you Islam as your religion. But as for him who is forced by severe hunger, with no inclination to sin (such can eat these above-mentioned meats), then surely, God is Oft-Forgiving, Most Merciful.; [Arberry] Forbidden to you are carrion, blood, the flesh of swine, what has been hallowed to other than God, the beast strangled; the beast beaten down, the beast fallen to death, the beast gored, and that devoured by beasts of prey - excepting that you have sacrificed duly -- as also things sacrificed to idols, and partition by the divining arrows; that is ungodliness. Today the unbelievers have despaired of your religion; therefore fear them not, but fear you Me. Today I have perfected your religion for you, and I have completed My blessing upon you, and I have approved Islam for your religion. But whosoever is constrained in emptiness and not inclining purposely to sin -- God is All-forgiving, All-compassionate. http://bit.ly/18WKKpS

Koran 16:106 [Hilali-Khan] Whoever disbelieved in Allah after his belief, except him who is forced thereto and whose heart is at rest with Faith but such as open their breasts to disbelief, on them is wrath from Allah, and theirs will be a great torment.; [Arberry] Whoso disbelieves in God, after he has believed -- excepting him who has been compelled, and his heart is still at rest in his belief -- but whosoever's breast is expanded in unbelief, upon them shall rest anger from God, and there awaits them a mighty chastisement; http://bit.ly/1frDJla

[5.] Joseph S. Douglass, Jr., *Why the Soviets Violate Arms Control Treaties*, 1988, Cambridge, MA.; see within, especially, Igor Lukes, "Linguistic Deception and U.S.-Soviet Arms Control Treaties," Appendix C, pp. 138-154; on p. 140 Lukes even notes the striking similarity between Soviet "linguistic maneuvers" and takiya/ kitman, the Islamic doctrine of deception:

> It is hard to ignore the existence of clear parallels between the defensive deceptions of Islamic kitman and the more global linguistic maneuvers of the Kremlin decision makers…[D]eception and conspiracy were to become a way of life of all communist movements. Indeed the long careers of Philby et al. [Harold Adrian Russell "Kim" Philby (d. 1988) was a high-ranking member of British intelligence, and Soviet double agent, who defected to the Soviet Union in 1963, having been an operative of the Soviet NKVD/KGB, as part the spy ring now known as the "Cambridge Five"] demonstrate that kitman is as Soviet as it is Middle Eastern.

6. "Iranian Political Analyst Mohammad Sadeq Al-Hosseini" http://bit.ly/1gDDcQS

7. Ibid.

8. Andrew Bostom, *The Legacy of Islamic Antisemitism*, Amherst, N.Y., 2008, pp. 149, 683; and Teitelbaum and Segall, "The Iranian Leadership's Continuing Declarations of Intent to Destroy Israel" http://bit.ly/1bT10bk

9. "Iranian Political Analyst Mohammad Sadeq Al-Hosseini" http://bit.ly/1gDDcQS

10. Ibid.; Koran 59:14 [Hilali-Khan]"They fight not against you even together, except in fortified townships, or from behind walls. Their enmity among themselves is very great. You would think they were united, but their hearts are divided, that is because they are a people who understand not."; [Arberry] "They will not fight against you all together except in fortified cities, or from behind walls. Their valour is great, among themselves; you think of them as a host; but their hearts are scattered; that is because they are a people who have no sense." http://bit.ly/J7HIYU

For exegeses of Koran 59:14—and indeed Koran 59:1 to 59:17—which relate these verses to the fate of Medinan Jewry, see *Tafsir al-Jalalayn*, pp. 1186-1191, and *Ma'ariful Qur'an*, pp. 366-400.; For relevant summary discussions of both Medinan Jewry, and the Jews of Khaybar, see Bostom, *The Legacy of Islamic Antisemitism*, pp. 67-76.

11. In addition to the previously cited "Six powers clinch breakthrough deal curbing Iran's nuclear activity" http://reut.rs/1gIefnl, see Robert Einhorn, "U.S., Israel spats blur simple truth: Neither wants Iran to have nukes,"*Haaretz*, November 24, 2013 http://bit.ly/1bYZHex; Susan Maloney, "Saved by the Deal—How Rouhani Won the Negotiations and Rescued His Regime," *Foreign Affairs*, November 27, 2013 http://fam.ag/19kpEaE; "A Breakthrough Agreement at Risk," The New York Times Editorial Board, *New York Times*, December 9, 2013 http://nyti.ms/JVfmSX; Even the *National Review's* Conrad Black opined, "I think the Geneva agreement over the Iranian nuclear program is progress," claiming moreover, that the interim deal, "creates a united front with the former roosters in the manger of collective security, China and Russia; and could conceivably be an unembarrassing avenue toward less dangerous and irresponsible behavior by the odious government in Tehran." Conrad Black, "Iran: Not That Bad a Start," *National Review*, November 27, 2013 http://bit.ly/197b2ZG

12. "Netanyahu says Iran nuclear deal is 'historic mistake'", http://bit.ly/1bSkxMq ; "Iranian President Hassan Rohani: Iran's Enrichment Activities Will Proceed Similar to the Past", http://bit.ly/1cCunQ9; "Pres. Rouhani: Deal with P5+1 'recognized Iran's nuclear rights'" http://bit.ly/18AL8zr; "Iranian FM: Iran to Continue Nuclear Activities"

[13.] "UANI Issues Statement Regarding P5+1 Deal with Iran," November 24, 2013, http://bit.ly/1a3vAPS

[14.] David Blair, "Iran nuclear deal – what are the terms of the agreement?", *The Telegraph* (London), November 24, 2013 http://bit.ly/18HO2Ct

[15.] "UANI Issues Statement Regarding P5+1 Deal with Iran"

[16.] "Letter from Ayatollah Khomeini regarding weapons during the Iran-Iraq war," 1988, reproduced via Iranian Labour News Agency (ILNA), Tehran, in Persian, September 29, 2006, and translated into English by the Council on Foreign Relations: http://on.cfr.org/IPnhAn;

As discussed (and referenced) by Mehdi Khalaji in his 2011 essay, "Shiite Jurisprudence, Political Expediency, and Nuclear Weapons," pp. 13-26 [in, Michael Eisenstadt and Mehdi Khalaji, *Nuclear Fatwa—Religion and Politics in Iran's Proliferation Strategy*, Policy Focus #115, September 2011, http://bit.ly/19k2YVA], Khomeini's 1988 responsive ruminations were disclosed in memoirs and diaries published by Ayatollah Ali Montazeri, and former Iranian President Rafsanjani. These references to Montazeri's and Rafsanjani's relevant works are from Khalaji's "Shiite Jurisprudence, Political Expediency, and Nuclear Weapons," note 5, p. 25: Hossein Ali Montazeri, *Memoire,*Paris: Entesharat-e Enghelab-e Eslami, 2001, p. 490.; Akbar Hashemi Rafsanjani, *Karnameh va Khaterat-e Hashemi Rafsanjani, Sal-e 1367*, ed. Alireza Hashemi, Tehran: Daftar-e Nashr-e Maref-e Enghelab, 2011, pp. 578–581.

[17.] "Letter from Ayatollah Khomeini regarding weapons during the Iran-Iraq war"

[18.] Khalaji, "Shiite Jurisprudence, Political Expediency, and Nuclear Weapons," p. 14

[19.] Glenn Kessler, "Did Iran's supreme leader issue a fatwa against the development of nuclear weapons?," The Washington Post, November 27, 2013 http://wapo.st/1kLmoop

[20.] Karim Sadjadpour, "Reading Khamenei: The World View of Iran's Most Powerful Leader," *Carnegie Endowment for International Peace*, 2009, p. 6. http://ceip.org/1c8vXfj

[21.] "Statement by the President" September 27, 2013 http://1.usa.gov/19s4RlP

[22.] Quoted in Kessler, "Did Iran's supreme leader issue a fatwa against the development of nuclear weapons?," http://wapo.st/1kLmoop

[23.] "Press Availability After P5+1 Talks," Remarks of John Kerry, Secretary of State, Geneva, Switzerland, November 24, 2013 http://1.usa.gov/1csbWkV

[23a.] Photo from cover, and caption from p. ii, *Nuclear Fatwa—Religion and Politics in Iran's Proliferation Strategy*.

[24.] Kessler, "Did Iran's supreme leader issue a fatwa against the development of nuclear weapons?," http://wapo.st/1kLmoop

[25.] Ibid.

[26.] A. Savyon and Y. Carmon, "Renewed Iran-West Nuclear Talks – Part II: Tehran Attempts to Deceive U.S. President Obama, Sec'y of State Clinton With Nonexistent Anti-Nuclear Weapons Fatwa By Supreme Leader Khamenei," *Middle East Media Research Institute*,

April 19, 2012, Inquiry & Analysis Series Report No. 825 http://bit.ly/1fLa8Df; "Release Of Compilation Of Newest Fatwas By Iranian Supreme Leader Khamenei – Without Alleged Fatwa About Nuclear Bomb," *Middle East Media Research Institute*, August 13, 2013, Special Dispatch No. 5406 http://bit.ly/1c9IcEW; Khalaji, "Shiite Jurisprudence, Political Expediency, and Nuclear Weapons," p. 14, and his note 17, p. 25, which includes Khamenei's own eponymous fatwa "How to Acquire the Fatwas of a Jurist?" (available at http://bit.ly/1cYp4L7)—which, when applied to the Supreme Leader's own alleged fatwa banning nuclear weapons, yields nothing concrete, certainly in writing!

[27.] Khalaji, "Shiite Jurisprudence, Political Expediency, and Nuclear Weapons," p.14

[28.] Kessler, "Did Iran's supreme leader issue a fatwa against the development of nuclear weapons?"; www.nuclearenergy.ir, includes an entire section on the putative fatwa against nuclear weapons—but no written fatwa itself http://bit.ly/19kOzFu

[29.] From US embassy cable - 04THEHAGUE1224 "CHEMICAL WEAPONS CONVENTION (CWC) - IRANIAN ANSWERS TO U.S. QUESTIONS," Identifier: 04THEHAGUE1224; Wikileaks: http://bit.ly/1boghRJ; Origin: Embassy The Hague http://bit.ly/1gUcfIE; Created: 2004-05-19 12:54:00; Classification: SECRET//NOFORN http://bit.ly/1ifzZqZ:

> Iran has acknowledged the existence of a past chemical weapons (CW) program and the production of chemical weapons.

[30.] Kessler, "Did Iran's supreme leader issue a fatwa against the development of nuclear weapons?"; Kessler's report provided this excerpt from a March 2003 speech by Khamenei in Persian, translated into English by Mehdi Khalaji:

> Nuclear technology is different than producing nuclear bomb. Nuclear technology is considered to be a scientific progress in a field that has lots of benefits. Those who want nuclear bomb can pursue that field and get the bomb. We do not want bomb. We are even against chemical weapons. **Even when Iraq attacked us by chemical weapons, we did not produce chemical weapons**. (emphasis added)

[31.] Ibid.

[32.] Ibid.

[33.] Khalaji, "Shiite Jurisprudence, Political Expediency, and Nuclear Weapons," pp. 14, 23-24.

[34.] Ibid., p. 14.

[35.] Ibid.

[36.] Ibid., p. 20; **Koran 3:151** http://bit.ly/1ehCDHE [Hilali-Khan] We shall cast terror into the hearts of those who disbelieve, because they joined others in worship with Allah, for which He had sent no authority; their abode will be the Fire and how evil is the abode of the Zalimun (polytheists and wrongdoers).; [Arberry] We will cast into the hearts of the unbelievers terror, for that they have associated with God that for which He sent down never authority; their lodging shall be the Fire; evil is the lodging of the evildoers.; **Koran 8:12** http://bit.ly/1cIfst9 [Hilali-Khan] (Remember) when your Lord inspired the angels, "Verily, I am with you, so keep firm those who have believed. I will cast terror into the hearts of those who have disbelieved, so strike them over the necks, and smite over all their fingers and toes."; [Arberry] When thy Lord was revealing to the angels, "I am with you; so confirm the believers. I shall cast into the unbelievers' hearts terror; so smite above the necks, and smite every finger of them!"; **Koran 8:60** http://bit.ly/KbE55J [Hilali-Khan] And make ready against them all you can of power, including steeds of war (tanks, planes, missiles, artillery, etc.) to threaten the enemy of Allah and your enemy, and others besides whom, you may not know but whom Allah does know. And whatever you shall spend in the Cause of Allah shall be repaid unto you, and you shall not be treated unjustly.; [Arberry] Make ready for them whatever force and strings of horses you can, to terrify thereby the enemy of God and your enemy, and others besides them that you know not; God knows them. And whatsoever you expend in the way of God shall be repaid you in full; you will not be wronged; **Koran 33:26** http://bit.ly/19u9yvm [Hilali-Khan] And those of the people of the Scripture who backed them (the disbelievers) Allah brought them down from their forts and cast terror into their hearts, (so that) a group (of them) you killed, and a group (of them) you made captives.; [Arberry] And He brought down those of the People of the Book who supported them from their fortresses and cast terror in their hearts; some you slew, some you made captive.; **Koran 59:2** http://bit.ly/19r3xtD [Hilali-Khan] He it is Who drove out the disbelievers among the people of the Scripture (**i.e. the Jews of the tribe of Bani An-Nadir**) from their homes at the first gathering. You did not think that they would get out. And they thought that their fortresses would defend them from Allah! But Allah's (Torment) reached them from a place whereof they expected it not, and He cast terror into their hearts, so that they destroyed their own dwellings with their own hands and the hands of the believers. Then take admonition, O you with eyes (to see).; [Arberry] It is He who expelled from their habitations the unbelievers among the People of the Book at the first mustering. You did not think that they would go forth, and they thought that their fortresses would defend them against God; then God came upon them from whence they had not reckoned, and He cast terror into their hearts as they destroyed their houses with their own hands, and the hands of the believers; therefore take heed, you who have eyes!; **Koran 59:13** http://bit.ly/1lo2S1q [Hilali-Khan] Verily, you (believers in the Oneness of Allah - Islamic Monotheism) are more awful as a fear in their (**Jews of Bani An-Nadir**) breasts than Allah. That is because they are a people who comprehend not (the Majesty and Power of Allah).; [Arberry] Why, you arouse greater fear in their hearts than God; that is because they are a people who understand not.

[37.]   Khalaji, "Shiite Jurisprudence, Political Expediency, and Nuclear Weapons," p. 20; "Top Cleric: Iran Has Right to 'Special Weapons'," *CBS News/Associated Press*, June 14, 2010 http://cbsn.ws/1h3XVxt

[38.] "Top Cleric: Iran Has Right to 'Special Weapons' "

[39.] Ibid.; (Title translation of Yazdi's book from Khalaji, "Shiite Jurisprudence, Political Expediency, and Nuclear Weapons," p. 20)

[40.] Khalaji, "Shiite Jurisprudence, Political Expediency, and Nuclear Weapons," p. 20.

[41.] "Top Cleric: Iran Has Right to 'Special Weapons'"

[42.] Khalaji, "Shiite Jurisprudence, Political Expediency, and Nuclear Weapons," p. 24.

[43.] Ibid., pp. 15-17, 19-20, 23-24.

[44.] Kessler, "Did Iran's supreme leader issue a fatwa against the development of nuclear weapons?"

[45.] Khalaji, "Shiite Jurisprudence, Political Expediency, and Nuclear Weapons," pp. 15-16.; For discussions of the nature of dar al-harb, and "harbis," see Bostom, *The Legacy of Jihad*, pp. v, 95-97, 301; For discussions of the absence of any true equivalent to Western just war theory in Islam, see *The Legacy of Jihad*, pp. 329-330, and Ella Landau-Tasseron, "Non-Combatants in Muslim Legal Thought," *Hudson Institute, Center on Islam, Democracy, and the Future of the Muslim World, Research Monographs on the Muslim World*, Series No. 1, Paper No. 3, December 2006. http://bit.ly/1ejBMXb (accessed December 29, 2013); and Joseph Spoerl, "Jihad and Just War," *The Levantine Review* Volume 2, Number 2 (Winter 2013), pp. 159-187. http://bit.ly/1d0IWNO

[46.] Khalaji, "Shiite Jurisprudence, Political Expediency, and Nuclear Weapons," p. 15, and Khalaji's related note 20, p. 26, which includes the following: Sayyed Ali Tabatabai, *Riaz al-Masael fi Tahqiq al-Ahkam bi Dalael*, vol. 8 (Qom: Moassassat Aal al-Bait li Ihyae Attorath, 1999), pp. 69–70. ***"The..Shiite jurist Allameh Helli* concurred that if defeating the enemy requires attacking and killing women, children, and elders, then such steps must be taken. Helli considered such an opinion the consensus among his jurist peers."*** See Muhammad Hasan Najafi, *Javaher al-Kalam fi Sharh-e Sharae al-Eslam*, vol. 21 (Beirut: Dar Ihya al-Torath al-Arabi, 1992), p. 71; Sad al-Din abu al-Qasem ibn Barraj, *al-Mohazzab*, vol. 1 (Qom: Jameat al-Modarressin, 1986), p. 302; Fakhr al-Din abu Abdullah ibn Edris, *al-Saraer al-Havi li Tahrir al-Fatawi*, vol. 3 (Qom: Jameat al-Modarressin, 1369), p. 7.;

*On "Allameh Helli," see also Sabine Schmidtke, "ḤELLI, ḤASAN B. YUSOF B. MOṬAHHAR," Iranicaonline.org, http://bit.ly/1czzzrW (accessed December 29, 2013). Jamal ad-Din Hasan ibn Yusuf ibn Ali ibn Muthahhar al-Hilli died December 18, 1325, and was one of the most renowned Shiite theologians and scholars of his era referred to as a Marja (Grand Ayatollah). His works expounded upon Islamic law, jurisprudence, theology and Koranic exegesis. Al-Hilli recorded all of his writings up to the year 1294 in his biographical work Khulasat ul-Aqwal ("The Summary of Opinions").

[47.] Khalaji, "Shiite Jurisprudence, Political Expediency, and Nuclear Weapons," pp. 15,16.; For two examples of accolades heaped upon Montazeri, see the remarks by neoconservative analysts Michael Rubin and Michael Ledeen in their respective eulogies: Michael Rubin, "Grand Ayatollah Hossein Ali Montazeri, R.I.P.," *National Review Online*, December 21, 2009 http://bit.ly/JHy3bW; Michael Ledeen, "Montazeri," *Pajamas Media*, December 21, 2009 http://bit.ly/1hcjEmW

[48.] Ibid., pp. 16,17

[49.] Ibid., p. 17; see also n. 40, p. 27, which cites, Abu Ali Tabarsi, *Majma al-Bayan fi Tafsir al-Quran*, vol. 1 (Beirut: Dar Ihya Attorath al-Arabi, 1995), p. 430.

[50.] Ibid.; see also n. 41, p. 27, which cites, Morteza Ansari, *al-Makasib al-Moharrama* (Qom: no publisher/date); p. 320.

[51.] Ibid.; see also n. 42, p. 27, which cites, Khomeini's July 31, 1981 speech from *Sahifeh-ye Nour*, vol. 15, p. 107.

[52.] Ibid., with reference again to Khomeini's July 31, 1981 speech

[53.] Blair, "Iran nuclear deal – what are the terms of the agreement?", *The Telegraph* (London)

[54.] "Text of Iran-Powers Nuclear Deal, Obama and Zarif Statements About Iran's Nuclear

Activities," *Al Jazeerah*, November 23, 2013; Michael Curtis, "Desperately Seeking Obama," *The American Thinker*, November 26, 2013 http://bit.ly/1dk9H39

[55.] A discussion by the World Nuclear Association about removing "highly enriched uranium" from weapons stockpiles in the U.S., and former Soviet Union, for use in nuclear power reactors, includes this observation:

> **The main weapons material is highly enriched uranium (HEU), containing at least 20% uranium-235**... ("Military Warheads as a Source of Nuclear Fuel," *World Nuclear Association*, updated, December 20, 2013 http://bit.ly/1kVkLr0)

[56.] Martin Sevior, "Could Iran be building nuclear weapons? A scientific perspective," *theconversation.com/uk*, March 6, 2012 http://bit.ly/19vRgtB

[57.] Jeremy Bernstein, "Iran's Plutonium Game," *The New York Review of Books Blog*, November 11, 2013 http://bit.ly/1cfIxWO

[58.] Curtis, "Desperately Seeking Obama"

[59.] Martin Sevior, "Uranium, plutonium, heavy water ... why Iran's nuclear deal matters," *theconversation.com/uk*, November 25, 2013, http://bit.ly/1ahdycX

[60.] Jonathan Spyer, "U.S. Blindspot Shows on the Iran Nuclear Deal," *Tablet Magazine*, November 25, 2013 http://bit.ly/1fUPscV

[61.] Ibid.

[62.] "Iranian FM: Iran to Continue Nuclear Activities" (no separate hyperlink available; cited within this *Al Jazeerah* report: http://bit.ly/18AJEFv)

[63.] Spyer, "U.S. Blindspot Shows on the Iran Nuclear Deal"

[64.] Bill Gertz, "Iran, North Korea Secretly Developing New Long-Range Rocket Booster for ICBMs," *The Washington Free Beacon*, November 26, 2013, http://bit.ly/JYNLjN

[65.] Khalaji, "Shiite Jurisprudence, Political Expediency, and Nuclear Weapons," p. 15, observes that the emblem logo on the Iranian Revolutionary Guard Corps uniform quotes Koran 8:60, a verse sanctioning jihad war, and terrorism [for contents of this verse, see note 36]

[66.] Gertz, "Iran, North Korea Secretly Developing New Long-Range Rocket Booster for ICBMs,"

[67.] Ibid.

[68.] This November, 2010 *New York Times* report, based upon the leak of a highly classified diplomatic cable, acknowledged Iran's procurement of North Korean missiles capable of carrying a nuclear warhead for 2000 miles.

> Secret American intelligence assessments have concluded that Iran has obtained a cache of advanced missiles, based on a Russian design, that are much more powerful than anything Washington has publicly conceded that Tehran has in its arsenal, diplomatic cables show. Iran obtained 19 of the missiles from North Korea, according to a cable dated Feb. 24 of this year [2010]…The missiles

could for the first time give Iran the capacity to strike at capitals in Western Europe or easily reach Moscow, and American officials warned that their advanced propulsion could speed Iran's development of intercontinental ballistic missiles...The Feb. 24 cable, which is among those obtained by WikiLeaks and made available to a number of news organizations, makes it clear that American intelligence agencies believe that the complete shipment indeed took place, and that Iran is taking pains to master the technology in an attempt to build a new generation of missiles. **The missile intelligence also suggests far deeper military — and perhaps nuclear — cooperation between North Korea and Iran than was previously known.** (William Broad, James Glanz, and David Sanger, "Iran Fortifies Its Arsenal With the Aid of North Korea" *The New York Times*, November 28, 2010 http://nyti.ms/1aiPEOe

Three years later, a December 7, 2013 *UPI* report, which focused on the likely attendance of Iranian scientists and military officials at an anticipated long-range ballistic missile test launch, noted,

> **For more than a decade, Iran and North Korea maintained what is in effect a joint missile development program**. ("Iran to observe North Korea missile test," *UPI*, December 7, 2012 http://bit.ly/19z9iWq

[69.] Gertz, "Iran, North Korea Secretly Developing New Long-Range Rocket Booster for ICBMs"

[70.] "Iran appoints pragmatist Salehi to head nuclear program," *Reuters*, August 16, 2013 http://reut.rs/1cD0GT0

[71.] Amir Taheri, "Iran nuke deal quietly collapses," *The New York Post*, December 16, 2013, http://bit.ly/1c9NFS9

[72.] Ibid.

[73.] Ibid.

[74.] Ibid.

[75.] "Transcript of interview highlights with Hassan Rouhani, Iranian president," *Financial Times.com*, November 29, 2013 http://on.ft.com/1by4PmB

[76.] "Senior Iranian MP: No Need to US Permission for Nuclear Enrichment," *Fars News Agency*, December 9, 2013 http://bit.ly/19Xg6R8

[77.] "Deputy FM: Iran Standing Firm on Uranium Enrichment Rights," *Fars News Agency*, December 7, 2013 http://bit.ly/1chX3AC

[78.] Taheri, "Iran nuke deal quietly collapses"

[79.] "Iran's nuclear activities not slowed down: Salehi," *IRNA*, December 12, 2013, http://bit.ly/1fYdu6e

[80.] Ibid.

[81.] "West's Lack of Cooperation Causes Iran to Enrich Uranium," *Fars News Agency*, December 16, 2013 http://bit.ly/19921lv; "Zarif Phones Kerry, Ashton to Stress Iran's

Protest against US Fresh Sanctions," *Fars News Agency*, December 16, 2013 http://bit.ly/1k8Vzgh

[82.] "FM: Pressures lead to production of 18,000 centrifuges," *IRNA*, December 17, 2013, http://bit.ly/1gjAywU

[83.] "Iran Says It Is Developing New Centrifuges", *The Associated Press*, December 27, 2013 http://nyti.ms/JwpAbu

[84.] "Iranian MP: Ratification of 60% Uranium Enrichment Bill Necessary," *Fars News Agency*, December 29, 2013 http://bit.ly/19uOiQn

[84a.] "Over 200 Iranian MPs Sign Draft Bill to Require Gov't to Enrich Uranium to 60%," *Fars News Agency*, January 4, 2014 http://bit.ly/JDmJxZ

[84b.] Adam Kredo, "Iranian Cleric: 'Having a Nuclear Bomb is Necessary to Put Down Israel'," *The Washington Free Beacon*, January 6, 2014, http://bit.ly/1aa9eQw

[84c.] @HassanRouhani, January 14, 2014, 3:36 AM http://bit.ly/19rQ4XL; Screen shot captured here: http://bit.ly/1aZsTzn

[84d.] "Iran's Foreign Minister Zarif lays a wreath at the grave of assassinated Hezbollah military commander Moughniyeh in the suburbs of Beirut," *Reuters*, January 13, 2014

http://bit.ly/1m6OOtu; Laila Bassam, Nadim Ladki, "Hezbollah's most wanted commander killed in Syria bomb," *Reuters*, February 13, 2008 http://reut.rs/LcmyL5; For the death toll from the embassy and Marine barracks attacks, see. Richard M. Gannon, "The Bombing of Embassy Beirut, 1983" in Joseph G.Sullivan, editor, *Embassies Under Siege*, 1995, Washington, DC.; and Timothy J. Geraghty, Alfred M. Gray Jr. (Foreword), *Peacekeepers at War: Beirut 1983—The Marine Commander Tells His Story*, 2009, Dulles, VA, p. xv.

[84e.] Matthew Levitt, David Schenker, "Who Was Imad Mughniyeh?," *The Washington Institute*, Policy #1340, February 14, 2008 http://bit.ly/1b4gp9E

[84f.] Marcelo Martinez Burgos, District attorney, Investigations Unit of the Office of the Attorney General, Alberto Nisman, Attorney general, Office of criminal investigations

"AMIA CASE," pp. 21-22 http://bit.ly/1m80jRz

[84g.] "Senior MP Reiterates Iran's Full Support for Anti-Israel Resistance Front," *Fars News Agency*, January 18, 2014 http://bit.ly/LjQzbl

[84h.] Avi Issacharoff, "Hezbollah digs in for more conflict with Israel," *The Times of Israel*, January 17, 2014 http://bit.ly/1dEgDdr

[84i.] Thomas Erdbrink, Alan Cowell, "Iran Says it Suspends Enrichment Under Deal with Powers," *The New Times*, January 20, 2014 http://nyti.ms/LuMEsj

[84j.] Tom Cohen, "Iranian official on nuke deal: 'We did not agree to dismantle anything'," *CNN*, January 23, 2014 http://cnn.it/1ipEvUe

[84k.] Joint Subcommittee Hearing: Implementation of the Iran Nuclear Deal, Subcommittee on Terrorism, Nonproliferation, and Trade, and Subcommittee on the Middle East and North Africa, 2172 House Rayburn Office Building Washington, DC 20515, January 28, 2014, 2:00pm http://1.usa.gov/1aCzmpJ

[84L.] "Written Statement of Gregory S. Jones," Senior Researcher, Nonproliferation Policy Education Center, House Foreign Affairs Committee, Hearing on: Implementation of the Iran Nuclear Deal , January 28, 2014 http://1.usa.gov/LdhYeJ

[84m.] Aaron Blake, "Kerry on Iran: 'We do not recognize a right to enrich,'" *The Washington Post*, November 24, 2013. http://wapo.st/1cyqBvH

[84n.] Jim Acosta, "White House prepared to allow limited Iran nuclear enrichment," CNN Political Ticker, December 3, 2013. http://cnn.it/18Z6NQ4

[84o.] "Written Statement of Gregory S. Jones"

[84p.] Adam Kredo, "Lawmaker: Iran Deal Being Kept in 'Super Secret Location'," The *Washington Free Beacon*, January 28, 2014 http://bit.ly/1b74mZu

[84q.] Ibid.

[84r.] Adam Kredo, "Iranian Ballistic Missile Program Can Continue Under Deal," *The Washington Free Beacon*, February 4, 2014 http://bit.ly/1k8q9Is

[84s.] Ibid.

[84t.] "FULL TRANSCRIPT: Obama's 2014 State of the Union address," *The Washington Post*, January 28, 2014 http://wapo.st/L1ZIR0

[84u.] "New Poll: Americans Show Overwhelming Support For Israeli Positions — Oppose Obama's Positions," *mclaughlinonline.com*, January 28, 2014 http://bit.ly/1besVqt

[85.] Christopher Hellman, "Iran Deal Could Lead To Scuttling Of The Great U.S. Oil Boom,"

www.forbes.com, November 25, 2013 http://onforb.es/1dXQkJu

[85a.] Ibid.

[85b.] Benoît Faucon, "Iran Deal Opens Door for Businesses," *The Wall Street Journal*, December 1, 2013, http://on.wsj.com/19DPf92; "Iran predicts growth rate 2.2% next year from current minus 5.8%," *IMRA*, December 1, 2013, http://bit.ly/1byUwOV; "South Korea Increases Oil Imports from Iran by 26 Percent," *Fars News Agency*, December 15, 2013 http://bit.ly/19zdoDz

[86.] Ilan Berman, "The Real Cost of Geneva," National Review Online, December 17, 2013, http://bit.ly/1hSgxhA

[87.] Taheri, "Iran nuke deal quietly collapses"

[88.] Ibid.

[89.] Lukes, "Linguistic Deception and U.S.-Soviet Arms Control Treaties," pp. 151-152.

[90.] Robert Conquest, *Reflections on a Ravaged Century*, New York, 2001, p. 121

[91.] Steven Plaut, "Collaborators in the War Against the Jews: Richard A. Falk," *Frontpage Magazine.com*, December 4, 2009 http://bit.ly/1cT5i7m; See also, "Canada calls for U.N. official Richard Falk's dismissal over accusing Israel of genocide," *JNS.org*, December 19, 2013 http://bit.ly/1lvYpN8

[92.] Falk, "Trusting Khomeini"

[93.] The late political scientist Samuel Huntington (d. 2008) validated this contention by adducing hard data. See, *The Clash of Civilizations and the Remaking of World Order*, New York, 1996, all quotes above from pp. 254ff.

[94.] Bostom, *The Legacy of Jihad*, especially, pp. 141-367.

[95.] As of February 26, 2014, an estimated 22,518 jihad terror attacks had been documented (a conservative estimate; see *thereligionofpeace.com* http://bit.ly/1989U8n) since September 11, 2001. These data are confirmed, independently, by both 2012, and longer term findings (i.e., dating back through the 1990s) from the National Consortium for the Study of Terrorism and Responses to Terrorism [START], reported (via data shared with CNN) in late October, 2013:

> More than 8,500 terrorist attacks killed nearly 15,500 people last year as violence tore through Africa, Asia and the Middle East, according to the National Consortium for the Study of Terrorism and Responses to Terrorism…**Six of the seven most deadly groups are affiliated with al Qaeda, according to START, and most of the violence was committed in Muslim-majority countries**… Beginning with the 1990s, South Asia, North Africa and the Middle East has seen steadily rising number of attacks, a trend that has accelerated in recent years. Although terrorism touched 85 countries last year, just three - Pakistan, Iraq and Afghanistan - suffered more than half of 2012's attacks (55%) and fatalities (62%). [Daniel Burke, "Terrorist attacks and deaths hit record high, report shows," *CNN Belief Blog*, October 28, 2013 http://cnn.it/1lKqwpg]

[96.] See reference 11.

[97.] Jacques Ellul, *Propaganda: The Formation of Men's Attitudes*, 1973, New York, p. 23.

[98.] Ryan Grim, "White House Dares Democratic Senators Pushing Iran Sanctions To Admit They Want War, " *The Huffington Post*, January 9, 2014, http://huff.to/1ksTnmq

[99.] "S. 1881: Nuclear Weapon Free Iran Act of 2013,"113th Congress, 2013–2015. Text as of 12/20/2013 (Placed on Calendar in the Senate). http://bit.ly/19j0M2Y

[100.] See this detailed chronology, annotated, and updated, through early January, 2014:

"Fact Sheets: The Failure of Sanctions Against Iran," *The Jewish Virtual Library*, http://bit.ly/1lZpdTf

[101.] "White House suggests Iran sanctions bill could draw U.S. into war"; The full exchange on this matter between White House Press Secretary Jay Carney, and Fox News Senior White House correspondent Ed Henry (reproduced from "Reporter to Carney: Why Is White House Accusing Democrats of Wanting to Go to War?," *The Washington Free Beacon*, January 10, 2014, http://bit.ly/1lZostB) is quite edifying:

ED HENRY: On Iran, got a lot of questions on that, but I wanted to be more specific on — there's an interesting story in Huffington Post where a White House official is quoted today as suggesting that people who support this sanctions bill on the Hill, Democrats and Republicans — the quote is, if certain members of Congress want the U.S. to take military action, they should be up front with the American public and say so. You're basically accusing Democrats like Bob Menendez of wanting to go to war. Is that really a fair characterization?

JAY CARNEY: I think we have said all along, Ed, that we have worked cooperatively and effectively with an excellent partner in Congress in building a sanctions regime against Iran the likes of which the world has never seen, more effective than the world has ever seen. And we share the same goals that members of Congress of both parties share, which is the absolute need to deprive Iran of acquiring a nuclear weapon. And our stated concern again and again is that pursuing sanctions now, new sanctions now, would actually undermine the objective here, the objective being that we can bring about, potentially, through negotiation, a peaceful resolution of this conflict between Iran and the rest of the world in a verifiable, transparent way that would, more effectively than a military action, assure the P-5 plus one, the United States, our allies and everybody in the world that Iran does not and is not — does not have and is not pursuing a nuclear weapon. So –

HENRY: **I understand you're saying this could blow up the diplomatic deal, but the thing is you're going further in this story. And a White House official on the record is saying that these lawmakers want the U.S. to take military action. Do you — can you say from the podium that you — that Democrat [New Jersey Senator] Bob Menendez wants to go to war?**

CARNEY: Look, I think that Senator Menendez — Chairman Menendez wants what we want, which is to prevent Iran from acquiring a nuclear weapon. He and many other in the Senate have been excellent partners in helping construct this sanctions regime which was designed to bring Iran to the negotiating table and which, thanks to the efforts of Congress, has achieved that. And I believe that, you know, when it comes — this isn't a debate about sanctions. Obviously this administration supports sanctions. We built the biggest, most effective sanctions regime in history. Our view of the current situation is that passing new sanctions legislation now would be counterproductive to the goal that we all share. And the problem — the obviously problem with that is that if we want, as everyone does, to prevent Iran from having a nuclear weapon, and we make it harder if not impossible to pursue achieving that goal peacefully, then we — our options become very limited. So it's not about motive; it's about, you know, the potential outcome that would be negative for the United States and our allies.

HENRY: **The president himself has repeatedly said he has the military option on the table, he should not take that off the table.**

CARNEY: And he won't.

HENRY: **So it would be unfair for people to suggest he wants to go to war, right? He's just saying I want to have that option. So how can you possibly accuse Democrats and Republicans on the Hill of wanting to take military action? That's what you're saying.**

CARNEY: Again, Ed, I think that –

HENRY: Are you running from that — (inaudible) — is my question.

CARNEY: No, I'm not. What I'm saying is — I mean, I don't know every one of a hundred senators, what their personal view is on whether or not military force ought to be used in Iran, so I can't give a blanket statement about how they all feel. What I do know is, when it comes to Senator Menendez and all of the partners who have assisted this administration over the years in building the sanctions regime, is that we share a common goal, which is to deprive Iran of the opportunity of acquiring a nuclear weapon, and to do so through negotiations. That's why we built the sanctions regime. And our strong concern is that passage of sanctions at this time would negatively affect and perhaps scuttle the negotiations that are underway, and then make it much harder, if not impossible, to achieve our objective peacefully.

[101a.] "MP: Iran Will End N. Talks if US Congress Approves Sanctions Bill," Fars News Agency, January 12, 2014 http://bit.ly/1eOBUOz

[101b.] Ibid.

[102.] John McDade, "Christians and Jews: Competitive Siblings or the Israel of God?" *New Blackfriars*, 2008, Vol 89, pp. 267–279, DOI: 10.1111/j.1741-2005.2008.00220.x; see pp. 267-268. McDade enumerates Conquest's "three laws," as follows:

1) Everyone is conservative about what he or she knows best.

2) Any organization not explicitly right-wing sooner or later becomes left wing. (Conquest gives as examples Amnesty International and the Church of England.)

3) The simplest way to explain the behaviour of any bureaucratic organization is to assume that it is controlled by a cabal of its enemies.

[103.] Falk, "Trusting Khomeini"

[104.] Reza Afshari, *Human Rights in Iran: The Abuse of Cultural Relativism*, 2001, Philadelphia, PA.

[105.] Elmer Swenson, "What Happens When Islamists Take Power? The Case of Iran," June 27, 2005, [gemsofislamism.tripod.com], http://bit.ly/19kHbiV

[105a.] Falk, "Trusting Khomeini"

[106.] D. G. Littman, "Jews under Muslim Rule: The Case of Persia," *Wiener Library Bulletin* 1979; vol. 32, pp. 5, 7–8. p. 5. Littman provides a very concise overview of the history of the Jewish community of Persia under Muslim rule, complemented by an impressive array of primary source documents from the archives of the Alliance Israélite Universelle (pp. 5–15), translated by the author into English, with but one exception, for the first time. The full text of Littman's landmark article, from which Bernard Lewis borrowed liberally for his discussion of Persian Jewry in *The Jews of Islam* (see especially pp. 181–83) is now available online at http://bit.ly/1lOjSRJ; "The Ancient Jewish Community of Iran and the Shiraz 'Show Trial,'" *United Nations Commission on Human Rights*, January 8, 2001 http://bit.ly/1har3AI

[107.] Afshari, *Human Rights in Iran: The Abuse of Cultural Relativism*; Eliz Sanasarian, *Religious Minorities in Iran*, 2000, Cambridge, MA.

[107a.] Falk, "Trusting Khomeini"

[108.] Afshari, *Human Rights in Iran: The Abuse of Cultural Relativism*, p. 22.

[109.] Afshari, *Human Rights in Iran: The Abuse of Cultural Relativism*, pp. 5, 8, 68, 87,110,112,123,139-141,144,206; Ann E. Mayer, *Islam and Human Rights*, 1999, Boulder, CO, pp. 13-14, 23, 24, 141-144, 151, 154, 165-168, 197, 237 note 48, 238 note 9; See also "Constitution of the Islamic Republic of Iran," Adopted: 24 October 24, 1979; Effective: 3 December 3, 1979; Amended: 28 July 28, 1989 http://bit.ly/1lOmHSE

[110.] Amir Taheri "Haunting Headlines from the Past," *Asharq Alawsat*, December 3, 2010 http://bit.ly/1m0ctfl; Relevant extracts from this essay are provided, below:

> One of the amazing gadgets that Sinbad the Sailor finds during his marvelous trips is a kaleidoscope that contains images of past and future life. Modern technology cannot offer the future in image. But images of the past are aplenty, and, thanks to Internet, are at anyone's disposal with the click of a button, causing pleasure or pain as the case may be. Last week, a friend in Tehran, a prankster in his youth, emailed me pictures of the front pages of Kayhan, the daily newspaper of which I was Editor in the 1970s. The front pages belong to the period October 1978 to February 1979, the Khomeinist revolution's decisive and ultimately successful phase. The front pages offer an almost surrealistic image of what was about to happen to Iran. A historian who depended on them would be led up the garden path. However, the cumulative image that the front pages provide offers an alternative, and perhaps more sobering, reading of a revolution based almost entirely on deception. Let us examine a few headlines from those heady days... "Full Freedom Is The First Goal of the Revolution." This banner is a quotation from Abol-Hassan Banisadr, then a student in Paris but also regarded as a spiritual son of Khomeini. Within less than a year, Khomeini had made him the first President of his Islamic Republic. A year and a half later, "Abol" had to flee back to Paris to save his life. To do so, "Abol" had to hitch a ride from one Massoud Rajavi, an Islamist-Marxist militant, who had hijacked a passenger aircraft to fly into exile. The next headline comes from Rajavi whose guerrillas had helped Khomeini by murdering policemen, robbing banks, and setting up roadblocks to terrorize the people. Here it is: "Under Islam All Parties Will Be Free." The last time I heard of Rajavi was in 2008 in Baghdad where he lived in a house that had once belonged to Izzat al-Duri, Saddam Hussein's vice president..."Parties of The Left Have Freedom To Operate." This comes from Nureddin Kianuri, leader of the pro-Soviet Communist Tudeh (Masses) Party, basing his claim on assurances from Khomeini. In the early phases of his regime, no political party helped Khomeini more than Tudeh did. Tudeh was especially useful in leading the regime's secret police to the hideouts of leftist groups that had broken with Khomeini. Three years later, however, the Tudeh was banned and Kianuri was in Evin Prison along with his entire Central Committee. Over 300 party cadres were executed while hundreds of others fled to exile. To save their lives, Kianuri and a few other top leaders converted to Shi'ism and appeared on television to confess to having spied for the KGB. According to the confessions, Kianuri received a monthly stipend of $800 from the Soviet secret police. Despite the confessions and demands of pardon from the "Imam," as Khomeini's devotees like to call him, Kianuri and other Tudeh

leaders were to die in prison or under house arrest. What about this headline? "The Revolution Will Create True Parliamentary Democracy." This claim comes from Karim Sanjabi who had briefly served as a minister of the Shah in the 1950s and was to become Khomeini's Foreign Minister for a fleeting moment. Sanjabi and his Mossadeqist friends had presented a kind of mild opposition to the Shah because, they claimed, he violated parliamentary rules. In 1978, they hoped that the ayatollah would restore what the Shah had taken away in 1953. Facing an arrest warrant, Sanjabi had to flee Iran in 1982, ending up in the United States where he died broken-hearted in 1995.

[110a.] Falk, "Trusting Khomeini"

[111.] See Bostom, *The Legacy of Jihad*, pp. 226-29 for Khomeini's pronouncements on jihad; Subsequent discussions herein elaborate his general views on non-Muslims, and Jews in particular, which essentially reiterate the traditionalist Shiite Islamic *Weltanschauung*; For Khomeini's misogyny, including promotion of female child abuse, and acceptance of animal sodomy, see, Parvin Darabi, "Leader Or Exterminator? Ayatollah Khomeini's Religious Teachings on Marriage, Divorce and Relationships," http://bit.ly/JQmM9I; and "Khomeini's Teachings on Sex with Infants and Animals" http://bit.ly/1cPfTPW; *Dr. Homa Darabi Foundation*

[112.] See reference 102.

[113.] See references 4 and 5 for previous discussions of takiya, and also: Czeslaw Milosz, *The Captive Mind*, translated from the Polish by Jane Zielonko, 1953, New York, Chapter III "Ketman" [kitman], http://bit.ly/1exzP9d

[113a.] Falk, "Trusting Khomeini"

[114.] "UANI Issues Statement Regarding P5+1 Deal with Iran"

[115.] John Bolton, "Abject Surrender by the United States. What does Israel do now?," *The Weekly Standard*, November 24, 2013 http://bit.ly/1dfFLWe; James Jay Carafano, "Munich II" *National Review Online*, November 24, 2013 http://bit.ly/1gxukJe; Benjamin Weinthal "Waltzing with the Mullahs to a Nuclear Bomb," *National Review Online*, November 24, 2013 http://bit.ly/1aU5W0p; Victor Davis Hanson, "Peace for Our Time," *National Review Online*, November 24, 2013 http://bit.ly/1eA89Ts; Dore Gold, "The Geneva Agreement: The Devil Is Not in the Details But in the Wider Picture," *National Review Online*, November 24, 2013

http://bit.ly/1he5mzN; Jack David "A Bad and Morally Indefensible Deal," *National Review Online*, November 24, 2013 http://bit.ly/1dnQPlX; Daniel Pipes, "A Foreign-Policy Disaster," *National Review Online*, November 24, 2013 http://bit.ly/19mUS0L

[116.] Anthony H. Cordesman, Chloe Coughlin-Schulte, Bryan Gold, "The US and Iran: Sanctions, Energy, Arms Control, and Regime Change," *Center for Strategic and International Studies*, December 17, 2013 http://bit.ly/1bk95pv

[117.] Ibid., p. 140. Rouhani was described as embodying a "measured pragmatism," while his appointments to key Iranian government administrative posts "further reflected this commitment to a technocratic over ideological government." The report added that many of these key appointees had previously served under the allegedly "moderate" former President, Ali Akbar Hashemi Rafsanjani.

[118.] Ibid., pp. xx, xxii include these comments, for example:

> There is no way of knowing how much weapons design data Iran has acquired from Pakistani or other sources, or whether it has carried out tests of nuclear designs using non-fissile materials at facilities like Parchin, but it certainly faced no technical barriers to covertly designing nuclear devices, bombs, and warheads. In short, Iran came as close to the point of nuclear "break out" as a nation could without actually producing weapons grade material or actually showing it could detonate some form of fissile event. It is unclear that any agreement (or any preventive strikes) can halt important aspects of Iran's nuclear weapons design efforts. Iran cannot be sure such post agreement activities will remain covert, but it can have reasonable confidence that they will…Iran can disperse design and test facilities, and carry out as much of the nuclear bomb and warhead modeling and testing it needs with little risk of detection. It can launch simulated nuclear warheads in its missile tests and nuclear bombs in simulated air exercises – testing the technology based on the results of physical recovery or highly encrypted telemetry. Unless the agreement brings a total halt to all Iranian Uranium enrichment activity, and firmly halts activation of the reactor at Arak or brings it under tight control, Iran will still have the ability to modify its use of such enrichment capabilities and produce weapons grade material. If Iran can continue to develop improved centrifuges, it will acquire both far greater ability to conceal a nuclear enrichment and the ability to produce significant stockpiles more quickly. There is also at least a minimal risk of some form of Iranian covert development of at least some form of nuclear weapon. Iran could potentially avoid the design ands testing complications in creating an implosion weapon by going for a gun device. The result would be much heavier, but still transportable by ship, and present the threat of some kind of rouge attack: A ship sailing into Haifa or a port in the Gulf. This kind of asymmetric threat may lack the credibility of serious nuclear forces, but would be impossible to dismiss.

> [I]t is still far from clear that they [i.e., sanctions and diplomacy] will stop Iran's progress toward a nuclear weapons capability or that successful negotiations may bring about long-term changes in the US-Iranian relationship. The US and its allies must continue to develop effective missile defenses. The US should continue key efforts to deter and contain Iran's missile defenses.

[119.] See references 115 and 116 for center-right assessments of the "P5 + 1" agreement; For Iran's hegemonic aspirations, see Khomeini's 1942 speech, "Islam Is Not A Religion of Pacifists," in Bostom, *The Legacy of Jihad*, p. 226, the "Constitution of the Islamic Republic of Iran," section, "An Ideological Army," and "Archival—Hassan Nasrallah in the Late 1980s: Lebanon Should Become Part of the Greater Islamic Republic Ruled by Leader of Iran, Who Should Appoint all Islamic Rulers," *The Middle East Media Research Institute*, Clip No. 2636 [Transcript] http://bit.ly/1hSQWru

[120.] Georges Vajda, "Juifs et Musulmans Selon Le Hadit," ("Jews and Muslims According to the Hadith"), *Journal Asiatique*, 1937, vol. 229, pp. 57-129, translated in full in Bostom, *The Legacy of Islamic Antisemitism*, with relevant English extracts about Islamic eschatology and the Jews on p. 246; David Cook, *Studies in Muslim Apocalyptic* (Studies in Late Antiquity and Early Islam, No. 21), 2002, Princeton, N.J., see section, "The Jewish Dajjal," pp. 110ff., and pp. 341, 367; See in addition, Cook's, " 'Hadith,' Authority and the End of the World: Traditions in Modern Muslim Apocalyptic Literature," *Oriente Moderno*, Nuova serie, Anno 21 (82), Nr. 1, *Hadith in Modern Islam*, 2002, p. 36; and his, "Dajjāl," *Encyclopaedia of Islam, Three*, edited by Gudrun Krämer, Denis Matringe, John Nawas, Everett Rowson. Brill Online, 2013, accessed December 25, 2013; See also, Moshe Sharon, "We only get one strike," *The Jerusalem Post*, July 16, 2008 http://bit. ly/1d3b02l; Mehdi Khalaji, "Apocalyptic Politics—On the Rationality of Iranian Policy," *Washington Institute for Near East Policy*, Iran Policy Focus #79, January 2008 pp. 30-31 http://bit.ly/1flV4KF

[121.] Cook, *Studies in Muslim Apocalyptic*, section 4, "Shi'i Apocalyptic," pp. 189ff.; For a thorough reconsideration of the importance of contemporary Shiite messianism/"Mahdism" in Iran, see the cogent argumentation in, Ze'ev Maghen, "Occultation in 'Perpetuum': Shi'ite Messianism and the Policies of the Islamic Republic," *Middle East Journal*, 2008, Vol. 62, No. 2, pp. 232-257 http://bit.ly/1eBCtLc

[122.] A. Savyon, Y. Mansharoff, "The Doctrine of Mahdism in the Ideological and Political Doctrine of Mahmoud Ahmadinejad and Ayatollah Mesbah-e-Yazdi," *The Middle East Media Research Institute*, Inquiry & Analysis # 357, May 2007 http://bit.ly/1eBDhQm

[123.] E. Zigron, A. Savyon, "The Image Of The Jew In The Eyes Of Iran's Islamic Regime – Part I: Theological Roots," *The Middle East Media Research Institute*, Inquiry & Analysis Series Report No. 922, January 27, 2013 http://bit.ly/1hmAXPR

[124.] See for example, Roger Savory, *Iran Under the Safavids*, 1980, Cambridge, U.K., chapter 2, "Theocratic State: the Reign of Shah Ismail I, 1501-1524," pp. 27-49.

[125.] Andrew Bostom, *Sharia Versus Freedom—The Legacy of Islamic Totalitarianism*, 2012, Amherst, N.Y., see especially pp. 100-160, 497-537.

[125a.] Abbas Amanat, *Apoclayptic Islam and Iranian Shi'ism*, 2009, London/New York, p. 194.

[126.] Ignaz Goldziher, *Introduction to Islamic Theology and Law*, Princeton, N.J., 1981, translated from the German *Vorlesungen über den Islam*, 1910, pp. 213ff.

[126a.] Edward G. Browne, *A Year Amongst the Persians—Impressions as to the Life, Character, and Thought of the People of Persia Received During Twelve Months Residence in That Country in the Years 1887-8*, 1893, London, U.K., pp. 371-372.

[126b.] Sorour Soroudi, "The concept of Jewish impurity and its reflection in Persian and Judeo-Persian traditions," *Irano-Judaica: studies relating to contacts with Persian culture throughout the ages*, 1994, Vol. 3, pp. 142-170; Sanasarian, *Religious Minorities in Iran*, pp. 23-24, 85-87, 108-109, 172 note 91, 198 notes 6 and 10; Afshari, *Human Rights in Iran*, pp. 136-137.

[127.] Cordesman, Coughlin-Schulte, Gold, "The US and Iran: Sanctions, Energy, Arms Control, and Regime Change"

[128.] Ibid., p. xxv

[129.] Ibid., p. 140

[130.] Ibid.

[130a.] Steven Stalinksy, "An Iranian Sermon Primer," *The New York Sun*, June 7, 2006 http://bit.ly/1a5GlBp

[130b.] Moojan Momen, *An Introduction to Shi'i Islam: The History and Doctrines of Twelver Shi'ism*, 1987 New Haven, CT; see chapter 8, "The Twelfth Imam, His Occultation, and Return," pp. 161 ff.

[130c.] Reza Khalili, "New Iran president thanks 'messiah' for victory," *WorldNet Daily*, June 23, 2013 http://bit.ly/1dsB9xy

[131.] Thomas Erdbrink, Jodi Rudoren, "Iran's President-Elect Provokes Furor Abroad With Remarks on Israel," *The New York Times*, August 2, 2013 http://nyti.ms/1eGcsfX; The Associated Press reported the same story, which I accessed online January 14, 2014, as it **still appeared**, then. Nasser Karimi, "Iran's new president calls Israel an 'old wound'," *The Associated Press*, August 2, 2013 http://yhoo.it/KgRMQ2; Here are the key extracts:

> "The Zionist regime has been a wound on the body of the Islamic world for years and the wound should be removed," Rouhani was quoted as saying by the semi-official ISNA news agency. However, Rouhani's official website later Friday published somewhat different comments, citing him only as saying that "the occupation of Palestine and Jerusalem ... is a wound on the body of the Islamic world," without any direct reference to Israel or saying that this wound should be removed. **The two versions of his comments could not immediately be reconciled.** [emphasis added]

[132.] Eberdink, Rudoren, "Iran's President-Elect Provokes Furor Abroad With Remarks on Israel". This comment—a *res ipsa loqitur* exercise in self-parody—was added to the "revised" account of Rouhani's remarks in the *New York Times*:

> **At least three Iranian news agencies appeared to misquote him** [emphasis added] as saying: the "Zionist regime is a sore which must be removed." Later in the day they posted corrections.

[133.] "Profile: Hassan Rowhani [Rouhani]," *Iran Election Watch*, http://bit.ly/KgSNaJ

[134.] Ibid.

[135.] Hasan Rouhani, "Islamic Political Thought, Volume I: Theory," 2009, *Center for Strategic Research*, (Tehran) http://bit.ly/19s2b7p (English translation by Amil Imani)

[136.] Quotations pooled from: A. Savyon, "Irans Nuclear Policy Crisis," *Middle East Media Research Institute*, Inquiry & Analysis Series Report No.189, September 21, 2004 http://bit.ly/1cj6dK6; Text of speech by Supreme National Security Council Secretary Hassan Rohani to the Supreme Cultural Revolution Council; place and date not given: "Beyond the Challenges Facing Iran and the IAEA Concerning the Nuclear Dossier," *Rahbord* (in Persian), September 30, 2005, pp. 7-38. FBIS-IAP20060113336001; Cited in, John W. Parker, *Persian Dreams: Moscow and Tehran Since the Fall of the Shah*, Dullers, VA, 2008, p. 376, note 29; Full translation accessed here: http://bit.ly/1kzZWUy; and Chen Kane, "Nuclear Decision-Making in Iran: A Rare Glimpse," *Middle East Brief*, May, 2006, Number 5, Crown Center for Middle East Studies, Brandeis University http://bit.ly/1d3wAUi

[137.] Mohamed Younis, "Iranians Feel Bite of Sanctions, Blame U.S., Not Own Leaders— Most support nuclear program despite sanctions," *Gallup World*, February 7, 2013 http://bit.ly/1m59HW3

[138.] Hafezi, Pawlak, "Six powers clinch breakthrough deal curbing Iran's nuclear activity"

[138a.] "Global Unease With The Major World Powers—Chapter 4: Views of Iran, Its Leader, and the Nuclear Question," 47-Nation Pew Global Attitudes Survey, Wednesday June 27, 2007, p. 53 http://bit.ly/1eUSmfX; Gil Ronen, "Poll: Most Israeli Arabs Support Violent Uprising—Most Israeli Arabs oppose a Jewish majority, support a Palestinian uprising and want Iran to have nukes," *Israel National News*, June 25, 2013 http://bit.ly/1eUSLz5

[139.] Andrew Bostom, "Yippee 'Hizbullahi' and 'Chaadoris'?—Some Sad Realities About Irredentist Iran," *www.andrewbostom.org*, Iran, June 20, 2009 http://bit.ly/1do3UtN; "Mullah's Milk," *www.andrewbostom.org*, June 21, 2009 http://bit.ly/JZ0mU2; "Perpetuating Iran's Islamic Culture of Hate," *www.andrewbostom.org*, June 22, 2009 http://bit.ly/1do5hsq; and "The Squandered Emancipation of Iranian Women," *The American Thinker*, July 1, 2009 http://bit.ly/1hnyGnj

[140.] A. Savyon, "Elections in Iran – Part V: The Waning of the Protest Movement," *The Middle East Media Research Institute*, Inquiry & Analysis Series Report No. 529, June 29, 2009, http://bit.ly/JZ3Zcr

[141.] Ibid.

[142.] Ibid.

[143.] Ibid.

[144.] Ibid.

[144a.] "Agreement Between the United States of America and the Republic of Iraq On the Withdrawal of United States Forces from Iraq and the Organization of Their Activities during Their Temporary Presence in Iraq"; Two concordant translations of the agreement can be found via McClatchy Newspapers, and The U.S. State Department. "Unofficial Translation of U.S.-Iraq Troop Agreement from the Arabic Text," *McClatchy Newspapers*, November 18, 2008 http://bit.ly/1dyz4vC; Here is the State Department pdf version: http://1.usa.gov/1k8vPCF

[144b.] Walter Pincus, "Gates on Bush: Who knew?," *The Washington Post*, January 27, 2014 http://wapo.st/1dyBCdd; Citing Pincus' report, see Diana West's own trenchant analysis of these revelations, which alerted me to them: Diana West, "So That's Why Bush Wanted to Prevent Israel From Attacking Iranian Nukes," http://www.dianawest.net, January 29, 2014 http://bit.ly/1llhgvJ

[145.] V. Minorsky, *Tadhkirat al-Muluk. A Manual of Safavid Administration* (1725; reprint, London: 1943); Walter Fischel, "The Jews in Medieval Iran from the 16th to the 18th Centuries: Political, Economic, and Communal Aspects," *Irano Judaica* (1982): 266; Al-Amili, *Jami i Abbasi*, discussed in E. G. Browne, *A Literary History of Persia* (Cambridge: 1930), vol. 4, p. 407; Al-Majlisi, *The Treatise Lightning Bolts against the Jews*, trans. V. B. Moreen, in *Die Welt des Islams* 32 (1992), pp. 187–93. Also see Bostom, *The Legacy of Jihad*, pp. 213–20, for an original English translation of Al-Amili and a reproduction of Moreen's translation of Al-Majlisi; Rainer Brunner, "The Role of Hadith as Cultural

Memory in Shi'i History," *Jerusalem Studies in Arabic and Islam*, 2005, Vol. 30, p. 322; Browne's comments in *A Literary History of Persia*, Vol. 4, pp. 371-372 apply through at least 1912 (and cover both the Safavid and Qajar periods, i.e., from 1501/1502-1924), establishing the continuum of Shiite theocratic influence over **"every department of human activity, form the minutest details of personal purification to the largest issues of politics."** For Nadir Shah's attempt to suppress overtly anti- Sunni elements of Twelver Shi'ism, and render this creed the "fifth" school of Sunni Islamic jurisprudence, dubbed the Ja'fari *madhab* [school], in tribute to the sixth Imam Ja'far al-Sadeq (d. 765), who was affirmed as its central authority, see Ernest Tucker, "NĀDER SHAH" ["Nadir Shah"] *www. iranicaonline.org*, August 15, 2006, http://bit.ly/1jGWdmV

[146.] F.R.C. Bagley, "The Iranian Family Protection Law of 1967: A Milestone in the Advance of Women's Rights," *Iran and Islam: In Memory of the Late Vladimir Minorsky*, edited by C. E. Bosworth, 1971, Edinburgh, pp. 47-64.; Laurence D. Loeb, *Outcaste—Jewish Life in Southern Iran*, 1977, New York, pp. 289-291.

[147.] Andrew Bostom, Alyssa A. Lappen, "A True Iranian Reformer, and His Movement?," *The American Thinker*, July 9, 2009 http://bit.ly/1eHum1M

[148.] "Iran's Gulag Archipelago," *FrontPageMagazine.com*, January 17, 2008

http://bit.ly/1amdngW

[149.] Afshari, *Human Rights in Iran: The Abuse of Cultural Relativism*; Swenson, "What Happens When Islamists Take Power? The Case of Iran"; Sanasarian, *Religious Minorities in Iran*

[150.] "Iranians' Views Mixed on Political Role for Religious Figures," *Pew Research Religion and Public Life Project*, June 11, 2013 http://bit.ly/1j6pDKH

[151.] Ibid.

[152.] Ahmed Shaheed, "Report of the Special Rapporteur on the situation of human rights in the Islamic Republic of Iran," October 4, 2013. http://bit.ly/1e85UZI; http://bit.ly/IXKxvY; Curiously, Mr. Shaheed's report discussed the plight of Bahai, Christian, and "Dervish" (Sufi) Muslim religious minorities in Iran, **but not the Jews.**

[153.] Ibid.

[154.] Ibid.

[155.] Raquel Maria Dillon, "Pastor Detained in Iran Set to Return to US," *The Associated Press*, October 22, 2013 http://abcn.ws/1iQFnyK

[156.] Ibid.

[157.] Heather Clark, "California Pastor Eddie Romero Released After Being Detained for Protesting Imprisonment of Iranian Christians," *Christian News Network*, October 24, 2013 http://bit.ly/1aDrrGk

[158.] "Californian activist pastor to be sent home after Iran protest," *The New York Daily News*, October 22, 2013 http://nydn.us/1eRoUHW

[159.] Naghmeh Abedini, "Grim anniversary -- one year in Iranian prison for my husband

Pastor Saeed Abedini," *Fox News*, September 25, 2013 http://fxn.ws/1dODspM

[160.] "Iran: Four Christians sentenced to 80 lashes each for drinking communion wine," *Christian Solidarity Worldwide*, October 23, 2013 http://bit.ly/1hoFxgs

[161.] Ibid.

[162.] Bostom, *Sharia Versus Freedom—The Legacy of Islamic Totalitarianism*

[163.] Shaheed, "Report of the Special Rapporteur on the situation of human rights in the Islamic Republic of Iran"

[164.] Benjamin Weinthal, "Iran's Continued War on Christians," *National Review Online*,

October 25, 2013 http://bit.ly/1hoGKEz

[165.] Benjamin Weinthal, "Iran gives Christians 80 lashes for communion wine as UN blasts human rights record," *Fox News*, October 24, 2013 http://fxn.ws/1m2ntvs

[166.] Michael Ledeen, "Montazeri," *Pajamas Media*, December 21, 2009 http://bit.ly/1hcjEmW

[167.] Michael Rubin, "Grand Ayatollah Hossein Ali Montazeri, R.I.P.," *National Review Online*, December 21, 2009 http://bit.ly/JHy3bW

[167a.] Reuel Marc Gerecht, "The Bill O'Reilly Fallacy," *The New Republic*, October 16, 2010 http://bit.ly/1n2gGT6

[168.] Khalaji, "Apocalyptic Politics—On the Rationality of Iranian Policy," pp. 30-31

[168a.] Koran 8:39—[Hilali-Khan] And fight them until there is no more Fitnah (disbelief and polytheism: i.e. worshipping others besides Allah) and the religion (worship) will all be for Allah Alone [in the whole of the world]. But if they cease (worshipping others besides Allah), then certainly, Allah is All-Seer of what they do.; [Arberry] Fight them, till there is no persecution and the religion is God's entirely; then if they give over, surely God sees the things they do. http://bit.ly/1h08UEM

[168b.] Soroudi, "The concept of Jewish impurity and its reflection in Persian and Judeo-Persian traditions," pp. 143-146, 155; Sanasarian, *Religious Minorities in Iran*, p. 85.

[169.] Soroudi, "The concept of Jewish impurity and its reflection in Persian and Judeo-Persian traditions," p. 144; Sanasarian, *Religious Minorities in Iran*, p. 85.

[170.] Mahmood T. Davari, The Political Thought of Ayatullah Murtaza Mutahari—An Iranian theoretician of the Islamic state, London, U.K., 2005, p. 156.

[171.] Kamran Hashemi, *Religious Legal Traditions, International Human Rights Law and Muslim States*, Leiden, The Netherlands, 2008, p. 37.; For a very concise primer on Islamic blasphemy law, and its modern relevance, see Andrew Bostom, "Ten Key Points on Islamic Blasphemy Law," *The American Thinker*, March 15, 2013 http://bit.ly/LizMpU

[172.] Ibid.

[173.] Ibid.

[174.] J. K. Choksy, Nina Shea, "Religious Cleansing in Iran," *National Review Online*, July 22, 2009, http://bit.ly/Kl7Lwg

[175.] Ibid.

[176.] Jamsheed K. Choksy, "Montazeri's Limited Tolerance of Non-Muslims," *The Huffington Post*, December 21, 2009 http://huff.to/19W8HRV

[177.] "Can a Nuclear Armed Iran Be Contained?," *The Morningside Post*, October 9, 2012 http://bit.ly/1kRyuzf; The Montazeri quote comes from, Ḥusayn 'Alī. Muntaẓirī [Hosayn Ali Montazeri], *Khāṭirāt-i Āyat Allāh Ḥusayn 'Alī Muntaẓirī : bih inẓimām-i kulliyah-i payvast'hā*, [Ayatollah Hossein Ali Montazeri, including all attachments] 2001, Los Angeles Ketab Corp., p. 405. Dr. Ze'ev Maghen was kind enough to provide me the page citation.

[178.] Ze'ev Maghen, "Eradicating the 'Little Satan'" *Commentary Magazine*, January 1, 2009 http://bit.ly/JllmUp

Chapter 2

Jihad, Dhimmitude, and Islamic Jew-Hatred: The Sunni-Shiite Continuum (From Tabari to Tabatabai)

¶ Translation in Bostom, *The Legacy of Jihad*, p. 213.

¶¶ Muhammad Husayn al-Tabatabai, *Al-Mizan—An Exegesis of the Holy Qur'an*, translated by Sayyid Saeed Akhtar Rizvi, World Organization for Islamic Services, Tehran, 2002, Volume 11, pp. 96-97 http://bit.ly/LK6Nvh

[179.] "Despite fewer attacks in Western world, global terrorism increasing—Al-Qaida associated groups are 2012's most deadly terrorist groups," *National Consortium for the Study of Terrorism and Responses to Terrorism*, December 19, 2013 http://bit.ly/1icddkd

[180.] Ibid.

[181.] Ibid.

[182.] *thereligionofpeace.com*, http://bit.ly/1989U8n

[183.] Ibid.

[184.] Ibid.

[185.] Orla Borg. "Islam er den mest krigeriske religion," ["Islam is the most warlike religion"] JP.dk, October 9, 2005, http://bit.ly/1cMPor6 [title translated by Peder Jensen].

[186.] Tina Magaard. "Fjendebilleder og voldsforestillinger i islamiske grundtekster," ["Images of enemies and conceptions of violence in Islamic core scriptures"] Acta Jutlandica: aarsskrift for universitetsundervisningen i Jylland, 2007, Vol. 82, No. 1, pp. 213-244 [title translated by Peder Jensen].

[187.] Borg, "Islam is the most warlike religion."

[188.] Magaard, "Images of enemies and conceptions of violence in Islamic core scriptures,"

p. 221 [English translation of excerpt by Lars Hedegaard].

[189.] Paul Stenhouse. "Muhammad, Qur'anic Texts, the Shari'a, and Incitement to Violence," made available as a pdf file, October 25, 2005, here http://bit.ly/1kQN8cu; Stenhouse, MSC, PhD, completed the first Arabic to English translation of the 16th century *Futuh al-Habasha*, "The Conquest of Abyssinia," by Shihab al-Din Ahmad bin Abdul Qader bin Salem bin Uthman (Hollywood, CA: Tsehai Publishers and Distributors, 2003). This text is essential to understanding contemporary events in the Horn of Africa. It provides an eye-witness account of the jihad campaigns waged by Muslims against Ethiopian Christians during the early part of the sixteenth century.

[190.] Edward William Lane. *An Arabic English Lexicon*, 6 volumes, London, 1865, p. 472. (Cited in Stenhouse)

[191.] "al-Azhar." Encyclopaedia of Islam, Second Edition. Edited by: P. Bearman, Th. Bianquis, C.E. Bosworth, E. van Donzel, W.P. Heinrichs. Brill Online, 2014. Reference. January 20, 2014 http://bit.ly/1eNwVNT; Skovgaard-Petersen, Jakob. "al-Azhar, modern period." Encyclopaedia of Islam, Three. Edited by: Gudrun Krämer, Denis Matringe, John Nawas, Everett Rowson. Brill Online, 2014. Reference. Brown University. January 20, 2014 http://bit.ly/1eNwGSX

[192.] Muhammad Abdul Lateef Al Sobki. "Al-Jihad in Islam," in *Proceedings of The Fourth Conference of the Academy of Islamic Research, September, 1968*, Cairo, 1970, pp. 157-158.

[193.] Moshe Gil, *A History of Palestine, 634-1099*, Cambridge, 1992, p. 11.

[194.] Ibid.

[195.] D.S. Margoliouth *Mohammed and the rise of Islam*, London, 1905, reprinted in New Delhi, 1985, pp. 355ff

[196.] Ibid., pp. 362-363.

[197.] Richard Bell. *The Origin of Islam in its Christian Environment*, London, 1926, pp. 134-135; 151; 159-161.

[198.] Richard Bell *The Qur'an*. Vol. 1, Edinburgh, 1937, p. 171ff; Stenhouse. "Muhammad, Qur'anic Texts, the Shari'a, and Incitement to Violence"

[199.] Ali Dashti. *Muhammad 23 Years: A Study of the Prophetic Career of Mohammad* Costa Mesa, CA, 1994, p. 97.

[200.] "The Prophet Muhammad as a Jihad Model" Middle East Media Research Institute, July 24, 2001 No.246. http://bit.ly/1bhQhs0

[201.] See Bostom, *The Legacy of Jihad*, pp. 141-220.

[202.] *Sahih Bukhari*, Translator: M. Muhsin Khan; Edited by: Mika'il al-Almany; 1st online edition October 2, 2009 http://bit.ly/16GJkUY; Khan's translations are also (largely) reproduced here: http://bit.ly/GAsiLN

[203.] *Sahih Muslim*, Translator: Abd-al-Hamid Siddiqui; Edited by: Mika'il al-Almany; 1st online edition October 2, 2009 http://bit.ly/1aRpRhE; Siddiqui's translations are also (largely) reproduced here: http://bit.ly/GCbuo4

204. Ibn Khaldun, *The Muqudimmah. An Introduction to History*, Translated by Franz Rosenthal. New York, 1958, vol. 1, p. 473. Ibn Khaldun (1332–1406) was born in Tunis, and died in Cairo. A jurist, qadi (Maliki), renowned philosopher, historian, and sociologist, Ibn Khaldun's vaunted historical writings included an analysis of the Berbers, and a universal history, preceded by an introductory volume, *al-Muquddimah*.

206. Armand Abel, "L'Etranger dans L'Islam Classique", *Recueils de la Societe Jean Bodin*, 1958, Vol. 9, pp. 332-333, 343-345. [English translation by Michael J. Miller]

207. C.E. Bosworth. "al-Ṭabari, Abu Djafar Muḥammad b. Djarir b. Yazid." *Encyclopaedia of Islam, Second Edition*. Edited by: P. Bearman; , Th. Bianquis; , C.E. Bosworth; , E. van Donzel; and W.P. Heinrichs. Brill, 2011. Brill Online. Brown University. July 30, 2011.

208. "Al-Tabari's *Book of Jihad*—A Translation from the Original Arabic" (translated by Yasir S. Ibrahim), Lewiston, 2007.

209. Ibid., p. 63.

210. Abel, "L'Etranger dans L'Islam Classique"

211. "Al-Qaradhawi Speaks In Favor of Suicide Operations at an Islamic Conference in Sweden" Middle East Media Research Institute July 24, 2003 http://bit.ly/1hLrjq1

212. D.S. Margoliouth *Mohammed and the rise of Islam*, London, 1905, reprinted in New Delhi, 1985, pp. 355ff.

213. Joseph Schacht, *An Introduction to Islamic Law*, Oxford, 1982, pp. 130-131.

214. Huntington, *The Clash of Civilizations and the Remaking of World Order*, pp. 254ff.

215. Ibid.

216. Ibid.

217. Ibn Hudayl (French translation by Louis Mercier), *L'Ornement des Ames*, Paris, 1939, p. 195. English translation by Michael J. Miller.

218. "Al-Tabari's *Book of Jihad*", pp. 235-236. These principles of Islamic jurisprudence derive in turn from the traditions of Islam's prophet Muhammad, and two of his proto-jihad campaigns—against the Jews of the Banu Nadir tribe, and during the siege of Taif. Examples of these traditions from the two most important canonical hadith collections, and the early Muslim biographies of Muhammad, are provided below:

> *Sahih Bukhari Volume 3, Book 39, Number 519*: Narrated Abdullah: The Prophet got the date palm trees of the tribe of Bani-An-Nadir burnt and the trees cut down at a place called Al-Buwaira . Hassan bin Thabit said in a poetic verse: "The chiefs of Bani Lu'ai found it easy to watch fire spreading at Al-Buwaira."; *Sahih Bukhari Volume 4, Book 52, Number 263*: Narrated Ibn Umar: The Prophet burnt the date-palms of Bani An-Nadir.; *Sahih Bukhari Volume. 5, Book. 59, Number 365*: Narrated Ibn Umar: Allah's Apostle had the date-palm trees of Bani Al-Nadir burnt and cut down at a place called Al-Buwaira. Allah then revealed: "What you cut down of the date-palm trees (of the enemy) Or you left them

standing on their stems. It was by Allah's Permission." (Koran 59:5) http://bit. ly/16GJkUY

Sahih Muslim Book 019, Number 4324: It is narrated on the authority of 'Abdullah that the Messenger of Allah (may peace be upon him) ordered the date-palms of Banu Nadir to be burnt and cut. These palms were at Buwaira. Qutaibah and Ibn Rumh in their versions of the tradition have added: So Allah, the Glorious and Exalted, revealed the verse: "Whatever trees you have cut down or left standing on their trunks, it was with the permission of Allah so that He may disgrace the evil-doers." (Koran 59:5).; *Sahih Muslim Book 019, Number 4325*: It is narrated on the authority of Ibn Umar that the Messenger of Allah (may peace be upon him) caused the date-palms of Banu Nadir to be cut down and burnt. It is in this connection that Hassan (the poet) said: It was easy for the nobles of Quraish to barn Buwaira whose sparks were flying in all directions.; *Sahih Muslim Book 019, Number 4326*: Abdullah b. Umar reported that Allah's Apostle (may peace be upon him) burnt the date-palms of Banu Nadir. http://bit.ly/1aRpRhE

"The Apostle then ordered that their palm trees be cut down and burned." (Al-Wakidi, "The Raid against the Banu Nadir (AH 3/625)," from Al-Waqidi, *Kitab al-Maghazi*, vol. 1, ed. Marsden Jones, London, 1966, pp. 363–75, quote reproduced in Bostom, *The Legacy of Jihad*, p. 273); "The Jews took refuge in their forts and the apostle ordered that the palm trees should be cut down and burnt." (*The Life of Muhammad—A Translation of Sirat Rasul Allah*, by A. Guillaume, 1955, London/2001, Karachi, p. 437; p. 871 refers to the use of catapults at the Taif siege.

[218a]. Joseph Schacht, "Abu Hanifa al-Numan b. Thabit," *Encyclopaedia of Islam, Second Edition*. Edited by: P. Bearman; , Th. Bianquis; , C.E. Bosworth; , E. van Donzel; and W.P. Heinrichs. Brill, 2011, Brill Online, Brown University. July 30, 2011.

[219]. Bostom. *The Legacy of Jihad*, Preface, pp. i-xiv.

[220]. Charles Emmanuel Dufourcq, *La Vie Quotidienne dans l'Europe Medievale sous Domination Arabe*, Paris: Hachette, 1978, p. 20. English translation by Michael J. Miller.

[221]. *Sahih Bukhari Volume 4, Book 52, Number 220*, http://bit.ly/16GJkUY

[222]. *The History of Al-Tabari: The Challenge to the Empires*. Khalid Yahya Blankinship, translator, SUNY Series in Near Eastern Studies, 1993, p.10.

[223]. S.K. Malik. *The Quranic Concept of War*, New Delhi (Indian reprint), 1986, 159 pp..

[224]. Ibid., Foreword and Preface, xi-xxv.

[225]. N.S. Rajaram. "A Quranic concept of terrorism." *The American Thinker*, July 22, 2005. http://bit.ly/1aKWvk5

[226]. Malik. *The Quranic Concept of War*, pp. 59, 143-144.

[227]. Franz Rosenthal. "On Suicide in Islam." *Journal of the American Oriental Society*, Vol. 66, 1946, pp. 243, 256.

[228]. Koran 9:111 [Hilali-Khan] http://bit.ly/1dOMzfr; [Arberry] "God has bought from the

believers their selves and their possessions against the gift of Paradise; they fight in the way of God; they kill, and are killed;" http://bit.ly/1imNzt7

[229.] Sura 33 of the Koran, from *Interpretation of the meanings of the noble Qur'ān in the English language:a summarized version of At [i.e. al.]-Tabarī, Al-Qurtubī, and Ibn Kathīr with comments from Sahīh Al-Bukhārī*, and *The Koran interpreted: a translation*; and "The Prophet Muhammad as a Jihad Model" *Middle East Media Research Institute*, July 24, 2001 No.246. http://bit.ly/1bhQhs0

[230.] Alfred Guillaume. *The Life of Muhammad: A Translation of Ishaq's Sirat Rasul Allah*, Oxford, 1979. (Originally published in 1956)

[231.] Arthur Jeffery. *The American Historical Review*, Vol. 61, No. 4, July, 1956, pp. 946-947.

[232.] W. H. T. Gairdner, in *The Vital Forces of Christianity and Islam: Six Studies by Missionaries to Moslems*. Humphrey Milford, London, 1915, p. 23.

[233.] *Sahih Bukhari, Volume 4, Book 52, Number 53*; *Sahih Bukhari: Volume 4, Book 52, Number 54* http://bit.ly/16GJkUY

[233a.] "The Prophet Muhammad as a Jihad Model"

[233b.] "Al-Qaradhawi Speaks In Favor of Suicide Operations at an Islamic Conference in Sweden"

[234.] John H. Sherburne, *Life and Character of John Paul Jones-A Captain in the Navy of the United States*, 1825, New York, p. 308.

[235.] *The Diplomatic Correspondence of the United States of America, From the Signing of the Definitive Treaty of Peace 10th September 1783, to the Adoption of the Constitution March 4, 1789*, Vol. 1, Washington, 1837, p. 605.

[236.] Edward Abbott Van Dyck, *Report of Edward A. Van Dyck, Consular Clerk of the United States at Cairo, Upon the Capitulations of the Ottoman Empire Since the Year 1150*, originally published 1881, Washington, D.C., U.S. Government Printing Office (reprinted 2010, Nabu Press), pp. 8-9.

[237.] Ibid., pp. 25-26.

[238.] "Quduri, al," In *The Oxford Dictionary of Islam*, edited by John L. Esposito. *Oxford Islamic Studies Online*, http://bit.ly/1bfRwl3 (accessed January 21, 2014).

[239.] *Report of Edward A. Van Dyck, Consular Clerk of the United States at Cairo, Upon the Capitulations of the Ottoman Empire Since the Year 1150*, pp. 25-27.

[240.] "Hidayah" ["Guidance"] in Thomas Patrick Hughes, *Dictionary of Islam*, 1895, London, (reprinted 1994, Chicago, IL) p. 174. This Hanafi compendium on Sunni Islamic Law was composed by Sheikh Burhanuddin Ali of Marghinan (d. 1196). An English translation of The Hidayah by Charles Hamilton was published during 1791, in London.

[241.] From Emile Tyan, "Le Système Monocratique Dans L'Islam Sunnite," *Recueil de la Société Jean Bodin*, V. 20, 1970, pp 503ff. (English translation by Nidra Poller, as "The Monocratic System in Sunni Islam")

242. From Emile Tyan, *Institutions du droit public musulman*, Vol. II *Sultanat et califat*, Paris, 1956, p. 250. English translation by Malcolm Kerr, in *Islamic Reform—The Political and Legal Theories of Muhammad Abduh and Rashid Rida*, Berkeley, CA, 1966, p. 28, note 17.

243. Emile Tyan, "Djihad" "[Jihad]," in *Encyclopaedia of Islam*, Edited by B. Lewis, Ch, Pellat, and J. Schacht; Assisted by J. Burton-Page, C. Dumont, and V. L. Menage; Volume II, C to G, Fourth Impression, Leiden, E.J. Brill 1991, pp. 538-39.

244. Bostom, *The Legacy of Jihad*, p. 28

245. Etan Kohlberg, "The Development of the Imami Shi'i Doctrine of Jihad", *Zeitschrift der Deutschen Morgenländischen Gesellschaft*, 1976, Vol.126, pp. 80-81. http://bit.ly/1biQBqw

246. Ibid., p. 80

247. Ibid.

248. Ann K. S. Lambton, "A Nineteenth Century View of Jihad," *Studia Islamica*, 1970, No. 32, p. 182 http://bit.ly/1g0LNNX

249. Ibid., p. 183

250. Kohlberg, "The Development of the Imami Shi'i Doctrine of Jihad", p. 81; also Bostom, *The Legacy of Jihad*, pp. 28,88, 213-220, 620-622.

251. Bostom, *The Legacy of Jihad*, p. 28.

252. Kohlberg, "The Development of the Imami Shi'i Doctrine of Jihad", pp. 81-83.

253. Ibid. p. 83.

254. Mehdi Khalaji, "Apocalyptic Politics—On the Rationality of Iranian Policy," *The Washington Institute for Near East Policy*, Policy Focus # 79, January, 2008, p. 30; Khalaji's note 19 on p. 30 cites, Ruhollah Khomeini, *Sahifeh-ye noor*, vol. 20, p. 27., and Ruhollah Khomeini, *Sho'oun va Ekhtiarat-e Vali-e Faqih* (Tehran: Vezarat-e farhang va Ershade

Eslami, 1995 [AHS 1374]). http://bit.ly/1fbANuj

255. Khomeini, "Islam Is Not a Religion of Pacifists"

256. Khalaji, "Apocalyptic Politics—On the Rationality of Iranian Policy," p. 30.

257. Ibid.

258. See earlier citations 168-177, and related text in the monograph, for relevant of discussion of Montazeri.

259. "Tabatabai, Muhammad Husayn," in *The Oxford Dictionary of Islam*., edited by John L. Esposito. *Oxford Islamic Studies Online*, http://bit.ly/1jUIDe1 (accessed December 12, 2013).; *Al-Mizan fi Tafsir-il-Qur'an* by Allamah as-Saiyed Mohammad Husain at-Tabataba'i, al-A'lami lil-Matbu'at, Beirut, Lebanon, 1972/1392 AH.

260. *Encyclopaedia of the Quran Online*, http://bit.ly/IJB37z

261. *The Cambridge Companion to the Qur'an*, edited by Jane Dammen McCauliffe, Cambridge, U.K., Cambridge University Press, 2006.

262. Jane Dammen McCauliffe, "Christians in the Quran and Tafsir", in *Muslim Perceptions of Other Religions—A Historical Survey*, New York, 1999, edited by Jacques Waardenburg, pp. 107-108.; Elsewhere, in Jane Dammen McCauliffe, *Qur'anic Christians—An Analysis of Classical and Modern Exegetes*, 1991, Cambridge, U.K., p. 85, **after dubbing the Sunni Sheikh, Rashid Rida (d. 1935), one of the "preeminent exegetes of this [the 20ᵗʰ] century," McCauliffe maintains, "Rashid Rida's counterpart for 20ᵗʰ century Shi'i commentary is undoubtedly Muhammad Husayn Tabatabai."**

263. Allamah Sayyed Muhammad Husayn Tabatabai, *Shi'ite Islam*, translated and edited by Seyyed Hossein Nasr, SUNY Press, 1975.

264. Ibid., p. 20.

265. Ibid., p. 19.

265a. W. Montgomery Watt, *Religious Studies*, 1977, Vol. 13, pp. 377-378, a review of *Shi'ite Islam* by Allāmah Ṭabāṭabā'ī; Seyyed Hossein Nasr, http://bit.ly/1i2Uvvk

266. "Introduction: Allameh Tabatabai University" http://bit.ly/1jqZPci

266a. "Allameh Tabatabaei's Interpretive Methods and Principles Nat'l Congress to be Held," *www.shahed.isaar.ir*, May 1, 2012 http://bit.ly/Meh9CO

267. Sayyid Muhammad Husayn at-Tabataba'i, *Al-Mizan fe Tafsir al-Quran*, translated by Sayyid Saeed Akhtar Rizvi, 1982, Vol. 3, Tehran, pp. 78-79. http://bit.ly/1cIpQf6

268. Sayyid Muhammad Husayn at-Tabataba'i, *Al-Mizan fe Tafsir al-Quran*, translated by Sayyid Saeed Akhtar Rizvi, 1990, Vol. 7, Tehran, p. 239. http://bit.ly/1aSeqpa

269. Muḥammad Ḥusayn Ṭabāṭabā'ī, [Muhammad Husain Tabatabai], *al-Mīzān fī tafsīr al-Qur'ān*, 2002, Beirut, Lebanon, Muassasat al-Alami, 22 volumes; Vol. 9, pp. 245-26. English translation by Sjimon R. den Hollander.

269a. Ibid., pp. 246-247.

269b. Ibid., pp. 247-248.

269c. Ibid., pp. 250-251.

269d. Al-Rāghib Abū l-Qāsim Hussein ibn Mufaddal ibn Muhammad al-Isfahāni (d. 1108), renowned for his Koranic commentary, *Al Mufradat fi Gharib al Quran*

269e. *Al-Mizan fe Tafsir al-Quran*, translated by Sayyid Saeed Akhtar Rizvi, 2001, Vol. 10, p. 23.; Koran 5:5 http://bit.ly/MgagkF [Hilali-Khan] Made lawful to you this day are At Tayyibat [all kinds of Halal (lawful) foods, which Allah has made lawful (meat of slaughtered eatable animals, etc., milk products, fats, vegetables and fruits, etc.). The food (slaughtered cattle, eatable animals, etc.) of the people of the Scripture (Jews and Christians) is lawful to you and yours is lawful to them. (Lawful to you in marriage) are chaste women from the believers and chaste women from those who were given the

Scripture (Jews and Christians) before your time, when you have given their due Mahr (bridal money given by the husband to his wife at the time of marriage), desiring chastity (i.e. taking them in legal wedlock) not committing illegal sexual intercourse, nor taking them as girl-friends. And whosoever disbelieves in the Oneness of Allah and in all the other Articles of Faith [i.e. His (Allah's), Angels, His Holy Books, His Messengers, the Day of Resurrection and Al-Qadar (Divine Preordainments)], then fruitless is his work, and in the Hereafter he will be among the losers.; [Arberry] Today the good things are permitted you, and the food of those who were given the Book is permitted to you, and permitted to them is your food; Likewise believing women in wedlock, and in wedlock women of them who were given the Book before you if you give them their wages, in wedlock and not in license, or as taking lovers. Whoso disbelieves in the faith, his work has failed, and in the world to come he shall be among the losers.

270. "Mohammad al-Husayni al-Shirazi," *Wikipedia*, http://bit.ly/1cbaOTh; "Ayatollah al-Udhma Sayyid Sadiq Hussaini Shirazi," *www.varesoon.ir*, http://bit.ly/1iuf18n

271. Afshari, *Human Rights in Iran*, p. 226.

272. Grand Ayatollah Sayyid Sadiq Husayni Shirazi, *Islamic Law Books One and Two. Handbook of Islamic rulings on Muslim's duties and practices*, 2013, Washington, D.C., pp. 383, 384 http://bit.ly/1mNjN0Y

273. "Constitution of the Islamic Republic of Iran," section, "An Ideological Army"

273a. Mordechai Nisan. Chapter 5: War. "The Islamic Assault on the West and Israel", in *Identity and Civilization*, 1999, Lanham, New York: University Press of America, p. 140

274. Esther Webman, *Anti-Semitic Motifs in the Ideology of Hizballah and Hamas*, Tel-Aviv, 1994, pp. 1-15; "Nass al-Risala al-Maftuha wajahaha Hizballah ila-l-Mustad'afin fi Lubnan wa-l-Alam" *al-Safir* (Beirut), February 16, 1985. English translation reproduced here: http://bit.ly/1fis6g3

275. "Archival—Hassan Nasrallah in the Late 1980s: Lebanon Should Become Part of the Greater Islamic Republic Ruled by Leader of Iran, Who Should Appoint all Islamic Rulers"

276. For biographical background on these jurists see Sabine Schmidtke, "Helli, Hasan b. Yusof b. Mottahar," www.iranicaonline.org, http://bit.ly/1czzzrW; Hossein Modarressi,

"Rationalism and Traditionalism in Shi'i Jurisprudence: A Preliminary Survey," *Studia Islamica*, No. 59. (1984), pp. 141-158; and Amanat, *Apocalyptic Islam and Iranian Shi'ism*, pp. 133,155; On p. 155 Amanat states Ali Tabatabai was "specialized in the method of [Islamic] jurisprudence."

277. For the specific doctrines of Allameh Helli and Ali Tabatabai mentioned, see Khalaji, "Apocalyptic Politics—On the Rationality of Iranian Policy," p. 29, and p. 29 note 15, [for Allameh Helli] Muhammad Hassan Najafi, *Javaher al-Kalam fi Sharh-e Sharae al-Eslam* (Beirut: Dar Ihya al-Torath al-Arabi, 1992), 21:71; Sad al-din Abul Qassem Ibn Barraj, *Al-Mohazzab* (Qom, 1406), 1:302; Fakhr al-Din Abu Abdullah Ibn Edris, *Al-Saraer Al-Havi li Tahrir al-Fatawi* (Tehran, 1901 [AHS 1280]), 3:7; See also Khalaji, "Shiite Jurisprudence, Political Expediency, and Nuclear Weapons," [for Ali Tabatabai] p. 15, and p. 26 note 20 citing [Ali] Tabatabai's *Riaz al-Masael fi Tahqiq al-Ahkam bi Dalael*, vol. 8, Qom, Moassassat Aal al-Bait li Ihyae Attorath,1999), pp. 69–70.

[278.] Khalaji, "Apocalyptic Politics—On the Rationality of Iranian Policy," p. 29.

[279.] See notes 36 and 218.

[280.] Khalaji, "Shiite Jurisprudence, Political Expediency, and Nuclear Weapons," p. 15.

[281.] Ibid.

[282.] "Understanding Iran's Assembly of Experts," Durham University, Centre for Iranian Studies, Policy Brief # 1, November, 2006 http://bit.ly/1jOZr52; Nima Malecki, "Ayatollah Ahmad Jannati, the head of Iran's Guardian Council," *rabble.ca*, July 12, 2009 http://bit. ly/1mWZ6zI; Meris Lutz, "Iranian clerics lash out on veiling," *The Los Angeles Times*, June 19, 2010, http://lat.ms/KV9854; "Guardian Council," *www.iranicaonline*, updated February 23, 2012 http://bit.ly/1d2wfSk ; "14th Summit of Assembly of Experts begins in Iran," Press TV, September 3, 2013, http://bit.ly/1ixHv0Q

[283.] Khalaji, "Shiite Jurisprudence, Political Expediency, and Nuclear Weapons," p. 15. Khalaji's note 24 on p. 26 adds this comment: "The Zoroastrian representative in Iran's Majlis officially protested against the ayatollah's statements. For his statement (in Persian) see http://bit.ly/1aygRmj."

[284.] "Ayatollah Ahmad Jannati, Chairman of the Iranian Guardian Council: The Time for America's Death Has Come," *The Middle East Media Research Institute*, Clip No. 1753, April 18, 2008. http://bit.ly/1aVp5PT Below are excerpts from Ayatollah Jannati's public address which aired on Channel 1, Iranian TV, April 18, 2008.

> *The military philosophy of Islam is to create a force within Islam that will be the most powerful force, which no one can defeat.[...] We must aspire to having in the not so distant future, Allah willing, military forces that are better trained than any other force in the world, and the most powerful military equipment in the world, so that no one will dare to consider violating the sanctity of the Islamic Republic. We will safeguard not only the sanctity of the Islamic Republic, but of Islam too, and we will defend oppressed Muslims throughout the world, so that all the Muslims will know that they have a strong protector. Thus, the enemies will not even dare to consider attacking Palestine, Afghanistan, Iraq, or anywhere else. We will support all the oppressed people and the oppressed Muslims in the world. We must aspire to such a future.[...] Yes, I must tell you that the time for America's death has come. You [audience] cried: "Death to the Shah," and indeed, he died. You cried: "Death to Israel," and it is now on its deathbed. You cry: "Death to America," and before long, Allah willing, the prayer for the dead will be recited over it.*

[285.] Khalaji, "Shiite Jurisprudence, Political Expediency, and Nuclear Weapons," p. 15, and note 23 p. 26, citing, Sayyed Javad Varai, "Mabani-ye Fiqhi-ye Amalyat-e Shahdat Talabaneh," *Hokoumat-e Eslami*, no. 27 (Spring 2003).

[286.] Al-Tabari, *The History of al-Tabari (Ta'rikh al rusul wa'l-muluk)*, vol. 12, *The Battle of Qadissiyah and the Conquest of Syria and Palestine*, translated by Yohanan Friedman, Albany, NY, 1992, p. 167.

[287.] Dufourcq, *La Vie Quotidienne dans l'Europe Medievale sous Domination Arabe*; Harry W. Hazard, *Atlas of Islamic History*, Princeton, New Jersey: Princeton University Press, 1951.; Al-Tabari, *The History of al-Tabari (Ta'rikh al rusul wa'l-muluk)*, vol. 12; vol. 13,

The Conquest of Iraq, Southwestern Persia, and Egypt. Translated by G.H.A. Juynboll, (Albany, NY.: State University of New York Press, 1989); Al-Baladhuri, *The Origins of the Islamic State* (*Kitab Futuh al-Buldan*), translated by Philip K. Hitti, New York.: Columbia, 1916; Al-Kufi, *The Chachnāmah, Part I: Giving the Mussulman period from the Arab conquest to the beginning of the reign of the Kalhorahs,* translated by Mirza Kalichbeg Fredunbeg, Delhi Reprint, 1979; Elliott and Dowson, *A History of India As Told by Its Own Historians,* Vols. 1-8, 1867-1877 (reissued Delhi Reprint, 2001); *Kanhadade Prabandha,* translated, introduced and annotated by V.S. Bhatnagar, New Delhi, 1991; *Biography of Dharmasvamin* (*Chag lotsava Chos-rje-dpal*), *a Tibetan Pilgrim,* English translation by G. Roerich, Patna, 1959; Mary Boyce, "Chapter Ten- Under the Caliphs", pp. 145-162, in *Zoroastrians-Their Religious Beliefs and Practices,* Routledge, London, 2001; Michael Morony, *Iraq After the Muslim Conquest,* Princeton, New Jersey: Princeton University Press, 1984, pp. 190-196, 381-382; Dimitar Angelov, "Certain aspects de la conquete des peuples balkanique par les Turcs", in *Les Balkans au moyen age. La Bulgarie des Bogomils aux Turcs,* London: Variorum Reprints, 1978, pp. 220-275; A.E. Vacalopoulos, *Origins of the Greek Nation-The Byzantine Period, 1204-1461,* New Brunswick, N.J., 1970, pp. 59-85; Speros Vryonis, Jr., *The Decline of Medieval Hellenism in Asia Minor and the Process of Islamization from the Eleventh through the Fifteenth Century,* Berkeley, CA.: University of California Press, 1971, pp.69-287; K.S. Lal, *The Legacy of Muslim Rule in India,* New Delhi.: Aditya Prakashan, 1992, pp. ; K.S. Lal, "Jihad Under the Mughals", from *Theory and Practice of Muslim State in India,* New Delhi, Aditya Prakashan, 1999, pp.62-68; Moshe Gil, *A History of Palestine, 634 -1099,* Cambridge: Cambridge University Press, 1992, pp. 11-74; Bat Ye'or, *The Decline of Eastern Christianity Under Islam,* Cranbury, NJ: Fairleigh Dickinson University Press, 1996, pp. 43-60, and Bat Ye'or, "The Ideology of Jihad, Dhimmitude, and Human Rights," Lecture, Georgetown University (Washington, D.C.), Reiss Building 103 , Moderator: Prof. Alan Parra (Human Rights Law), October 22, 2002, and Bat Ye'or, Andrew Bostom, "Jihad and Dhimmitude: Victimless Islamic Institutions?," *FrontPageMagazine.com,* December 3, 2002 http://bit.ly/1csUIHX ; Demetrios Constantelos, "Greek Christian and other accounts of the Moslem conquests of the near east", in Christian Hellenism : essays and studies in continuity and change. New Rochelle, N.Y.: A.D. Caratzas, 1998, pp. 125-144.; *A Chronicle of the Early Safawis-Being the Ahsanu't-Tawarikh of Hasan-I-Rumlu,* Volume II, translated by C.N. Seddon, Baroda, 1934, pp. 135, 143, 159, 168-169.

[288.] Ibid.

[289.] Savory, *Iran under the Safavids,* Chapter 3, "Internal dissensions and external foes: the Safavid state from 1524-1588," pp. 50-75

[290.] Ibid., p. 65

[291.] Roger Savory, "Hasan-I-Rumlu", *The Encyclopaedia of Islam,* Edited by

B. Lewis, V. L. Menage, Ch. Pellat, and J. Schacht, 1986, Leiden, Vol. 3, p. 253

[292.] *A Chronicle of the Early Safawis- Being the Ahsanu't-Tawarikh of Hasan-I-Rumlu,* Volume II, translated by C.N. Seddon, Baroda, 1934, pp. 135, 143, 159, 168-169.

[293.] Roger Savory, "Iskandar Beg Munshi", *The Encyclopaedia of Islam,* Edited by E. Van Donzel, B. Lewis, and Ch. Pellat, 1997, Leiden, Vol. 4, pp. 130-131.

[294.] Iskandar Munshi, *The History of Shah Abbas the Great* (*Tārīk-e 'ālamārā-ye 'Abbāsī; [a 17ᵗʰ century Persian chronicle]*), English translation, 1978, Boulder, CO, p. 140

295. Mihailo D. Stojanovic, *The Great Powers and the Balkans*, 1939/1968, Cambridge, U.K, pp. 1, 183.

296. Ignaz Goldziher. "*A Muhammedan Kozvelemenyrol*" ["Muhammadan Public Opinion"], *Budapesti Szemle*, 1882 (January), Vol. 30, pp. 234-265. Translated by Jerry Payne and Philip Sadgrove as "Muhammadan Public Opinion," *Journal of Semitic Studies*, Vol. 38, pp. 97-133; Extracts quoted from pp. 97-98.

297. Ibid.

298. Ibid.

299. Ibid.

300. C. Snouck Hurgronje, *Mohammedanism*, New York, 1916, pp. 105-106.

301. Ibid.

302. Ibid.

303. P.C. Bamford, *Histories of the Non-co-operation and Khilafat Movements*, 1925/1985, Delhi, India, p. 110

304. Richard P Mitchell. *The Society of the Muslim Brothers*, London, Oxford University Press, 1969; Hasan al-Banna. Translated by Charles Wendell. *Five tracts of Hasan al-Banna a selection from the Majmu at Rasa'il al-Imam al-Shahid Hasan al-Banna*, Berkeley, CA, 1978.; Brynjar Lia. *The Society of the Muslim Brothers in Egypt—The Rise of an Islamic Mass Movement, 1928-1942*, Reading, UK, 1998.

305. Wendell, *Five tracts of Hasan al-Banna*

306. Ignaz Goldziher, *Schools of Koranic Commentators*, edited and translated by Wolfgang H. Behn, Wiesbaden, Germany, 2006. First published as *Die Richtungen der Islamischen Koranaslegung*, Leiden, 1920. See especially pp. 203, 204, 212, 213-214, and 222-223 from Behn's 2006 translation; Charles C. Adams, *Islam and Modernism in Egypt*, New York, 1933, especially pp. 15-16, and 59-60.; Johannes J.G. Jansen, *The Dual Nature of Islamic Fundamentalism*, Ithaca, New York, 1997, pp. 38-40. Jansen concludes his analysis of the Manar modernists—their own legacy, and direct linkage to Hasan al-Banna's Muslim Brotherhood movement—with this apt, if unromantic appraisal:

> *In retrospect it is evident that Rida shared these popular feelings about the Koranic punishments [i.e., the so-called hadd punishments, wherein according to the Sharia, the acts of unlawful sexual intercourse, false accusation of unlawful sexual intercourse, drinking wine, theft, and highway robbery, as well as unrepentant apostasy, are punishable by flogging, limb amputation, or death] Moreover, he appears to have subscribed to the radical view that condemns modern heads of state in the Arab world as apostates from Islam, **and it is difficult today, to see why an earlier generation of orientalists [Note: but certainly not Goldziher!] regarded Al-Afghani, Abduh, and Rida as modernizing, westernizing liberals.** The desire for the return of the glory of Islam, which these three reformers felt so strongly, and the particular socio-political circumstances in which they lived made them not [emphasis in original] into liberal modernizers but into the founding fathers of Islamic fundamentalism. In October 1941 the Egyptian*

government suppressed Al-Manar ["The Lighthouse," a publication originally produced by Abduh and Rida], which a certain Hasan al-Banna had recently taken over from the heirs of Rashid Rida [d. 1935]. It is with Hasan al-Banna that professional violence became part and parcel of the movement we now call Islamic fundamentalism.

307. Wendell, *Five tracts of Hasan al-Banna*, pp. 3-8.

308. "August 27, 1947, Memorandum of Conversation between Shaikh Hassan Al Banna, Supreme Leader of Ikhwan Al Muslimin, and Philip W. Ireland, First Secretary of Embassy," Enclosure No. 1 to Despatch no. 2866, August 29, 1947, from the American Embassy, Cairo, Egypt. Ireland's comment appears on p. 4 of the Enclosure.

309. Farhad Kazemi, "The Fada'iyan-e-Islam: Fanaticism, Politics, and Terror," in Said Amir Arjomand, Editor, *From Nationalism to Revolutionary Islam*, 1984, Albany, N.Y. p. 160.

310. Ibid., pp. 175-176, note 46

310a. Mitchell, *The Society of the Muslim Brothers*, p. 126 note 60.

311. Kazemi, "The Fada'iyan-e-Islam: Fanaticism, Politics, and Terror," p. 160.

312. Ibid., p. 162.

313. Farhad Kazemi, "Fedāʾīān-e Eslām," *www.iranicaonline.org*, http://bit.ly/MqMRhb

314. Ibid.

315. Ibid.

316. Ibid.

317. Ibid.

318. Ibid.

319. Hurgronje, *Mohammedanism*, pp. 105-106.

320. "Muslim Public Opinion on US Policy, Attacks on Civilians and al Qaeda,"

WorldPublicOpinion.Org, A Project of The Program in International Policy Attitudes, The University of Maryland, April 24, 2007 http://bit.ly/1feD0mF; "The World's Muslims: Religion, Politics and Society," *Pew Research Center*, April 30, 2013 http://bit.ly/1eiFNxe

321. "Muslim Public Opinion on US Policy, Attacks on Civilians and al Qaeda"

322. "The World's Muslims: Religion, Politics and Society"

323. Ibid.

324. Ibid.

325. See: "The Future of the Global Muslim Population—Sortable Data Tables," *Pew Research Center*, January, 2011, http://bit.ly/1dQyl7G; "The Future of the Global Muslim

Population—Region: Middle East-North Africa," *Pew Research Center*, January 27, 2011 http://bit.ly/1gtHprc; "Islam by Country," *en.wikipedia.org*, http://bit.ly/11nWlcl

326. "The World's Muslims: Religion, Politics and Society"

327. For the designation "Lewis Doctrine," see Peter Waldman, "A Historian's Take on Islam Steers U.S. in Terrorism Fight: Bernard Lewis's Blueprint—Sowing Arab Democracy— Is Facing a Test in Iraq," *The Wall Street Journal*, February 3, 2004 http://on.wsj. com/1idALmb; For a critical analysis of this "doctrine," see Andrew Bostom, "What Went Wrong With Bernard Lewis?," *The American Thinker*, March 17, 2013 http://bit. ly/1fpR9Q4; And for a more extensive analysis of the pitfalls in Lewis's conceptions, see my "A Legacy of Islamic Confusion," in, Bostom, *Sharia Versus Freedom*, pp. 51-98.

328. Diana West, "Why they fight (No, really, why?)," *www.Townhall.com*, May 1, 2006 http://bit.ly/1lo1aCu; Andrew Bostom, "Making the World Safe for Shari'a?," The American Thinker, August 18, 2006 http://bit.ly/1aK5UOB

329. "The World's Muslims: Religion, Politics and Society"

330. Ibid.

331. Ibid.

332. See reference 151.

333. Brendan O'Leary, "Ernest Gellner Remembered," 1995, http://bit.ly/1cz0DIn

334. Ernest Gellner, *Muslim Society*, 1981, Cambridge, U.K. Cambridge University Press

335. O'Leary, "Ernest Gellner Remembered"

336. Ernest Gellner. "Islam and Marxism: Some Comparisons", *International Affairs*, 1991,Vol. 67, No. 1, p. 2

337. Ibid.

338. See references 151 and 320.

339. Osama Saeed, "The return of the caliphate—There is no reason why the west should set its face against the vision of a reunited Islamic world," *The Guardian*, October 31, 2005, http://bit.ly/L8AFjE (Osama Saeed, was identified as "a spokesman for the Muslim Association of Britain," when this essay appeared)]

340. Bostom, *The Legacy of Jihad.*

341. Alfred von Kremer, *Geschichte der herrschenden Ideen des Islams: der Gottesbegriff. die Prophetie und Staatsidee* ["History of the dominant ideas of Islam: the concepts of God, prophecy, and the state"]1868, Leipzig, pp. 332ff. http://bit.ly/1aHx5ti

342. Ibid.

343. Bostom, *The Legacy of Jihad*, p. 396

344. Ibid.

[345.] Ibid.; see also *The Origins of the Islamic State*, being a translation of Al-Baladhuri's, *Kitab Futuh al-Bildan*, by Philip K. Hitti, 1916, reprinted 2002 by Georgias Press, N.J., pp. 48, 103; and the canonical hadith, *Sahih Bukhari, Volume 3, Book 39, Number 531*: Narrated Ibn 'Umar: Umar expelled the Jews and the Christians from Hijaz. When Allah's Apostle had conquered Khaybar, he wanted to expel the Jews from it as its land became the property of Allah, His Apostle, and the Muslims. Allah's Apostle intended to expel the Jews but they requested him to let them stay there on the condition that they would do the labor and get half of the fruits. Allah's Apostle told them, "We will let you stay on thus condition, as long as we wish." So, they (i.e., Jews) kept on living there until 'Umar forced them to go towards Taima' and Ariha' http://bit.ly/16GJkUY

[346.] Bostom, *The Legacy of Jihad*, p. 396

[347.] Andrew Bostom, *The Legacy of Islamic Antisemitism*, 2008, Amherst, N.Y., p. 577.

[348.] Bostom, *Sharia Versus Freedom*, pp. 140-150.

[349.] Al-Mawardi [Mawerdi] (d. 1058) was a famous Shafiite jurist of Baghdad, who authored a seminal legal study which elucidated the workings of the Caliphate system, *Al-ahkam as-Sultaniyya*, and a treatise on morality.; Sayyid Abul Ala Mawdudi (1903–1979) was a major twentieth-century Indo-Pakistani Islamic revivalist ideologue whose prolific output shaped modern efforts to restore the Sharia, for its potential global application (see E. I. J. Rosenthal, *International Affairs* [*Royal Institute of International Affairs*] Vol. 38, No. 3, July, 1962, pp. 365-368). Mawdudi's "magnum opus," *Tafhim Al-Quran* (*Understanding the Koran*), remains one of the most important works of modern Koranic exegesis, or interpretation.; For their respective references to Koran 4:59, see Al-Mawardi, *Al Akham as-Sultaniyyah* [*The Laws of Islamic Governance*], English translation by Dr. Asadullah Yate, London, 1996, pp. 10-11, and Sayyid Abul Ala Mawdudi. *Toward's Understanding the Qur'an*, Vol. 2, Surahs 4-6, London, 1988, pp. 50-53.

[350.] Mawardi, *The Laws of Islamic Governance*, pp. 10-11.

[351.] Mawdudi, *Understanding the Koran*, pp. 50-53.

[352.] Robert Reilly, *The Closing of the Muslim Mind: How Intellectual Suicide Created the Modern Islamist*, pp. 2-3, 203-204. For a thorough debunking of Reilly's very flawed analysis of the Mutazilites, see Andrew Bostom, "Mutazilite Fantasies," in *Sharia Versus Freedom*, pp. 383-389.

[353.] Fazlur Rahman. "Non-Muslim Minorities in an Islamic State," *Journal Institute of Muslim Minority Affairs*, Volume 7, Issue 1, 1986, pp. 13-24.

[354.] Bostom, *The Legacy of Jihad*, pp. 127-135.

[355.] Rahman, "Non-Muslim Minorities in an Islamic State," p. 20.

[356.] Ibid.

[357.] Ibid., pp. 13-24.

[358.] See Bostom, *The Legacy of Jihad*, pp. 29-37, 178-179, 196-198, 199, 200-201, 205-211, 213-215, 216-220; and also *The Legacy of Islamic Antisemitism*, pp. 481-488.

[359.] Bostom, *The Legacy of Jihad*, p. 29.

[360.] Mawdudi, *Towards Understanding the Quran*, vol 3, Surahs 7-9, p. 202.

[361.] Mawardi, *The Laws of Islamic Governance*, pp. 60; 77-78; 200-201.

[362.] "The Meeting between the Sheik of Al-Azhar and the Chief Rabbi of Israel" *Middle East Media Research Institute*, Special Report No. 3, January 8, 1998 http://bit.ly/1fmbofv

[363.] Mawardi, *The Laws of Islamic Governance*, p. 211; Bat Ye'or, *The Dhimmi: Jews and Christians Under Islam*, 1985, Cranbury, NJ: Fairleigh Dickinson University Press, p. 169; Lal, *The Legacy of Muslim Rule in India*, p. 237.

[364.] Al-Ghazali (d. 1111*). Kitab al-Wagiz fi fiqh madhab al-imam al-Safi'i*, Beirut, 1979, pp. 186, 190-91; 199-200; 202-203. [English translation by Dr. Michael Schub.] Al-Ghazali (1058–1111) was born at Tus in Khurasan, near modern Meshed, and became a renowned theologian, jurist, and mystic. His early training was as a jurist, and he continued to have an interest in jurisprudence throughout his career, writing a work, the *Wadjiz*, dated 1101, that is, in the last decade of his life. W. M. Watt wrote of Al-Ghazali, "acclaimed in both the East and West as the greatest Muslim after Muhammad, and he is by no means unworthy of that dignity. . . . He brought orthodoxy and mysticism into closer contact . . . the theologians became more ready to accept the mystics as respectable, while the mystics were more careful to remain within the bounds of orthodoxy."

[365.] A.S. Tritton, *The Caliphs and Their Non-Muslim Subjects*, London, 1930, pp. 232-233. Arthur Stanley (A.S.) Tritton, (1881-1973) succeeded Sir Hamilton Gibb as Professor of Arabic and Head of Department at the School of Oriental and African Studies, London, in 1938. He retired in 1946 but continued to teach for a time as a part-time lecturer. Tritton was made an Honorary Fellow of the School in 1946 and Professor Emeritus in the following year. His obituarist in the *Bulletin of the School of Oriental and African Studies*, C.F. Beckingham, described Tritton, thusly:

> Tritton was a painstaking teacher, a helpful colleague, and an industrious author. He published six books, *The rise of the Imams of Sanaa* (1925), based on his doctoral thesis, *The Caliphs and their non-Muslim subjects* (1930), which has been reprinted and translated into Arabic, *Teach yourself Arabic* (1947), *Muslim theology* (1947), *Islam: beliefs and practices* (1951), and *Materials on Muslim education in the Middle Ages* (1957). He contributed numerous articles to academic periodicals, especially to this Bulletin and the *Journal of the Royal Asiatic Society*, and to encyclopaedias, acting on occasion as English editor of the *Encyclopaedia of Islam* in Gibb's absence. He reviewed 140 books for the Bulletin alone. His scholarship was wide and accurate...("Obituary: Arthur Stanley Tritton," *Bulletin of the School of Oriental and African Studies, University of London*, 1974, Vol. 37, No. 2, pp. 446-447 http://bit.ly/1eqQhe3)

[366.] Tritton, *The Caliphs and Their Non-Muslim Subjects*, pp. 232-233.

[367.] Jadunath Sarkar, *History of Aurangzib, Vol. III- Northern India, 1658-1681*, Chapter XXXIV, "The Islamic State Church in India", excerpts from pp. 283-297. The scholar K.S. Lal, records this translation, **"...and should the collector choose to spit into his mouth, opens the same without hesitation, so that the official may spit into it.."** Lal notes, further that , **"Actual spitting in the mouth of the non-Muslims was not uncommon."** Lal cites a poem by Vijaya Gupta (1493-1519 C.E.), which includes the line, "The peons employed by the qazis tore away the sacred threads of the Brahmans and spat saliva in their mouths." From, *Theory and Practice of Muslim State in India*, pp. 238-39, note 124.; Sir Jadunath Sarkar, (born December 10, 1870, Karachmaria, Bengal [now in Bangladesh], knighted in 1929, and died May 15, 1958, Calcutta, India), is recognized as the foremost Indian historian of the Mughal dynasty (1526–1857). Aurangzeb [Aurangzib], the last major Mughal emperor, became the object of his life's work. Sarkar's initial book, *India of Aurangzib*, was published in 1901. It took Sarkar 25 years to complete his five-volume *History of Aurangzib*, which was published in 1924. Sarkar then devoted another 25 years to his *Fall of the Mughal Empire*, a four-volume work, completed in 1950. The consensus view is that Sarkar's works "demonstrate his vast knowledge of Persian-language sources and are skillfully written in English." His residence at 10 Lake Terrace, Calcutta housed the *Centre for Studies in Social Sciences*, Calcutta, an autonomous research centre from 1973 to 2000, and currently houses the newly established *Jadunath Sarkar Resource Centre for Historical Research*.

[368.] Antoine Fattal, *Let Statut Legal de Musulmans en Pays'd'Islam*, Beirut, 1958; pp. 369-370. (English translation by Nidra Poller)

[369.] Goitein was Professor Emeritus of the Hebrew University, and a scholar at the Institute for Advanced Study in Princeton. The *New York Times* obituary for Professor Goitein (published in February, 1985) noted, appositely, that his renowned (and prolific) writings on Islamic culture, and Muslim-Jewish relations, were "standard works for scholars in both fields."; "Shelomo D. Goitein, A Hebraic Scholar, Dies." *The New York Times*, February 10, 1985 http://nyti.ms/1eiiUvj

[370.] S.D. Goitein. "Minority Self-rule and Government Control in Islam" *Studia Islamica*, No. 31, 1970, pp. 101, 104-106.

[371.] A genizah or geniza is the storeroom or depository in a synagogue, usually for worn-out Hebrew-language books and papers on religious topics that were stored there before they could receive a proper cemetery burial, it being forbidden to throw away writings containing the name of God (even personal letters and legal contracts could open with an invocation of God). But in practice, genizot [plural] also contained writings of a secular nature, with or without the customary opening invocation, and also contained writings in other languages that use the Hebrew alphabet (Judeo-Arabic, Judeo-Persian, Ladino, Yiddish). The Cairo Geniza is an accumulation of almost two hundred thousand Jewish manuscripts that were found in the geniza of the Ben Ezra synagogue (built 882) of Fostat, Egypt (now Old Cairo); the Basatin cemetery east of Old Cairo; and a number of old documents that were bought in Cairo in the later nineteenth century. These documents were written from about 870 to as late as 1880 CE.

The importance of these materials for reconstructing the social and economic history for the period between 950 and 1250 cannot be overemphasized; the index Goitein created covers about thirty-five thousand individuals, which included about 350 "prominent people" (including Maimonides and his son Abraham), 200 "better-known families," and mentions of 450 professions and 450 goods. He identified material from Egypt, Palestine, Lebanon, Syria (but not Damascus or Aleppo), Tunisia, Sicily, and even covering trade with India. Cities mentioned range from Samarkand in Central Asia to Seville and Sijilmasa, Morocco to the west; from Aden north to Constantinople; Europe not only is represented by the Mediterranean port cities of Narbonne, Marseilles, Genoa, and Venice, but even Kiev and Rouen are occasionally mentioned.

[372.] Lambton's obituarist, Burzine K. Waghmar, noted (on August 1, 2008),

Lambton was unrivalled in the breadth of her scholarship, covering Persian grammar and dialectology; medieval and early modern Islamic political thought; Seljuq, Mongol, Safavid, Qajar and Pahlavi administration; tribal and local history; and land tenure and agriculture. Her association with SOAS (School of Oriental and Asiatic Studies) in London, which lasted from her time as an undergraduate in 1930 until her death as Professor Emerita, aged 96, was one of the longest and most illustrious, and Lambton became acknowledged as the dean of Persian studies in the West. Without hyperbole, an era has passed in Middle Eastern studies. (Burzine K. Waghmar, "Professor Ann Lambton: Persianist unrivalled in the breadth of her scholarship whose association with Soas was long and illustrious." *The Independent*, August 1, 2008, http://ind.pn/1afeNyV)

[373.] Ann Lambton. *State and Government in Medieval Islam*, Oxford, U.K., 1981, pp. 206-208.

[374.] See Bat Ye'or's major works in English cited earlier, *The Dhimmi, The Decline of Eastern Christianity Under Islam*, and her more recent *Islam and Dhimmitude—Where Civilizations Collide*, 2001, Cranbury, N.J., Fairleigh Dickinson University Press, and *Understanding Dhimmitude*, 2013, New York, N.Y., RVP Publishers

[375.] Bat Ye'or, *The Dhimmi*, p. 67; Bat Ye'or, *The Decline of Eastern Christianity under Islam*, pp. 252, 254.

[376.] Mary Boyce, *Zoroastrians: Their Religious Beliefs and Practices*, London, 1979, 2001, and *A Persian Stronghold of Zoroastrianism* (based on the Ratanbai Katrak lectures, 1975), Lanham, Maryland, 1989; During the initial jihad conquest of Persia, for example, 40,000 Zoroastrians were killed defending the royal city of Istakhr, where the religious library was housed.; Boyce (1920-2006) was the preeminent 20th century scholar of Zoroastrianism and its relevant languages, and Professor of Iranian Studies at the School of Oriental and African Studies (SOAS) of the University of London. She produced the groundbreaking works, *A Persian stronghold of Zoroastrianism*, based on her 1963-64 field-work in Iran (presented as the *Ratanbai Katrak Lectures* at the University of Oxford, 1975), and *Zoroastrians: their religious beliefs and practices* (1979). As per her biography at *Encyclopaedia Iranica*, "The range of her contributions to the study of Iran in general, and Zoroastrianism in particular, is inestimable." http://bit.ly/Lov6O6

[377.] Boyce, *A Persian Stronghold of Zoroastrianism*, pp. 7-8; Napier Malcolm lived among the Zoroastrians in the central Iranian town of Yezd at the end of the 19th century. He documented the following in his narrative, *Five Years in a Persian Town*, New York, 1905, pp. 45-50:

Up to 1895 no Parsi (Zoroastrian) was allowed to carry an umbrella. Even during the time that I was in Yezd they could not carry one in town. Up to 1895 there was a strong prohibition upon eye-glasses and spectacles; up to 1885 they were prevented from wearing rings; their girdles had to be made of rough canvas, but after 1885 any white material was permitted. Up to 1896 the Parsis were obliged to twist their turbans instead of folding them. Up to 1898 only brown, grey, and yellow were allowed for the qaba [outer coat] or arkhaluq [under coat] (body garments), but after that all colors were permitted except blue, black, bright red, or green. There was also a prohibition against white stockings, and up to about 1880 the Parsis had to wear a special kind of peculiarly hideous shoe with a broad, turned-up toe. Up to 1885 they had to wear a torn cap. Up to 1880 they had to wear tight knickers, self-colored, instead of trousers. Up to 1891 all

Zoroastrians had to walk in town, and even in the desert they had to dismount if they met a Mussulman of any rank whatsoever. During the time that I was in Yezd they were allowed to ride in the desert, and only had to dismount if they met a big Mussulman. There were other similar dress restrictions too numerous and trifling to mention.

Then the houses of both the Parsis and the Jews, with the surrounding walls, had to be built so low that the top could be reached by a Mussulman with his hand extended; they might, however, dig down below the level of the road. The walls had to be splashed with white around the door. Double doors, the common form of Persian door, were forbidden, also rooms containing three or more windows. Bad-girs [Air-shafts] were still forbidden to Parsis while we were in Yezd, but in 1900 one of the bigger Parsi merchants gave a large present to the Governor and to the chief mujtahid (Mohammedan priest) to be allowed to build one. Upper rooms were also forbidden.

Up to about 1860 Parsis could not engage in trade. They used to hide things in their cellar rooms, and sell them secretly. They can now trade in the caravanserais or hostelries, but not in the bazaars, nor may they trade in linen drapery. Up to 1870 they were not permitted to have a school for their children.

The amount of the jaziya, or tax upon infidels, differed according to the wealth of the individual Parsi, but it was never less than two tomans [a sum of money, 10,000 dinars]. A toman is now worth about three shillings and eight pence, but it used to be worth much more. Even now, when money has much depreciated, it represents a laborer's wage for ten days. The money must be paid on the spot, when the farrash [literally, a carpet sweeper. Really a servant, chiefly, outdoor], who was acting as collector, met the man. The farrash was at liberty to do what he liked when collecting the jaziya. **The man was not even allowed to go home and fetch the money, but was beaten at once until it was given. About 1865 a farrash collecting this tax tied a man to a dog, and gave a blow to each in turn.**

About 1891 a mujtahid caught a Zoroastrian merchant wearing white stockings in one of the public squares of the town. He ordered the man to be beaten and the stockings taken off. About 1860 a man of seventy went to the bazaars in white trousers of rough canvas. They hit him about a good deal, took off his trousers, and sent him home with them under his arm. Sometimes Parsis would be made to stand on one leg in a mujtahid's house until they consented to pay a considerable sum of money.

In the reign of the late Shah Nasiru'd Din, Manukji Limji, a British Parsi from India, was for a long while in Tehran as Parsi representative. Almost all the Parsi disabilities were withdrawn, the jaziya, the clothes restrictions, and those with regard to houses, but the law of inheritance was not altered, according to which a Parsi who becomes a Mussulman takes precedence of his Zoroastrian brothers and sisters. The jaziya was actually remitted, and also some of the restrictions as to houses, but the rest of the firman was a dead letter.

In 1898 the present Shah, Muzaffaru'd Din, gave a firman to Dinyar, the present Qalantar [Head Man] of the Parsi Anjuman, or Committee, revoking all the remaining Parsi disabilities, and also declaring it unlawful to use fraud or deception in making conversions of Parsis to Islam. This firman does not appear to have had any effect at all.

About 1883, after the firman of Nasiru'd Din Shah had been promulgated, one of the Parsis, Rustami Ardishiri Dinyar, built in Kucha Biyuk, one of the villages near Yezd, a house with an upper room, slightly above the height to which the Parsis used to be limited. He heard that the Mussulmans were going to kill him, so he fled by night to Tehran. They killed another Parsi, Tirandaz, in mistake for him, but did not destroy the house.

So the great difficulty was not to get the law improved, but rather to get it enforced. When Manukji [British Parsi and 'consul' in Tehran] was at Yezd, about 1870, two Parsis were attacked by two Mussulmans outside the town, and one was killed, the other terribly wounded as they had tried to cut off his head. The Governor brought the criminals to Yezd, but did nothing to them. Manukji got leave to take them to Tehran. The Prime Minister, however, told him that no Mussulman would be killed for a Zardushti, or Zoroastrian, and that they would only be bastinadoed. About this time Manukji enquired whether it was true that the blood-price of a Zardushti was to be seven tomans. He got back the reply that it was to be a little over.

The Yezd Parsis have been helped considerably by agents from Bombay, who are British subjects, and of late years things have improved slightly.

Finally, Kestenberg Amighi (Janet Kestenberg Amighi. *The Zoroastrians of Iran: conversion, assimilation, or persistence.* New York, NY: AMS Press, 1990, pp. 85) has argued that the Zoroastrians were the lowest non-Muslim caste in Shiite Iran, and accordingly, subjected to the most severe najis-related restrictions:

In Yezd and Kerman (through the early 20th century), Moslem pollution prohibitions were strictly observed and extended to most aspects of life. A Moslem would not eat out of a dish touched by a Zoroastrian nor permit even his garment to be touched by a Zoroastrian. Zoroastrians were forbidden the use of most community facilities such as barber shops, bath houses, water fountains, and tea houses. Water and wetness were considered to be particularly strong carriers of pollution. Zoroastrians were not permitted to go to the market in the rain. They could not touch fruit when shopping in the bazaar, although the dry goods could be touched.

[378.] Bostom, *The Legacy of Islamic Antisemitism*, pp. 31-32, 34-35, 57-63, 221-228, 235-262, 299-314, 481-488.

[379.] Ibid., pp. 56-57.; Allamah Tabatabai's *Al-Mizan* acknowledged that the hadith remained an authoritative source of Islamic Law, inseparable from the Koran itself:

tradition is the companion of the Koran and they are not separate from each other in being authoritative sources of the law. (*Al-Mizan fe Tafsir al-Quran*, translated by Sayyid Saeed Akhtar Rizvi, 2001, Vol. 10, p. 21.)

A contemporary report, "The hadith is the second type of revelation," *The Gulf Times*, Thursday October 23, 2008, http://bit.ly/1e3XzT9, confirmed the ongoing importance of the hadith from a modern Islamic perspective, stating:

Adherence to the Sunnah is an obligation. So there must be a means by which

Muslims could fulfill their obligation. The only way to completely do so is to know exactly what the Prophet said and did. This cannot be fulfilled by following or reading the Koran alone, therefore we must turn to the reports and record of the Prophet's words and deeds, meaning the hadith. The hadith is the second type of revelation from Allah the Almighty. From the hadith do we derive the sunnah of the Prophet.

[380.] Bostom, *The Legacy of Islamic Antisemitism*, pp. 64-65.

[381.] Ibid., p. 144.

[382.] Ibid.

[383.] Ibid.

[384.] Robert L. Pollock, "A Dialogue With Lebanon's Ayatollah," *The Wall Street Journal*, March 14, 2009 http://on.wsj.com/1eNnCvX

[385.] Ibid.

[386.] Bassem Mroue, "Lebanon's top Shiite cleric Fadlallah dies at 75," *The Associated Press*, July 4, 2010 http://usat.ly/LHYvDK

[387.] Bostom, *The Legacy of Islamic Antisemitism*, p. 145; Here is the gloss on Koran 5:60 from the authoritative, classical commentary *Tafsir al-Jalalayn* [see reference 4], p. 259:

> those whom Allah has cursed and put far away from His mercy and with whom he is angry — turning some of them into monkeys and into pigs by transmogrification — and who worshipped false gods. **These are the Jews** ... "False gods" refers to Shaytān [Satan]. They [the Jews] worship him by obeying him. Such people are in a worse situation — because they will be in the Fire — and further from the right way (the Path of the Truth) [i.e., Islam].

See the contemporary glosses on Koran 2:96, 4:53, and 59:13-14, from March, 2004, by the former head of Al-Azhar University's fatwa committee in *The Legacy of Islamic Antisemitism*, p. 461. Koran 4:53 is adduced as evidence of the Jews' real world miserliness, while 2:96 demonstrates their "greediness" for life, fearing eternal damnation in the afterlife. These modern interpretations are entirely concordant with the classical exegeses on these verses in *Tafsir al-Julalayn* p. 34 (Koran 2:96), p. 194 (Koran 4:53), and p. 1189 (Koran 59:13-14).

[388.] Ibid.

[389.] See references 262-266.

[390.] *Al-Mizan*, (translated by Rizvi), 1983, Vol. 1, p. 256.;

Koran 2:40 [Hilali-Khan] O Children of Israel! Remember My Favour which I bestowed upon you, and fulfill (your obligations to) My Covenant (with you) so that I fulfill (My Obligations to) your covenant (with Me), and fear none but Me.; [Arberry] Children of Israel, remember My blessing wherewith I blessed you, and fulfill My covenant and I shall fulfill your covenant; and have awe of Me. http://bit.ly/1cUl8uf

Koran 2:41 [Hilali-Khan] And believe in what I have sent down (this Qur'an), confirming that which is with you, [the Taurat (Torah) and the Injeel (Gospel)], and be not the first to disbelieve therein, and buy not with My Verses [the Taurat (Torah) and the Injeel (Gospel)] a small price (i.e. getting a small gain by selling My Verses), and fear Me and Me Alone.; [Arberry] And believe in that I have sent down, confirming that which is with you, and be not the first to disbelieve in it. And sell not My signs for a little price; and fear you Me. http://bit.ly/KOgjNB

Koran 2:42 [Hilali-Khan] And mix not truth with falsehood, nor conceal the truth [i.e. Muhammad Peace be upon him is Allah's Messenger and his qualities are written in your Scriptures, the Taurat (Torah) and the Injeel (Gospel)] while you know (the truth); [Arberry] And do not confound the truth with vanity, and do not conceal the truth wittingly. http://bit.ly/1gTZcoj

Koran 2:43 [Hilali-Khan] And perform As-Salat (Iqamat-as-Salat), and give Zakat, and Irka' (i.e. bow down or submit yourselves with obedience to Allah) along with ArRaki'un.; [Arberry] And perform the prayer, and pay the alms, and bow with those that bow. http://bit.ly/1cK17tH

Koran 2:44 [Hilali-Khan] Enjoin you Al-Birr (piety and righteousness and each and every act of obedience to Allah) on the people and you forget (to practise it) yourselves, while you recite the Scripture [the Taurat (Torah)]! Have you then no sense? [Arberry] Will you bid others to piety, and forget yourselves while you recite the Book? Do you not understand? http://bit.ly/1d75OPh

[391.] Ibid., p. 357.;

Koran 2:75 [Hilali-Khan] Do you (faithful believers) covet that they will believe in your religion inspite of the fact that a party of them (Jewish rabbis) used to hear the Word of Allah [the Taurat (Torah)], then they used to change it knowingly after they understood it?; [Arberry] Are you then so eager that they should believe you, seeing there is a party of them that heard God's word, and then tampered with it, and that after they had comprehended it, wittingly? http://bit.ly/1n9bSsa

[392.] Ibid., pp. 317, 321, 371-373; *Al-Mizan*, 1984, Vol. 2, pp. 282-284, 286.;

Koran 2:61 [Hilali-Khan] And (remember) when you said, "O Musa (Moses)! We cannot endure one kind of food. So invoke your Lord for us to bring forth for us of what the earth grows, its herbs, its cucumbers, its Fum (wheat or garlic), its lentils and its onions." He said, "Would you exchange that which is better for that which is lower? Go you down to any town and you shall find what you want!" And they were covered with humiliation and misery, and they drew on themselves the Wrath of Allah. That was because they used to disbelieve the Ayat (proofs, evidences, verses, lessons, signs, revelations, etc.) of Allah and killed the Prophets wrongfully. That was because they disobeyed and used to transgress the bounds (in their disobedience to Allah, i.e. commit crimes and sins). [Arberry] And when you said, "Moses, we will not endure one sort of food; pray to thy Lord for us, that He may bring forth for us of that the earth produces - green herbs, cucumbers, corn, lentils, onions." He said, "Would you have in exchange what is meaner for what is better? Get you down to Egypt; you shall have there that you demanded." And abasement and poverty were pitched upon them, and they were laden with the burden of God's anger; that, because they had disbelieved the signs of God and slain the Prophets unrightfully; that, because they disobeyed, and were transgressors. http://bit.ly/1boRuya

Koran 2:88 [Hilali-Khan] And they say, "Our hearts are wrapped (i.e. do not hear or understand Allah's Word)." Nay, Allah has cursed them for their disbelief, so little is that which they believe. [Arberry] And they say, "Our hearts are uncircumcised." Nay, but God has cursed them for their unbelief; little will they believe. http://bit.ly/Ms7oBC

Koran 2:89 [Hilali-Khan] And when there came to them (the Jews), a Book (this Qur'an) from Allah confirming what is with them [the Taurat (Torah) and the Injeel (Gospel)], although aforetime they had invoked Allah (for coming of Muhammad Peace be upon him) in order to gain victory over those who disbelieved, then when there came to them that which they had recognized, they disbelieved in it. So let the Curse of Allah be on the disbelievers. [Arberry] When there came to them a Book from God, confirming what was with them -- and they aforetimes prayed for victory over the unbelievers -- when there came to them that they recognized, they disbelieved in it; and the curse of God is on the unbelievers. http://bit.ly/1n9dAKa

Koran 2:90 [Hilali-Khan] How bad is that for which they have sold their ownselves, that they should disbelieve in that which Allah has revealed (the Qur'an), grudging that Allah should reveal of His Grace unto whom He will of His slaves. So they have drawn on themselves wrath upon wrath. And for the disbelievers, there is disgracing torment. [Arberry] Evil is the thing they have sold themselves for, disbelieving in that which God sent down, grudging that God should send down of His bounty on whomsoever He will of His servants, and they were laden with anger upon anger; and for unbelievers awaits a humbling chastisement. http://bit.ly/MZdiuT

Koran 2:91 [Hilali-Khan] And when it is said to them (the Jews), "Believe in what Allah has sent down," they say, "We believe in what was sent down to us." And they disbelieve in that which came after it, while it is the truth confirming what is with them. Say (O Muhammad Peace be upon him to them): "Why then have you killed the Prophets of Allah aforetime, if you indeed have been believers?"; [Arberry] And when they were told, "Believe in that God has sent down," they said, "We believe in what was sent down on us"; and they disbelieve in what is beyond that, yet it is the truth confirming what is with them. Say: "Why then were you slaying the Prophets of God in former time, if you were believers?" http://bit.ly/1e1Snfz

Koran 2:92 [Hilali-Khan] And indeed Musa (Moses) came to you with clear proofs, yet you worshipped the calf after he left, and you were Zalimun (polytheists and wrong-doers).; [Arberry] And Moses came to you with the clear signs, then you took to yourselves the Calf after him and you were evildoers. http://bit.ly/LNujaj

Koran 2:93 [Hilali-Khan] And (remember) when We took your covenant and We raised above you the Mount (saying), "Hold firmly to what We have given you and hear (Our Word). They said, "We have heard and disobeyed." And their hearts absorbed (the worship of) the calf because of their disbelief. Say: "Worst indeed is that which your faith enjoins on you if you are believers." [Arberry] And when We took compact with you, and raised over you the Mount: "Take forcefully what We have given you and give ear." They said, "We hear, and rebel"; and they were made to drink the Calf in their hearts for their unbelief. Say: "Evil is the thing your faith bids you to, if you are believers." http://bit.ly/1eRRcjU

Koran 3:112 [Hilali-Khan] Indignity is put over them wherever they may be, except when under a covenant (of protection) from Allah, and from men; they have drawn on themselves the Wrath of Allah, and destruction is put over them. This is because they disbelieved in the Ayat (proofs, evidences, verses, lessons, signs, revelations, etc.) of Allah and killed the Prophets without right. This is because they disobeyed (Allah) and used to transgress beyond bounds (in Allah's disobedience, crimes and sins). [Arberry] Abasement shall be pitched on them, wherever they are come upon, except they be in a bond of God, and a bond of the people; they will be laden with the burden of God's anger, and poverty shall be pitched on them; that, because they disbelieved in God's signs, and slew the Prophets without right; that, for that they acted rebelliously and were transgressors. http://bit.ly/1gKHNS5

Koran 3:113 [Hilali-Khan] Not all of them are alike; a party of the people of the Scripture stand for the right, they recite the Verses of Allah during the hours of the night, prostrating themselves in prayer. [Arberry] Yet they are not all alike; some of the People of the Book are a nation upstanding, that recite God's signs in the watches of the night, bowing themselves, http://bit.ly/1fsNjDD

Koran 3:114 [Hilali-Khan] They believe in Allah and the Last Day; they enjoin Al-Ma'ruf (Islamic Monotheism, and following Prophet Muhammad) and forbid Al-Munkar (polytheism, disbelief and opposing Prophet Muhammad); and they hasten in (all) good works; and they are among the righteous. [Arberry] believing in God and in the Last Day, bidding to honor and forbidding dishonour, vying one with the other in good works; those are of the righteous. http://bit.ly/1kPdg3W

Koran 3:115 [Hilali-Khan] And whatever good they do, nothing will be rejected of them; for Allah knows well those who are Al-Muttaqun [Arberry] And whatsoever good you do, you shall not be denied the just reward of it; and God knows the godfearing. http://bit.ly/1imc6LM

Koran 3:116 [Hilali-Khan] Surely, those who reject Faith (disbelieve in Muhammad as being Allah's Prophet and in all that which he has brought from Allah), neither their properties, nor their offspring will avail them aught against Allah. They are the dwellers of the Fire, therein they will abide. [Arberry] As for the unbelievers, their riches shall not avail them, neither their children, against God; those are the inhabitants of the Fire, therein dwelling forever. http://bit.ly/1e1UQqu

392a. "Protection," as we have seen is a pious Islamic euphemism for the humiliating system of dhimmitude. Even most generously interpreted, it refers to "protection," most commonly, not from outside enemies to the Islamic state, but from the resumption of the jihad against the subjugated dhimmis by their Muslim overlords for any real or perceived "breaches" of the pact of submission, or "dhimma," per Koran 9:29.

393. *Al-Mizan*, 1990, Vol. 7, pp. 120-121.;

Koran 3:181 [Hilali-Khan] Indeed, Allah has heard the statement of those (Jews) who say: "Truly, Allah is poor and we are rich!" We shall record what they have said and their killing of the Prophets unjustly, and We shall say: "Taste you the torment of the burning (Fire)." [Arberry] God has heard the saying of those who said, "Surely God is poor, and we are rich." We shall write down what they have said, and their slaying the Prophets without right, and We shall say, "Taste the chastisement of the burning." http://bit.ly/1fFJQ7d

Koran 3:182 [Hilali-Khan] This is because of that (evil) which your hands have sent before you. And certainly, Allah is never unjust to (His) slaves. [Arberry] that, for what your hands have forwarded, and for that God is never unjust unto His servants. http://bit.ly/MsTpeC

Koran 3:183 [Hilali-Khan] Those (Jews) who said: "Verily, Allah has taken our promise not to believe in any Messenger unless he brings to us an offering which the fire (from heaven) shall devour." Say: "Verily, there came to you Messengers before me, with clear signs and even with what you speak of; why then did you kill them, if you are truthful?" [Arberry] Those same men said, "God has made covenant with us, that we believe not any Messenger until he brings to us a sacrifice devoured by fire." Say: "Messengers have come to you before me bearing clear signs, and that you spoke of; why therefore did you slay them, if you speak truly?" http://bit.ly/1nSU73x

Koran 3:184 [Hilali-Khan] Then if they reject you (O Muhammad), so were Messengers rejected before you, who came with Al-Baiyinat (clear signs, proofs, evidences) and the Scripture and the Book of Enlightenment [Arberry] But if they cry lies to thee, lies were cried to Messengers before thee, who came bearing clear signs, and the Psalms, and the Book Illuminating. http://bit.ly/N1GFfV

Koran 3:185 [Hilali-Khan] Everyone shall taste death. And only on the Day of Resurrection shall you be paid your wages in full. And whoever is removed away from the Fire and admitted to Paradise, he indeed is successful. The life of this world is only the enjoyment of deception (a deceiving thing). [Arberry] Every soul shall taste of death; you she surely be paid in full your wages on the Day of Resurrection. Whosoever is removed from the Fire and admitted to Paradise, shall win the triumph. The present life is but the joy of delusion. http://bit.ly/1bu015X

Koran 3:189 [Hilali-Khan] And to Allah belongs the dominion of the heavens and the earth, and Allah has power over all things [Arberry] To God belongs the Kingdom of the heavens and of the earth; and God is powerful over everything. http://bit.ly/Ly49aQ

394. *Al-Mizan*, 2002, Vol. 11, p. 41.;

Koran 5:64 [Hilali-Khan] The Jews say: "Allah's Hand is tied up (i.e. He does not give and spend of His Bounty)." Be their hands tied up and be they accursed for what they uttered. Nay, both His Hands are widely outstretched. He spends (of His Bounty) as He wills. Verily, the Revelation that has come to you from Allah increases in most of them their obstinate rebellion and disbelief. We have put enmity and hatred amongst them till the Day of Resurrection. Every time they kindled the fire of war, Allah extinguished it; and they (ever) strive to make mischief on earth. And Allah does not like the Mufsidun (mischiefmakers). [Arberry] The Jews have said, "God's hand is fettered." Fettered are their hands, and they are cursed for what they have said. Nay, but His hands are outspread; He expends how He will. And what has been sent down to thee from thy Lord will surely increase many of them in insolence and unbelief; and We have cast between them enmity and hatred, till the Day of Resurrection. As often as they light a fire for war, God will extinguish it. They hasten about the earth, to do corruption there; and God loves not the workers of corruption. http://bit.ly/1c3gWsT

395. Ibid., p. 82.;

Koran 5:71 [Hilali-Khan] They thought there will be no Fitnah (trial or punishment), so they became blind and deaf; after that Allah turned to them (with Forgiveness); yet again many of them became blind and deaf. And Allah is the All Seer of what they do. [Arberry] And they supposed there should be no trial; but blind they were, and deaf. Then God turned towards them; then again blind they were, many of them, and deaf; and God sees the things they do. http://bit.ly/N1I5XQ

396. Ibid., p. 95.;

Koran 5:78 [Hilali-Khan] Those among the Children of Israel who disbelieved were cursed by the tongue of Dawud (David) and Iesa (Jesus), son of Maryam (Mary). That was because they disobeyed (Allah and the Messengers) and were ever transgressing beyond bounds. [Arberry] Cursed were the unbelievers of the Children of Israel by the tongue of David, and Jesus, Mary's son; that, for their rebelling and their transgression. http://bit.ly/1gM5utv

[397.] Ibid., pp. 96-97

Koran 5:82 [Hilali-Khan] Verily, you will find the strongest among men in enmity to the believers (Muslims) the Jews and those who are Al-Mushrikun, and you will find the nearest in love to the believers (Muslims) those who say: "We are Christians." That is because amongst them are priests and monks, and they are not proud. [Arberry] Thou wilt surely find the most hostile of men to the believers are the Jews and the idolaters; and thou wilt surely find the nearest of them in love to the believers are those who say "We are Christians"; that, because some of them are priests and monks, and they wax not proud; http://bit.ly/1g1rZpq

[398.] *Islam and Revolution—Writings and Declarations of Imam Khomeini (1941-1980)*, Translated and Annotated by Hamid Algar, 1981, North Haledon, NJ, pp. 89, 27.

[399.] See reference 191.

[400.] "Sheik of Al-Azhar Ahmad Al-Tayeb Justifies Antisemitism on the Basis of the Koran," *The Middle East Media Research Institute*, October 25, 2013, Clip No. 4048 http://bit.ly/1nUh1rs

[401.] Bostom, *The Legacy of Islamic Antisemitism*, p. 37, and p. 175, notes 50-53.; for Koran 2:90-91, 3:112, and 3:181, see references 392 and 393;

Koran 4:155 [Hilali-Khan] Because of their breaking the covenant, and of their rejecting the Ayat (proofs, evidences, verses, lessons, signs, revelations, etc.) of Allah, and of their killing the Prophets unjustly, and of their saying: "Our hearts are wrapped (with coverings, i.e. we do not understand what the Messengers say)" - nay, Allah has set a seal upon their hearts because of their disbelief, so they believe not but a little.; [Arberry] So, for their breaking the compact, and disbelieving in the signs of God, and slaying the Prophets without right, and for their saying, "Our hearts are uncircumcised" -- nay, but God sealed them for their unbelief, so they believe not, except a few -- http://bit.ly/LQAOZY

[402.] See reference 4.

[403.] *Maariful Qur'an*, Vol. 3, pp. 235, 237-239.

[404.] Andrew Bostom, *The Mufti's Islamic Jew-Hatred—What The Nazis Learned From the Muslim Pope*, 2013, Washington, D.C., Bravura Books, http://amzn.to/1cVyQCe; The proclamation is translated in full on pp. 25-32. An introductory discussion briefly elucidating el-Husseini's jihadism can be found on pp. 19-24.

[405.] Ibid., p. 31

[406.] "Egypt's top Muslim cleric dies of heart attack," *www.alarabita.net*, March 10, 2010 http://bit.ly/1kdlVyg

[407.] Muhammad Sayyid Tantawi, *Banu Isra'il fi al-Qur'an wa al-Sunna* [*The Children of Israel in the Qur'an and the Sunna*] (Cairo: Zahraa' lil-I`laam al-`Arabi, 1986–87), pp. 107–26, 129–46; English translation by Dr. Michael Schub, in Bostom, *The Legacy of Islamic Antisemitism*, pp. 391-401.; quote from p. 394.

[408.] See for example *Tafsir al-Jalalayn*, p. 147. The gloss on Koran 3:113 cites Abdullah ibn Salam, as an example of those "who are upright," and in the commentary's words, "straight and holding firm to the truth," i.e., Islam. He was one of the *rare* Jewish converts to Islam described in the hadith and sira. See in addition the discussion of Koran 5:82 by Maulana Muhammad Shafi cited in reference 403, which also mentions Abdullah ibn Salam.

[409.] Tantawi, in Bostom, *The Legacy of Islamic Antisemitism*, p. 394.

[410.] Camilla Adang, "Medieval Muslim Polemics Against the Jewish Scriptures," in *Muslim Perceptions of Other Religions—A Historical Survey*, edited by Jacques Waardenburg, New York, 1999, p. 143.

[411.] Bostom, *The Legacy of Islamic Antisemitism*, pp. 34-35

[412.] Andrew Bostom "Confronting Hamas' Genocidal Jew-Hatred", *The American Thinker*, January 02, 2009 http://bit.ly/LC355M

[413.] *Sunan Abu Dawud*, Vol. 3, 1990/2007. New Delhi, English translation by Ahmad Hasan, Chapter 1603, Command and Prohibition, Number 4322, p. 1207; also available as *Sunan Abu Dawud, Book 37, Number 4322*, here: http://bit.ly/1jiEv9b

[414.] Herman Bernstein. *The History of a Lie*, New York, 1921; and *The Truth About the "Protocols of Zion"—A Complete Exposure*, New York, 1935.

[414a.] Bostom, *Legacy of Islamic Antisemitism*, pp. 144-145.

[415.] Aaron Klein, "Abbas urges: 'Raise rifles against Israel' " *WoldNet Daily*, January 11, 2007 http://bit.ly/1ixhFak

[416.] "Saul S. Friedman," *Youngstown News*, www.vindy.com, May 17, 2013 http://bit.ly/1av6Aae

[417.] Educated at al-Azhar University, Sheikh Atiyyah Saqr (d. 2006) was a prolific writer, and consultant for the Egyptian Ministry of Awqaf (the ministry of religious endowments). Sheikh Saqr belonged to various esteemed Al-Azhar religious councils, such as Al-Azhar's Islamic Research Academy, Higher Council for Islamic Affairs, and Fatwa Committee. Saqr also served as a member of the Religious Committee in the Egyptian government's People's Assembly. ("Atiyyah Saqr," www.islamopediaonline.org, http://bit.ly/1ix9cny)

[418.] Saul S. Friedman, "The Myth of Islamic Toleration," in *Without Future: The Plight of Syrian Jewry*, 1989, New York, N.Y., pp. 2–3.

[419.] "Former Al-Azhar Fatwa Committee Head Sets Out the Jews' 20 Bad Traits As Described in the Qur'an," *The Middle East Media Research Institute*, Special Dispatch No. 691, April 6, 2004 http://bit.ly/1kW8X73; For a litany of 25 pejorative (and inveterate) traits of the Jews depicted in the Koran, and published nearly four decades earlier, see: Sheikh Abd Allah Al Meshad, "Jews' Attitudes Toward Islam and Muslims In the First Islamic Era," *Proceedings of The Fourth Conference of the Academy of Islamic Research*,

September, 1968, pp. 460-464.

[420.] Friedman, "The Myth of Islamic Toleration," p. 3

[421.] Haggai Ben-Shammai. "Jew Hatred in the Islamic Tradition and Koranic Exegesis", originally in Antisemitism through the Ages, editor, Shmuel Almog, Oxford, 1988, pp. 161-169, reproduced in Bostom, *The Legacy of Islamic Antisemitism*, pp. 221-225, with various extracts included earlier in the compendium.

[422.] Bostom, *The Legacy of Islamic Antisemitism*, p. 34

[423.] Ibid.

[424.] Andrew Bostom, "Ecumenical Editing of the Navy's Muslim Sea Burial Prayer Service", May 12, 2011 http://bit.ly/19wrHHA

[425.] *The Qur'an: An Encyclopedia*, edited by Oliver Leaman, 2006, Routledge, New York, N.Y., p. 614.; Koran 1:7 [Hilali-Khan] The Way of those on whom You have bestowed Your Grace, not (the way) of those who earned Your Anger (such as the Jews), nor of those who went astray (such as the Christians). [Arberry 1:7] the path of those whom Thou hast blessed, not of those against whom Thou art wrathful, nor of those who are astray. http://bit.ly/Nf7vRU

[426.] *Tafsir Ibn Kathir*, Vol. 1, p. 50.

[427.] Bostom, *The Legacy of Islamic Antisemitism*, p. 35

[428.] Bostom, *The Legacy of Islamic Antisemitism*, p. 54

[429.] *Sunan Abu Dawoud, Book 37, Number 4322* http://bit.ly/17P73A4

[430.] Bostom, *The Legacy of Islamic Antisemitism*, p. 35

[431.] Ibid.

[432.] Ibid.

[433.] Ibid. p. 38

[434.] Edward William Lane. *An Account of the Customs of the Modern Egyptians*, New York, 1973, pp. 553–56.

[435.] "A Risala of Al-Jahiz," translated by Joshua Finkel, *Journal of the American Oriental Society*, Vol. 47, 1927, pp. 311–34. Al-Jahiz (776–868/869), born in Basra, Iraq, was a prolific Arabic prose writer, historian, and author of works of literature, theology, and politico-religious polemics. He authored two hundred books throughout his lifetime that discuss a variety of subjects, including Arabic grammar, zoology, poetry, lexicography, and rhetoric. Extracts from pp. 322–24, 326, and 327–28 of his "A Reply to the Christians," (in "A Risala of Al-Jahiz,") are included on pp. 317-318 of *The Legacy of Islamic Antisemitism*, and referenced earlier in the book, as well.

[436.] Bostom, *The Legacy of Islamic Antisemitism*, p. 38

[437.] Ibid.

[438] Ibid., p. 39

[439] Ibid.

[440] Ibid.

[441] Ibid.

[442] Ibid., p. 31; (Note: The primary source for this reference, and the two following references [443-444] is the discussion in Goitein's, *A Mediterranean Society*, encompassing pp. 278-283, and pp. 586-587, notes 14-25.)

[443] Bostom, *The Legacy of Islamic Antisemitism*, p. 31

[444] Ibid., p. 32

[445] Lane, *An Account of the Customs of the Modern Egyptians*, p. 554

[446] Ibid., pp. 554-555.

[447] Gregory Wortabet, *Syria and the Syrians*, London, 1856, vol. 2, pp. 263–64.

[448] Moshe Perlmann, "Introduction to Samau'al al-Maghribi's Ifham al-Yahud (Silencing the Jews)," *American Academy for Jewish Research*, Vol. 32, 1964, p. 19.

[449] Bostom, *The Legacy of Islamic Antisemitism*, p. 35

[450] Ibid., pp. 74, 229, 232-234

[451] The relevant hadith are:

Sahih al-Bukhari, Volume 5, Book 59, Number 713 http://bit.ly/GCu2nw

Sahih Muslim, Book 026, Number 5430 http://bit.ly/175J2Ap

Sahih al-Bukhari, Volume 5, Book 59, Number 551 http://bit.ly/GCu2nw

Sahih al-Bukhari, Volume 7, Book 71, Number 669 http://bit.ly/1dZeVR7

[452] *The Life of Muhammad—A Translation of Sirat Rasul Allah*, p. 516.

[453] Ibn Sa'd. *Kitab Al-Tabaqat Al-Kabir*, pp. 249-252.

[454] Bostom, *The Legacy of Islamic Antisemitism*, pp. 66-74, 265-278, 283-287.

[455] Ibid.

[456] Ibid., p. 54

[457] Summarized, here: M.J. Kister, "The massacre of the Banū Qurayẓa: a re-examination of a tradition" *Jerusalem Studies in Arabic and Islam*, Vol. 8, 1986, pp. 61-96.

[458] Abu Yusuf Ya'qub *Le Livre de l'impot foncier*, Translated from Arabic and annotated by Edmond Fagnan. Paris, 1921. English translation in Bat Ye'or, *The Dhimmi- Jews and*

Christians Under Islam, 1985, Cranbury, New Jersey, pp. 172-173.

459. Kister, "The massacre of the Banū Qurayẓa", p. 69.

460. Kister, "The massacre of the Banū Qurayẓa", p. 70.

461. W.H. T. Gairdner, "Muhammad Without Camouflage", *The Moslem World*, Vol. 9, 1919, p. 36.

462. Bostom, *The Legacy of Islamic Antisemitism*, pp. 66-76, 229, 231, 233.

463. Salo Baron. "The Historical Outlook of Maimonides," *Proceedings of the American Academy for Jewish Research*, vol. 6, 1934-35, p. 82; Bostom, *Legacy of Islamic Antisemitism*, p. 21.

464. Bostom, *Legacy of Islamic Antisemitism*, pp. 66-76.

465. Hartwig Hirschfeld. "Essai Sur l'Histoire des Juifs de Medina", *Revue des Etudes Juives*, Vol. 7, 1883, pp. 192-193, and Vol. 10, 1885, pp. 10-31. A full English translation of the text and notes appears in *The Legacy of Islamic Antisemitism*, pp. 299-312, with various extracts included earlier in the compendium. These extracts are from p. 67.

466. Georges Vajda. "Juifs et Musulmans selon Le Hadit" (Jews and Muslims according to the Hadith), *Journal Asiatique*, Vol. 229, 1937, pp. 57-129; A full English translation of the text and notes appears in *The Legacy of Islamic Antisemitism*, pp. 235-260, with various extracts included earlier in the compendium.

467. *The Legacy of Islamic Antisemitism*, p. 63.

468. Ibid.

469. Ibid.

470. Meir Bar-Asher, "La Place du Judaîsme et des Juifs dans le shi'isme duodécimain, " ("The Place of Judaism and Jews in Twelver Shi'ism") in *Islam: identite et alterite: Hommages au Pere Guy Monnot* (*Islam: identity and otherness: Tributes to Father Guy Monnot*), edited by M.A. Amir-Moezzi, 2013, Paris, pp. 57- 82.

471. Ibid., p. 57

472. Ibid., p. 58

473. Ibid., p. 57

473a. For the Sunni perspective, see the gloss on Koran 2:40, which makes quite plain Islam's supersession of Judaism, from *Tafsir al-Jalalayn*, p. 16:

> Tribe of Israel (descendants of Yaqub [Jacob])! Remember the blessing I conferred on you, meaning your ancestors, by rescuing you from Pharoah, parting the sea, and sending the manna and quail and other things for **which you should show gratitude by obeying Allah. Honor My contract which I made with you to believe in Muhammad** and I will honor your contract which I made with you to reward you for that by admitting you into the Garden. Have dread of Me alone, **meaning fear not fulfilling your contract with Me by preferring something else to it.**

[473b.] Ibid., pp. 68-70.

[474.] Ibid., p. 60

[475.] See reference 378.

[476.] Bar-Asher, "The Place of Judaism and Jews in Twelver Shi'ism," p. 60.

[477.] Bostom, *The Legacy of Islamic Antisemitism*, p. 63.

[478.] Armand Abel, "al-Dadjdjal" *Encyclopedia of Islam*, Edited by B. Lewis, Ch. Pellat, and J. Schacht, 1991, Leiden, E.J. Brill, Vol. II C-G, pp. 77-78. For additional confirmation that the Muslim Antichrist "Dajjal" is accompanied by Jews, and may be indentified as "Jewish," see Cook, "Dajjāl,"; Cook, *Studies in Muslim Apocalyptic* section, "The Jewish Dajjal," pp. 110ff., and pp. 341, 367; and Cook's, "'Hadith,' Authority and the End of the World: Traditions in Modern Muslim Apocalyptic Literature," p. 36;

[479.] abu-Mansur abd-al-Kahir ibn Tahir al-Baghdadi (d. 1037) was a Muslim theologian, esteemed for his erudition in Islamic law and the hadith, as well as a noted mathematician; See the introduction *to Moslem Schisms and Sects* (*Al-Fark Bain Al-Firak*) *by abu-Mansur abd-al-Kahir ibn Tahir al-Baghdadi (d. 1037)*, translated by Kate Chambers Seelye, 1920, New York, Columbia University Press, pp. 7-8.

[480.] Mark Durie, "Isa, the Muslim Jesus," in *The Myth of Islamic Tolerance*, edited by Robert Spencer, 2005, Amherst, NY, pp. 541–55.

[481.] James Robson, "The material of Tradition II," *The Muslim World*, 1951, Vol. 41, pp. 257–270; p. 259 http://bit.ly/11Wt6xQ

[482.] Bostom, *The Legacy of Islamic Antisemitism*, p. 63.

[483.] *Sahih Muslim, Book 041, Number 7034* http://bit.ly/MFKE17; *Sahih Bukhari, Volume 4, Book 52, Number 177* http://bit.ly/1ga214L; *Sahih Muslim, Book 041, Number 6985.* http://bit.ly/19pfcHZ

[484.] *Tafsir Ibn Kathir*, Volume 3, p. 34

[485.] Bostom, *The Legacy of Islamic Antisemitism*, p. 63.; Regarding the ransoming of prisoners of Muslim enemies vanquished by jihad (see Bostom, *The Legacy of Jihad*, p. 149), the great Maliki jurist and polymath Averroes (d. 1198), wrote:

> Most scholars are agreed that, in his dealings with   captives,   various policies are open to the Imam [head of the Islamic state, caliph]. He may pardon them, kill them, or release them . . . on ransom . . .

[486.] Andrew Bostom, "Islam's Jew-Hating Hadith In Context," *The Jewish Press*, April 17, 2013 http://bit.ly/1bIT4Le

[487.] Bostom, *The Mufti's Islamic Jew-Hatred*, p. 31.

[488.] "The Covenant of the Islamic Resistance Movement–Hamas", *Middle East Media Research Institute*, February 14, 2006, Special Dispatch No.1092 http://bit.ly/GLLLtJ

[489.] Itamar Marcus, Nan Jacques Zilberdik, "Muslims' destiny is to kill Jews," *Palestinian*

Media Watch, January 15, 2012, http://bit.ly/1h87yvU

> The following is an excerpt from the Fatah ceremony broadcast on PA TV: Moderator at Fatah ceremony: "Our war with the descendants of the apes and pigs (i.e., Jews) is a war of religion and faith. Long Live Fatah! [I invite you,] our honorable Sheikh." **PA Mufti Muhammad Hussein** comes to the podium and says: "47 years ago the [Fatah] revolution started. Which revolution? The modern revolution of the Palestinian people's history. In fact, Palestine in its entirety is a revolution, since [Caliph] Umar came [to conquer Jerusalem, 637 CE], and continuing today, and until the End of Days. The reliable Hadith (tradition attributed to Muhammad), [found] in the two reliable collections,

> Bukhari and Muslim, says: "The Hour [of Resurrection] will not come until you fight the Jews. The Jew will hide behind stones or trees. Then the stones or trees will call: 'Oh Muslim, servant of Allah, there is a Jew behind me, come and kill him.' Except the Gharqad tree [which will keep silent]." Therefore it is no wonder that you see Gharqad [trees] surrounding the [Israeli] settlements and colonies…[PA TV (Fatah), Jan. 9, 2012]

490. "Antisemitism in Al-Azhar University's Friday Sermon: The Jews Are The Muslims' Worst Enemies," *The Middle East Media Research Institute*, Clip No. 3871, May 10, 2013 http://bit.ly/1kyQjEE

> Following are excerpts from a Friday sermon at Al-Azhar University in Cairo, delivered by Muhammad Al-Mukhtar Al-Mahdi, which aired on Channel 1, Egyptian TV, on May 10, 2013: Muhammad Al-Mukhtar Al-Mahdi: The Islamic nation, which is the guardian of Truth, must be aware of the conspiracies of Falsehood, and of the snares of those who lie in wait. **Allah has taught [Muslims] that their worst enemies are those about whom He said: "You shall find the Jews and the polytheists to be the most hostile towards the believers" [Koran 5:82].** Thus, Allah made Jihad for His sake and endurance of pain and hardship effective means to fight the people of Falsehood. [...] The confrontation [with the Jews] is inevitable. **Our Prophet does not lie. He told us that there would be a confrontation between the Muslims and the Jews before the Day of Judgment, and that the Muslims would vanquish them to the point that the Jews would hide behind the stones and the trees, but the stones and the trees would say: "Oh Muslim, oh servant of Allah, there is a Jew behind me, come and kill him."** Prepare for that day, for it will surely arrive, because the divine revelation harbors no lies.

491. Cook, *Studies in Muslim Apocalyptic*, chapter 4, "Shi'i Apocalyptic," pp. 189-229.

492. Ibid., p. 226.

493. Ibid.

494. Ibid.

495. Ibid., pp. 213, 222.

496. Ibid., p. 222, note 132.; Muhammad Baqir al-Majlisi, *Bihar al-anwar*, 1957 ff., Tehran, Vol. 52, p. 192; English translation by Yigal Carmon. http://bit.ly/1bKbgnH

Mulla Muhammad Bakr Majlisi (1627–1699) was an authoritative jurist and prolific hadith collector. He was also well educated in Islamic philosophy and mysticism. During the late Safavid period, Majlisi became a dominant authority in politics, and social and judicial matters.

Majlisi's professed goal in his Persian writings was to disseminate the Shi'a ethos to "the masses of believers and common Shiites who had "no familiarity with the Arabic language." Majlisi had very close relationships with at least two of the Safavid monarchs, Shah Sulayman (d. 1694) and Shah Sultan Husayn (d. 1713). In 1686 he was appointed the Shaykh al-Islam by Shah Sulyaman. Upon Shah Husayn's accession to the throne in 1694, his title was changed to Mullabashi. Majlisi personally undertook legal matters and proceedings while holding these supreme institutionalized clerical offices. During the last four years in this official state office under Shah Sultan Husayn, Majlisi was the de facto ruler of Iran.

Etan Kohlberg characterized Majlisi's magnum opus, *Bihar al-anwar* ("Oceans of Light"), as follows (in Kohlberg's, "Majlisī, al-," *Encyclopedia of Religion*. Ed. Lindsay Jones. 2nd ed. Vol. 8. Detroit: Macmillan Reference USA, 2005. 5623. *Gale Virtual Reference Library*. Web. December 25, 2013. http://bit.ly/M9SMqy):

> [H]e [Majlisi] is best known for his *Bihar al-anwar* ("Oceans of Light"), a voluminous encyclopedia containing a vast number of Shi'i traditions from various sources. As such, it spans virtually all major aspects of Twelver Shi'i religious thought: the unity of God and the divine attributes; the concepts of knowledge, belief and unbelief, and free will and predestination; the lives of the prophets and imams and the pilgrimages to their graves; the position of the Qur'an; and positive law. Thanks to the Bihar, much of the corpus of Shi'i tradition was saved from oblivion and returned to center stage. In preparing the work, al-Majlisi relied heavily on the help of pupils and enlisted the financial backing of the Safavid court to obtain manuscripts of rare or inaccessible works. The first volume of the Bihar appeared in 1666, and by the time of al-Majlisi's death seventeen of the twenty-six projected volumes had been finished. The rest were completed by his pupil Abd Allah Efendi. A lithograph edition of the entire work was first published between 1885 and 1897, and a new edition containing 110 volumes has been published in Tehran. Various volumes of the Bihar have been translated into Persian, and the many excerpts, abridgments, and supplements in existence attest to the continuing influence of the work.

[497.] Khalaji, "Apocalyptic Politics—On the Rationality of Iranian Policy," p. 34; Khalaji cites as his primary sources, on p. 34, notes 5-8, Muhammad Baqer Majlesi, *Behar al-Anwar fi Dorar-e Akhbar-e Aimat-e al-Athar* (Tehran: Manshourat-e Ketabchi, 2004 [AHS 1383]), Vol. 51, pp. 89, 69, 94, 105, 93.

[498.] Maghen, "Occultation in 'Perpetuum': Shi'ite Messianism and the Policies of the Islamic Republic"

[499.] Ibid., p. 234.

[500.] Ibid.

[501.] Ibid., p. 235.

[502.] Ibid., pp. 235-236.

[503.] Bernard Lewis, "Does Iran have something in store?," *The Wall Street Journal*, August 8, 2006 http://bit.ly/1kBSCXy; See also "Mi'radj," *The Shorter Encyclopaedia of Islam*, pp. 541-542, which refers to,

> **The experience alluded to in (Koran) Sura 17:1**...[Arberry translation: **Glory be to Him, who carried His <u>servant</u> by night from the Holy Mosque to the Further Mosque** the precincts of which We have blessed, that We might show him some of Our signs. He is the All-hearing, the All-seeing. http://bit.ly/ NClEJa]... **That Muhammad is meant by the "servant" is generally assumed** and there is no reason to doubt it...**Muhammad probably meant by al-Masdjid al-Aksa [the Further Mosque] a place in heaven**, such as the place in the highest of the seven heavens in which the angels sing praises of Allah...**Hadith gives further details of the Prophet's ascension. Here the ascension is usually associated with the nocturnal journey to Jerusalem, so that the ascent to heaven takes place from this sanctuary. We also have accounts preserved which make the ascension start from Mecca and make no mention of the journey to Jerusalem**.

[504.] Maghen, "Occultation in 'Perpetuum': Shi'ite Messianism and the Policies of the Islamic Republic," p. 236, note 8.

[505.] Ibid., p. 243.

[506.] Ibid., pp. 248-249.

[507.] Ibid., p. 250.

[508.] Ibid.

[509.] Ibid.

[510.] Ibid., pp. 252, 253.

[511.] Andrew Bostom, "Ashura, Shi'ism,...and Yet Another 'Jewish Conspiracy Against Islam'," *Pajamas Media*, November 18, 2013 http://bit.ly/1kD1MTr

[512.] Maghen, "Occultation in 'Perpetuum': Shi'ite Messianism and the Policies of the Islamic Republic," p. 256, note 69.

[513.] Ibid.

[514.] Ibid.

[515.] David Cook, *Contemporary Muslim Apocalyptic Literature*, 2005, Syracuse, N.Y., p. 232.

[516.] Ibid.

[517.] Gil Hoffman. "6 in 10 Palestinians reject 2-state solution, survey finds", *The Jerusalem Post*, July 15, 2011 http://bit.ly/18lgxUN

[518.] Ibid.; For relevant statements and sermons alluded to, see references 487-490.

[519.] Hoffman, "6 in 10 Palestinians reject 2-state solution, survey finds", and references

487-490.

[520.] Bostom, *The Legacy of Islamic Antisemitism*, pp. 41,100, 319, 337, 389-390.; Sean W. Anthony, *The Caliphs and the Heretic: Ibn Saba, The Sabaiya and Early Shi'ism Between Myth and History*, Ph.D. Dissertation, University of Chicago, August, 2009 http://bit. ly/1ckyFfF; Sean W. Anthony, "The Legend of Abdallāh ibn Saba and the Date of Umm al-Kitāb," *Journal of the Royal Asiatic Society*, 2011, Vol. 21, pp. 1-30 http://bit.ly/1eG7rpy

[521.] Anthony, *The Caliphs and the Heretic: Ibn Saba, The Sabaiya and Early Shi'ism Between Myth and History*, p. 68.

[522.] See especially, Bostom, *The Legacy of Islamic Antisemitism*, pp. 41,100, 319, 337, 389-390.

[523.] Ibid., p. 319.

[524.] Ibid., pp. 389-390.

[525.] "2008 Update: Saudi Arabia's Curriculum of Intolerance," *Center for Religious Freedom of Hudson Institute*, http://bit.ly/1iD4KV0

[526.] Anthony, *The Caliphs and the Heretic: Ibn Saba, The Sabaiya and Early Shi'ism Between Myth and History*, p. vii; Anthony, "The Legend of Abdallāh ibn Saba and the Date of Umm al-Kitāb," p. 2.

[527.] Anthony, *The Caliphs and the Heretic: Ibn Saba, The Sabaiya and Early Shi'ism Between Myth and History*, pp. 167-168.

[528.] Ibid., p. 75.

[529.] Bostom, *The Legacy of Islamic Antisemitism*, pp. 85-86.

[530.] Ibid.

[531.] Ibid.

[532.] Ibid.

[533.] Ibid.

[534.] Andrew Bostom, "The Cordoba House and the Myth of Cordoban Ecumenism," in Bostom, *Sharia Versus Freedom*, pp. 367-377.

[535.] Bostom, *The Legacy of Islamic Antisemitism*, p. 46.

[536.] The entry "Crusades, The" from the *Jewish Encyclopedia.com—The unedited full-text of the 1906 Jewish Encyclopedia*, maintains: "The Jews of the Rhine district were decimated: it has been calculated that about 4,000 were killed or slew themselves." http:// bit.ly/1nvTytF; Ibn Warraq's 2013, *Sir Walter Scott's Crusades and Other Fantasies*, New English Review Press, pp. 149-157, confirms these estimates.

[536a.] Bostom, *The Legacy of Islamic Antisemitism*, p. 46.

[537.] Ibid.

[538.] Ibid., p. 54

[539.] Ibid.

[540.] Ibid., p. 47.

[541.] Ibid.

[542.] Ibid.

[543.] Ibid.

[544.] Ibid.

[545.] Ibid.

[545a.] Ibid.

[546.] Ibid.

[547.] Ibid.

[548.] Ibid.

[549.] Ibid.

[550.] Ibid.

[551.] Ibid.

[552.] Ibid., pp. 47-48.

[553.] Ibid., p. 48.

[554.] Ibid.

[555.] Ibid.

[556.] Ibid.

[557.] Ibid.

[558.] Ibid., p. 54.

[559.] Ibid., p. 50

[560.] Mordechai Hakohen, *The Book of Mordechai: Study of the Jews in Libya—Selections from the "Highid Mordekhai" of Mordechai Hakohen*, Harvey E. Goldberg (Editor) 1993, London, p. 55.

[561.] Bostom, *The Legacy of Islamic Antisemitism*, see especially pp. 76-164, 481-610, 655-678.

[562.] For the Alexandrian and Cairene anti-Jewish pogroms of 1047, 1168, 1265, and 1324, and the 13th century anti-Jewish persecutions of Sultan Baybars, see Saul S. Friedman, *A History of the Middle East*, Jefferson, N.C., 2006, p. 142.

[563.] The following eyewitness account in the New York Times of August 28, 1929 was reported by a surviving American student at the Slobadka Rabbinical College of Hebron (Hebron is noted, appositely, as, "the burial place of Jewish patriarchs, and the first capital of Judea"), which was a prime target of the Muslim attackers:

> The real massacre began Saturday about 11 o'clock in the morning when 73 were butchered as only Arabs could do it. Doors were smashed and infants, children, women, and men without distinction butchered in a manner incredible even in the blackest day of the Spanish Inquisition. The secretary of the college was murdered as well as the town Shochet [kosher butcher] with his wife, children, and brother. The rest of the Jewish population is being held in police headquarters for protection. ("STUDENT SLAUGHTER SHOCKS JERUSALEM; Hundreds, Awaiting News of Wounded Relatives, Shriek at Reports of Hebron Tragedy. VICTIMS KILLED LIKE SHEEP General Mourning Will Be Proclaimed Throughout All Synagogues and Rabbinical Colleges," *The New York Times*, August 28, 1929, http://bit.ly/1gfQ3oG)

During May, 2011, The Middle East Media Research Institute excerpted a *res ipsa loquitur* interview of a 92-year-old Palestinian Arab Muslim woman who witnessed the murderous1929 anti-Jewish ethnic cleansing pogrom in Hebron. She openly celebrated the slaughter of the Jews of Hebron as an appropriate paradigm for the present, while being interviewed during her participation in a so-called a "Right-of-Return Demonstration." The extracts are reproduced below ("92-Year-Old Palestinian Woman in a Right-of-Return Demonstration: Palestinians Should Massacre the Jews Like We Massacred Them in Hebron," *The Middle East Media Research Institute*, Clip No. 2929, May 13, 2011 http://bit.ly/1gfSZl6):

> Interviewer: Please tell us who you are.
>
> Sara Jaber: I am from Hebron. The Jaber family.
>
> Interviewer: What is your name?
>
> Sara Jaber: Sara Muhammad 'Awwadh Jaber.
>
> Interviewer: How old are you?
>
> Sara Jaber: I am 92.
>
> Interviewer: So you remember May 15, 1948, the day of the Nakba.
>
> Sara Jaber: Why wouldn't I remember? May Allah support us. I hope we forget those days. **Allah willing, you will bury [Israel], and massacre the Jews with your own hands. Allah willing, you will massacre them like we massacred them in Hebron.**
>
> Interviewer: What does this day mean to you? You have lived 63 years since the Nakba. You have experienced the entire Nakba...
>
> Sara Jaber: 92 years. That's 92. I lived through the British era, **and I lived through the massacre of the Jews in Hebron. We, the people of Hebron, massacred the Jews. My father massacred them, and brought back some stuff...**

Interviewer: Thank you very much.

564. David G. Dalin, John F. Rothmann, *Icon of Evil: Hitler's Mufti and the Rise of Radical Islam*, Brunswick, N.J, 2008/2009, p. 30.

565. Bostom, *The Legacy of Islamic Antisemitism*, p. 168.

566. Friedman, *Without Future—The Plight of Syrian Jewry*, p. 9

Chapter 3

The *Dhimmi* Condition for Iranian Jewry Under Shiite Theocratic Rule: A Half-Millennial Past as Prolugue

567. Minorsky. *Tadhkirat al-Muluk. A Manual of Safavid Administration*; Fischel. "The Jews in Medieval Iran from the 16th to the 18th centuries: Political, Economic, and Communal aspects", Al-Amili (d. 1622), Jami i Abbasi; discussed in Browne, *A Literary History of Persia*, vol. IV, p. 407; Al-Majlisi (d. 1699), *The Treatise Lightning Bolts Against the Jews*. Translated by V.B. Moreen, in: *Die Welt des Islams*, Vol. 32, 1992, pp. 187-193. Also, see Bostom, *The Legacy of Jihad*, pp. 213-220 for an original English translation of Al-Amili, and a reproduction of Moreen's translation of Al-Majlisi.; Savory, *Iran Under the Safavids*, chapter 2, "Theocratic State: the Reign of Shah Ismail I, 1501-1524," pp. 27-49.; Brunner, "The Role of Hadith as Cultural Memory in Shi'i History"; pp. 318-319, 322.

568. i.e., the combined Safavid (1501-1722) and Qajar (1795-1925) periods comprised 350 years of Shi'ite theocracy. This period was characterized, initially by Sunni Afghan invasion, and then both Ottoman and Russian advances. Under Nadir Shah (r. 1734-1747)—who was of Turkmen descent—Persian sovereignty was restored, but upon his accession to the throne:

> He announced that…his subjects would abandon certain religious practices that had been introduced by Shah Ismail I (r. 1501-24) and had plunged Iran into disorder, such as *sabb* (ritual cursing of the first three caliphs Abu Bakr, Omar, and 'Othman, termed "rightly guided" by the Sunnites) and *rafz* (denial of their right to rule the Muslim community). Nadir decreed that Twelver Shi'ism would become known as the Ja'fari *madhab* (legal school) in honor of the sixth Imam Ja'far al-Sadeq (d. 765), who would be recognized as its central authority. Nadir asked that this *madhab* be treated exactly like the four traditionally recognized legal schools of Sunnite Islam… Nadir departed substantially from Safavid precedent by redefining Shi'ism as the Ja'fari *madhab* of Sunni Islam and promoting the common Turkmen descent of the contemporary Muslim rulers as a basis for international relations. Safavid legitimacy depended on the dynasty's close connection to Twelver Shi'ism as an autonomous, self-contained tradition of Islamic jurisprudence as well as the Safavids' alleged descent from the seventh Imam Musa al-Kazem (died between 779 and 804). Nadir's view of Twelver Shi'ism as a mere school of law within the greater Muslim community (*umma*) glossed over the entire complex structure of Shi'ite legal institutions…(Tucker, "NĀDER SHAH" ["Nadir Shah"])

569. Browne, *A Literary History of Persia*, Vol. 4, pp. 371-372.

570. Fischel, "The Jews in Medieval Iran", p. 266.

571. Tome Pires. *Suma Oriental* (1512-1515), Vol. I (London, 1944), p. 27.

[572.] Raphael. du Mans. *Estat de la Perse*, 1660, ed. Schefer (Paris, 1890), pp. 193-194; cited in, Fischel, "The Jews in Medieval Iran", p. 266.

[573.] Samuel C. Chew. *The Crescent and the Rose*, Oxford University Press, 1937, p. 211.

[574.] Laurence Loeb. *Outcaste- Jewish Life In Southern Iran*, New York, 1977, p. 292.

[575.] Benjamin, *Eight Years in Asia and Africa- From 1846-1855*, pp. 211-213.

[576.] D.G. Littman. "Jews Under Muslim Rule: The Case of Persia" *The Weiner Library Bulletin*, 1979, Vol. 32, pp. 7-8. http://bit.ly/1lOjSRJ

[577.] Ibid., p. 7.

[578.] Fischel, "The Jews in Medieval Iran", p. 275.

[579.] Thévenot, cited in Ibid, p. 275

[580.] Fryer, cited in Ibid., p. 275

[581.] Fischel, "The Jews in Medieval Iran", p. 275

[582.] Ibid., pp. 275-276

[583.] W.F. Fischel, "Isfahan- The Story of a Jewish Community in Persia", *The Joshua Starr Memorial Volume, Jewish Social Studies, Publication No. 5*, 1953, pp. 122-123.

[584.] Ibid., pp. 123, 124; and Fischel, "The Jews in Medieval Iran", pp. 279-280.

[585.] Fischel ignores this earlier more apposite Muslim equivalent (and possible learned prototype) of the persecutions in late 15th century Spain, i.e., the Muslim Almohad persecutions in both Spain and North Africa, of the mid to late 12th century. See Bostom, *The Legacy of Islamic Antisemitism*, pp. 102-104.

[586.] Fischel, "Isfahan- The Story of a Jewish Community in Persia", p. 124.; This threat is confirmed in an independent account from the *Kitab-i-Anusi*, excerpts translated by V.B. Moreen, *Iranian Jewry's Hour of Peril and Heroism- A Study of Babai Ibn Luft's Chronicle (1617-1662)*, New York-Jerusalem, 1987, p. 188.

[587.] English translation from Bat Ye'or, *The Decline of Eastern Christianity Under Islam*, pp. 372-373.

[588.] *A Chronicle of the Carmelites in Persia and the Papal Mission of the 17th and 18th Centuries* 1939, London, pp. 364-366.

[589.] Arnold T. Wilson. "History of the Mission of the Fathers of the Society of Jesus, Established in Persia by the Reverend Father Alexander of Rhodes" *Bulletin of the School of Oriental Studies*, 1925, Vol. 3, p. 695.

[590.] Kohlberg, "Majlisī, al-,"

[591.] D.M. Donaldson, *The Shiite Religion. A History of Islam in Persia and Iran*

1933, London, pp. 303-304. http://bit.ly/M2cWCh

[592.] Rainer Brunner, "The Role of Hadith as Cultural Memory in Shi'i History," *Jerusalem Studies in Arabic and Islam* 2005, Vol. 30, p. 20.

[593.] Ibid.

[594.] From, Bar-Asher, "La Place du Judaîsme et des Juifs dans le shi'isme duodécimain, " ("The Place of Judaism and Jews in Twelver Shi'ism"), p. 60, especially notes 9-11; Bar-Asher cites Majlisi's *Bihar al-anwar*, Beirut, 1983, 110 volumes, specifically vol. 77, p. 44 lines 18, 7, and 6, respectively, for the quoted text.

[594a.] Al-Majlisi, *The Treatise Lightning Bolts Against the Jews*, pp. 187-193

[595.] Loeb, *Outcaste- Jewish Life In Southern Iran*, p. 21.

[596.] Al-Majlisi, *The Treatise Lightning Bolts Against the Jews*, pp. 187ff.

[597.] Daniel Tsadik, *Between foreigners and Shi'is: nineteenth-century Iran and its Jewish minority*, 2007, Stanford, CA, p. 17.

[598.] Ibid.

[599.] Goldziher. *Introduction to Islamic Theology and Law*, p. 213.

[600.] Malcolm, *Five Years in a Persian Town*, p. 107.

[601.] Soroudi. "The Concept of Jewish Impurity and its Reflection in Persian and Judeo-Persian Traditions," p. 156, and p.156, footnote 36.

[602.] Loeb, *Outcaste- Jewish Life In Southern Iran*, p. 21.

[603.] Fischel, "The Jews in Medieval Iran", p. 281.

[604.] Ibid.

[605.] *A Chronicle of the Carmelites in Persia and the Papal Mission of the 17ᵗʰ and 18ᵗʰ Centuries* p. 408, July 29, 1678; and p. 474, June 13, 1702.

[606.] Fischel, "The Jews in Medieval Iran", p. 282.

[607.] Ibid., p. 283.

[608.] Fischel. "Isfahan- The Story of a Jewish Community in Persia", p. 126.

[609.] Ibid., p. 127, and W. F. Fischel, "The Jews of Persia, 1795-1940", *Jewish Social Studies*, 1950, Vol. 12, p. 121.

[610.] John Malcolm, *The History of Persia*, 1829, London, Vol. 2, p. 301.

[611.] David. d'Beth Hillel. *The Travels of Rabbi David d'Beth Hillel: from Jerusalem, through Arabia, Koordistan, Part of Persia, and India to Madras*. p. 115; cited in, W.J. Fischel *The Jews of Kurdistan A Hundred Years Ago*, New York, 1944, Reprinted from Jewish Social Studies, Vol. VI, No.3, p. 223.

[612.] James B. Fraser. *Narrative of a Journey into Khorasan in the Years 1821 and 1822*,

London, 1825, p. 182.

613. Henry A. Stern. *Dawnings of Light in the East*, London, 1854, pp. 184-185.

614. Malcolm, *Five Years in a Persian Town*, p.108.

615. Reverend Isaac Adams. *Persia by a Persian*, Washington, D.C., 1900, p. 120.

616. Soroudi, "The Concept of Jewish Impurity", p. 157.

617. d'Beth Hillel, *The Travels of Rabbi David d'Beth Hillel*, pp. 74-75, cited in Fischel W.J. *The Jews of Kurdistan*, pp. 223-224.

618. A. Grant. *The Nestorians*, New York, 1841, pp. 382-383.

619. Fischel, *The Jews of Kurdistan*, pp. 224-225, and Fischel, *The Jews of Persia*, p. 124. After exhaustive research on the late 18th century fate of the Jews of Tabriz, Amnon Netzer concluded [A. Netzer, "The Fate of the Jewish Community of Tabriz", in: *Studies in Islamic History and Civilization in Honor of Professor David Ayalon*, Jerusalem, 1986, p. 419.],

> … that there was, indeed, a terrible massacre of the Jews in Tabriz at some time between the years 1790-1797, and that Tabriz ceased to become a dwelling place where Jews could have a communal life for many generations to come

620. Cited in G.N. Curzon. *Persia and the Persian Question*, 1892, Vol. 1, p. 166.

621. W.J. Fischel. "Secret Jews of Persia", *Commentary*, January 1949, p. 29.

622. Fischel, *The Jews of Persia*, pp. 124-125.

623. Loeb, *Outcaste- Jewish Life In Southern Iran*, p. 57.

624. C.J. Wills, *Persia As It Is*, London, 1887, pp. 229-230.

625. Ibid, pp. 23, 24.

626. Fischel, *The Jews of Persia*, pp. 134,137.

627. Cyrus Adler, Aaron Margalith, *With Firmness in the Right—American Diplomatic Action Affecting Jews, 1840-1945*, New York, 1946, p. 11.

628. Ibid., p. 14.

629. Mr Tyler to Mr. Olney. No. 260, Dip Ser., Legation of the United States, Teheran, Persia, October 7, 1896, *Foreign Relations of the United States*, http://bit.ly/1dZInUo; Tyler comments, pejoratively, that the Jews exercise "the same methods of doing business [in Persia] as elsewhere," adding, they might escape their "indignities and suffering" would that they behaved "with a little more prudence in business matters."

630. "Persecution of Jews," Mr. McDonald to Mr. Sherman, No. 294, Legation of the United States, Teheran, Persia, May 17, 1897, *Foreign Relations of the United States*, http://bit.ly/1dZInUo

[631.] Fischel, *The Jews of Persia*, p. 121.

[632.] Tsadik, *Between foreigners and Shi'is: nineteenth-century Iran and its Jewish minority*, p. 12.

[633.] Ibid., p. 10

[634.] Ibid, pp. 13-14.

[635.] Ibid., p. 5.

[636.] Ibid.

[637.] Ibid., p. 125.

[638.] Ibid., p. 126.

[639.] Ibid.

[640.] Ibid., p. 29.

[641.] See reference 269c.

[642.] Tsadik, *Between foreigners and Shi'is: nineteenth-century Iran and its Jewish minority*, pp. 29-30.

[643.] Ibid., pp. 176-177.

[644.] Ibid., p. 8.

[645.] Ibid.

[646.] Ibid., p. 142.

[647.] Claude Anet, *Through Persia in a Motor-Car*, translated by M. B. Ryley, London, 1907.

[648.] Ibid, p. 221.

[649.] Littman, "Jews Under Muslim Rule: The Case of Persia," pp. 12-14.

[650.] Fischel, *The Jews of Persia*, pp. 143-144, and Loeb, *Outcaste- Jewish Life In Southern Iran*, pp. 289-290.

[651.] Loeb, *Outcaste- Jewish Life In Southern Iran*, p. 291.

[652.] Farideh Goldin, *Wedding Song—Memoirs of an Iranian Jewish Woman*, 2003, Lebanon, NH.

[653.] Ibid., pp. 75, 72.

[654.] Ibid., p. 72.

[655.] Ibid., pp. 121-122.

[656.] Ibid., p. 43.

657. Ibid., p. 158.

658. Ibid., pp. 167-168.

659. Ibid., pp. 195-196.

660. Littman, "Jews Under Muslim Rule: The Case of Persia," p. 5., from which Bernard Lewis borrowed liberally in *The Jews of Islam* http://bit.ly/1lOjSRJ

661. Ibid., p. 5.

662. Ibid.

663. Ibid.

664. "Iran young, urbanised and educated: census," *Agence France Presse* (AFP) – July 29, 2012 http://bit.ly/1bhMpg8

665. Sultanhussein Tabandeh, *A Muslim Commentary on the Universal Declaration of Human Rights*, English translation by F. J. Goulding, London, 1970.

666. Sanasarian, *Religious Minorities in Iran*, p. 173, footnote 92.

667. Tabandeh, *A Muslim Commentary on the Universal Declaration of Human Rights*, p. 4.

668. Netzer, "The Fate of the Jewish Community of Tabriz", p. 413. See also references 571, 572.

669. Sanasarian, *Religious Minorities in Iran*, p. 25.

670. Tabandeh, *A Muslim Commentary on the Universal Declaration of Human Rights*, pp. 17,18, 37.

671. Sanasarian, *Religious Minorities in Iran*, p. 28.

672. Ibid., p. 85.

673. S.R. (Ayatollah) Khomeini. *Principles, Politiques, Philosophiques, Sociaux et Religieux.* Translated into French and edited by J.-M. Xaviere, Paris, 1979, English translation of these excerpts in, Bat Ye'or, *The Dhimmi*, pp. 396-397.

674. See references 259-265; 266

675. Tabatabai, *al-Mīzān fī tafsīr al-Qur'ān*, p. 236. English translation by Sjimon R. den Hollander.

676. See references 166-169.

677. See reference 169.

678. See references 382-386.

679. Bar-Asher, "La Place du Judaîsme et des Juifs dans le shi'isme duodécimain," ("The Place of Judaism and Jews in Twelver Shi'ism"), p. 65, citing in note 33, Fadlallah's *Min*

wahy al-qur'an, Beirut, 1987-1989, 10 volumes. ; vol. 3, part VIII, p. 74, from the author's commentary on Koran 5:5

[680.] Ibid., p. 65.

[681.] See reference 4.

[682.] See references 270, 271.

[683.] Bar-Asher, "La Place du Judaîsme et des Juifs dans le shi'isme duodécimain, " ("The Place of Judaism and Jews in Twelver Shi'ism"), pp. 65-66.

[684.] Shirazi, *Islamic Law Books One and Two. Handbook of Islamic rulings on Muslim's duties and practices*, pp. 23, 697-698.

[685.] Thomas L. Friedman, "A Nobel for Sistani," *The New York Times*, March 20, 2005

http://nyti.ms/L8qlIr

[686.] "Window on The Week," *National Review Online*, February 10, 2006, http://bit.ly/1fbJ1Au

[687.] "Dennis has memorable dialogue with Fouad Ajami, noted expert on Middle East politics," *www.dennisprager.com*, June 15, 2007 http://bit.ly/1bpIga9

[688.] Reuel Marc Gerecht, "The Bill O'Reilly Fallacy," *The New Republic*, October 16, 2010 http://bit.ly/1n2gGT6

[689.] L. Paul Bremer III, Malcolm McConnell, *My Year in Iraq: The Struggle to Build a Future of Hope*, 2006, New York, p. 190.

[690.] Ibid., p. 166.

[691.] Ibid.

[692.] Andrew Bostom, "Is Paul Bremer 'Unclean'?", *FrontPageMagazine.com*, February 20, 2004 http://bit.ly/1llO09c

[693.] "Najis things—Kafir," *www.sistani.org*, http://bit.ly/1aSvhO4

[694.] John Agresto, *Mugged By Reality—The Liberation of Iraq and te Failure of Good Intentions*, 2007, New York, N.Y.

[695.] Ibid., p. 101.

[696.] Ibid., p. xx, note 4.

[697.] Ibid., p. 101.

[698.] Ibid., p. 184.

[699.] Sanasarian, *Religious Minorities in Iran*, pp. 84-85.

[700.] See reference 398.

[700a.] Sanasarian, *Religious Minorities in Iran*, p. 29.

[701.] See references 424-426.

[702.] Pooya Dayanim, "Imagine Being a Jew in Iran" *The Iranian* March 12, 2003. http://bit.ly/1dHq0bv

[703.] Ibid., p. 111.

[704.] Afshari, *Human Rights in Iran-The Abuse of Cultural Relativism*, p.136.

[705.] Sanasarian, *Religious Minorities in Iran*, p. 113.

[706.] Afshari, *Human Rights in Iran*, p. 165.

[707.] English translation from Mark Durie, "Dhimmitude and Ibn Ajibah on the Death of the Non-Muslim Soul," *markdurie.com blog*, June 12, 2011 http://bit.ly/1hEmgLi; The original Arabic commentary on Koran 9:29 from Ibn 'Ajiba's *Al-Bahr Al-Madid* , which was the source of Durie's published translation, can be found at *www.altafsir.com*, http://bit.ly/1jnyVjc; For biographical/historical background on Ibn Ajiba, see *Autobiography of a Moroccan Soufi: Ahmad Ibn 'Ajiba* (1747-1809), translated from the Arabic by Jean-Louis Michon and David Streight, Fons Vitae, Louisville KY, 1999

[707a.] Jovan Cvijic, *La Peninsule Balkanique*, Paris, 1918, pp. 387-388 ff. English translation by Michael Miller.

[708.] Dayanim, "Imagine Being a Jew in Iran"

[709.] Brian Murphy, "Iran's Jews Caught Again in No Man's Land" *Associated Press*, July 30, 2006. http://fxn.ws/1mwOt93; Shortly afterward (August 3, 2006), three representatives of the small remnant Moroccan Jewish community—mimicking the *dhimmi* behaviors of the Jews of Shiraz, Iran—emerged from their own usual state of self-imposed political silence to file a petition in Rabat's high court against Moroccan-born Israeli Defense Minister Amier Peretz, accusing him of "war crimes" committed during the same July 2006 confrontation with Hezbollah, on the Lebanon-Israel northern border. ("Moroccan Jews Ask Court to Try Amir Peretz For War Crimes," *Haaretz*, August 3, 2006. http://bit.ly/MFnMyQ)

[710.] See references 274, 275, 382, 383.

[711.] Ann E. Mayer, *Islam and Human Rights*, Boulder, Colorado, 1999, p. 141.

[712.] Ibid., p. 142.

[713.] Ibid., p. 143.

[714.] Ibid.

[715.] Dayanim, "Imagine Being a Jew in Iran"

[716.] Ibid.

[717.] Murphy, "Iran's Jews Caught Again in No Man's Land"

[718.] Dayanim. "Imagine Being a Jew in Iran"

[719.] Chris Wattie, "Iran Eyes Badges for Jews—Law Would Require non-Muslim Insignia", *National Post*, May 19, 2006. http://bit.ly/1hdWOb1

[720.] Chris Wattie, "Experts Say Report of Badges for Jews in Iran is Untrue", *National Post*, May 19, 2006. http://bit.ly/1bsB6C6

[721.] Amir Taheri, "Press Release: Amir Taheri Addresses Queries About Dress Code Story," *Benador Associates*, May 22, 2006, http://bit.ly/1edpwFM

[722.] No further information on this matter emerged from the Iranian committee Mr. Taheri cited.

[723.] Al-Majlisi, "Lightning Bolts Against the Jews", cited in Bostom, *The Legacy of Jihad* , p. 218

[724.] Loeb, *Outcaste- Jewish Life In Southern Iran*, p. 21.

[725.] Wattie, "Iran Eyes Badges for Jews"; Andrew Bostom, "The Yellow Badge of Denial" *The American Thinker*, May 23, 2006. http://bit.ly/1nT26L2

[726.] "Howard compares Iran to Nazi Germany," *The Sydney Morning Herald*, May 20, 2006. http://bit.ly/1p0R89K

[727.] Wattie, "Iran Eyes Badges for Jews"

[728.] Bostom, "The Yellow Badge of Denial"

[729.] "Howard compares Iran to Nazi Germany"

[730.] Ibid.

[731.] Ibid.

[732.] "Iran 2012—International Religious Freedom Report," *The U.S. Department of State*. http://1.usa.gov/Ojef1M

[733.] Ibid.

[734.] Ilan Ben Zion, "Jewish woman brutally murdered in Iran over property dispute," *The Times of Israel*, November 28, 2012 http://bit.ly/1f4ekLK

[735.] Ibid.

[736.] Ibid.

[737.] Karmel Melamed, "A Jew murdered in Iran," *The Jewish Journal*, December 11, 2012 http://bit.ly/1jVpIRX

[738.] Ibid.

[739.] See reference 653.

[740.] Melamed, "A Jew murdered in Iran"

[741.] "If You Were Involved in Killing a Jew, You Did a Good Deed," *The Algemeiner*, January 3, 2013, http://bit.ly/1fq7JzC

[742.] Sanasarian, *Religious Minorities in Iran*, p. 198, note 6.

[743.] "Iranian President Ahmadinejad on the 'Myth of the Holocaust'", *Middle East Media Research Institute*, Special Dispatch Series No. 1091, February 14, 2006. http://bit.ly/1cbibql; Justus Reid Wiener et al., "Referral of Iranian President Ahmadinejad on the Charge of Incitement to Commit Genocide" *The Jerusalem Center for Public Affairs*, Jerusalem, Israel, 2006 http://bit.ly/1nWqXxR; Matthias Kuntzel, "Iran's Obsession with the Jews" *The Weekly Standard*, February 19, 2007 http://tws.io/1hi46KN

[743a.] "Iranian Supreme Leader Khamenei Denied Holocaust—MEMRI Disproves Iranian FM Zarif's Claim To ABC That Khamenei's Statements About Holocaust 'Myth' Were 'A Bad Translation'; Khamenei Also Praised French Holocaust Denier Roger Garaudy," *The Middle East Media Research Institute*, Special Dispatch No. 5621, January 26, 2014 http://bit.ly/1fidWgS; The report summary notes:

> In a September 29, 2013 interview with ABC's George Stephanopoulos, in which Iranian Foreign Minister Mohammad Javad Zarif was questioned about Iranian Supreme Leader Ali Khamenei's statements that the Holocaust is a "myth," Zarif claimed that Khamenei is not a Holocaust denier and that the statements – which can be found in English on his official English-language website – were a "bad translation" and "out of context." Khamenei had made the statements in a February 2006 speech to Iranian Air Force officers. However, a MEMRI investigation reveals that FM Zarif's claim is false; in Khamenei's original statements, which can be accessed on Khamenei's official Persian-language website, Khamenei did indeed call the Holocaust a "myth." Furthermore, in mid-December 2013, Khamenei's office re-released Khamenei's 1998 statements of praise for the work of the late convicted French Holocaust denier Roger Garaudy, on the occasion of the anniversary of Garaudy's 1998 trial in France.

[744.] "Fomer Iranian President Rafsanjani on Using a Nuclear Bomb Against Israel", *Middle East Media Research Bulletin*, Special Dispatch No. 325, January 3, 2002 http://bit.ly/1egGUcv; Nazila Fathi, "Iran's President Says Israel Must Be Wiped Off the Map" *The New Tork Times.com*, October 26, 2005 http://nyti.ms/1fIeQQw; "Iranian President at Tehran Conference" *Middle East Media Research Institute*, Special Dispatch Series No. 1013, October 28, 2005 http://bit.ly/1dfLqsq; Wiener et al, "Referral of Iranian President Ahmadinejad on the Charge of Incitement to Commit Genocide"; Kuntzel, "Iran's Obsession with the Jews"

[745.] Gary Sick, "US can exploit peaceful Iran revolution," *Newsday*, June 11, 1997, A42.

[746.] "Iran's Mushrooming Threat" *The Washington Times*, June 15, 2004. http://bit.ly/1f8XbR7

[747.] Michael Rubin, "Iran's Burgeoning WMD Programs", *Middle East Intelligence Bulletin*, 2002, Volume 4, Number 3, March-April http://bit.ly/1e3uw4a

[748.] "Fomer Iranian President Rafsanjani on Using a Nuclear Bomb Against Israel"

[749.] Kuntzel, "Iran's Obsession with the Jews"; Matthias Kuntzel, "Unholy Hatreds: Holocaust Denial and Antisemitism in Iran" December 11, 2006 http://bit.ly/1mA22oi

[750.] "Iran's President Says Israel Must Be Wiped Off the Map"

[751.] "Iranian President at Tehran Conference"

[752.] "Iranian President Ahmadinejad on the 'Myth of the Holocaust'"

[753.] Kuntzel, "Iran's Obsession with the Jews"

[754.] "President Ahmadinejad: 'I Have a Connection With God, Since God Said that the Infidels Will Have No Way to Harm the Believers...'" *Middle East Media Research Institute*, Special Dispatch Series No. 1328, October 19, 2006 http://bit.ly/1hi8gT1

[755.] Wiener et al., "Referral of Iranian President Ahmadinejad on the Charge of Incitement to Commit Genocide"

[756.] Ibid.

[757.] See reference 131.

[758.] "US, Israel hampering regional revolutions: Larijani," *www.presstv.ir*, February 8, 2014. http://bit.ly/1kLGy5Y

[759.] "Iran: We will help 'cut out the cancer of Israel'" *The Telegraph* (London), February 3, 2012 http://bit.ly/1diSnZD

[760.] Ibid.

[760a.] Ariel Ben Solomon, "Khamenei: 'Israeli regime is doomed to failure, annihilation'" *The Jerusalem Post*, November 20, 2013, http://bit.ly/1elS2qA

[761.] Rahimian's November, 2006 statements were published by the *Iranian Student News Association (ISNA)*, November 16, 2006, then translated and quoted by the Iran research section of *Honestly-Concerned.org*, November 17, 2006. "Iran: Antijüdische Parolen und Kriegsdrohungen, " ["Iran: Anti-Jewish slogans and threats of war, "] November 17, 2006 http://bit.ly/1djRAaJ. German analyst Matthias Kuntzel provided a German to English translation of Rahimian's statements in his "Unholy Hatreds: Holocaust Denial and Antisemitism in Iran," published December 11, 2006. Kuntzel was apparently unaware that Rahimian's statement, "The Jew is the most obstinate enemy of the devout," was a direct reference to Koran 5:82

[762.] "Senior Iranian Official Mohammad Hassan Rahimian: Our Missiles Can Cause "Big Holocaust" in Israel," *The Middle East Media Research Institute*, Clip No. 2342, January 12, 2010 http://bit.ly/1gucbva

[763.] See references 498-514.

[764.] See reference 508.

[765.] See reference 178.

[766.] Maghen, "Occultation in 'Perpetuum': Shi'ite Messianism and the Policies of the

Islamic Republic," p. 256.

767. Ibid, pp. 256-257.

768. Jules Monnerot, *Sociology and Psychology of Communism*, 1953, Boston.

769. Bertrand Russell, *The Practice and Theory of Bolshevism*, 1920, London.

770. Ibid., pp. 5,114-115.

771. G.K. Chesterton, *The New Jerusalem*, 1921, New York, pp. 262-263.

772. Monnerot, *Sociology and Psychology of Communism*, p. 5.

773. Ibid., pp. 18-19.

774. Ibid., p. 19; See Bostom, *The Legacy of Jihad*, for discussion of the jihad campaigns of Mahmud of Ghazni, pp. 80, 382, 440-445, 551, 632-640; For discussion of the jihad campaigns of Togrul [Tughril] Beg, see pp. 382, 447, 605, 607; For discussion of the jihad campaigns of Alp Arslan, see pp. 382, 608.; See also Andrew Bostom, "Sufi Jihad?," *The American Thinker*, May 15, 2005. http://bit.ly/1f1fxNp

775. Alexis Lacroix, "Maxime Rodinson: 'Islam et communisme, une ressemblance frappante'," ["Islam and Communism, A Striking Resemblance"] *Le Figaro*, September 28, 2001. http://bit.ly/NxEFff; English extracts translated from the French by Ibn Warraq.

776. Ibid.

777. Ibid.

778. Ibid.

779. Reuel Mark Gerecht. "The Last Orientalist—Bernard Lewis at 90," *The Weekly Standard*, Vol. 11, No. 36, June 5, 2006. http://tws.io/MuKlFN

780. Bernard Lewis. "Communism and Islam," *International Affairs*, Vol. 30, No. 1(Jan., 1954), pp. 7, 9-10. http://bit.ly/1hhsnTj

781. Sayyid Abul Ala Mawdudi [Maudoodi], *Islamic Law and Constitution*, Lahore, 1960, p. 154.

782. See reference 84d.

783. See reference 84h.

784. Farideh Goldin, "Iran on My Mind" *Jewish Quarterly* 204 (Winter, 2006): 88. Extracts available at *Jewish Refugees Blogspot.com* http://bit.ly/1dh3AN5

785. Norman Podhoretz, "Norman Podhoretz: Strike Iran Now to Avert Disaster Later," *The Wall Street Journal*, December 11, 2013 http://on.wsj.com/1cDirRG

786. Ibid.

Index

A

314

Index

Index

Index

Index

C

319

Index

Index

Index

Index

F

Index

Index

Index

J

Index

K

Index

Index

Index

Index

Index

Index

Index

338

Index

Ne'ematullahi
Sultanalishahi Sufi
Order, 204
Nehdaran, Toobah, 224
Netanyahu, Benjamin
(Prime Minister), 26,
237, 244
Netzer, 303, 305
New York Times
Editorial Board, The,
244
New York Times, The,
19, 37, 42-44, 49-50,
208, 235-236, 244,
249-250, 260, 279, 299,
306
Nigeria, 104
Night flight of the
prophet Muhammad,
151
Ninety-two-year-old
Palestinian Woman in
a Right-of-Return
Demonstration, 299
Nini, Yehuda, 159
Nisan, Mordechai, 271
Nisman, Alberto, 251
NKVD, 244
Nobel Peace Prize, 208
Non-Muslim Minorities
in an Islamic State,
277
Nonproliferation Policy
Education Center, 38,
252
North Korea, 33, 249-250

North Korean missiles,
249
Nuclear Weapon Free
Iran Act of 2013, 43,
253
Nuclear weapons, 17,
24-31, 38, 40, 43,
47-48, 50, 52, 60, 226,
234, 236, 245-249, 258,
271-272

O

O'Donoghue, Daniel, 241
Obama, 18-19, 24, 27-29,
38-40, 43-44, 52-53,
234-237, 245, 248-249,
252
Obama's 2014 State of
the Union address, 252
Old Dominion
University, 202
Omidi, Mehdi Reza
(Youhan), 55
On Suicide in Islam, 70,
267
Origins of the Islamic
State, The, 273, 277
Ottoman Empire, 74, 98,
117, 268

Index

Index

342

Index

Index

Index

Index

Index

U

V

W

Index

Z

Y

Made in the USA
Las Vegas, NV
04 July 2021